TEACHING SCIENCE
TO CHILDREN
An Integrated Approach

Alfred E. Friedl
Emeritus Professor of Education
Kent State University

TEACHING SCIENCE TO CHILDREN

AN INTEGRATED APPROACH

Third Edition

McGraw-Hill, Inc.
New York St. Louis San Francisco Auckland Bogotá
Caracas Lisbon London Madrid Mexico City
Milan Montreal New Delhi San Juan Singapore
Sydney Tokyo Toronto

This book was developed by Lane Akers, Inc.

TEACHING SCIENCE TO CHILDREN
An Integrated Approach

1 2 3 4 5 6 7 8 9 0 SEM SEM 9 0 9 8 7 6 5

 This book is printed on recycled paper
containing 10% postconsumer waste.

ISBN 0-07-022455-2

This book was set in Electra by J. M. Post Graphics, a Division of
    Cardinal Communications Group, Inc.
The editor was Lane Akers;
the production supervisor was Margaret Boylan.
The cover was designed by Rafael Hernandez.
Semline, Inc., was printer and binder.

Library of Congress Catalog Card Number: 95-75169

About the Author

Alfred E. Friedl is Emeritus Professor of Education at Kent State University. He began his teaching career as an elementary school teacher in Minnesota and California and later began teaching extension classes for San Diego State University and U.C.L.A. After receiving his Doctorate in Education from Colorado State University, he moved to Kent State University where he has taught for the past twenty years. In addition to winning an "outstanding teacher" award from Kent State, he also won a national teaching award for writing and presenting a 13-week television series entitled, "Teaching Children about Space Science."

Professor Friedl has written extensively for more than three decades—authoring or coauthoring more than twenty books. He coauthored his first book, *Your Science Fair*, while still a sixth-grade teacher. His most recent books include *Modern Physical Science* and *Exercises and Investigations*, both high school science texts.

Contents

Preface   **xi**

1. The Methods   **1**

Process-Content   1
The Role of the Textbook in the Classroom   2
What Is a Discrepant Event?   3
How to Use Discrepant Events in Promoting the Processes of Science   4
How to Use This Book   7

2. Teaching Children about the Characteristics of Matter   **9**

Democritus and the Atom   9
The Model of an Atom   9
Terms   11
Spaces between Molecules   11
Molecular Motion   15
The Phases (or States) of Matter   17
Changes in Matter   22
Adhesion   23
Cohesion   26

3. Teaching Children about Heat Energy   **30**

Measuring Heat and Temperature   30
Heat of Fusion and Heat of Vaporization   33
Sources of Heat   35
Conduction   37
Convection   40
Radiation   42
Expansion and Contraction   43
Fire   47

4. Teaching Children about Static Electricity   **50**

From Amber to Electrons   50
Charged Objects Attract Uncharged Objects   51
Like Charges Repel   53
Unlike Charges Attract   57
Charging by Induction   58
How to Build an Electroscope   59

5. Teaching Children about Magnetism   60

From Lodestones to Domains   60
What Do Magnets Attract?   61
Magnetism Is a Force   62
Attraction and Repulsion   64
Temporary and Permanent Magnets   67

6. Teaching Children about Current Electricity   68

The Discovery of Current Electricity   68
What Is Current Electricity?   69
Sources of Electricity   71
Circuits   74
Uses of Electricity   78
Things to Make   80

7. Teaching Children about Sound   82

What Is Sound?   82
How Does Sound Travel?   84
The Speed of Sound   90
Volume (Loudness)   92
Pitch   96
Music   99

8. Teaching Children about Light, Lenses, and Color   101

What Is Light?   101
Brightness of Light   106
Light Can Be Reflected   107
Light Can Be Refracted   110
Color   116
Optical Illusions   120

9. Teaching Children about Air and Air Pressure   124

Air Is a Real Substance and Occupies Space   124
Air Exerts Pressure   128
Air Expands and Contracts   133

10. Teaching Children about Weather and Climate   137

What is Weather? What Is Climate?   137
Convection Currents   138
The Water Cycle   142
The Seasons   149

11. Teaching Children about Flight through the Air   152

Forces of Flight   152
Streamlining for Speed   155
How Airplanes Are Controlled   156
Supersonic Flight   158

12. Teaching Children about Space Science   **162**

From Firecrackers to Spaceflight   162
Power for Flight   163
Gravity and Inertia   166
Trajectories, Orbits, and Reentry   171
Astronauts in Space   174

13. Teaching Children about the Sun, Moon, and Stars   **176**

Concepts of Number, Size, and Distance   176
The Earth and Moon   182

14. Teaching Children about the Earth (Geology)   **188**

The Structure of the Earth   188
Surface Features of the Earth   189
Rocks and Minerals   192
Weathering and Erosion   196
Soils   200

15. Teaching Children about the Oceans   **204**

Why Turn to the Oceans?   204
The Motions of the Oceans   207
Living under the Sea   214

16. Teaching Children about the Plant Kingdom   **217**

Seeds   217
Seedless Reproduction of Plants   222
The Parts of a Plant   223
Microscopic Plants   227

17. Teaching Children about the Animal Kingdom   **231**

Animals with Backbones   231
Adaptations of Nature   239
Insects   242
Insect Cages and Collections   244

18. Teaching Children about Nutrition and Health   **245**

Cell Growth   245
Growth Rates   246
Food Tests and Tastes   248
Foods and Diets   251

19. Teaching Children about Fitness: The Heart, Lungs, and Muscles   **263**

Measuring Fitness   263
The Heart and Circulatory System   266
Lungs and Respiration   270
Muscles, Bones, and Skin   273
Effects of Tobacco on the Body   276

20. Teaching Children about Energy, Environment, and Pollution   **281**

How Opinions Change   283
Energy Use in the United States   286
Nuclear Energy   288
Radiation   291
Conservation   297

Index   311

Preface

What should a text for teachers of elementary school science contain? Should it contain lengthy descriptions of instructional methodologies, scientific procedures, and other complexities? Should it show you how difficult it is to teach science?

Should it have instructional methods in the first half of the book and science content in the back half? Should you be expected to put the methods and content halves together yourself...even if the author could not seem to do it?

We think not.

This book is different. Instead of showing you how difficult it is to teach science, it shows you how *simple* it is. Instead of many complex steps, there are only three manageable ones. Instead of focusing mostly on theory, the book focuses on practical exercises that work in the classroom.

Not only are the methods simple, but so are the activities. Most of the activities in the book can be presented by a typical elementary schoolteacher without a strong science background, special in-service work, or extra course work.

We feel that instructional methods, when presented in isolation from science content, are of limited value. That is why methods and content are combined throughout this text. Only Chapter 1 is different. It is an introduction. The rest of the book is filled with hundreds of classroom activities that show how the Chapter 1 methodology can be used to teach all areas of science content. Most of these activities can be presented as *discrepant events* (the outcome is unexpected and surprising), thus increasing student interest and motivation.

The methods and activities in this text have been used with thousands of pre-service and in-service teachers for more than 25 years. The activities and steps have been tested and retested. We hope that the reader will find this book a real help in teaching science to children.

Alfred E. Friedl

TEACHING SCIENCE TO CHILDREN

An Integrated Approach

The Methods

This is a rather short chapter. Instead of spending much time discussing methods in isolation, we find it is better to combine the methods with the content (as is done in the remaining content chapters). However, some basic information is needed to set the stage for the methods used in this book.

For example, it is useful to know what is meant by *process* and *content* and how some national science programs affected the balance between these two factors. It is also important to know the advantages inherent in *discrepant events* (that is, events that are unexpected or surprising to the viewer). Finally, the simple three-step approach used throughout the book is clearly explained.

Science teaching in the elementary school has changed greatly during the past 35 years. At one time most of the science teaching focused on the *content* of science. Then after the launching of the *Sputnik* satellite by the Soviet Union in 1957, America took a new look at science education.

PROCESS-CONTENT

Federal funds were authorized to support a number of major national programs in science education. All these programs shifted the emphasis away from content and toward *process*.

What is process? Process is how a scientist works, thinks, and studies problems. In other words, it is a *method of investigating*. The process approach includes many specific skills including, for example, the following:

classifying
comparing
contrasting
controlling variables
demonstrating
describing
estimating
experimenting
forming theories
generalizing

graphing (a way of recording data)
identifying
inferring
interpreting
measuring
observing
predicting outcomes
recording data
verifying

The federal infusion of funds to promote the "new science" continued for many years. What were the results? Most educators concede that the results were somewhat disappointing. The bright hopes evoked by the new programs were, too often, not realized.

Why the disappointing results? There are many likely reasons. It is generally believed that most teachers found the new programs too demanding, too complex, too costly, and too time-consuming. In addition, some programs virtually ignored science content. Process had taken over completely. Many teachers found that process without content did not produce results. Consequently, most of the programs disappeared. Very few remain today.

Overall, the new programs tended to be too difficult to use in the classroom. The typical elementary teacher is, after all, responsible for many different subjects. To make matters worse, science is often the teacher's greatest weakness. As a result, success in elementary science is not easy to achieve.

In this book we try to make it easier to teach science well. We try to take away the complexity that is so often part of science teaching. In this book you need not worry about how to teach the process approach: it is built right into the content chapters. (It is step 2 of the three-step approach.)

Nor will you need to worry about combining the methods with the content; that is done for you in every chapter. The book provides teachers with many simple, concrete, and easy-to-use examples of events or situations that encourage good teaching practices.

The Role of the Textbook in the Classroom

The emphasis on the national programs during the past three decades tended to work against the use of a textbook in the classroom. In fact, many programs are clearly opposed to the use of texts.

The weaknesses of the textbook approach are well known. For example, a text is normally too content-oriented. In fact, content is often the only goal when using a text. In lesson after lesson pupils are asked to memorize facts.

Another weakness of the typical textbook approach is that pupils are often asked to read about science when they should be *doing* science. Pupils should be involved in direct hands-on investigation. All too often science classes have become nothing more than a succession of reading lessons. Presented that way, even good readers may find the content to be abstract and difficult to understand. For poor readers, of course, this approach is a disaster.

In summary, the textbook approach often tends to focus too much on content while ignoring both the activities and *processes* of science. In such cases the text approach is seriously restricting and inflexible.

Despite all the weaknesses of texts, and despite the major attempts to replace them with the national programs, textbooks still prevail. In most classrooms it was the national programs that disappeared, not the books. Why does the textbook survive? Probably because teachers find teaching science easier with a text than without it. The national programs were much more difficult than a text.

If the textbook approach led to such poor teaching, we can easily understand the attempts to replace it. Yet it survives. How should the problem be viewed now?

The basic view offered in this book is threefold: (1) Recognize the fact that the basic text will continue to be a major factor in the classrooms of the future. It is not realistic to suggest otherwise. (2) Make it possible to teach science effectively, even if a textbook is used. (3) Simplify good teaching. In other words, make "good teaching" easier to achieve by typical elementary teachers.

Perhaps we should also recognize that the text approach is not all bad. One of its greatest values is that it relieves teachers of the task of organizing the body of scientific knowledge. There is really nothing wrong with that particular benefit. We can easily work from such a base and expand it to bring in supplementary materials than to expect teachers to do the original organizing themselves.

Another benefit of a text is that it provides a common source of data for all pupils. We know that supplementary materials should be provided for your classes. However, there is really nothing wrong with having at least one common source of information for all pupils. It helps in organizing the lessons and provides a stable base from which to prepare the lessons.

The major focus of this book, however, is not to argue for or against the merits of a text or nontext approach. It is to help teachers regardless of what approach they use in their classrooms. If a text is used, the limitations that are often associated with texts can be upgraded greatly by following a few simple steps.

These steps are outlined in detail in a later section of this chapter ("How to Use Discrepant Events in Promoting the Processes of Science"). For now it is sufficient to say that the textbook approach can be improved by selecting appropriate activities for pupils to investigate.

Finally, the teaching method advocated in this book is not limited to the upgrading of the text approach. The method stands alone. It can be used with or without a textbook. It can be used to improve a course of study or to improve teacher-made units. The teacher needs only to look over the chapters of this book and to select those activities that fit his or her classroom.

WHAT IS A DISCREPANT EVENT?

Everyone has seen water run downhill. The fact is hardly surprising or unusual. However, if you were to see water run *uphill*, it would be an entirely different matter! Water flowing *against* the force of gravity is a discrepancy. (To see just such an event, refer to *Event 9–J. Antigravity Fountain.*)

Most people know that water freezes at 0 degrees Celsius (32° Fahrenheit). But what if you were to see ice *melt* at 10 or 15 degrees *below* the freezing point? What would you think? Again, there would be feelings of surprise and curiosity.

The surprise is even greater when, upon closer inspection, frost is seen forming on the outside of the beaker while ice is melting on the inside! (See *Event 3–C.*)

Water is expected to run downhill, not uphill; ice is expected to melt at 0 degrees Celsius, not 10 or 15 degrees below 0. These are examples of discrepant events. Such events are best described as being unexpected, surprising, or paradoxical.

A good discrepant event tends to create a strong feeling in the observer. Generally, there will be an inner feeling of "wanting to know." As children stare in disbelief at some of the events, they simply *have* to know how they work.

It is obvious that when pupils are strongly motivated, conditions are favorable for learning. Therefore, special emphasis was placed on selecting discrepant events whenever possible throughout this book. Such events capitalize on the curiosity of pupils and lead them to gain a better understanding of science.

Although there is much value in the use of discrepant events, it is evident that these cannot be developed for every conceivable topic or scientific principle. In the absence of an appropriate discrepant event, it is quite acceptable to present a nondiscrepant event. The pupils will still have a chance to observe or perform some kind of investigation. The main point to remember is that the event is used as an incentive to get pupils involved.

The various lessons in this text contain a carefully chosen selection of discrepant and nondiscrepant events. Discrepant events are used whenever possible, supplemented with nondiscrepant events whenever needed.

HOW TO USE DISCREPANT EVENTS IN PROMOTING THE PROCESSES OF SCIENCE

Discrepant events become quite useful when care is taken to initiate a lesson properly and time is allowed for student investigation. The teaching lessons can become effective when the following three general steps are employed:

1. SET UP A DISCREPANT EVENT. In this step the event (or events) are presented to gain attention, increase motivation, and encourage pupils to seek ways of solving the discrepancy. The stage is set for learning because pupils are confronted with questions or problems that they will want to resolve. They will *want to know* the answer to a good discrepant event.

2. PUPILS INVESTIGATE TO SOLVE THE DISCREPANCY. After the event is properly introduced, pupils will be anxious to seek an answer. In attempting to resolve the discrepancy, pupils will often engage in purposeful activities.

   They will be active in observing, recording data, classifying, predicting, experimenting, and doing whatever tasks are needed to solve the problem. (Notice that these tasks are the processes that were discussed earlier in this chapter in the section on "Process-Content".) In addition, it is likely that pupils will learn much of the real scientific content of the lesson.

3. RESOLVE THE DISCREPANCY. With some luck pupils will resolve the events themselves as a result of their own investigations. In other words, by their own direct activities and experiences they will find the answers to many of the questions posed by the discrepant event. And again, they will have learned something about how to observe, experiment, gather data, and perform other related processes of science.

If pupils are not successful in finding all the answers, they will still be ready to benefit from a more traditional treatment of the topic at this time. Even if the teacher merely explains the answer, the explanations will no longer be abstract. By this time pupils having put so much effort into the event will have a vested interest in the outcome. That is far better than merely listening to an explanation of some abstract principle found in a book.

To help you understand how the three steps are used, we will use and explain them more thoroughly in the following examples:

1. SET UP A DISCREPANT EVENT. Place a coin under a clear beaker or jar and tell the children to watch the coin closely. It is easily visible when viewed through the side of the glass. Now pour water into the tumbler and "presto" the coin disappears! Repeat several times to be sure that everyone can see. (See Fig. 1–1.)

   An event such as this has great value in motivating children. Even adults who see this activity are generally quite surprised to see the coin disappear and will want to know how it works. As a result, such an activity is ideal for introducing a science lesson. From this point on the "wanting to know" comes from the pupils.

Fig. 1–1. **Why does the coin "disappear" when water is poured into the beaker?**

2. PUPILS INVESTIGATE TO SOLVE THE DISCREPANCY. At what better point can we involve the children! They are self-motivated and are eager to find out "how it works."

   The pupils' involvement at this stage of a lesson is likely to be quite purposeful and will include questioning, recording data, graphing, predicting, experimenting, reading, theorizing, and doing many of the processes of science so strongly advocated by the national science programs.

   In this particular event pupils will observe that the coin disappears from view when the tumbler is filled with water but only if viewed through the side of the tumbler. The coin is still visible if viewed from above.

   They will find that it makes no difference whether the water is poured quickly or slowly. (Although if poured slowly, the coin seems to move upward slightly before it vanishes.)

3. RESOLVE THE DISCREPANCY. Under an ideal setting pupils will gradually resolve the questions as they work on step 2. Their findings should then be placed into the proper context in step 3. They should be led to see how the event relates to a broader scientific framework.

   The event with the disappearing coin is taken from Chapter 8 (*Event 8–K*) and pertains to the refraction (or bending) of light. Refraction occurs when light moves at an angle from one medium (a substance that allows light to pass through it) to another.

   When viewed through the side of the glass, the light travels through several different mediums (glass, water, and glass again) and is bent so much that the light from the coin never reaches the outside of the glass.

When viewed from the top, however, the coin is still visible because there are only two mediums. Also, since the light travels from one medium to another at only a slight angle, there is not as much bending as when it passes through at a sharp angle.

In this sample lesson we used only a single event to keep things simple. In a typical classroom setting we would probably present several related events at the same time, as long as they all pertained to the same topic of refraction. Let's trace the method through a second example.

Fig. 1–2. **A paradox of high and low sounds can be produced by striking the bottles and blowing across the mouth of each.**

1. SET UP A DISCREPANT EVENT. Select two identical bottles (such as soft-drink bottles). Fill one about one-half to two-thirds full of water. Leave the other empty. Blow across the mouth of the empty bottle and listen to the tone that is created. (See Fig. 1–2.)

   Now ask the pupils to predict the tone that will be created when you blow across the other bottle. Will the tone be higher, lower, or the same? Confirm their prediction by blowing across the partially filled bottle. The tone is higher.

   Ask the pupils to generalize. Why is the sound higher in the bottle containing water? They will probably say that the higher the water, the higher the pitch.

   Repeat the event several times so that everyone is sure of the results. Then tell the pupils that we need to check the results just once more, but in a slightly different way.

   This time, instead of blowing across the tops of the bottles, tap them with a small object such as a pen or the handle of a spoon. Surprisingly, this time the results will be just the opposite of what they were earlier! Now, the higher the water, the *lower* the pitch.

2. PUPILS INVESTIGATE TO SOLVE THE DISCREPANCY. At first glance the discrepancy is baffling to pupils. They will want to repeat the event themselves to check the results. They probably will want to try various bottles filled with different amounts of water. In summary, they will be using many of the processes of science while searching for a solution.

3. RESOLVE THE DISCREPANCY. This event is taken from Chapter 7 (*Event 7–X*). A single scientific principle explains both the first and second set of sounds from the bottles. The basic principle is that the greater the mass, the lower the sound; or, the smaller the mass, the higher the sound.

   That principle is verified, not contradicted, by this event. By blowing across the top, the air produces the sound. When striking the bottles, the bottles themselves, plus the contents, produce the sounds.

   In each case, the more substance there was, the lower the sound;

the less substance there was, the higher the sound. When blowing across the bottle, the "more" was the air; when striking the bottle, the "more" was the bottle-plus-water.

As in the first sample lesson, this event should be used along with other events that also relate to the same basic concept of sound. The explanation would then receive a more thorough treatment and be better related to a continuous discourse of science content.
Let's try a third example.

1. SET UP A DISCREPANT EVENT. This discrepancy is set up in problem form. Give a set of two tumblers each to several committees and ask them to pour *air* (not water) from one tumbler to another. Have available an aquarium or large glass container filled with water.

2. PUPILS INVESTIGATE TO SOLVE THE DISCREPANCY. Pupils are likely to say that it cannot be done. Some will make pouring motions with the tumblers but will concede they are not pouring anything. Tell them that it really can be done. In fact, if they do it right, there will be no doubt that air is actually being poured.

3. RESOLVE THE DISCREPANCY. The solution is very simple. Merely invert one tumbler and lower it into the water, leaving it filled with air. Lower the other tumbler underwater and invert it, filling it with water. Then tilt the tumbler that is full of air so that bubbles of air rise from it. Hold the other tumbler so that it catches the rising bubbles. (See Fig. 1–3.) In this way it is quite apparent that air is transferred (or poured) from one tumbler to another. (This example is taken from Chapter 9, *Event 9–C. Pouring Air*.)

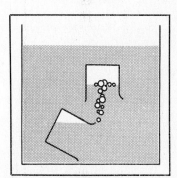

Fig. 1–3. **Pour air from one beaker to another underwater.**

This activity is related to one of the important properties of air. When this event is solved, the children will readily know that *air is a real substance and occupies space.*

Again, as stated in the first two examples, the lesson may include other related events, as long as those events all pertain to the same topic.

One final comment is necessary. The three steps are important only insofar as they are useful in permitting teachers to acquire techniques that promote good instructional practices. The steps are really only generalized procedures for setting up the beginning, middle, and end of a good lesson. The steps should not be regarded as restrictive in any way. Within the three steps teachers should feel free to use a wide range of variations in teaching any given lesson.

The steps of teaching a lesson are found, not only in this chapter, but are also built into all the content chapters of this book. You will find that the first two steps are incorporated in the "Discrepant Events and Pupil Investigations" sections. The third step is built into "Events Explained in Contexts" sections of each chapter.

HOW TO USE THIS BOOK

Teachers who depend mostly on science textbooks in their classrooms will find this book helpful in supplying challenging classroom activities in which children use the inquiry approach to science. For example, suppose a textbook lesson pertains to a topic on sound. The teacher can refer to Chapter 7 of this book ("Teaching Children About Sound") and select activities to introduce the topic, to heighten interest, and get pupils directly involved in science.

Their involvement in solving the problems will enable pupils to experience some of the processes of science. Furthermore, they will be in a much better position to understand what they read in the text.

Similarly, teachers who devise their own units or rely on courses of study may find that this book can supply them with a variety of useful activities that will help pupils to learn the process skills. In addition, the events are carefully explained in an appropriate context.

Finally, teachers who are actively working with one of the national programs in elementary science may find that the events and explanations are a useful supplement to the regular project materials.

Teaching Children about the Characteristics of Matter

During the Golden Age of Greece a philosopher named Democritus gave us the first look at the subject of "matter." He wondered about the smallness of things. How small can a bit of matter be? Can something be so tiny that it could not be divided? Suppose, for example, that we had a bucket of water and that it could be divided and redivided until the amounts would be too small to be seen.

If we had a magic knife, could those tiny bits be divided further, or is there a limit to how small something can be? Democritus thought that, yes, there must be a limit. Beyond a certain point, he reasoned, it could not be divided further. For this smallest of all parts he gave the name *atom*.

Today we know from one point of view that Democritus was right. There is, indeed, a limit to smallness. In the case of water, for example, the smallest part is called a *molecule*. It contains two atoms of hydrogen and one atom of oxygen (H_2O). If it is divided any further, it is no longer water. Thus, there *is* a limit to how tiny a substance can be *and still retain the properties of that substance*. When molecules and atoms are divided still further, the divided parts no longer have the characteristics of the original substance. (See Fig. 2–1.)

Until the mid-1800s scientists believed that the *atom* was the smallest possible particle. They then discovered that the atom was made of even tinier parts. Today scientists are aware of dozens of subatomic particles, and they continue to find ever smaller bits of matter.

Will we ever discover the elusive "smallest of all possible parts"? The subject calls to mind a poem by an unknown poet:

> Do fleas have little fleas
> Upon their backs to bite 'em.
> And these little fleas have littler fleas
> In ad infinitum?

How do we know what an atom looks like? Although the atom is too small to be seen, scientists have learned much about its structure. For example, we

DEMOCRITUS AND THE ATOM

Fig. 2–1. **When one molecule of water is divided, it ceases to be water. Instead, it becomes two atoms of hydrogen and one atom of oxygen.**

THE MODEL OF AN ATOM

Fig. 2–2. **Rutherford's experiments gave evidence that atoms contained mostly space.**

know that an atom is mostly space. Even dense materials like iron, lead, bricks, and stone contain atoms made up mostly of space.

How do we know this? Many of the explanations about the structure of an atom are too complex to discuss here. However, there was one important experiment performed by an English physicist in 1901 that gives us a clue as to how scientists "looked" inside the atom. Ernest Rutherford designed an experiment as shown in Fig. 2–2. He decided to test a sample "target" by "shooting" it with atomic "bullets." The target was a piece of gold foil, the gun was a bit of a radium, and the bullets were alpha particles from the radium.

He drilled a hole into the center of a block of lead and dropped a bit of radium inside. Lead is a shield against radiation, so no alpha particles came out except through the drilled hole. The hole was like the barrel of a rifle, and the atomic particles came out like bullets from a gun.

He aimed the atomic bullets toward a screen coated with a phosphorescent material that glowed when struck by radiation. In this way it was easy to see where the atomic bullets were hitting.

Rutherford then placed the thin piece of gold foil between the barrel and the screen to see what might happen. To his surprise the screen continued to glow as if the foil did not even exist! The atomic particles went right through the foil.

He observed the event for a long time. Then he noticed that from time to time a tiny fleck of light appeared on the phosphorescent screen *outside* the target area. This meant that on rare occasions an atomic particle hit something inside the foil and was deflected.

Careful study showed that only about 20 out of every million bullets were deflected. He concluded that (1) since most bullets went right through the foil, atoms consisted mostly of space; (2) since it was seldom hit, an atom must have a very small nucleus; and (3) since the nucleus was able to deflect the bullets, the nucleus must be very heavy as compared to the rest of the atom.

Rutherford's experiment can be compared to placing a chunk of metal inside a bale of straw and firing rifle bullets through it. Most of the bullets go right through the straw, but a few will hit the metal and be deflected. By studying the pattern of deflected bullets, we can estimate the size and shape of the unseen metal.

The comparison, to be accurate, would require a huge bale with a mass of 1000 kilograms. Of that total mass the chunk of metal would have 999.5 kilograms, whereas the rest of the bale would have only 0.5 kilogram. Most surprising of all, the heavy nucleus would be so tiny that it could hardly be seen.

If the nucleus of an atom were 1 centimeter in diameter, the outer part of that atom would be 120 meters away, or farther than the length of a football field. These figures show that an atom is made up mostly of space. Only about one part in 50,000 is actually solid.

It is easy to see from the figures that making an accurate classroom model of an atom is very difficult. Still, diagrams can be used if we are careful to

Fig. 2–3. **A two-dimensional model of an atom may be helpful in showing some relationships.**

stress the limitations. In other words, a diagram or model of an atom such as that shown in Fig. 2–3 is quite inaccurate with respect to scale, and it gives a poor representation of motion. However, the diagram can be helpful in showing some relationships.

Two terms can be used to describe every substance in the universe. All matter is made up either of *elements* or *compounds*.

TERMS

ELEMENT: A substance made up of only one kind of atom. It cannot be separated by ordinary chemical means into anything other than a sample of that element. There are 103 known elements. Some well-known examples are iron, carbon, uranium, hydrogen, oxygen, gold, and silver.

COMPOUND: A substance made up of two or more kinds of atoms. There are countless numbers of compounds. Some well-known examples are water, made up of two atoms of hydrogen and one atom of oxygen (H_2O); carbon dioxide (CO_2); and sugar; made up of atoms of carbon, hydrogen, and oxygen. Some complex compounds (such as synthetics) contain thousands of atoms.

Two additional terms can be used to describe the smallest parts of elements and compounds. They are atoms and molecules. They are not the smallest particles in the universe. But they are the smallest parts of matter that can exist alone or in combinations.

ATOM: The smallest part of an element. For example, you can have a single atom of the elements of hydrogen and oxygen, but not of the compound water (H_2O).

MOLECULE The smallest part of a compound. For example, the smallest part of water is a single molecule (H_2O) containing two atoms of hydrogen and one atom of oxygen. Some complex molecules contain thousands of atoms.

Another way to describe the structure of matter is to look at the order of size from the largest to the smallest.

COMPOUND: Made up of molecules.
MOLECULES: Made up of atoms.
ATOMS: Made up of electrons and nucleus (of many parts).
NUCLEUS: Made up of protons and neutrons (plus many other parts).

Discrepant Events and Pupil Investigations

SPACES BETWEEN MOLECULES (EVENTS 2–A THROUGH 2–D)

Event 2–A. Does 2 + 2 = 3½? Before the class begins, pour about 50 milliliters of rubbing alcohol (or you can use spirit duplicator "ditto" fluid that was once commonly used in schools) into a graduate cylinder. This should be an "unknown" liquid as far as the pupils are concerned.

Later, while the class is observing, pour about 50 milliliters of "known" liquid, identified as water, into another cylinder. Measure the volumes carefully and write the number on the chalkboard. Add a drop or two of food coloring to the containers to make the liquids easier to see. (It is not necessary to have exactly 50 milliliters in each container. But read the values carefully and add them together.)

Now pour the contents of one cylinder into the other and mix well. Check the volume of the combined liquids. Surprisingly, the sum will be about 2 to 4 milliliters *less* than the total of the two liquids measured separately. What happened to the missing liquid?

Pupil Investigations (may include the following processes):
1. Identifying by smell the "unknown" liquid as alcohol
2. Observing traces of liquid inside the emptied cylinder and theorizing (incorrectly) that this accounts for the loss in volume. (Students should be encouraged to check this theory. When they pour together two volumes of the "known" liquid, water, there is no measurable loss of volume.)
3. Graphing the volume of the combined liquids at 5-minute intervals for 30 minutes to see if the liquid is lost by evaporation. (Students will find that there is no measurable loss of volume after the initial mixing of the two liquids.)
4. Detecting the correct level of the liquid; take this opportunity to teach pupils how to read the level of a liquid. (See Fig. 2–4.)

Event 2–B. Where Does the Water Go? Fill a narrow-necked flask about one-fourth to one-half full of water-softener salt pellets. Then add warm water to nearly fill the flask. Mark the water level with a grease pencil or with tape. (See Fig. 2–5.)

After a few minutes the level will have dropped noticeably. Why? (*Note:* You can use table salt for this activity, but it tends to cake together if you let it stand for a few days.)

Pupil Investigations (may include the following processes):
1. Observing that the flask is warm to the touch (Some pupils may conclude incorrectly that the heat is produced by a chemical reaction. However, other pupils will have noticed that the water was added from the hot water faucet.)
2. Measuring the level of the water at periodic intervals for 40 to 60 minutes (Pupils will notice that most of the decline in the level occurs in the first 10 to 20 minutes and then stabilizes.)
3. Observing that the pellets become smaller (Pupils may conclude correctly that the pellets are dissolving.)
4. Forming a theory (incorrectly) that the loss in volume is due to the fact that the pellets are absorbing the water (Have pupils check this theory. Empty the liquid from the flask and refill with warm water.

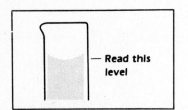

Fig. 2–4. **The level of liquid in the container should be read at its lowest point in the curve.**

Fig. 2–5. **Why does the water level go down? Use a grease pencil to mark the original level.**

The water level drops again, even when you start with saturated salt pellets.)

5. Forming a theory (incorrectly) that the water level drops because of evaporation (Pupils can check this theory by measuring the water level every 5 minutes for 40 to 60 minutes. Evaporation would cause a uniform rate of decline during the entire period.)

Safety Note: Some pupils may want to taste the liquid. Be sure to impress upon the pupils that unknown liquids should *never* be tasted. An unknown liquid could be poisonous.

Event 2–C. Pour Salt into a "Full" Tumbler. Fill a tumbler level-full with warm water. Then slowly add a measured amount of table salt. How much can be added without causing the tumbler to overflow? (See Fig. 2–6.)

Fig. 2–6. **How much salt can you pour into a "full" tumbler?**

Pupil Investigations (may include the following processes):
1. Measuring the amount of salt that can be poured into the tumbler before it overflows
2. Observing that the top surface of the water will stand above the rim of the tumbler after enough salt is added to the water

3. Concluding (incorrectly) that the amount of salt is equal to the amount of water standing above the rim of the tumbler (Pupils can check this theory by using a second tumbler and adding water instead of salt. They can add more salt than water before the tumbler overflows.)

Event 2–D. The Shrinking Balloon. Fill a balloon and tie it shut. Measure the distances around its length and width with a string. Put the balloon aside for a few days. Then measure again. The balloon will get smaller each day. Where does the air go?

Pupil Investigations (may include the following processes):
1. Predicting that the balloon will get smaller each day
2. Measuring to confirm the predictions
3. Inferring that the loss of size is due to a loss of air
4. Controlling variables: avoiding air loss at the neck by sealing the balloon securely

Events 2–A Through 2–D Explained in Context (Spaces Between Molecules)

It is difficult to show the size and shape of atoms and molecules in the classroom. Those particles are too small to be seen with ordinary lab equipment. Yet surprising as it may seem, the first four events in this chapter show us something about the makeup of molecules.

Event 2–A. Does 2 + 2 = 3½? shows that the two volumes do not add up. Some volume is lost when alcohol and water are mixed. When 50 milliliters of water are added to 50 milliliters of alcohol, we are surprised to find that the total adds up only to about 96 to 98 milliliters.

What happened to the missing liquid? It went into the spaces *between* the molecules. When mixed, the combined molecules fit together better than when they were alone, so that they take up less space. It is similar to mixing 50 milliliters of marbles and 50 milliliters of fine sand. The mixed volume will be much less than 100 milliliters because some of the sand will find room in the spaces between the marbles.

In *Event 2–B. Where Does the Water Go?* volume is lost again. The salt dissolves and the ions of sodium and chloride find room in the spaces *between* the molecules of water. If a narrow-necked flask is used, it is possible to see the level drop by as much as 3 centimeters in 30 minutes.

Sometimes pupils will say that the water is absorbed by the pellets. To test this theory, pour out the water after the level has dropped and refill the container with fresh warm water. This time the pellets are already saturated, but the water level drops again. (You can also use cold water, but it takes longer for the level to go down.)

In *Event 2–C. Pour Salt into a "Full" Tumbler* the dissolving salt again fills the spaces between molecules of water. This is part of the reason that you can add salt to a "full" tumbler. However, it is not the entire reason.

Another factor, cohesion (to be discussed in more detail later in this chapter), is also responsible. Cohesion is a force that causes water to "heap up" somewhat over the rim of a tumbler before it overflows.

Thus, because of these two factors—spaces between molecules and cohesion—a surprising amount of salt can be added to a "full" tumbler before it overflows. Pupils will have somewhat better success with this activity if the water is warm and the salt is added slowly so that it dissolves quickly.

Event 2–D. The Shrinking Balloon is an activity that almost all pupils will predict correctly. They seem to know instinctively that the balloon will be smaller after a few days. Yet many will not know why. The main reason for the loss of size is the loss of air. Molecules of air slowly escape through the spaces between the molecules of rubber or plastic.

All four of the events give evidence that there are spaces between molecules.

Discrepant Events and Pupil Investigations

Event 2–E. The "Smell" Box. Place a cut onion into a small cardboard box. Cut a hole in the box and place a barrier inside it so that the onion cannot be seen. Do not tell pupils what is in the box. Ask them to identify the object by using the sense of smell. (You can use other substances such as mothballs or a vinegar-soaked cloth in place of the onion.)

Pupil Investigations (may include the following processes):
1. Identifying the object in the box by smelling it (Most pupils will be able to identify an onion by its odor.)
2. Experimenting to see how far away the onion can be detected

Event 2–F. Pollen Jitter. Place some pollen or dust particles in a container of water. Let the water become very still and observe the pollen with a strong magnifying glass. It is possible to see the pollen vibrate in random motion. (See Fig. 2–7.)

Pupil Investigations (may include the following processes):
1. Observing the pollen specks with the magnifying lens
2. Forming a theory (incorrectly) that the specks are alive (Pupils can check this theory by boiling the water to kill all possible animal life.)
3. Concluding that some other force causes the specks to move.

Event 2–G. The "Hot" Rod. Place small bits of wax at 1-centimeter intervals along a copper or other metal rod. Heat one end of the rod and observe what happens. (See Fig. 2–8.)

Pupil Investigations (may include the following processes):
1. Observing that the wax bits melt, first close to the heat source and then progressively along the rod
2. Inferring that the heat travels along the rod to melt the wax
3. Comparing the rate of heat travel among different metals

MOLECULAR MOTION (EVENTS 2–E THROUGH 2–H)

Fig. 2–7. **If you look closely, you can see the pollen move. Where does that motion come from?**

Fig. 2–8. **What happens to the little blobs of wax as the heat moves along the rod?**

Event 2–H. How Does the Ink Spread? Place a drop of ink into a still glass of water. Do not stir the water. After a day or so the jar is uniformly colored. Why? (You can use food coloring in place of ink.)

Pupil Investigations (may include the following processes):
1. Recording data describing how much of the ink has dispersed through the liquid at periodic intervals (Hourly data for one school day is often enough.)
2. Forming a theory (incorrectly) that the ink mixes because of very slow currents in the water
3. Concluding that some other force spreads the ink throughout the water

Events 2–E Through 2–H Explained in Context (Molecular Motion)

Molecules are in constant motion. This motion is generally undetected by most of us because the molecules are too small to be seen. However, we have all seen and heard certain effects of random molecular motion without being aware of it. Random molecular motion causes electronic interference on television and radio receivers. The interference is seen as "snow" on television and is heard as "hiss" on radio.

Molecular motion increases when the temperature rises and decreases when the temperature falls. As a result, electronic interference can be reduced by cooling down the equipment. Such cooling is not practical in home television or radio equipment. However, liquid helium is used to cool some very costly equipment that is used in satellite communication systems. At that very cold temperature the motion of molecules is so slow that "hiss" is almost totally eliminated.

Evidence of molecular motion is shown in *Event 2–E. The "Smell" Box.* Many pupils will be able to identify an onion by smell alone. Almost everyone will be able to smell something, even if they cannot tell what it is. The event almost seems too simple.

The point of the event, however, is not to detect the onions. Instead, it is to find out *how the onion travels from the box to your nose.* Are there little bits of the onion that jump from the box and go to your nose? (Pupils usually laugh when you ask that question.) Yet, in a way, the answer is yes!

The event is meant to show that *molecules travel through gases.* The molecules are too small to be identified by sight, but, in the case of onions, they can be identified by smell. Molecules of the onion evaporate. That is, the liquid parts of the onion change to a gas and escape into the air. The gaseous onion molecules can then be detected by smell.

Further evidence of molecular motion is shown in *Event 2–F. Pollen Jitter.* By careful observation through a magnifying glass, we can sometimes see a random movement ("jittering") of the pollen. The motion is caused by molecules that keep bumping into the tiny pollen bits.

Larger particles do not show the jittery motion because they are hit by so many molecules from all sides that the effect of the bumps evens out, leaving no net effect. The random motion of the tiny bits is called the *Brownian movement*, named for Robert Brown, the scientist who discovered it.

In *Event 2–G. The "Hot" Rod* we see that heat is sent from molecule to molecule along the rod. This movement of heat through a substance is called *conduction*. This topic will be studied in greater detail in Chapter 3. At this point we are only concerned with the evidence that molecules move in solids.

Finally, we see evidence that molecules move in liquids in *Event 2–H. How Does the Ink Spread?* The molecules of ink are bumped by the molecules of water and gradually spread evenly throughout the container.

Note: Care must be taken to avoid heating the liquid because then the liquid will begin to develop a slow movement (or convection current). That current will obviously mix the liquids. In this event you want to see if the mixing will occur even if the water remains totally still. It does. Molecular motion will eventually disperse the ink evenly throughout the water. It will take from several hours to several days for the mixing to occur.

Discrepant Events and Pupil Investigations

THE PHASES (OR STATES) OF MATTER (EVENTS 2–I THROUGH 2–L)

Event 2–I. Make Ice Disappear. Put some crushed ice into a Pyrex beaker and heat it. Record the temperature of the contents at 1- or 2-minute intervals. Make a graph to show the results. At what point does ice melt? How many phases of matter are shown by this activity?

Pupil Investigations (may include the following processes):
1. Observing the temperatures at regular intervals
2. Recording the readings on a graph
3. Interpreting the graph to note the effects of melting and boiling

Event 2–J. Liquid to Gas to Liquid. Boil some water in a teakettle. Hold a cold piece of glass or small mirror over the spout and observe.

Pupil Investigations (may include the following processes):
1. Observing that a "cloud" forms above the spout of the teakettle
2. Observing that the pane of glass or mirror becomes fogged and that drops of water fall from it
3. Inferring that water (liquid phase) is formed from steam (gaseous phase)
4. Comparing this activity with the water cycle

Event 2–K. What Put Out the Fire? Place a small candle inside a beaker and add a small amount of baking soda and water. Then light the candle and pour about 2 or 3 cubic centimeters of vinegar ("unknown" liquid to pupils) into the beaker, being careful not to touch the candle flame. Soon the flame goes out. Why? (See Fig. 2–9.)

Fig. 2–9. **Why does the flame go out when you pour the liquid into the beaker?**

Pupil Investigations (may include the following processes):
1. Observing a foaming action as the unknown liquid touches the baking soda solution
2. Identifying, by smell, the unknown liquid as vinegar
3. Inferring that there is a substance produced by the foaming action that causes the flame to go out

Event 2–L. Solids to Liquids. Place a variety of solids on a round copper plate. Include such solids as wax, solder, ice, and lead, if available. Be sure that all items are at equal distances from the center. Heat the plate at the center and observe.

Pupil Investigations (may include the following processes):
1. Observing that different substances melt at different times
2. Recording the times at which the different solids melt
3. Inferring that the different solids have different melting points

Events 2–I Through 2–L Explained in Context (The Phases of Matter)

Just about all matter on earth exists in one of three forms: *solid*, *liquid*, or *gas*. (There is a fourth state called plasma that is found in the sun and stars. It can also be formed on earth but is not commonly found outside the lab.) Some characteristics and definitions of solids, liquids, and gases are shown in Table 2–1.

Table 2–1. **Phases of Matter**

Solid	Liquid	Gas
Definite volume and definite shape	Definite volume but no definite shape	No definite volume or shape
High cohesive force	Low cohesive force	Cohesive force almost nonexistent
Molecules tightly packed	Molecules not tightly packed	Molecules fairly far apart
Easily visible	Easily visible	Almost always invisible
Example: ice	Example: water	Example: steam

Event 2–I. Make Ice Disappear is excellent because it shows all three states of matter. It also gives us some evidence of the melting and boiling points of water.

Students will find that the temperature of the water will remain more or less stationary at the *melting point* until all the ice is melted. Then the temperature will rise rapidly until it boils. At the *boiling point* the temperature will again remain stationary as the water boils away. (See Fig. 2–10.) All three states are evident: ice (solid), water (liquid), and steam (invisible gas).

Not all substances go through the liquid state when they change from a solid to a gas. Some materials, such as mothballs and dry ice, change directly from a solid to a gas.

Even ordinary ice can change directly from a solid to a gas. Ice and snow will gradually disappear in very cold weather, even if temperatures do not go above freezing.

This direct change from solid to gas is called *sublimation*. The reverse can also happen. A gas (such as water vapor) can change directly into solids (such as snow and frost) without going through the intermediate liquid phase.

MOST GASES ARE INVISIBLE. Students are often surprised to discover that most gases are invisible. They commonly believe that fog, clouds, and steam are visible gases. Of course, fog and clouds are visible, but they are not gases. They are liquids. And although steam is a gas, it is not visible.

Pupils will question the invisibility of steam. If it is supposed to be invisible, *why can we see steam coming from a teakettle?* We have all seen the cloud that forms over the spout of a teakettle. If that cloud is not steam, what is it?

Fig. 2–10. **Study the graph. What are the effects of the heat of fusion and heat of vaporization?**

Fig. 2–11. **The steam coming from the strongly boiling teakettle is invisible. The visible cloud consists of tiny droplets of liquid that are condensed when the steam is cooled by the air in the room.**

The answer is simple. The visible cloud is not steam. It is a *cloud*. The cloud above the spout is formed just like the clouds in the sky. It is mostly liquid, consisting of tiny floating drops of water. In both cases the cloud forms, not when H_2O is heated up, but when the H_2O cools down.

Just follow the path of the H_2O in the kettle from water to steam to cloud. As the water boils inside the kettle, it is changed to steam. Then as the steam travels up the spout, it is chilled by the much colder room temperature . . . and condenses into a cloud. (See Fig. 2–11.) Once you are able to see something, it has already changed from steam (an invisible gas) to a cloud (a visible liquid). Outside, the clouds in the sky are formed in the same way. Water vapor rises high into the sky and is chilled. As it cools, the water vapor (a gas) is changed into tiny droplets of water to form a cloud (a liquid).

Sometimes the air is very dry and the steam will go directly to ordinary water vapor without forming a cloud and nothing will be visible. (Remember that water vapor is already in the air, and that steam only adds to it. The only difference between steam and ordinary water vapor is that steam is hot and water vapor is not.) In that case, using a mirror or pane of glass, as suggested in *Event 2–J. Liquid to Gas to Liquid*, will still show the formation of a liquid.

If you hold the glass in the steam long enough, you will see not only fog, but possibly rain as well. The droplets sometimes gather and grow until they combine into drops of water. That is an example of how rain forms in nature. The tiny droplets in the clouds combine until they become large enough so that they no longer float in the air. When those drops fall, they form rain.

Another simple experiment can be done to show that water vapor is invisible. Just wipe a chalkboard with a damp cloth. The dampness that is visible is a liquid. However, the damp spot quickly disappears. Where does it go? It evaporates into a gas (water vapor) and mixes with the air. It is still in the room but is no longer visible.

Event 2–K. What Put Out the Fire? also shows the existence of an invisible substance—one that put out the fire. When the vinegar is poured into the dissolved baking soda, carbon dioxide is released. It fills the container, pushing out the oxygen. Thus, deprived of its oxygen, the flame goes out.

In summary, the event is an indirect way of proving the existence of a substance that you cannot see. You can tell it is there *by what it does*: It puts out the fire. (This event can also be used to show that oxygen is necessary to support combustion.)

All common gases (such as oxygen, nitrogen, hydrogen, carbon dioxide, and water vapor) are invisible. Only a few rare gases, such as iodine vapors, can be seen.

Even invisible gases can sometimes cause visible effects. For example, you may notice a shimmering effect if you look at an object through the rising air currents directly over a hot stove or above a candle flame. Also, on a very hot day you may notice that objects in the distance appear to "dance." That, too, is caused by rapidly rising air currents.

CHANGES OF PHASE. When a substance is heated, its molecular action increases. This action, in turn, weakens the forces that hold a substance together. If enough heat is applied, the molecular action becomes so strong that the substance can no longer hold itself together. It changes from a solid to a liquid. In other words, it melts.

If the substance is heated still more, it eventually becomes a gas. At that point molecular action is much greater than when the substance was a liquid or a solid. Probably the simplest example of these changes is the melting of ice and heating it to form steam. It changes from a solid (ice) to a liquid (water) and then to steam (a gas).

A change of a solid to a liquid is shown in *Event 2–L. Solids to Liquids.* Pupils will see that the solids have different melting points. The first substance to melt is ice. Ice is followed by wax, solder, then lead. It is not too important which substances you use. The event is merely intended to show that different substances have different melting points.

THE BOILING POINT OF WATER. In this chapter we have discussed boiling and melting points. Normally, those terms are used as if they represent fixed points on the thermometer. In fact, those points are not fixed: They change if air pressure changes.

The boiling point, especially, is affected by pressure. At sea level pure water boils at 100 degrees Celsius. At higher elevations the boiling point is lower. In fact, the boiling point drops about 1 degree for every 300 meters gain in altitude. Thus, water boils at about 95 degrees Celsius in Denver, at 86 degrees Celsius on top of Pike's Peak, and at 74 degrees Celsius on top of Mount Everest.

At even greater heights reached by plane or spacecraft, water boils at still lower temperatures. At 19,000 meters water boils at body temperature (37 degrees Celsius). This means that body fluids of an unprotected astronaut will boil at that altitude. At 27,000 meters water will boil at room temperature (22 degrees Celsius). Astronauts are protected from those dangers by wearing pressurized suits.

The opposite effect occurs as pressure is increased: The greater the pressure, the higher the boiling point. For example, a cook can obtain a higher boiling point by using a pressure cooker. The effect of pressure on the boiling point has even been observed in undersea labs where the boiling point of water was raised to almost 130 degrees Celsius. (See Fig. 2–12.)

27,000 m	22°C	
19,000 m	37°C	
Mt. Everest	9600 m	74°C
Pike's Peak	4400 m	86°C
Denver	1600 m	95°C
Sea level		100°C
Undersea lab		130°C

Fig. 2–12. **The boiling point of water decreases as air pressure decreases (at higher altitudes).**

CHANGES IN MATTER (EVENTS 2–M AND 2–N)

Discrepant Events and Pupil Investigations

Event 2–M. Separate the Materials. Mix together sand, sugar, iron filings, bits of cork, and marbles. Let students separate them. Do not tell them ahead of time what the materials are or how many different ones are in the mixture.

Pupil Investigations (may include the following processes):
1. Devising a procedure to separate the materials
2. Recording data of the materials separated
3. Concluding that the mixing did not change the materials

Event 2–N. Rearrange Some Molecules. Mix together some iron filings and sulfur. Show that the two elements can be separated because each element still retains its own properties. (Use a magnet to pull out the iron filings.)

Then remix the substances and heat them in a well-ventilated area (an offensive odor will be produced). If heated enough, the mixture is changed to iron sulfide. Let it cool and check it with a magnet.

Pupil Investigations (may include the following processes):
1. Observing that the magnet will have no effect on the substance after the mixture is heated
2. Forming a theory (incorrectly) that the sulphur acts like glue to hold the iron particles (The magnet would still be attracted to iron even if the iron were held in glue.)
3. Concluding that the materials have been greatly changed

Events 2–M and 2–N Explained in Context (Changes in Matter)

Matter can be changed in three fundamental ways: physical, chemical, and nuclear. The three types are explained in Table 2-2.

Two of the three types of changes can be shown in the classroom. For example, *Event 2–M. Separate the Materials* focuses on the physical differences of matter. All the substances in this mixture can be separated by using only physical means. The marbles can be picked out by hand and the iron filings drawn out by a magnet. The bits of cork will float to the top if the mixture is dumped into a bowl of water, and the sugar that dissolves in water can be crystallized again by letting the water evaporate.

All the substances are located in a grouping called a *mixture*. A mixture is a collection of matter in which each substance keeps its own property.

Event 2–N. Rearrange Some Molecules represents a chemical change. Before the heat is applied the two substances are still only a mixture and can be separated by physical means. After the mixture is heated enough, it becomes a *compound* called iron sulfide. Iron sulfide is quite different from either iron or sulfur. A magnet will no longer pull out the iron because the iron no longer exists.

Table 2–2. **Changes in Matter**

Types of Change	Definition	Examples
Physical	A change in appearance only; the substance is still the same after the change takes place	Cutting paper Melting butter Dissolved salt in water Breaking glass
Chemical	A substance is changed into one or more different substances; change is at the molecular level	Rusting Fire Heating iron and sulfur Overcooking food (change to carbon)
Nuclear	A rearrangement of the nuclei of atoms to form new atoms	Radioactivity Atomic fission Nuclear fusion Energy of sun and stars

Discrepant Events and Pupil Investigations

ADHESION (EVENTS 2–O THROUGH 2–R)

Event 2–O. Why Does the Water Climb? Place capillary tubes of varying sizes into a jar of water and observe how high the liquid climbs up the tubes. What causes the differences in height? (Mix some food coloring into the water so that the liquid is easier to see in the tiny tubes.)

Pupil Investigations (may include the following processes):
1. Observing that the water level inside each tube is above the water level in the bottle
2. Measuring the height of the liquid in each tube
3. Inferring a relationship between the diameter of a tube and the height of the liquid in that tube
4. Forming a theory (incorrectly) that air pressure is causing the water to climb the tubes (Point out that the tubes are all open on top so that the air pressure pushes down equally on all of them.)

Event 2–P. What Pulls Out the Water? Drape a washcloth over the edge of a partially filled bowl of water. Leave it for about an hour. Why does the water leave the bowl?

Pupil Investigations (may include the following processes):
1. Observing that the water climbs up the cloth and over the edge of the bowl
2. Investigating to see if water climbs other materials
3. Measuring how water will climb in different materials

Event 2–Q. Get a Lift. Fill a tin can with pieces of cardboard. Then add water and place a heavy weight on top of the cardboard. Observe for an hour. Soon the weight is lifted up by swelling and expanding cardboard.

Pupil Investigations (may include the following processes):
1. Measuring how much the weight is lifted at equal time intervals and plotting the readings on a graph
2. Repeating the activity using different weights
3. Inferring correctly that there is a relationship between the water and the swelling cardboard

Event 2–R. Make a Cork Stay in the Middle. Place a cork into the middle of a partly filled glass of water. What happens to the cork? Ask the pupils to find a way to make the cord float in the middle.

Pupil Investigations (may include the following processes):
1. Observing that the cork moves to the side of the glass even when the cork is placed in the center
2. Observing that the water level in the middle of the tumbler is slightly lower than the water touching the side of the glass
3. Trying (unsuccessfully) to keep the cork in the middle by floating it at all angles (on either end, on its side, etc.)
4. Experimenting with corks and containers of varying sizes and filled to different heights

Events 2–Q Through 2–R Explained in Context (Adhesion)

Fig. 2–13. Think of a piece of sticky adhesive tape. Adhesion is the attraction of two different substances for each other—like adhesive tape and skin.

Why does paint stick to a wall? Why does glue hold things together? Why does a paper towel get wet (but not a sheet of wax paper)? All the questions have the same answer: *adhesion.* Adhesion is the attraction between unlike substances.

Another way to remember this topic is to think about an old sticky piece of adhesive tape that is being pulled from the skin. Why does adhesive tape stick? Because of adhesion. (See Fig. 2–13.)

The force of adhesion varies greatly among different substances. In most of the preceding examples the adhesion is quite strong. In other cases it is quite weak. For example, water does not stick very well to other substances. It does not stick to a wall, for example, as well as paint sticks to a wall. Indeed, the attraction between water with most other substances is so weak that most people do not think that there is any attraction at all.

Surprisingly, water *does* attract other substances. In fact, all four events in this section are related to adhesion. Go back to Fig. 2–4. Remember that the water in the test tube was lower in the middle and was curved up at the sides? This upward curve is caused by an attraction between glass and water.

The force of adhesion becomes more evident when tubes of smaller sizes are used. Hence, in *Event 2–O. Why Does the Water Climb?* the smaller the tube, the higher the water level. Those fine hairlike tubes are called *capillary tubes,* and the upward climb of liquids in those tubes is called *capillary action.*

Capillary action also occurs in *Event 2–P. What Pulls Out the Water?* The fibers of the washcloth contain thousands of tiny hairlike passages that act as capillary tubes to attract water. Thus, the water is pulled out of the bowl, eventually draining it.

The strength that can be generated by adhesion becomes more apparent in *Event 2–Q. Get a Lift.* As the water soaks into the cardboard, it swells up and lifts the weight. The force is so great that it can lift a fully grown adult standing on the cardboard. (Unfortunately, the action is so slow that few would be willing to stand on the cardboard long enough to find out.)

It is the adhesion between the water and wood that causes wood to swell. Thus, damp floors sometimes bulge, and during humid summers windows and doors sometimes expand so that they are hard to open and close.

Event 2–R. Make the Cork Stay in the Middle also shows the force of adhesion. Regardless of how carefully you put the cork into the middle of the tumbler, the cork will slide off to the side and attach itself to the glass (unless you use a large container and a small cork).

The reason for the cork's movement is really quite simple. The cork is light and it floats to the top. If you look closely, the water is higher at the edge of the glass than at the middle. Thus, the "top" of the water is along the side where it touches the glass. As explained earlier, the water is pulled upward because of adhesion (attraction) between the glass and water.

As long as the cork is fairly large and the tumbler fairly small, it is almost impossible to keep the cork from moving to the side. However, if you have a large container, then the middle becomes fairly flat and the cork might stay there.

The "trick" in getting the cork to stay in the middle is merely to fill the tumbler "heaping" full. Now the high point of the water is in the middle, not the sides. Again, the cork just floats to the top, but in this case the top is in the middle. (See Fig. 2–14.)

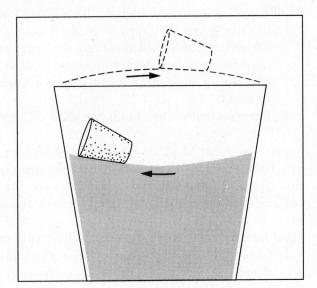

Fig. 2–14. **The cork in this activity always goes to the highest point of the water. As long as the tumbler is not full, the highest part is along the edges. If the glass is "heaping" full, the highest part is in the middle.**

COHESION (EVENTS 2–S THROUGH 2–X)

Discrepant Events and Pupil Investigations

Event 2–S. Pour Water at an Angle. Anyone can pour water that falls straight down, but use a string and pour water *at an angle*. Have available a full glass of water, an empty glass, some string, and some weights. Try the event over a sink or large pan to collect spills.

Pupil Investigations (may include the following processes):
1. Observing that water does not flow along a dry string
2. Experimenting with ways of pouring water along the string
3. Observing that water tends to "stick" to a wet string and to flow along it even at an angle

Event 2–T. Join the Water. Punch several holes close together along the bottom of an empty milk carton. Fill the carton with water and observe how the water comes out of the holes. Under certain circumstances the streams will join together to form a single stream.

Pupil Investigations (may include the following processes):
1. Experimenting to see the effects of high and low water levels on the stream
2. Devising a procedure of separating and joining the streams
3. Experimenting to see the effects of holes farther apart and closer together
4. Forming a theory that the streams will join together because of an inner force or attraction in water

Fig. 2–15. **Why does salad oil form spheres in the water-alcohol solution?**

Event 2–U. Suspended Drops. Mix together a combination of two-thirds alcohol and one-third water. Place a few drops of salad oil into this solution. Enlarge the drops with a medicine dropper. What shape do the drops take? (See Fig. 2–15.)

Pupil Investigations (may include the following processes):
1. Observing that the drops of salad oil assume a spherical shape
2. Observing that the salad oil remains more or less suspended in the solution (the drops do not move up or down very much.)
3. Comparing these drops to the shape of typical raindrops as described in books
4. Inferring that a force holds the salad oil together

Event 2–V. Float Metal on Water. Carefully lower a metal screen onto water in a bowl. If this is done with care, the screen will float. A needle, paper clip, tin-can lid, pepper, sawdust, feather, or string should float also. Then add a drop of soap or detergent and see how many items sink.

Pupil Investigations (may include the following processes):
1. Observing that the surface of the water is pushed down, or forms a depression, by the weight of some objects

2. Inferring that some objects float even though they seem to be heavier than the water
3. Observing that many of the objects sink after the soap is added
4. Inferring that the soap reduces the lifting power of water

Event 2–W. What Keeps the Water In? Fill a flask or bottle with water. Cover the container with a metal screen or piece of cloth and invert it over a sink. Initially, a few drops of water may spill, but then the water will not run out. Why not?

Pupil Investigations (may include the following processes):
1. Observing that the water will not run through the screen or cloth as long as it is held tightly against the inverted flask
2. Testing to see if the screen or cloth is clogged (It is not.)
3. Forming a theory to explain what keeps the water in the flask and the air out of it

Event 2–X. Sink the Pepper. Sprinkle some pepper on the surface of a bowl of water. Then place a drop of liquid soap on the water near one edge of the bowl. What happens?

Pupil Investigations (may include the following processes):
1. Observing that most of the pepper floats on the water before the soap is added
2. Observing that the water "explodes" away from the point where the soap is added to the water
3. Observing that the pepper falls like rain after the soap is added
4. Inferring that the soap has an effect on the water that reduces its "lifting" power

Events 2–S Through 2–X Explained in Context (Cohesion)

Why does your desk stay together? Why doesn't a chunk of iron fall apart? Why can you push your hand through water but not through a board?

The answers to these questions all relate to cohesion. *Cohesion is the attraction of like molecules for each other.* Refer to the discussion about the phases of matter earlier in this chapter. Recall that there are differences in the cohesive forces of solids, liquids, and gases. In solids the force is strongest. *It is cohesion that holds a solid together.*

The cohesive force of liquids, however, is so weak that they have no definite shape of their own. Furthermore, you can easily push your hand through a liquid.

Gases have the least cohesion of all. Gas molecules have so little attraction for each other that a gas will not even stay in an open container. It just floats out.

We mentioned the effect of cohesion briefly during our discussion of adhesion; water is affected by both forces. That is, water is attracted to many substances (adhesion), while there is also an attraction among water molecules for each other (cohesion).

If you can reduce the effect of one force, then the effect of the other force is easier to observe. For example, water is not attracted to wax paper. Thus, if you put a drop on wax paper, you see only the effect of cohesion.

What is the shape of that drop? The water "beads up" because cohesive forces pull the water as close together as possible. If you put the drop on a blotter, however, adhesive forces (along with gravity) quickly spread out the water. Cohesion is not strong enough to keep the drop together in such a situation.

The events in this section pertain mostly to the cohesive forces within the water. As a matter of fact, go back to the last event before this section (Event 2–R), where we saw the cork move to the middle when the tumbler was filled heaping full. What caused the water to "heap up" over the rim of the glass? Why didn't the water overflow? The answer: cohesion. The attraction within water is great enough to overcome (somewhat) the force of gravity.

Cohesion is also the explanation for *Event 2–S. Pour Water at an Angle.* Water can be poured along the string, but only if the string is wet. If you try to pour along a dry string, there is no cohesion and the water just spills. If the string is wet, however, it works nicely because the poured water is attracted (by cohesion) to the water that is already on the string. With some care and practice you can pour water at quite an angle. (See Fig. 2–16.)

Note: Be sure that the string touches the lip of the top beaker but does *not* touch the lip of the bottom beaker. It is easier to do this event if you tie a weight to each end of the string.

Event 2–T. Join the Water also shows the cohesive forces within water. The water will flow out of the holes at the bottom of the milk carton in separate streams until you use your fingers to pull the streams together. Once joined, they tend to "stick" together to form a single stream. That "sticking" is due to cohesion. (See Fig. 2–17.)

In *Event 2–U. Suspended Drops* another example of cohesion is seen. In this event the salad oil weighs just about the same as the water-alcohol mixture. Thus, the salad oil will tend to float within the mixture without either rising or settling. (If you find that your salad oil tends to rise too quickly, increase the ratio of alcohol in the mixture. If the salad oil sinks too quickly, increase the ratio of water.)

Since the force of gravity of both the oil and the mixture are almost exactly the same, gravity exerts no net force. Cohesion is the only force that exerts itself in the drops of oil. Cohesion will pull the oil as closely together as possible, and thus the drops will form into round spheres. (There is very little, if any, adhesive forces between oil and water, so adhesion is no factor in this event.)

A special form of cohesion called *surface tension* occurs along the surface of a liquid. Its special effects can be noted in the three remaining events of this section. In *Event 2–V. Float Metal on Water,* for example, the metal floats because of surface tension.

We all know that metal is heavier than water. Yet a metal screen, needle, tin-can lid, or paper clip will float if placed carefully on the surface of water.

Fig. 2–16. **Water flows along a wet string. The string must touch the lip of the top beaker but not the rim of the lower one. Hold the string in place by attaching weights to both ends.**

Fig. 2–17. **The water from the three holes tends to stay together because of the cohesive attraction of water molecules for one another.**

The molecules of water on the surface hold together so well that they often keep heavier objects from breaking through. In fact, the surface acts as if it has a "skin" on it.

Once the object breaks through the surface, however, the cohesive force of the water below the object is the same as the cohesive force of the water above it. The cohesive forces are equalized, leaving only gravity to act on the object. Therefore, it sinks to the bottom.

When soap is added, however, the floating objects sink right away. Why? Because soap lowers the cohesive forces of water. In a washing machine soap reduces the cohesion of water. This means that water no longer "sticks together," so it can enter fibers and fabrics more easily to flush out the soil and grime.

Surface tension is an important factor in *Event 2–W. What Keeps the Water In?* For water to flow out it must break up into tiny streams and pass through the openings of the screen or through the openings between the fibers of the cloth. However, the cohesive force of water is strong enough to keep it from separating into the tiny streams. (Another factor, air pressure, is also involved in this event. Air trys to enter the bottle to replace the water going out, so that air exerts a pressure against the water.)

Finally, *Event 2–X. Sink the Pepper* shows another example of surface tension. Or, more accurately, it shows what happens when the surface tension is broken.

As soon as a drop of soap hits the water, the pepper seems to "explode" away. That happens because the soap reduces cohesion (or attraction). The water no longer has any cohesion where the soap hits it but is still attracted at all points away from the soap. This causes the "explosion."

As soon as the soap spreads out across the surface of the water, the surface tension is lost and can no longer hold up the heavier pepper. In fact, the pepper seems to "rain" down.

The events show that cohesion is a form of attraction among molecules of the same substance. Cohesion is very strong in solids—strong enough for a solid to hold its shape. Cohesion is quite weak in liquids but is still evident if shown in the right way. In summary, cohesion is molecular attraction that holds things together.

CHAPTER

3

Teaching Children about Heat Energy

MEASURING HEAT AND TEMPERATURE (EVENT 3–A)

Fig. 3–1. **Does the bolt or nail contain more heat? How will they affect the temperatures of the lower containers?**

Discrepant Event and Pupil Investigations

Event 3–A. Heat or Temperature? For this event you will need three beakers, one large bolt, and one small nail. Fill three beakers about half full of tap water. Measure the temperature of the water.

Place the bolt and nail into the first beaker and heat until the water boils. Then, with tongs, place the bolt into the second beaker and the nail into the third beaker. (See Fig. 3–1.) Record the temperature of the water in those beakers at 30-second intervals for a few minutes.

The containers should be small and have only enough water to cover the objects completely. Otherwise the temperature will not be affected very much.

Pupil Investigations (may include the following processes):
1. Recording the temperature of the water in the containers at periodic intervals
2. Graphing the readings to show the temperature changes
3. Observing that the bolt raised the temperature of the water more than the nail did
4. Forming a theory to explain the differences that were observed and recorded

Event 3–A Explained in Context (Measuring Heat and Temperature)

Heat is a form of energy. It is the energy that a substance has because of the motion of its molecules. When a substance gains heat, the motion of its molecules becomes more vigorous. Conversely, when a substance loses heat, its molecular action decreases.

If a substance were to lose *all* of its heat, all molecular motion would stop. That point is called *absolute zero*. Absolute zero is −459.6 degrees on the Fahrenheit scale and −273 degrees on the Celsius scale. Absolute zero has never been reached, but scientists have gotten to within a fraction of a degree of that figure.

HOW HEAT IS MEASURED. Since heat and temperature are different, they are measured differently. Heat is measured in calories, British thermal units (Btu), or joules. A *calorie* is the amount of heat needed to raise the temperature of 1 gram of water by 1 degree Celsius. A Btu is the heat needed to raise 1 pound of water by 1 degree Fahrenheit. The joule, a unit used to measure work, can also be used to measure heat.

The calorie is a fairly common unit; the other two are not. However, the Btu is still the standard unit used to measure the heat output of home furnaces. Look at the label fixed to your home furnace. You will find the Btu rating listed. The joule is used mostly in the scientific community.

HOW TEMPERATURE IS MEASURED. *Temperature* is a measure of how hot or cold something is. It is measured in degrees. However, the *size* of the degree varies, depending on which temperature scale that is used.

A number of scales have been developed since 1714 when Gabriel Daniel Fahrenheit developed the first scale to be widely used. He decided that a scale should have three major reference points: (1) a boiling point, (2) a freezing point, and (3) a zero point.

Absolute zero could not be the zero point because in those days nobody knew where it was. It could not be measured. The only sure reference points known at that time were the boiling and freezing points of water. The boiling point was no good because it would make the cooler temperatures of ordinary weather read in minus values (or below zero). Fahrenheit did not like the freezing point either. In the winter time the temperature would still go below freezing and he felt that people would be confused by "below zero" numbers.

To avoid the confusion, Fahrenheit decided to invent a zero point that would be low enough so that minus values would not normally be needed to measure winter weather. His solution was to mix together equal amounts of salt and crushed ice. The temperature of such a mixture drops far below freezing. It became his zero point.

The next step was to choose the *size* of the degree. He could have chosen any size at all because the degree is an arbitrary unit. If he wanted to, Fahrenheit could have chosen a degree so large that only five degrees would have fit between the boiling and freezing points. Or he could have chosen a size that would allow hundreds of degrees to fit.

He decided to use a size that permitted 180 degrees. He felt that 180 was a convenient number because it seemed to fit into the world of mathematics. After all, if you go in one direction and then turn around and go in the opposite direction, that is a 180-degree turn. He reasoned that boiling and freezing were opposites also, so 180 degrees seemed to be just right.

Once he selected 180 degrees to measure the difference between the boiling and freezing points, it was simply a matter of arithmetic to find how many of those degrees fit between the freezing and zero points. He found that there were 32 degrees between those points. Thus, starting with the zero point, the freezing point became 32 degrees and the boiling point (180 degrees higher) became 212 degrees.

Fahrenheit's scale was certainly useful and was quickly adopted by all the civilized countries of the world. As useful as it was, however, it was not without problems. First of all, the zero point was not really a fixed value. It could not be accurately duplicated around the world. The temperature of an ice-salt mixture varies depending on the size of the crushed ice and the size and type of the salt. Thus, the zero point meant different temperatures in different places. It was not a fixed value.

Second, although the 180 degrees seemed to imply "opposite," it had no practical meaning in this case. It did not fit into the decimal system and scientists had to apply conversion formulas to use them.

Third, although Fahrenheit wanted to avoid the use of minus numbers in measuring winter temperatures, that problem was not avoided either. In many countries winter temperatures went below zero anyway.

Because of these problems, it took only 28 years for another scale to be introduced. In 1742 Anders Celsius, a Swedish astronomer, invented a scale that was originally named the *Centigrade scale*. Later it was renamed *Celsius scale* in honor of its author. It used the freezing point of water as its zero point, a fixed point anywhere in the world. The Celsius scale used 100 degrees between boiling and freezing, a value that fit into the decimal system. Scientists all over the world quickly adopted it.

A third major scale was developed by Lord Kelvin of England. His scale became possible when scientists discovered absolute zero. Remember that in the times of Fahrenheit and Celsius that point was unknown.

Once absolute zero was known, Kelvin moved the zero point down to it. Thus, he had a scale in which a temperature below zero could not exist. Moving the zero was the only thing that Kelvin did. He kept the size of the degree the same as the Celsius degrees. In other words, there were 100 degrees between the freezing and boiling points.

He found that there were 273 degrees between absolute zero and the freezing point. The boiling point was 100 degrees higher, or 373 degrees. You can see that the *Kelvin scale* is the same as the Celsius scale, except that in the Kelvin scale the zero point starts 273 degrees lower.

A summary of the three scales is shown in Table 3–1.

Table 3–1. Temperature Scales

	Fahrenheit	Celsius	Kelvin
Boiling point	212	100	373
Freezing point	32	0	273
Fahrenheit's ice-salt mixture	0	−18	255
Absolute zero	−460	−273	0

Event 3–A. Heat or Temperature? shows the difference between heat and temperature. Both the large bolt and the small nail have the same temperature—the boiling point of water. But do they have the same heat? No, the large bolt has more heat because it is bigger. The bolt will raise the temperature of an equal amount of water more than will the nail.

Another way of showing the difference between heat and temperature is to compare a match flame with the air in the room. Which is hotter? Of course the flame is hotter. It has a higher temperature. But does the flame have much heat? No. Even if it burned for hours, the flame would not warm up the air in the room. There is just not enough of it.

To summarize, temperature refers to how hot or how cold something is in degrees. Heat refers to a quantity of energy—its total energy, measured in calories, Btus, or joules.

Discrepant Events and Pupil Investigations

Event 3–B. Cooling Breezes? Place one thermometer into the breeze of a fan and another near the fan but not in the breeze. Let pupils predict which of the two thermometers will show a cooler temperature after the fan is turned on for several minutes.

Pupil Investigations (may include the following processes):
1. Predicting (incorrectly) that the breeze will cool off the one thermometer
2. Observing either that there is no difference in the temperatures, or, possibly, that the one in the breeze is slightly warmer
3. Contrasting the observations with our own experience—that a breeze makes us feel cooler

Event 3–C. Melt Ice . . . Below Its Freezing Point. Fill a beaker about one-third full of crushed ice. Carefully pour 4 to 8 tablespoonsful of salt onto the crushed ice. Then add another one-third beaker of crushed ice on top. Prepare the ice-salt mixture ahead of time so that pupils are not aware that salt was used. If done correctly, the salt will not be visible to the observer. (See Fig. 3–2.)

Show the beaker with the mixture to the pupils. Point out that liquid is collecting at the bottom of the beaker. Ask them at what temperature ice melts. Most pupils know that it melts at 0 degrees Celsius (32 degrees Fahrenheit). Have pupils check the temperature of the melted liquid with a thermometer.

Surprisingly, the pupils will find that the temperature is well *below* the freezing point. Ask them how it is possible for ice to melt below freezing.

Pupil Investigations (may include the following processes):
1. Observing that the temperature of the liquid in the beaker is many degrees below freezing
2. Forming a theory (incorrectly) that the thermometer does not work and that the temperature is actually at the melting point (Even without a thermometer, pupils can see that *frost* forms on the *outside* of the beaker!)
3. Recording and graphing the temperature at periodic intervals
4. Forming a theory that the beaker might contain something other than pure ice (If pupils suggest that salt melts ice, respond by asking, "But why is the temperature so cold?")

HEAT OF FUSION AND HEAT OF VAPORIZATION (EVENTS 3–B AND 3–C)

Fig. 3–2. **When salt is poured on crushed ice, what happens to the temperature?**

Events 3–B and 3–C Explained in Context (Heat of Fusion and Heat of Vaporization)

Which contains more heat—a gram of ice at 0 degrees Celsius or a gram of water at 0 degrees Celsius? Surprisingly, they are not the same. Try another example. Which contains more heat—a gram of water or a gram of steam if both are at 100 degrees Celsius? Again, they are not the same.

Why the difference? Because heat is needed to melt the ice. Thus, after it is melted, a gram of water has more heat than a gram of ice *even if the temperatures are the same in both cases (0 degrees Celsius)*. The same principle applies to the water and steam. Heat is needed to change the water into steam. Thus, once converted to steam, the steam has more heat than water *even if their temperatures are the same* (100 degrees Celsius).

The heat that is needed to melt ice is called the *heat of fusion*, and the heat needed to change water to steam is called the *heat of vaporization*. (The terms are also used if the processes are reversed; freezing instead of melting and condensing instead of forming steam.)

It may be easier to understand these processes if we add heat to a gram of ice and follow its path as it moves from a solid at 10 degrees *below zero* to a gas at 110 degrees. (See Fig. 3–3.) It takes 1 calorie of heat to raise the temperature of ice by 1 degree. By adding 10 calories of heat, the ice is raised 10 degrees, from 10 *below zero* to 0, its melting point. *But it still remains ice.* It does not change to water (at 0 degrees) unless more heat is added.

How much heat is needed to change 1 gram of ice to water? A large amount—80 calories! Once the ice has changed to water, then any additional

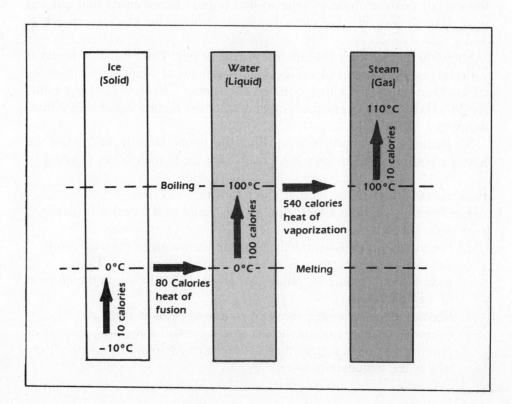

Fig. 3–3. **Heat energy is needed to raise the temperature of H$_2$O *and* to change it from one phase to another.**

heat will again raise its temperature. As stated earlier, 1 calorie of heat raises the temperature of 1 gram of water by 1 Celsius degree. Thus, to heat 1 gram of water, the 100 degrees from freezing to boiling takes 100 calories.

Now, how many calories are needed to change that 1 gram of water to steam without any increase in temperature? An amazing 540 calories! Once the H_2O is steam, any additional heat again raises its temperature.

Where does the heat come from that is used in the processes just described? Normally, we think of a heat source like a stove, hot plate, or burner. But the heat that melts ice can come from any source such as air or even from your body. If you put an ice cube on your hand, will it melt? Will it make your hand feel cold? Yes, because the heat is being used to melt the ice.

It should be noted that the heat of vaporization applies at any temperature, not just at the boiling point. Thus, any change of H_2O from a liquid to a gas requires the heat of vaporization. For example, if 1 gram of water evaporates at room temperature, 540 calories are still needed to change it from a liquid to a gas. That is why you feel cool when you step out of a shower, bath, or pool. The heat used in the evaporation process comes from your body.

Since pupils have all felt the cooling effect of evaporation, it is easy to see that *Event 3–B. Cooling Breezes?* comes as a surprise to them. Many will predict that the thermometer in the breeze will be cooler than the thermometer in the still air. Nevertheless, the event does not work out that way. Both readings will be the same.

Why is there no change? Because there is no moisture being evaporated. The temperature of air does not change just because it is moved by the fan. In fact, if the electric motor gives off some heat, the air that it sets in motion may actually be slightly warmer.

The heat of fusion accounts for the apparent discrepancy in *Event 3–C. Melt Ice . . . Below Its Freezing Point.* Most pupils who live in cold climates know that salt is sprinkled on roads to melt ice. As a result, they are not surprised to find that salt will cause ice to melt. They assume that the ice melts because the temperature warms up. The surprise comes when they see that the temperature goes down instead of up.

Why does the mixture get so cold? Remember the heat of fusion? Heat (80 calories) is needed to change 1 gram of ice to a liquid. Where does that heat come from? It comes from the contents of the beaker. Thus, when salt causes the ice to melt, huge amounts of heat energy are absorbed by the process, leaving the beaker and its contents far below freezing. That gives us a paradox of ice melting inside the beaker while frost forms on the outside.

The forced melting of the ice has a cooling effect just like evaporation has a cooling effect. In both cases heat is absorbed during a change of phase.

Discrepant Events and Pupil Investigations

SOURCES OF HEAT
(EVENTS 3–D AND 3–E)

Event 3–D. Shake Heat into a Bottle. Take a baby-food bottle or similar container, fill it three-quarters full of sand, and wrap it with insulation. (Many layers of paper will do.) Have students take turns shaking the contents vigorously for 4 to 5 minutes. Compare the temperature of the sand before and after the shaking.

Pupil Investigations (may include the following processes):
1. Measuring the temperature of the sand before, during, and after shaking it
2. Graphing the data obtained in process 1
3. Experimenting to compare results when no insulation is used
4. Forming a theory to account for the changes in temperature

Fig. 3–4. **What happens to the temperature of the wire if it is bent a number of times?**

Event 3–E. Wire Heater. Take a short length of wire such as that used in a coat hanger. Bend it back and forth a number of times and touch it at the point where it was bent. What do you feel? (See Fig. 3–4.)

Pupil Investigation (may include the following processes):
1. Observing that the point where the wire was bent becomes hot
2. Experimenting with different wires
3. Generalizing that some energy has been changed into heat

Events 3–D and 3–E Explained in Context (Sources of Heat)

Where does heat come from? There are many sources of heat, but they can all be grouped into the four categories shown in Table 3–2.

Table 3–2. **Sources of Heat**

Mechanical	Chemical	Electrical	Nuclear
Friction	Rearrangement of molecules	Lights	Sun and stars
Bending	Flame of any kind	Toasters	Atomic fission
Hammering	Water and plaster of Paris	Heaters	Atomic fusion
Pressure	Sulfuric acid and sugar	Stoves	Nuclear power reactor

Most students will already be familiar with chemical and electrical sources of heat. They probably know about nuclear sources, too, but that source is not practical for classroom demonstration. Mechanical sources, however, are often not known. Fortunately, they can be shown easily.

Remind pupils that friction produces heat. Many of them will have experienced minor burns or will have felt heat that has resulted from friction. Ask them to rub their hands together firmly and briskly. It is surprising how warm the hands can become.

Friction also produces the heat that is slowly developed in *Event 3–D. Shake Heat into a Bottle.* It is likely that some of the heat is also caused by the pressure of sand striking the top and bottom of the bottle during brisk shaking. To get a measurable gain in temperature, be sure that pupils shake the bottle vigorously for a long enough time.

It is important to use insulation so that the heat from your hands does not enter the bottle; that would obscure the effect of the friction in producing the heat.

Another form of mechanical heat is produced in *Event 3–E. Wire Heater.* When the wire is bent back and forth a number of times, the point where the wire is bent becomes warm to the touch. If the wire is bent fast enough and often enough, it becomes quite hot.

Heat can be produced by other mechanical means. For example, when a nail is driven into a board, the nail head becomes warm from the blows, and the shank of the nail gets hot from the friction. Some nails are designed to make use of this heat in a clever way. They are coated with a dry adhesive, which is not active at room temperature. When driven into wood, however, the friction between the nail and wood produces enough heat to melt the adhesive. As a result, those coated nails hold very well.

Discrepant Events and Pupil Investigations

Event 3–F. Ice Preservation Race. Select several teams of three or four pupils each and give each team an ice cube in a tin can. Ask them to figure out a way to keep the ice from melting. Let the teams work for 5 or 10 minutes and then set the samples aside.

After a specified period of time (perhaps an hour or two) check the results. One way to determine the success of the team efforts is to pour the melted water into test tubes.

Pupil Investigations (may include the following processes):
1. Experimenting with various types of insulation
2. Experimenting with different containers (Okay, if your rules permit that)
3. Measuring the melted water to compare results
4. Generalizing about the conditions that keep the ice from melting (or how to keep heat from traveling)

Event 3–G. The Two-Toned Paper. Place a wooden dowel against the end of a solid copper rod of the same diameter. Wrap and tape the joint using a single thickness of paper. Apply heat from a flame to scorch the paper. Observe the pattern of the scorch marks. What caused the paper to scorch more on the wooden side of the joint than on the copper side? (See Fig. 3–5.)

Pupil Investigations (may include the following processes):
1. Observing that there is a sharp line of demarcation between the scorched and unscorched parts of the paper
2. Forming a theory (incorrectly) that the heat was applied only to the part of the paper that was scorched

CONDUCTION (EVENTS 3–F THROUGH 3–I)

Fig. 3–5. **The paper scorches more easily where it covers the wood than where it covers the copper.**

Fig. 3–6. The copper coil puts out a small candle flame.

Fig. 3–7. This activity shows that water transmits heat poorly by conduction. However, it transmits heat well by convection currents.

3. Generalizing (correctly) that the scorching of the paper was related to the substance under the paper

Event 3–H. Candle Snuffer. Place a coil of copper wire over the flame of a small birthday candle as shown in Fig. 3–6. Why does the flame go out? (Use a candle with only a small flame. A large flame will not work.)

Pupil Investigations (may include the following processes):
  1. Performing the activity a number of times to see if the flame goes out each time
  2. Observing that sometimes the flame appears to be out but reappears when the coil is lifted
  3. Generalizing (incorrectly) that the flame goes out due to a lack of oxygen
  4. Inferring a relationship between the type of metal used and how heat is conducted

Event 3–I. Can Ice Water Boil? Push a small chunk of ice down to the bottom of a water-filled test tube by shoving a rock against it. Then apply heat to the water at the *top* of the test tube. The water at the top of the test tube will boil while the ice remains at the bottom. (See Fig. 3–7.)

(*Caution:* Do not use a Bunsen burner or similar heat source, unless you are very sure that you will not overheat the water. The Bunsen burner produces so much heat that the water may boil explosively and blast out of the test tube. Hold the test tube far enough above the flame so that the water is brought to a boil slowly, and always aim the mouth of the tube away from people.)

Pupil Investigations (may include the following processes):
  1. Observing that the water is actually boiling
  2. Verifying that the test tube actually contains ice
  3. Inferring that heat does not travel down to the ice
  4. Generalizing that in water heat travels poorly by conduction

Events 3–F Through 3–I Explained in Context (Conduction)

How does the heat from a stove travel up through a frying pan to fry an egg? Why does smoke go up a chimney? How does the heat of the sun reach us here on earth? These and many other questions are related to a topic of how heat travels.

Heat travels in three ways: *conduction, convection,* and *radiation.* The three methods are compared in Table 3–3.

We will discuss the three methods of heat transfer separately. The events in this section pertain only to conduction. Convection and radiation will be treated in separate sections with events related only to those topics.

Table 3–3. **How Heat Travels**

	Conduction	Convection	Radiation
Definition	Transfer of heat from one molecule to another	Transfer of heat by movement of fluids	Transfer of energy by waves through space
Examples	Copper Aluminum Cookware	Winds (weather) Chimney draft Boiling water	Sun's heat Heat lamp Electric heater

CONDUCTION. One way to introduce the topic of conduction is to perform *Event 3–F. Ice Preservation Race.* Divide the class into teams and have each team try to preserve the ice.

The event can be successful even if performed after the section has been discussed. However, if presented in the beginning, the results are likely to be more diverse. Pupils will have to "fend for themselves," and it tends to prepare them for the information about heat transfer that will follow.

It is important that a few rules are established to assure success in the activity.

1. Do not allow pupils to use refrigerators, buckets of ice, or (in the winter) the out-of-doors. The containers should all be stored at room temperature.
2. Teams must not lose any of the melted water (that is how the results will be measured). This means that no paper, cloth, or other materials can be wrapped directly around the ice, because they would soak up melted water.
3. An optional rule may be made about the use of the tin can. Generally, it is best to require the use of the can. However, the ice cube can first be put into a waterproof plastic bag, small glass jar, or small plastic container. Then surround the container with paper and stuff it into the tin can. Some of the greatest benefits result by giving only the first two rules and nothing more.

Best results in this activity are attained by focusing on two factors—size and conductivity.

First of all, reduce the area that needs to be protected. This means that the ice cube should be placed into a very small container. (Since the "melt" needs to be saved for measurement later, the container must be waterproof.) A small jar, plastic bag, or other such container will work well.

Secondly, get rid of good conductors. The tin can is an excellent *conductor*. It will bring heat to the ice quickly. Keep as much material as possible between the ice and tin can.

At the end of the allotted time, have each team pour its melted water into test tubes. It is easy to compare the results of the teams in this way.

The purpose of the lesson is to learn about the movement of heat by conduction. That is the most likely way in which heat gets to the ice. The most successful teams will be those that reduced conduction the most.

The best conductors are generally metals. As stated earlier, the metal of the tin can is an excellent conductor as compared to the other substances used in the event. The best metallic conductors are copper, silver, and aluminum.

Once pupils know how heat travels, they may also learn how to keep it from traveling. This is done by using materials that are poor conductors. Poor conductors are also termed *insulators*. Glass, paper, wood, plastics, and rubber are examples of insulators.

We can see the effects of good and poor conductors in *Event 3–G. The Two-Toned Paper*. The paper on the wood side of the wood-copper joint will scorch more quickly than the paper on the copper side. The paper on the copper side does not get as hot from a flame because the copper carries away the heat very quickly. Wood, however, does not conduct the heat away, so the paper quickly gets hot enough to scorch.

Event 3–H. Candle Snuffer also demonstrates the effects of a good conductor. At first some pupils will think that the candle goes out because the flame cannot get oxygen. But since the snuffer is a coil, air can enter between the coils as well as from above and below. Instead, the fire goes out because the copper carries away the heat so quickly.

It is important that a small candle (such as a birthday candle) be used. Large candles produce too much heat for this event to work well. Also, once the coil gets too hot, it can no longer carry away enough heat to put out even a small flame. *Caution:* Be careful not to touch the heated coil.

A final example of conduction is shown in *Event 3–I. Can Ice Water Boil?* At first glance this looks like an impossible activity, yet it can be done. Normally, ice floats on top of water. But by using a rock, or other weight, the ice can be pushed down to the bottom of the test tube and kept there. Then, by applying heat (carefully) near the *top* of the tube, the water can be made to boil *even though the ice still remains at the bottom of the tube*.

This event shows that water is a poor conductor of heat. Water is usually heated from the bottom. It then churns to distribute its heat quickly throughout the container. (This churning is called convection, the next topic in this chapter.) However, when water is heated at the top, it does not churn. Thus, it gets hot enough to boil on top, but the heat does not travel down to melt the ice at the bottom.

CONVECTION (EVENTS 3–J THROUGH 3–M)

Discrepant Events and Pupil Investigations

Event 3–J. The Mixed-Up Bottles. Set up four wide-mouth bottles in pairs as shown in Fig. 3–8. Start with two bottles of hot water and two of cold water. Mix food coloring into the lower bottle of each pair. Use an index card to keep the water from spilling while inverting each of the top two bottles.

The finished arrangement should have one pair with hot water over cold and the other pair just the opposite. Pupils should *not* be told that the water is at different temperatures.

When the arrangement is set up, carefully pull out the index cards and observe. The food coloring mixes quickly in one pair of bottles but not in the other. Ask the students to try to learn why.

Pupil Investigations (may include the following processes):
1. Observing that the water is mixing in both the top and bottom bottles of the rapidly mixing side
2. Measuring the temperature of each bottle by touching the bottles
3. Observing closely to see if anything is blocking the water in the side that is not mixing (Nothing is blocking it.)
4. Predicting what will happen if the unmixed side is turned over

Fig. 3–8. **The food coloring mixes quickly in one pair of bottles because there are convection currents in them.**

Event 3–K. The Circling Sawdust. Drop some sawdust into a beaker of water that is being heated. Set up the beaker so that it is heated at the edge as shown in Fig. 3–9. Observe the motion of the sawdust as the water is being heated.

Pupil Investigations (may include the following processes):
1. Observing the motion of the sawdust in the water
2. Drawing a diagram to show the movement of the water
3. Generalizing that water rises when it is heated

Event 3–L. Does Air Move In or Out? This is an activity that should be done (for a short time only) on a cool winter day. If you have windows in your room to allow it, open them slightly on top and on the bottom. Have the pupils determine how the air moves.

Pupil Investigations (may include the following processes):
1. Observing that cool air comes into the room at the bottom opening
2. Observing that warm air escapes from the room at the top
3. Inferring that the temperature of the air is related to its weight
4. Generalizing that the movement of air is based on its weight and temperature

Fig. 3–9. **Heat the edge of the beaker and you can see a convection current in the water.**

Event 3–M. Convection Tester. (*Caution:* Do this event as a demonstration and use it only if you feel that the class is mature enough to observe an activity in which matches are used.) Slowly bring a match head toward a candle flame. See how close the match head must be brought to the flame before it ignites. Hold matches near the base, along the side, and over the top of the flame. (See Fig. 3–10.)

Pupil Investigations (may include the following processes):
1. Predicting the distances at which the matches will ignite at different points around the candle flame

Fig. 3–10. **This activity shows that warm air rises. See how closely the match can be held to the side of the flame.**

2. Recording the observations by drawing diagrams
3. Generalizing that air rises when heated

Events 3–J Through 3–M Explained in Context (Convection)

Convection is the transfer of heat by the movement of fluids. (A fluid is either a gas such as air or a liquid such as water.) When a fluid is heated, it expands and becomes lighter per given volume. Being lighter, it then rises and is replaced by cooler, heavier fluid. This motion of fluids is called a *convection current.*

A convection current is shown clearly in *Event 3–J. The Mixed-Up Bottles.* In the pair of bottles where the mixing takes place, you start with the warm water in the bottom bottle and the cold water on top. When the index card is removed from between the bottles, the warm water rises and the cold water descends. In a minute or two the water is totally mixed. In the other pair the top bottle has warm water and the lower bottle has cold water. No mixing takes place because the warm (or lightweight) water is already on top and the cold (or heavy) water is already on the bottom.

Event 3–K. The Circling Sawdust also shows a convection current. The sawdust is so light that it is carried along by the moving water. The water rises when it is heated, and cold water descends to take its place. This action continues so that the water can be seen to move in a constant circle while the container is being heated.

Convection currents are also present in the air, as is shown in *Event 3–L. Does Air Move In or Out?* Many pupils will be able to predict that cold air will move in from the lower opening of the window. Many of them will have had experience with cold drafts coming in through doors and windows.

However, the motion at the top of the windows will be another matter. Ask them to predict what will happen. Many will say that cold air will also enter there. Ask them where the air goes that is already in the room. It has to go somewhere when cold air enters. It goes out on top because warm air rises when cold air descends.

If you decide to demonstrate *Event 3–M. Convection Tester,* pupils will again see an example of warm air rising. The match will ignite fairly high above the tip of the flame because heat rises. Along the side and bottom of the flame, however, the match can be held very closely without igniting.

RADIATION (EVENT 3–N)

Discrepant Event and Pupil Investigations

Event 3–N. Which Is the "Warmer" Color? Obtain two cans that are alike. Paint one can black and the other white. Fill them with equal amounts of water and place the cans in direct sunlight. Measure the temperature of the water at periodic intervals for about an hour or two.

Pupil Investigations (may include the following processes):
1. Making a graph of the water temperatures taken at 15- to 30-minute intervals for an hour or two
2. Observing that the water in the black can warms up more than the water in the white can
3. Inferring that there is a relationship between sunlight, warmth, and color

Event 3–N Explained in Context (Radiation)

Radiation is a third method of heat transmission. In that method energy travels at the speed of light from a source, through space, to an object. The best example is the heat from the sun.

Radiant energy does not warm up any transparent substance. It is converted to heat only when it strikes an object that is not transparent. Thus, the air above the earth is not heated by the sun, but the ground on the earth's surface is. Likewise, on a cold winter day the sun's light warms up the inside of a windowsill, but the transparent glass through which the energy travels is quite cold.

Of course, the sun is not the only example of heat transmission by radiation. All objects above absolute zero actually radiate some heat, but such radiation cannot be felt until the temperatures get quite hot. Hold your hand a few inches *below* a clothes iron. The heat you feel is due to radiation. (Remember that if you hold your hand *above* the iron, the heat you feel is due to convection currents, not radiation.) Another example is to hold your hand close to a car's headlight. You should be able to feel the radiant heat.

Substances vary in their ability to absorb and reflect radiation. We can see in *Event 3–N. Which Is the "Warmer" Color?* that black absorbs heat well but white does not. White reflects much of the energy that strikes it. As a result, the water in the black can gets warmer than the water in the white can.

Discrepant Events and Pupil Investigations

Event 3–O. "Dancing" Dimes. Cool off some large soft-drink bottles in a refrigerator. When they are cooled, place them on a table and cover each with a dime or penny. Moisten the edge between the coin and bottle with a drop of water. Wait and watch. (Students should not be told that the bottles have been cooled.)

Pupil Investigations (may include the following processes):
1. Observing that again and again the coins rise slowly and then fall back with a "plink"
2. Measuring the length of time that the coins continue to dance (They stop plinking after a while.)

EXPANSION AND CONTRACTION (EVENTS 3–O THROUGH 3–S)

3. Discovering that the bottles feel cool to the touch
4. Generalizing about air expanding when heated

Event 3–P. Jumping Juice. Pour some colored water into a flask. See Fig. 3–11. It appears that a single tube is pushed all the way through the one-hole stopper. It is not. That is unsafe. If you push too hard, the tube could break and plunge through your hand. It is safer to use two tubes, with one tube extending down into the flask and the other extending upward about 20 to 30 centimeters. In this event they act as a single tube.

Pour hot water over the outside of the flask. The colored water inside the flask will rise up the tube. Pour cold water from a different beaker and the colored water will go down. Have the pupils investigate the activity and find out what caused the colored water to rise and fall. (Do not tell the pupils that the waters are different temperatures.)

Pupil Investigations (may include the following processes):
1. Observing that one beaker of water was used to make the colored water rise up the tube and that another beaker of water was used to make it go down
2. Checking to find out if there is a difference in the water used in the two beakers
3. Inferring a relationship between the temperature of the water in the beakers and the action of the colored water in the tube

Event 3–Q. The Sagging Solid. Everyone knows that when a metal is heated hot enough, it can become weak and sag. Tell the students that you can show how heat causes a special metallic strip to "sag," even if it is just held in a candle flame for a short time. (Do not mention at this time that the device is a *bimetallic strip.*) Then tell them that you will do it again, just to be sure it works. This time, however, turn the strip over (do not let class notice this turn). They will be amazed to see the strip bend *upward!* (See Fig. 3–12.)

Pupil Investigations (may include the following processes):
1. Observing whether or not the heat is applied to the same place on the strip with each trial
2. Observing how the strip is straightened between trials (The strip straightens out by itself when cooled. Water cools it quickly.)
3. Generalizing that the metal strip is not actually sagging (losing strength) when it bends downward but that the bend is caused by something else

Event 3–R. Expansion Meter. Attach a metal rod to one end of an apparatus as shown in Fig. 3–13. Rest the other end of the rod loosely on a straw to which a pointer has been glued. Light the candles and observe the results. As the metal expands, it causes the straw to rotate. This, in turn, shows the degree of expansion. Compare the expansion rates of various metals.

Fig. 3–11. **The water inside the tube rises and falls as the air inside expands or contracts.**

Fig. 3–12. **Does this metal strip really sag? Why does it sometimes go upward?**

Fig. 3–13. **The expansion of the metal rod causes the pointer to turn.**

Pupil Investigations (may include the following processes):
1. Recording the expansion of various metals and comparing those results with published indices of expansion
2. Comparing the expansion figures for long and short bars of the same metal (It is likely that these figures will not be consistent.)
3. Generalizing that the expansion of metal is affected by how much it is heated
4. Inferring that all metals expand when heated

Event 3–S. Expansion of Gases. This is an expansion meter for gases. Set up an arrangement as shown in Fig. 3–14. (*Caution*: Double check to be sure that the bottles are *not* sealed. If they are, the bottles will explode when heated.) The bottle that is placed on the heat source has a one-hole stopper and an open tube that is run into the open second container. The inverted second container is filled with water at the start of the test.

Fig. 3–14. **The expanded gases move through the tube into the inverted bottle where they displace the water. (*Caution*: Bottles must *not* be sealed.)**

Pupil Investigations (may include the following processes):
1. Observing bubbles rising into the second bottle when the first bottle is heated
2. Recording the amount of expansion of several gases
3. Concluding that all gases have about the same rates of expansion

Events 3–O Through 3–S Explained in Context (Expansion and Contraction)

One characteristic of almost all substances is that they expand when heated and contract when cooled. The degree to which substances expand and contract is referred to as the *index of expansion*.

It is generally believed that expansion is caused by the increased activity of molecules when they are heated. When heated, they vibrate more vigorously and take up more space.

Water is a well-known exception to the rule. Like other substances, water expands when heated and contracts when cooled. But it does so only as long as the temperature remains above 4 degrees Celsius.

Below 4 degrees, however, water reverses itself. It will then expand when *cooled*. (This oddity of water is very handy. It allows ice to form on top of a lake instead of at the bottom. If ice were to form at the bottom of a lake in winter, not only would it make for some rather tough skating, but heat would not likely get down to the ice in the summer to melt it.)

Expansion and *contraction* are important factors to consider in constructing roads, buildings, and other projects. Here are a few surprising examples:

1. The Sears Tower in Chicago (the tallest building in the world) is about 15 centimeters taller on a hot summer day than on a cold winter day.

2. A 2-kilometer bridge may expand and contract as much as a meter between summer and winter.
3. Concrete highways and sidewalks are built with separations or joints to allow them to expand and contract without breaking up.
4. Electric power lines, telephone lines, and railroad tracks must be built with provisions for expansion and contraction.

Expansion is the principle that explains *Event 3–O. "Dancing" Dimes*. To get the dimes to dance, we must start with cool bottles. When the bottles are brought into a warm room, they warm up, causing the air inside to expand.

Since the air has to go somewhere, it pushes the coin aside long enough to escape. Then the coin "plinks" back down. The air in the bottle warms slowly, so that the coin plinks many times before the air inside finally reaches room temperature.

For the activity to work the coin must have an airtight seal on top of the bottle. Just moisten the edge between the coin and bottle with a drop or two of water. This provides the seal.

The answer to the mystery of *Event 3–P. Jumping Juice* is again related to expansion and contraction of air. The air inside the bottle expands when hot water is poured over the flask. Thus, the air expands and forces the colored water up the glass tube. However, when cool water is used, the air inside contracts and the colored water in the tube drops quickly. (Be sure to do the activity without telling the pupils ahead of time that you have used hot and cold water. Let them discover that for themselves.)

In *Event 3–Q. The Sagging Solid* the metal strip does not really sag. It just bends in response to expansion and contraction. The event can only be done with a special bimetal strip—a sandwich of two metals (usually brass and iron) joined together to look like a single strip. (Such a bimetal strip can be obtained from a science supply house.)

The strip bends when heated because the metals have different rates of expansion. One of the metals expands much more than the other. To allow for the different rates of expansion, the strip must bend.

The two metals can be compared to two runners in a track meet. If one runner runs the curve in the outside lane, he or she must run farther than the runner in the inside lane. Likewise, the metal in the strip that expands more is on the "outside lane" as it bends.

To cause the strip to bend down, just hold the strip one way; and to cause it to bend upward, just turn it around. A little deftness is needed in handling so that it is not obvious to pupils that you just turned the strip over. Let them discover the details in their investigations.

Events 3–R. Expansion Meter and *3–S. Expansion of Gases* can be used to compare the expansion rates of different substances. The metal expansion meter is not very accurate, but it shows relative differences between metals. The reason it lacks accuracy is that it is difficult to heat the entire length of the rod uniformly during each trial. The gas measuring device is somewhat more accurate. Pupils should be able to tell that all gases have about the same index of expansion.

Discrepant Events and Pupil Investigations

Event 3–T. Water from Fire? Invert a cold tumbler over a candle flame for a few seconds and observe. What is seen to form on the inside of the glass? Ask the pupils to explain what they see. (See Fig. 3–15.)

Pupil Investigations (may include the following processes):
1. Observing that the glass becomes fogged on the inside
2. Inferring that there is a relationship between fire and the fog
3. Forming a theory that water is an end product of fire

Event 3–U. Boil Water in a Paper Cup. Fill a paper cup with water and set it on a screen over an open flame from a Bunsen burner. If you have no Bunsen burner, you can use some other heat source; but an open flame works the best. If you decide to try a stove or heater, use an empty iron or steel pan or tray and set the cup in it. (Do not use copper or aluminum utensils because they will melt from the intense heat.) Observe until the water boils in the cup.

Pupil Investigations (may include the following processes):
1. Observing that the water actually boils in a paper cup
2. Observing that the cup leaks slightly after heating
3. Inferring (incorrectly) that the cup is not really made of paper
4. Generalizing about the factors that support combustion

Event 3–V. Kindling Temperatures. On a large metal plate place small bits of coal, sulfur, sugar, candle wax, paper, wood, bread, and a match head. Arrange them around the outer edge of the plate so that they are all equal distances from the center. Apply heat to the center of the plate and note the order in which they start to burn. (*Caution:* Be sure to do this event in a well-ventilated place.)

Pupil Investigations (may include the following processes):
1. Predicting the order in which the materials will ignite
2. Recording the order in which the substances actually ignite
3. Listing the substances according to their kindling temperatures

Event 3–W. The Hottest Part of a Flame. Place a match into the base of a Bunsen burner flame and see how quickly it ignites. See how fast the match ignites when placed in other parts of the flame. You can suspend a match over a Bunsen burner by using a pin as shown in Fig. 3–16. Then when you light the flame, see how long it takes for the suspended match to ignite. If you have no Bunsen burner, try a candle flame.

Pupil Investigations (may include the following processes):
1. Recording the length of time needed to ignite the match in various parts of the flame

FIRE (EVENTS 3–T THROUGH 3–W)

Fig. 3–15. **What forms on the inner surface of a cold glass when it is held over a candle flame for a few seconds?**

Fig. 3–16. **Suspend a match in the opening of a Bunsen burner and ignite the gases in the burner. What happens to the match?**

2. Diagraming the flame and identifying its hottest and coolest parts
3. Generalizing about factors that support combustion
4. (If you use a candle) Observing that there is a tiny space between the top of the wick and the bottom of the flame

Events 3–T Through 3–W Explained in Context (Fire)

WHAT IS FIRE? We have all seen fires burn. Now we will take a more scientific look at what is needed to allow a fire to burn.

We saw earlier in this chapter that fire is a common source of heat energy. You may recall that it is a chemical source of energy. Just how does it release energy? Let us look at a typical example—a candle. A candle is an example of a hydrocarbon. That is, it contains mostly hydrogen (H) and carbon (C) atoms; and when the candle burns, it unites with oxygen (O). Thus, you start with H plus C, and O.

The end products contain the same atoms but in different arrangements: carbon dioxide (CO_2) and water (H_2O). Surprising as it may seem to pupils, fire releases water, which becomes visible as it condenses on the tumbler in *Event 3–T. Water from Fire?*

Fig. 3–17. **All three parts of the fire triangle are needed to support a fire.**

THE FIRE TRIANGLE. Three things are necessary to permit a fire to burn: (1) fuel, (2) oxygen, and (3) kindling temperature. The three factors are referred to as the *fire triangle*, and there cannot be any fire unless the triangle is complete. (See Fig. 3–17.)

Event 3–U. Boil Water in a Paper Cup is easier to understand if you think about the fire triangle and decide *what is missing*. This event is quite surprising to most pupils. They expect to see the cup burst into flame. They are amazed that the cup does not burn and that you can boil water in it.

The reason the cup does not burn is that the kindling temperature is missing from the fire triangle. The flame is very hot, but the water in the cup takes the heat away from the paper so quickly that the cup never reaches the kindling point. Even when the water is boiling, the temperature of the paper is no greater than the temperature of water, or 100 degrees Celsius.

One note of caution: Be sure to use only paper cups, not plastic. Most plastic drinking cups will melt below the boiling point of water. Also, some plastics are such effective insulators that the water cannot take the heat away fast enough, and the outside of such a cup can actually burn, filling the room with acrid fumes.

Two other notes: Most paper cups have a rim around the bottom. You will see that this rim will burn away immediately because it is too far from the water to be cooled by it. The cup will still hold together, however, and the lack of a rim does not affect the experiment. Finally, paper drinking cups are coated with wax to make them waterproof. The wax melts in the boiling water, and the cup then begins to leak slowly. This also does not harm the experiment.

In *Event 3–V. Kindling Temperatures* we saw that different substances have different *kindling temperatures*. That is, different materials will ignite at different temperatures: some ignite quickly at low kindling temperatures; others ignite much later at high kindling temperatures. Be sure to do this activity in an area with plenty of ventilation. Some of the substances give off offensive fumes and odors.

Finally, *Event 3–W. The Hottest Part of a Flame* shows that a flame has relatively cool spots in it. If you have a Bunsen burner, you will find that the gases that come out of the burner are cool and keep the match head from burning. Only after the gases reach several centimeters above the top of the burner do they get hot enough to ignite. It isn't until you reach the tip of the flame that you find its hottest part.

A candle flame works much the same way. The heat of the flame is enough to melt the candle wax. This wax travels up the wick and is turned into a gas. However, the gas does not ignite until it rises a centimeter or two above the wick. Then it gets hot enough to burn.

If you place a match head into the flame right above the wick (at the base of the flame), it will not ignite quickly because it is too cool. The hottest part of the candle flame is its tip.

4

Teaching Children about Static Electricity

FROM AMBER TO ELECTRONS

When working with this topic, we can use many discrepant events to show pupils what *static electricity* is and how it works. However, let us look into some background information before beginning the activities. How did early scientists learn about static electricity?

The earliest known reference to static electricity goes back at least 2600 years. In 600 B.C. the Greeks discovered that, when rubbed, the hardened resin from a tree, called *amber,* would attract bits of lint, dust, and paper. In fact, the term *electron* comes from the Greek word *amber.*

Knowledge about static electricity did not increase rapidly as the centuries passed. Very little new information was discovered except that more and more materials were found that could be attracted to amber.

Not until 1672 did the next real breakthrough come. Up to this time it had always been necessary to charge a rod by actually rubbing it. But in that year Otto Van Guericke, a German physicist, built a machine to do the rubbing for him.

Less than 80 years later another important invention followed. Two scientists discovered the same thing at almost the same time. In 1745 E. G. Kleist, a German clergyman, and in 1746 Pieter von Musschenbroek of Holland, built devices to *store* electricity. Although Kleist's invention came earlier, it was Musschenbroek who first reported his. Thus, the invention became known as the *Leyden jar,* named for Musschenbroek's hometown in Leyden, Holland.

There is an interesting sidelight to the story of the Leyden jar. Why did scientists use a jar or bottle to store electricity? After all, there is no reason for bottles to be used for that purpose, and today none is used in any electronic devices.

The answer is simple. In those days scientists thought that electricity was a form of weightless, invisible fluid. So, it was natural to use a container to collect that fluid. What kinds of containers did they have? Glass jars were very common. And that is how a glass jar became the first container to store electricity.

The Leyden jar was referred to as an electrical *condenser* for much the same reason. If electricity was an invisible fluid, scientists reasoned that it might be a gas that had to be condensed. Today we still refer to tiny electronic devices that can store charges as condensers, although it is now more common to refer to them as *capacitors.*

Another leader in the field of static electricity was Benjamin Franklin. He is well known for discovering that *lightning* in an electrical storm is the same form of energy as the static charges that he developed in his lab.

It is important to note that Franklin was very cautious when conducting his famous kite experiment during an electrical storm. He was well aware of the danger of lightning. After all, lightning was known to kill people and start fires, so he had great respect for its power.

First of all, Franklin did not stand in the rain. He stood on dry ground under an overhanging roof. Second, the kite was attached to a thin wire, but Franklin did not touch the wire. He attached a short piece of dry string to the end of the wire and held on to the string.

During the experiment Franklin held up an empty Leyden jar so that it touched a key that was suspended from the end of the wire. He wondered if the energy in the clouds would fill the jar with the same energy that he generated in the lab. Was it the same as the energy he created when he rubbed amber with wool? It turned out that the charges were the same. He proved that lightning was really just a powerful form of static electricity.

Franklin was lucky that a lightning bolt did not follow the wire to where he stood. For even with his precautions he was in great danger and could have been killed. Franklin's experiment should *never* be attempted as a school or individual project.

Franklin was responsible for perhaps the first practical use that was ever made of the research in static electricity. Scientists had worked with this form of energy for centuries but discovered only uses that were of interest to other scientists. No practical use existed outside the lab. What was Franklin's discovery? The *lightning rod*. He noticed that an object in the lab would quickly lose its charge if it had a pointed tip. He reasoned, therefore, that the idea might work for lightning too. He put a pointed tip on a house, connected it to a cable, and anchored the cable deeply into the ground. It worked.

A lightning rod offers protection in two ways. First, electrons escape from the tip of the rod, just like they did from a pointed object in the lab. Thus, a charge that normally would form on a building will leak off instead. If the charge does not form, there is less chance that lightning will strike. Second, if lightning strikes anyway, the violent charge does not enter the building. It follows a path along a heavy copper cable straight to the ground without damaging the building.

Franklin's invention came shortly before the discovery of current electricity. Keep in mind that despite all the discoveries about static electricity, there was still no way in which it could be released in a continuous, controlled flow. Everything was still static—a charge that could only be released in a single instant. The big discoveries about current electricity were yet to come.

Discrepant Events and Pupil Investigations

Event 4–A. The Balloon and Its Invisible Shelf. Rub a balloon with wool and touch the balloon to the wall. Does the balloon stay as if it were on an invisible shelf?

CHARGED OBJECTS ATTRACT UNCHARGED OBJECTS (EVENTS 4–A THROUGH 4–C)

Pupil Investigations (may include the following processes):
1. Verifying the activity to see if pupils can also make the balloon stick to the wall
2. Observing that the balloon does not stick unless it is rubbed
3. Inferring a relationship between rubbing the balloon and its attraction to the wall

Event 4–B. Make the Water Bend. Turn on a faucet so that a very thin stream of water is flowing from it. Provide a rubber or plastic comb and some wool. Ask pupils to figure out a way to get the comb to attract the water without touching it.

Pupil Investigations (may include the following processes):
1. Observing the water bend when the comb is held near the stream
2. Testing to see if the experiment will work if the comb is not rubbed (It does not.)
3. Generalizing that the rubbing does something to the comb to cause it to attract water

Event 4–C. Pepper and Salt. Sprinkle some pepper and salt on a sheet of paper. Ask if anyone can separate the two by using just a comb and wool cloth.

Pupil Investigations (may include the following processes):
1. Observing that the comb attracts *both* the pepper and the salt
2. Predicting that slight taps of the comb will cause the salt to drop off before the pepper does
3. Comparing the heights at which the pepper and salt are attracted

Events 4–A Through 4–C Explained in Context (Charged Objects Attract Uncharged Objects)

WHAT CAUSES STATIC CHARGES? A typical explanation of this event usually includes a statement that the charges are caused by rubbing. This is not completely true. The charges are actually caused by bringing the right substances close together. Rubbing is just a way to accomplish this task.

Some substances tend to gain electrons easily, whereas other substances tend to lose them easily. Thus, when two such different substances are brought close to each other (by rubbing, for example), the electrons move from one to the other.

When an object gains electrons, it has a surplus of electrons and is said to have a *negative charge*. When an object loses electrons, it has a shortage of electrons and is considered to have a *positive charge*.

When working with static electricity, one word of caution is needed. Weather conditions can have a major effect on experiments with such charges. The activities work best on cold winter days. (It is easy to get shocks on those days just by shuffling across a rug.) Warm and humid days in the summer are the very worst for such experiments.

The reason for the problems during warm weather is that moisture can carry charges. Thus, moisture in the air will discharge negative and positive charges quickly on a warm day. In winter, when the air is cold, it is very dry. On warm summer days, even when it appears to be dry, the air carries much more moisture than on any cold winter day.

CHARGED OBJECTS ATTRACT UNCHARGED OBJECTS. Let us see what objects can be charged and what effects these objects have on uncharged objects. With little effort we can see that many things can be charged and attracted. In fact, almost anything will generate a charge of some sort when rubbed. Even liquids and gases can be charged; and just about anything can be attracted, including solids, liquids, and gases.

It is easy to demonstrate static charges in the elementary classroom. For example, in *Event 4–A. The Balloon and Its Invisible Shelf* the balloon becomes charged when rubbed with wool. It is attracted to the uncharged wall. The balloon often sticks for hours because the electrons do not move very well on the balloon. (The balloon is a poor conductor.)

Eventually, however, the electrons migrate from the balloon to the wall. When this happens, the charge is lost (or neutralized) and the balloon falls to the floor. As stated earlier, the charges are lost much more quickly on warm, moist days than on cold, winter days.

In *Event 4–B. Make the Water Bend* we see another example of an object being attracted by a charged object. The charged comb attracts the uncharged stream of water. With some practice the water can be pulled dramatically off course. (See Fig. 4–1.)

The purpose of *Event 4–C. Pepper and Salt* is to show two more examples of materials that are attracted by a charged object. Both the salt and pepper are attracted, so how can they be separated? The grains of pepper are lighter than the salt so the pepper is attracted first. Also, if both substances are on the comb, the salt tends to drop off, with light tapping, before the pepper.

All the events in this section show that many different materials can be attracted by static electricity. Perhaps your pupils will discover additional examples of that principle.

Fig. 4–1. **A charged comb will attract a stream of water.**

Discrepant Events and Pupil Investigations

Event 4–D. Attraction or Repulsion? Rub a comb with wool and ask the pupils to decide what will happen when the comb is brought near to (but not touching) a pith ball hanging on a threat. (A *pith ball* is very sensitive to static charges and can be obtained from a science supply house.)

After the pupils make a prediction, bring the comb near the ball to show that there is an attraction. Do this several times to be sure that the attraction is seen by everyone. Then do the activity once more and allow the comb to touch the ball.

LIKE CHARGES REPEL (EVENTS 4–D THROUGH 4–I)

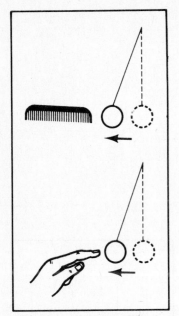

Fig. 4–2. **A charged comb will attract the pith ball, and a charged ball will be attracted to your hand.**

Fig. 4–3. **Rub the pane of glass with silk, and the bits of paper and tinfoil will "dance."**

After the comb and ball touch for a moment the ball jumps away. The two *repel* each other! The activity is quite surprising to most pupils. One additional feature can be added to this event if you wish. Show that sometimes the ball is (and sometimes is not) attracted to your hand. (See Fig. 4–2.)

Pupil Investigations (may include the following processes):
1. Predicting the action of the ball in various circumstances
2. Observing that the comb attracts the pith ball as long as they do not touch each other
3. Discovering that once the comb and ball touch, they repel each other
4. Concluding that the ball is attracted to your hand only after the ball has been touched by the comb
5. Forming a theory about the attraction and repulsion of static charges

Event 4–E. Make the Paper "Dance." Place a pane of glass on two thin books, as shown in Fig. 4–3. Place bits of paper (tinfoil or thread will also work) in the space under the glass. Provide a silk or nylon cloth and ask children to make the paper "dance." (*Note:* This activity needs ideal conditions to work effectively.)

Pupil Investigations (may include the following processes):
1. Observing that the bits of paper jump up when the glass is rubbed with silk, wool, and paper (Some other substances will also work.)
2. Discovering that the bits of paper jump up to the glass, stick for a while, and then jump down, only to repeat the cycle again
3. Inferring a relationship between rubbing the glass and attracting the paper
4. Forming a theory that accounts for both the attraction and repulsion of the paper

Event 4–F. The Tinsel Tree. Hang several strands of tinsel on a thread and have pupils decide how to make the tinsel spread apart. Provide students with a wool cloth. This activity can also be performed using polyethylene strips and wool.

Pupil Investigations (may include the following processes):
1. Observing that the tinsel strips spread apart after they have been rubbed with the cloth
2. Inferring that each strip of tinsel has the same charge
3. Generalizing that like charges repel each other

Event 4–G. Fill the Stocking. Let pupils decide how to fill a silk or nylon stocking *without putting anything into it.* Then let them decide how to "empty" it. Have a polyethylene bag available.

Pupil Investigations (may include the following processes):
1. Observing that the stocking "fills out" when rubbed with the polyethylene bag

2. Experimenting with a variety of materials
3. Inferring that the effect is caused by the repulsion of like charges
4. Discovering that the stocking is "emptied" by running your hand along the entire length of the stocking

Event 4–H. Leaping Leaves. Let pupils decide how to make the leaves of an electroscope spread apart. (An *electroscope* is a device that can detect static charges.) Have a comb and a woolen cloth available for pupils to use. If pupils succeed in causing the leaves to move apart, ask them to find a way to cause them to return to normal again. (See "How to Build an Electroscope" at the end of this chapter.)

Pupil Investigations (may include the following processes):
1. Discovering that the comb influences the leaves even before the comb touches the knob on top of the electroscope
2. Observing that when a charged comb touches the electroscope knob, the leaves spread apart
3. Discovering that the leaves are also attracted when the comb is held near the glass side of the electroscope
4. Discovering that the leaves collapse when the knob is touched with a finger
5. Generalizing that the comb gives the leaves like charges and that like charges repel

Fig. 4–4. **A thin strip of newspaper, when rubbed, will act like the leaves of an electroscope.**

Event 4–I. Newspaper Electroscope. Cut a long thin strip of newspaper and hang it over the edge of a ruler as shown in Fig. 4–4. Ask pupils to see if they can make the paper act just like the leaves of the electroscope. Provide pupils with woolen cloth.

Pupil Investigations (may include the following processes):
1. Experimenting by rubbing the paper with a cloth to see if the leaves spread apart
2. Inferring that the movement of the paper is similar to the movement of the leaves of the electroscope in Event 4–H
3. Testing to see if other substances can be used in place of paper

Events 4–D Through 4–I Explained in Context (Like Charges Repel)

We have seen that a charged object, either negative or positive, will attract an uncharged object. But what happens when two like charges are brought close together? *Event 4–D. Attraction or Repulsion?* shows what can happen. The sequence of six steps in that activity is shown in Fig. 4–5. Let's go over the steps one by one:

A. When a charged comb is held near the ball, there is an attraction between them because *a charged object (comb) attracts an uncharged object (ball).*

A. Charged comb attracts uncharged ball

B Charged comb transfers like charge to ball

C. Now ball is repelled because it has same charge as comb

D. Charged ball is attracted to uncharged hand

E. After ball is discharged it is not attracted or repelled by uncharged hand

F. Now cycle can be repeated

Fig. 4–5. **The steps of the attraction-repulsion activity are explained.**

B. As soon as the comb touches the ball, the charge moves from the comb to the ball. Now both have the same charge.

C. Once the ball has the same charge as the comb, the ball jumps away because *like charges repel each other.*

D. If your hand is held near the ball, the ball is attracted to the hand because a *charged object (ball) is attracted to the uncharged object (hand).*

E. When the ball touches the hand, the ball is discharged (or "neutralized," or "grounded"). Your body is so large that it acts as a reservoir that is able to absorb any excess electrons on the ball. (Be sure to show that an uncharged ball is neither attracted nor repelled by the hand. The attraction occurs only when the ball is charged.)

F. Once the ball is discharged, the entire sequence can be repeated. The ball is again attracted to the charged comb. The conditions are again the same as they were in step 1.

The little balls can be made with a variety of materials. The best are *pith* balls (made from the inside of corn stalks). Other materials that can be used are puffed wheat, puffed rice, bits of foam plastic, or carbon ends of burnt matches, and probably many other things. If a tiny bit of foil is wrapped around the pith ball, the responses will be very rapid.

Without the foil the ball is a poor conductor and electrons are gained or lost slowly: The ball "hugs" the plastic comb for a moment or two before it is repelled. When it is coated with foil, however, it jumps away at once.

The other events in this section also demonstrate that like charges repel. *Event 4–E. Make the Paper "Dance"* does not start out that way, but it ends that way. First of all, by rubbing the glass with silk or wool, the glass becomes charged. It, in turn, attracts the paper bits. At this point it simply shows that a charged object (glass) attracts an uncharged object (paper).

After a while the bits of paper jump off again. Why? Once those bits of paper touch the glass, they gradually take on the same charge as the glass. At that point they have like charges. Since like charges repel, the paper jumps down again. *Event 4–F. The Tinsel Tree* also shows that like charges repel. Once charged, the individual strands of tinsel repel each other.

Event 4–G. Fill the Stocking works best when the toe of a nylon stocking is held against a wall and the polyethylene is rubbed down along the stocking against the wall. (You can tell if a plastic bag is polyethylene by its stretch. If it stretches easily, it is probably polyethylene.)

Pull the stocking off the wall and hold it up to see if it "fills out." Since all the fibers of the stocking have the same charge, all the fibers repel each other into a round shape, causing the "filling" action. The stocking can be "emptied" again by merely pulling it loosely through your fingers. Your fingers and hand will neutralize the charge on the stocking.

Event 4–H. Leaping Leaves shows another example of how like charges repel. The leaves of the electroscope move apart when the knob on top is touched with either a positive or negative charge.

As the charge is placed on the knob, it travels down to the leaves. Since both leaves receive the same charge, they are repelled and move apart from each other. The leaves collapse again when the charge is neutralized. This can be done easily by just touching the knob with your finger.

Even strips of newspaper, as used in *Event 4–I. Newspaper Electroscope,* can be used as an electroscope. Rub the newspaper with wool and you will notice that the paper, at first, seems to stick together. However, as soon as a small space develops between the strips, they jump apart. Again, the newspaper event shows that like charges repel each other.

Discrepant Event and Pupil Investigations

Event 4–J. Unlike Charges Attract. Charge one pith ball with a glass rod rubbed with silk. Charge another pith ball with a plastic rod rubbed with wool or fur. Slowly bring the two suspended balls close together. What happens? (See Fig. 4–6.)

Pupil Investigations (may include the following processes):
1. Observing that the balls attract each other
2. Comparing the attraction to that observed when an uncharged object was brought near a charged object
3. Experimenting to discover that one ball is attracted and the other is repelled by a charged rod
4. Forming a theory that the balls carry unlike charges and that such charges attract each other
5. Discovering that after the balls touch, they are neutral

UNLIKE CHARGES ATTRACT (EVENT 4–J)

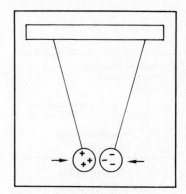

Fig. 4–6. **Unlike static charges attract each other.**

Event 4–J Explained in Context (Unlike Charges Attract)

We have seen that (1) charged objects attract uncharged objects and (2) like charges repel each other. The third fundamental law of static electricity states that *unlike charges attract each other*. This law is shown in *Event 4–J. Unlike Charges Attract.*

One pith ball takes on a positive charge when touched by the glass rod; the other ball takes on a negative charge when touched by the plastic rod. The attraction between these two balls is greater than the attraction either ball has toward an uncharged object.

It is not particularly important for pupils to memorize which object receives what charge. Instead, they should focus on the three basic principles of static charges presented in this chapter.

CHARGING BY INDUCTION (EVENT 4–K)

Discrepant Event and Pupil Investigations

Event 4–K. Induce a Charge. Follow these steps to induce a static charge on an object:
1. Bring a negatively charged rod *near,* but not touching, an object.
2. Ground (neutralize) the object with your finger. Negative charges leave the object.
3. Remove the ground (your finger).
4. Remove the rod. The object now has a charge. Which charge is it?

Pupil Investigations (may include the following processes):
1. Experimenting with charged glass and plastic rods to determine what charge the object has
2. Comparing the charge with another object that is charged by contact instead of by induction
3. Concluding that charging by induction gives a charge opposite to that which is given when charging by contact

Event 4–K Explained in Context (Charging by Induction)

This topic is usually not taught in the elementary grades. However, it is a subject that a gifted pupil might find challenging.

We saw earlier that when an object is charged by contact, the object receives the same charge as the rod. However, when an object is charged *by induction,* it gets the opposite charge. This is shown in *Event 4–K. Induce a Charge.*

In this particular example the negatively charged rod is brought near to, but not touching, the ball. The negative charge on the rod repels the negative charge on the ball. Thus, when a finger is touched to the ball, the repelled electrons have a chance to escape. When these electrons have gone, the finger is removed. With the electrons gone, the charge that remains is positive. (See Fig. 4–7.)

If a positively charged rod is used instead of a negatively charged rod, the

Fig. 4–7. **Charging by induction. When a negatively charged rod is brought *near* the grounded ball, a positive charge is induced.**

electrons will enter the ball instead of leave it. Thus, the ball would get a negative charge.

Notice that by induction we get a charge that is opposite to the charge on the rod, whereas by contact we get a charge that is the same as the one on the rod.

An electroscope is a device that detects a static charge. You can make an electroscope by using a bottle or flask, a cork or rubber stopper, a coat hanger wire, and some foil. (See Fig. 4–8.)

Heat the bottle in an oven (on low heat) or on a radiator to be sure that it is totally dry. Otherwise the device will not work. Insert the wire through the cork or one-hole stopper as shown in the diagram. Use wax to seal the wire where it passes through the cork or stopper. Be sure that you bend the wire that is inside the bottle so that two leaves can be hung alongside each other.

For the leaves use very thin foil, such as that found on some chewing gum wrappers. It is thinner and more sensitive than regular kitchen foil (although kitchen foil will work if necessary). Be sure to peel away the paper backing from the gum foil.

To make the electroscope more sensitive, cut two leaves and hang them on separate supports (instead of making one long leaf and bending it in the middle to make two leaves). Best results are obtained when the end of each leaf is bent and hung loosely on the support. Do not fasten the end of the leaves solidly to the support. Just drape the ends loosely over the wires.

Finally, take some foil (kitchen foil is fine), form it into a ball, and press it around the top of the wire. Why? Do you remember the discovery by Benjamin Franklin? He found that charges leak away from sharp objects quickly. The wire is a sharp object that would cause the electroscope to lose whatever charge that was put on it. Thus, you can eliminate the sharp object by merely fastening a round ball of foil to the wire. In that way the charges stay inside the bottle and can be measured.

HOW TO BUILD AN ELECTROSCOPE

Metal foil ball

Wax to seal

Coat hanger rod

1½"

Foil from chewing gum wrapper

Fig. 4–8. **A simple electroscope.**

5

Teaching Children about Magnetism

FROM LODESTONES TO DOMAINS

Before going into some events about magnets, we will present a brief history of how they were discovered and used. The history of magnets goes back more than 3000 years. Ancient civilizations discovered that certain types of rock seemed to attract bits of natural iron. The rock was actually *magnetite* (Fe_3O_4), a mineral that is very rich in iron.

It is believed that magnetite was formed during the slow hardening of the earth's crust as it cooled down from its molten state. The rock was magnetized by the earth's magnetic field. This magnetic action does not occur in ordinary iron or steel during steelmaking because the metal hardens far too fast.

At first the magnetic rock was merely a curiosity. By A.D. 1200, however, it became quite important. Sailors found that when the rock was placed on a small floating raft in a pool of water, the rock would line up in a north-south direction.

Sailors could use magnetite to tell direction. All they had to do was mark one of the ends to know always which way they were headed, even if they were out in the high seas beyond the sight of land. Because it was used to lead a ship safely to its destination, magnetite became known as the *lodestone* (or "lead-stone").

WHAT CAUSES MAGNETISM? There is still much to learn about the causes of magnetism. However, it is generally believed that magnetism comes from certain properties within the atom.

Since all materials are made up of atoms, you might think that all things are magnetic. But that does not happen. No such properties are evident in many substances such as paper, glass, silver, wood, plastic, and ordinary rocks. Why not?

The answer is thought to be that atoms often are grouped in opposite pairs so that they cancel each other out. That is what probably happens in those substances that have no net magnetic effect. Such substances are called non-magnetic.

In other substances the magnetic fields of their individual atoms are not fully paired, so that a net magnetic field remains. In these magnetic substances the atoms group themselves into small regions known as *magnetic domains* ranging in size from 0.01 to 0.1 centimeters across.

Nonetheless, even these substances (such as iron or steel) do not *appear* to be magnetic. For example, ordinary iron and steel do not attract each other.

That is because the *domains* are scattered in a random order and cancel each other out. (Remember that in nonmagnetic objects the *atoms*, not domains, cancel out each other.) However, when an external magnetic force is brought near, the domains line up and the substance is attracted to the magnet.

Discrepant Event and Pupil Investigations

WHAT DO MAGNETS ATTRACT? (EVENT 5–A)

Event 5–A. What Materials Are Attracted? There are many variations of this activity. Basically, it is designed to test a variety of materials to see if they are attracted to a magnet. Eventually, pupils should be able to classify objects according to whether they are attracted or not attracted by a magnet.

If you use a list such as the one in Fig. 5–1, ask the class to make predictions about which are and which are not attracted. Do *not* let the pupils try the items with a magnet at this point of the activity. Just ask them to predict on the basis of their past experiences. Then summarize the predictions on the chalkboard.

Of the items on the list, silver is perhaps the hardest to get. Use an old, unclad dime or quarter if you can find one. It contains about 90 percent silver. A Canadian nickel is a good source of nickel. (The U.S. nickel does not contain enough nickel.)

Pupil Investigations (may include the following processes):
1. Predicting which materials are attracted by a magnet
2. Classifying materials according to which are and which are not attracted by a magnet
3. Discovering that many metals are not attracted by a magnet

Item	Yes	No
Copper (penny)	?	?
Silver ("unclad" dime)	?	?
Nickel (Canadian nickel)	?	?
Juice can	?	?
Aluminum foil	?	?
Etc.	?	?

Fig. 5–1. Summarize class responses on a chart like this.

Event 5–A Explained in Context (What Do Magnets Attract?)

There are relatively few pure substances that are attracted by a magnet. *Event 5–A. What Materials Are Attracted?* calls attention to those materials that are attracted. In this activity you may wish to have the students test many additional items to see if a pattern develops. They can place those items that are attracted in one pile and those that are not in another.

After a while most pupils will see some patterns develop. For example, they will see that *nonmetallic objects are not attracted* to magnets. Even kindergarten pupils will be able to understand this. Metallic objects, however, will be more difficult. Most students believe that *all* metallic objects are attracted by magnets. Here they will discover that this is not the case.

In fact, only iron, nickel, and cobalt are attracted to a *magnet*. All other metals are not. However, some combinations of metals (alloys), such as iron, aluminum, nickel, and cobalt (alnico), are also magnetic.

In lower grades it may be fun to make a "fishing" game out of this activity. Use a magnet instead of a hook, a string for a line, and a ruler for the pole. Use a wide variety of common items around the classroom as the "fish."

Spread out the items on a table and allow each child to fish for one item. The pupil should tell which item he or she will fish for and predict whether it will be attracted to the magnet. Then, if the item is magnetic, it is picked up by the magnet. The pupil puts the object on the magnetic pile. If it is not magnetic, the student should test with the magnet, and finally pick the object up with his or her fingers and put it on the nonmagnetic pile. Eventually, all the items are checked and classified into magnetic and nonmagnetic substances.

An interesting variation of this activity is to build a discrepancy into the collection of materials. For example, hide a thin iron plate inside a note pad, and see the surprise on pupils' faces when the paper note pad "sticks" to the magnet.

Another idea is to use a "tin" can. Most cans contain no tin. They are made of nonmagnetic substances such as aluminum and even cardboard. However, many cans have a lid that contains iron to allow it to stick to the magnetic holder of a can opener. Let the pupils investigate.

MAGNETISM IS A FORCE (EVENTS 5–B AND 5–C)

Discrepant Events and Pupil Investigations

Event 5–B. Lines of Force. Place some magnets on a flat surface as shown in Fig. 5–2 and cover them with a pane of glass. Then sprinkle some iron filings on the top of the glass. Observe the formation of lines between like poles and unlike poles.

Fig. 5–2. **The lines of force show attraction between unlike poles and repulsion between like poles.**

Pupil Investigations (may include the following processes):
1. Observing that lines between unlike poles connect each other
2. Observing that lines do not connect between like poles
3. Generalizing that unlike poles attract and like poles repel

Event 5–C. Levitation. Set up an arrangement similar to that shown in Fig. 5–3. Place a strong magnet inside the plastic cup and cover the magnet with tissue, cotton, or some other material (to hide the magnet). Attach a thread to a paper clip so that the clip is held down. Do not tell the pupils that there is a strong magnet in the cup. Ask them to decide what holds up the paper clip.

Another part of this event is to insert sheets of various materials such as glass, paper, aluminum foil, plastic, copper, and iron between the paper clip and the cup. Ask pupils to predict if the paper clip will fall as each of the sheets are carefully inserted between the cup and clip, one sheet at a time.

Pupil Investigations (may include the following processes):
1. Observing that there is nothing holding up the paper clip
2. Predicting which sheets will cause the clip to fall
3. Inferring that there is a magnet inside the cup
4. Generalizing that there is a relationship between sheets that cause the clip to fall and those that are attracted by a magnet

Events 5–B and 5–C Explained in Context (Magnetism Is a Force)

SEEING MAGNETIC LINES OF FORCE. *In Event 5–B. Lines of Force* the magnetic force acts upon the iron filings to show how the lines of force look. This is a rather traditional activity and is quite worthwhile. Note that the *lines of force* show attraction between unlike poles.

Fig. 5–3. **What is holding up the paper clip? What happens when paper, glass, and other substances are inserted between the paper clip and the cup?**

However, if like poles face each other, there seems to be a wall or fence formed between them. The lines of force deflect away from the like poles and show that like poles repel each other.

The iron filings hold the shape of the lines only as long as the magnets are there. Once removed, the filings are easily disturbed and lose the pattern of the lines. A more permanent picture of the lines of force can be obtained by placing wax paper on top of the glass and heating the wax after the filings have formed a pattern. When the wax cools, the filings will stick well enough to hold the magnetic pattern even if the paper is moved.

Another way to obtain a permanent picture of the lines of force is to substitute a sheet of paper for the wax paper and spray the filings with a fine mist of water. If the filings are kept wet for some time, they will rust quickly, forming a stain that forms a pattern on the sheet. Try to use paper that is somewhat resistant to moisture for this variation.

MAGNETISM TRAVELS THROUGH SOME MATERIALS. *Magnetism* is a force that acts through space. We also know that it acts through certain materials as if those materials did not exist. Some materials are, therefore, "transparent" to magnetic lines of force. This principle is shown in *Event 5–B. Levitation.*

Pupils tend to guess rather quickly that there must be a magnet inside the cup. Even primary grade pupils will come to that conclusion after a few moments. This prepares them for the lesson to follow.

The purpose of this lesson is to show that magnetism is a force that extends beyond the ends of a magnet, that is, to show that there is something called a *magnetic field.* How can the magnet affect the paper clip if it does not touch it? Because the magnet sends lines of force out through space to "grab" the paper clip.

Another purpose of the lesson is directed at middle and upper grades. We see that magnetic lines of force go through some materials and are blocked by others. Since the magnet is inside the cup, it is obvious that the lines of force go through the cup (as if the cup did not exist) to attract the paper clip.

Placing thin sheets of paper, glass, copper, wood, aluminum foil, and plastic between the cup and clip does not affect the magnetic force. They are all transparent to the magnetic forces. A sheet of iron, however, cuts the lines of force and the paper clip falls.

Students will find that any sheet that is attracted to a magnet will cut the lines of force to the paper clip. Any sheet that is not attracted will have no effect on those forces. Given that information, ask how an object can be shielded from magnetic forces. The answer is to surround the object with a magnetic material, such as iron or steel.

One final note is directed to the primary grade teacher who wishes to be more creative in doing this event. Replace the cup with a crepe paper "flower" in which a magnet is hidden. Cover the paper clip with tissue paper wings to transform it into a "bee."

Ask the pupils why the bee goes to the flower. Do not be surprised to hear an automatic response, "Because the bee *likes* the flower." That comment is likely to be followed by exclamations that "it is not a real bee and it is not a real flower." They soon conclude that there must be a magnet in there.

ATTRACTION AND REPULSION (EVENTS 5–D THROUGH 5–G)

Discrepant Events and Pupil Investigations

Event 5–D. Feel Magnetic Forces. There is no substitute for actual experience. Have the pupils experiment with two magnets. Let them hold the ends together so that they can actually feel the forces of attraction and repulsion. Be sure that the force of repulsion is not overlooked. Almost all pupils know about attraction because magnets "pick things up." Many, however, are not aware that magnets also repel.

Pupil Investigations (may include the following processes):
1. Observing that like poles of a magnet repel each other and that unlike poles attract
2. Experimenting with and feeling the forces produced by magnets
3. Observing that the force decreases as the distance between the poles increases

Fig. 5–4. **What causes these special rings to float when dropped on the peg?**

Event 5–E. Floating Rings. Drop rings onto a peg as shown in Fig. 5–4. Drop them one way and they pile up neatly. Drop them another way and the rings will float. Ask the children to figure out how it is done and why the rings float.

Pupil Investigations (may include the following processes):
1. Observing and feeling the rings that float on the peg
2. Inferring that the rings are actually magnets
3. Generalizing that when the rings float, it is because like poles of the magnets face and repel each other
4. Generalizing that when the rings do not float, it is because unlike poles face and attract each other

Fig. 5–5. **What rules about like and unlike poles can we discover by studying pairs of compasses?**

Event 5–F. Compasses and Magnetic Forces. Let pupils observe the poles of a pair of compasses. Most compass poles are identified by color, although some have the initial N stamped on one end of the needle. Will the north pole of one compass attract the north or the south pole of another compass? (See Fig. 5–5.)

Pupil Investigations (may include the following processes):
1. Observing that unlike poles attract each other
2. Verifying the initial results with other magnets and compasses
3. Discovering that not all compasses and magnets are correctly marked
4. Inferring that compass needles are actually floating magnets

Event 5–G. Magnetic Mixup. If like poles repel each other, why does the "north" magnetic pole of the compass point to the North Pole of the earth? This question produces a real dilemma. Up to this point students have learned that like poles repel each other. In this example, however, it seems that like poles attract each other.

This event should be used only in the upper grades. Let students check references to see if they can solve the riddle. (See Fig. 5–6.)

Fig. 5–6. **Is this diagram correct? Does the north pole of a compass point to the North Pole of the earth?**

Pupil Investigations (may include the following processes):
1. Inferring that the north pole of a compass is really just the north-*seeking* pole (or, incorrectly, that it is really just a south pole)
2. Testing to see if a suspended bar magnet lines up the same way as the needle of a compass
3. Verifying the results with other compasses and magnets to see if they "agree" with each other (They do not.)

Events 5–D Through 5–G Explained in Context (Attraction and Repulsion)

Every magnet has a north pole and a south pole. We find that when two like poles are brought together they repel each other, but two unlike poles attract each other. This principle is presented in *Event 5–D. Feel Magnetic Forces.*

Although most pupils have handled magnets at one time or another, they probably have focused only on how two magnets "stick together" or attract each other. In this exercise they should also handle the magnets so that they experience the push or repulsion between them.

Ask if they can separate two magnets just by pulling on them, not wiggling or sliding them as they pull. Then see if they can place two like poles directly together. It will be very difficult to do so. As they try to bring the poles together, the repelling forces will push the magnets to the side.

The forces of attraction and repulsion can also be observed by suspending a bar magnet on a string and bringing other magnets close by. The results of this activity can be recorded on a table such as Table 5–1. Let pupils tabulate the results of many attempts of the four possible combinations.

A sample tabulation of 24 trials is shown in Table 5–1. By the time the activity is completed, it will be obvious to the pupils that *like poles repel* and *unlike poles attract.*

Event 5–E. Floating Rings is explained by the "like poles repel" principle. The rings are really magnets with the poles on their flat surfaces. When placed over the peg with like poles facing each other, the rings repel each other and "float" in the air. If they are placed so that unlike poles face each other, the rings stick together.

Table 5–1. **Magnetic Poles**

Pole of Swinging Magnet	Pole of Hand-held Magnet	Tabulate Numbers of Trials	
		Attract	Repel
North	North		‖‖ (5)
North	South	‖‖ 11 (7)	
South	South		‖‖ 111 (8)
South	North	1111 (4)	

Event 5–F. Compasses and Magnetic Forces also shows the effects of attraction and repulsion. If the compasses are properly marked, we will see that unlike poles attract and like poles repel. (Compasses are not always marked correctly, so check the compasses that you plan to use for this event.)

After you present the lessons on the poles of a magnet, a pupil may ask a question about the earth's *magnetic poles*. That question can be quite difficult to answer. It poses a real discrepancy: If like poles repel, why does the north pole of a compass needle point to the North Pole of the earth? (See *Event 5–G. Magnetic Mixup.*)

Some pupils will merely respond, "Because the compass is built to point that way." However, after spending so much time learning that like poles repel, the answer should be better than that. In this case it seems that like poles are attracting.

The answer is not particularly simple. You will find that the explanations vary in different textbooks. The most common explanation seems to be that the "north" pole of a compass needle is, in reality, the north-*seeking* pole. In other words, the claim is made that the north pole of the compass is really a south pole!

Unfortunately, that explanation is not accurate. Just check the compass needle with a magnet. The north pole of the compass is attracted to the south pole of a magnet (if the magnet is marked correctly). To make matters worse, magnets are often incorrectly marked. In fact, you cannot rely on the accurate markings of either the magnets or compasses found in a typical elementary school.

Still, the confusion remains. What is the real answer to the question about the poles of the compass and the earth? The confusion began when compasses were originally made.

The first compasses were lodestones, or magnetic rocks. They were set on floating supports and used on ancient ships to aid in navigation. Sailors noticed that the lodestone lined up so that one end always pointed north. It was not surprising that they called that end the "north" pole. In those days they knew nothing about like poles repelling each other.

Geologists have decided that the rules of magnets can be applied accurately if the needle that points north is labeled "north," just as the early sailor had done. Then to make all the rules agree, the point of the earth near the *north geographic* pole is, in reality, the south *magnetic* pole. (See Fig. 5–7.)

At any rate, it is probably just as well to avoid this discussion in the elementary school. This explanation is presented here as background information for teachers in case the question is asked by pupils.

Fig. 5–7. **Strange as it may seem, the earth's south *magnetic* pole is located in the *Northern* Hemisphere. The north pole of a compass points to it, in keeping with the rule that opposite poles attract.**

TWO KINDS OF MAGNETS. Magnets are often classified as "permanent" or "temporary." *Permanent magnets* retain their magnetism for long periods of time. They are used in the activities in this chapter.

A *temporary magnet* is one in which the magnetic force can be turned on and off by using an electric current. It is called an *electromagnet* and will be investigated in greater detail in the next chapter.

You can make a permanent magnet in the classroom. This requires the use of a hard steel—such as a hacksaw blade, darning needle, or a workshop file. Hold the object to be magnetized, and stroke it 20 or 30 times with a magnet. That is all it takes. The object becomes a magnet, provided it is made of the right steel.

Despite being called permanent, such a magnet is not really permanent. It retains its magnetism only if handled with care. The magnet can lose magnetism in several ways, including (1) placing it in a powerful external magnetic field, (2) heating the magnet until it is too hot, and (3) hitting or dropping it.

HOW TO MAKE A COMPASS. Use a magnetized needle to make a compass. Make a "raft" from a slice of cork and place the needle on it. Set the cork in a plastic or glass container and observe.

If there is no interference from magnets, metal, or electrical wires, the needle will be influenced only by the earth's field. Thus, the needle should line up in a north-south direction, just like the needle of a compass.

TEMPORARY AND PERMANENT MAGNETS

Teaching Children about Current Electricity

THE DISCOVERY OF CURRENT ELECTRICITY

The history of current electricity goes back to the late 1700s when two Italian scientists became involved in a great debate. Luigi Galvani, a doctor of medicine, made a startling discovery while dissecting a frog. He noticed that the frog's leg twitched while he was dissecting it.

Since the frog was dead, what caused the twitch? The leg could be made to twitch when sparks crackled from a static electricity machine nearby or during an electrical storm, so Galvani concluded that the twitch must be related to electricity.

After many further attempts Galvani could get the frog's leg to twitch even when the weather was nice. Finally, Galvani reported his findings and advanced the theory that the electricity came from the frog. He called it "animal electricity."

Galvani was a respected scientist and his report was widely accepted by the scientific community. However, there was one notable exception—a young Italian physicist named Alessandro Giuseppe Antonio Anastasia Volta. He insisted that the source of the twitch was not in the frog, but outside it.

Volta showed that the muscular twitch could not be produced unless dissimilar metals were used in the dissecting knife and probe. He claimed that it was not the frog's leg but the dissimilar metals that caused the twitch, and he called the energy "contact electricity."

Galvani double-checked and refined his work. Eventually, he was able to get the frog's leg to twitch even when he used similar metals in the knife and probe. This appeared to overcome Volta's objections. Volta, however, countered with evidence that the similar metals had to be dissimilar in some way for the leg to twitch. He still insisted that the energy came from the dissimilarity in the metals, not from the frog.

Finally, Galvani countered with a startling and convincing new discovery. He got rid of the metals altogether! He was able to get the leg to twitch by just touching the end of one nerve to the end of another. The proof seemed overwhelming: If nothing else was used, the energy must have come from the frog. It must be animal electricity!

In the face of Galvani's discovery, what could Volta do? Amazingly, he got rid of the frog!

Volta used only dissimilar metals in a liquid, and produced an even greater discovery. In fact, it was overwhelming! It wiped away all debate. By using only dissimilar metals, he produced a large amount of energy.

Remember that scientists working with static electricity had looked for current electricity for centuries. Now Volta had found it. Keep in mind that with static electricity the energy could only be discharged in a flash or spark. It was not a continuous current. (Even the words "static" and "current" describe the difference between the two types of electricity.)

Volta's discovery was so spectacular that it swept the scientific world by storm. First of all, it was easy for any scientist around the world to duplicate. (In comparison, Galvani's work required a surgeon's skill to duplicate.) Second, Volta produced a large amount of energy, not just something to make a frog's leg twitch.

The story of the two Italian scientists has a sad ending. Galvani admitted the greatness of Volta's discovery but suffered a personal loss of face. He felt disgraced by having led so many of his friends on a false path. He died within a year, a broken man.

Had Galvani been able to look into the future, he would have been pleasantly surprised. Today we know that an electrical current *does* come from individual cells! For example, the *electrocardiogram* and the *electroencephalogram* are measurements of the electricity produced by the cells in the heart and brain, respectively. Also, electricity produced by our body's pacemaker regulates the ticking of the heart. It seems that Galvani was right after all. They were *both* right!

Discrepant Events and Pupil Investigations

Event 6–A. The Mysterious Marbles. Arrange a row of marbles as shown in Fig. 6–1. Snap a marble against one end of the row. What happens to the other marbles? How does the activity relate to current electricity?

Pupil Investigations (may include the following processes):
1. Observing that the last marble moves away as soon as the first marble strikes the front of the row
2. Inferring that the energy moves through the marbles instantly
3. Comparing the movement of marbles to the movement of electrons in a conductor

Event 6–B. Conduction Tester. Set up an arrangement as shown in Fig. 6–2. Place the material to be tested across the gap between the two terminals on the board. If the bulb lights up, the material is a conductor; if it does not light, the material is a nonconductor.

Pupil Investigations (may include the following processes):
1. Testing various substances to see if they are conductors
2. Classifying materials into conductors and nonconductors
3. Generalizing that all metals are conductors

WHAT IS CURRENT ELECTRICITY? (EVENTS 6–A AND 6–B)

Fig. 6–1. **What happens when a marble is snapped into the row?**

Fig. 6–2. **Use this device to test the conductivity of materials.**

Events 6–A and 6–B Explained in Context (What Is Current Electricity?)

DIFFERENCE BETWEEN STATIC AND CURRENT ELECTRICITY. The work of Volta and Galvani opened up a spectacular new field in science. Prior to this time there was only static electricity with little practical value. Now there was current electricity!

In static electricity the energy that accumulated in objects was stationary, moving only during the instant of discharge, often appearing as a spark or flash. Static electricity had a few interesting lab applications but provided almost no practical uses. Franklin's lightning rod was about the only exception.

By contrast, current electricity was a *continuous controlled flow of electrons*, kept moving by a kind of electrical "pressure" between dissimilar metals. This continuous flow was soon harnessed to do useful work. Today current electricity is used for heat, light, motors, electronics, and many other applications.

At one time electricity was believed to be an invisible, weightless fluid, so fine that it passed through the densest materials in conductors. Words expressing the early thinking can even be found today. For example, the movement of electricity is referred to as a "current" or "flow," and electricians still refer to it as "juice."

HOW DO ELECTRONS FLOW? Electrical current moves along a conductor at great speed. Yet there is relatively little motion of individual electrons. The action is similar to pushing beans through a bean shooter. When the shooter is full, you only need to push one bean into one end of the shooter to cause another bean immediately to come out of the other end. The individual beans do not move very much, but the motion goes all the way through.

A good way to show the motion of electrons is to do *Event 6–A. The Mysterious Marbles*. Place a few marbles in the groove of a ruler or between two rulers, and roll another marble so that it strikes the others in the row. As soon as the first marble strikes the row, the end marble jumps away. As with the bean shooter example, the energy moves through the row quickly, but the individual marbles do not move very much.

Table 6–1. **Electrical Terms**

Term	Defined	Compared to Water
Volt	Potential difference or "electrical pressure" (volts are equal to amperes times ohms)	Water pressure in pounds per square inch
Ampere	A unit of current flow (one ampere lights a 100-watt bulb)	Gallons per second
Ohm	Resistance depends on the composition, length, thickness, and temperature of a substance	Resistance of the pipe
Coulomb	A specific quantity of charge (6 billion, billion electrons)	A specific number of gallons such as "5 gallons"

Some electrical currents are large, some small. Some currents have great pressure, others do not. Currents flow through some substances easily, but not through others. There are special terms used to describe the flow of current. These terms are listed in Table 6–1. In the table the electrical units are also compared to water to help us understand the meaning of the terms.

WHAT IS A CONDUCTOR? An electrical current does not travel through all materials. Substances that are good carriers of electricity are called *conductors*. Those that are very poor carriers are called *nonconductors*. What are some good conductors? *Event 6–B. Conduction Tester* is designed to help children find out. A substance that is a good conductor will allow the current to flow. You will know if the current flows because it lights the bulb. All metals are good enough conductors to light the bulb, but the best common conductors are copper and aluminum.

Even better conductors are uncommon gold and silver. Those precious metals are far too expensive to be widely used. They are used only in places where amounts needed are small, where extreme conductivity is required, and where the product is very expensive. Gold and silver are used in space satellites, and silver is sometimes used in computers and sophisticated electronic devices.

The atoms that allow current to flow are those with a number of free or loosely held electrons. Copper, for example, has 29 electrons. Twenty-eight are held tightly in the first three atomic shells. However, the last one is all by itself in the fourth shell. This single loose electron is the one that transmits electrical energy.

Materials that are nonconductors include paper, rubber, plastic, glass, and wood. Nonconductors are also called *insulators*.

Discrepant Events and Pupil Investigations

Event 6–C. Current from Coins. This is a good activity if you can get an old unclad silver dime. Clean a penny and a silver dime in detergent. Drop them into a dish or tray, and pour in enough saltwater to cover the coins. Connect wires to the terminals of a galvanometer, and touch the loose ends to the two coins. (A *galvanometer* is a device that can detect very tiny electrical currents.) Observe the meter. What happens to the needle? Reverse the coins and observe the meter again. What happens? (See Fig. 6–3.)

Pupil Investigations (may include the following processes):
1. Observing that the meter moves when the coins are touched with the wires
2. Observing that the meter moves in the opposite direction when the coins are reversed
3. Experimenting to see the effects of different metals and coins
4. Forming a theory about the sources of the electrical energy
5. Comparing results when distilled water instead of saltwater is used

SOURCES OF ELECTRICITY (EVENTS 6–C, 6–D, AND 6–E)

Fig. 6–3. **A penny and a pre-1964 silver dime will produce an electric current when they are soaked in saltwater.**

Event 6–D. Potato Power! Insert a copper strip and a zinc strip into a raw potato, and attach wires from the strips to a galvanometer. (Zinc can be obtained by cutting up the outside shell of a dry cell; copper can be obtained from a hardware store.) What does the galvanometer show? Use different materials and observe the reaction on the meter.

Pupil Investigations (may include the following processes):
1. Observing that the meter is deflected when the strips are inserted into the potato
2. Experimenting with different substances to see which will produce electrical current
3. Forming a theory about the source of the current

Event 6–E. Current from a Coil? Wrap about 25 turns of bell wire around a tin can or box of salt and carefully remove the wire. You now have a coil. In making the coil, leave the ends long enough to attach to a galvanometer. Push a magnet through the coil and observe the meter. Then pull out the magnet and observe the meter again. Turn the magnet around and try again. Observe the results. (See Fig. 6–4.)

Fig. 6–4. **When the magnet is inserted into the coil, a current is generated.**

Pupil Investigations (may include the following processes):
1. Observing that the needle of the meter moves one way when the magnet is pushed in and the other way when the magnet is pulled out
2. Observing that when the magnet is reversed the readings are reversed
3. Comparing the size of the meter reading with the speed of the magnet's insertion into the coil
4. Discovering that the meter shows pulses of energy instead of a continuous flow
5. Generalizing about the source of energy

Events 6–C, 6–D, and 6–E Explained in Context (Sources of Electricity)

There are several different sources of electricity. They are listed in Table 6–2. Some sources are fairly easy to duplicate, especially the chemical and *electromotive sources,* but others are more complex. It is generally too difficult to produce photoelectric and piezoelectric sources of electricity in the elementary classroom, although some examples can be shown. The *electrothermal source* is somewhat less difficult to produce but is still not easy. See Fig. 6–5 for details on setting up the activity.

If you do not have a galvanometer, it is possible to make one using a coil and a good compass. Just wrap about 20 to 30 turns of bell wire around a compass leaving the ends about half a meter long. Attach the free ends to the metal strips in the potato. If the compass is held carefully so that the needle is floating freely, it is often sensitive enough to detect the current that comes from the potato.

Fig. 6–5. **When dissimilar metals (wires) are heated and cooled at different points of the circuit, an electric current is produced.**

Table 6–2. **Sources of Electricity**

Source	Examples
Chemical (or electrochemical)	Dry cell, potato battery, wet cell, silver dime and a penny
Mechanical (or electromotive)	Coils and magnet
Heat (or electrothermal)	Thermocouple
Light (or photoelectric)	Electric eye, photo cell, solar cell, light meter
Pressure (or piezoelectric)	Crystal detectors for radios, microphones, and headsets

CHEMICAL SOURCES OF ELECTRICITY. The first kind of current electricity that was discovered was a chemical source. The energy comes mostly from dissimilar metals but can also include some nonmetals such as carbon. The basic energy comes from atomic differences within substances.

Some substances tend to lose electrons easily. Other substances tend to gain electrons easily. When there is a path between the two types of substances, there is a tendency for the electrons to move from one to the other. That movement is called an *electrical current*.

Volta produced electricity using a chemical source. *Event 6–C. Current from Coins* is a fairly good example of Volta's original cell. If the event is done correctly, the energy from the penny and dime is quite apparent on the meter.

If the old silver dimes are not available, you can use other metals such as zinc, aluminum, brass, or tin. Experiment to see which metals produce the best currents. Another version, as shown in Fig. 6–6, is to use strips of copper and zinc in beakers of saltwater.

Fig. 6–6. **Wet cells, made of dissimilar metals dipped into saltwater, produce an electrical current.**

The cell shown in *Event 6–D. Potato Power!* is still another example of getting electricity from a chemical source. The potato contains dissimilar metals and the juices needed to carry the current.

In a sense the potato cell is really a form of *dry cell*. A dry cell is not *really* dry inside. It is called "dry" because it can be tipped over without leaking any liquids. The potato cell can work in the same way. Regardless of how the potato is held, it does not spill.

In the place of a potato you may use a lemon. In fact, a lemon works better in some ways. The lemon juice is a better conductor, so it produces a somewhat stronger current. Unfortunately, the juices tend to run and drip.

ELECTROMOTIVE SOURCE OF ELECTRICITY. The most common source of electricity today is not chemical. It is electromotive. This is the form that is generated by power stations and sent to your homes.

It is easier to understand this form of electricity by performing *Event 6–E. Current from a Coil?* In the activity a magnet is thrust into and out of a coil of wire. When this happens, a current is produced in the coil and can be seen on the meter.

Note that the meter moves in one direction when the magnet is pushed into the coil but goes in the opposite direction when the magnet is pulled out. Then when the magnet is reversed, the meter readings are reversed also. This shows that polarity and direction affect the direction of the current. The current that is produced in this way is called *alternating current (AC)*. All other sources of electricity produce *direct current (DC)*.

Today most of our electrical energy comes from magnets and coils. Of course, the magnets and coils in a power station are so much larger and more complex that we would not recognize them as being similar to the ones in our simple experiment.

CIRCUITS (EVENTS 6–F THROUGH 6–I)

Discrepant Events and Pupil Investigations

Event 6–F. Light the Bulb. Divide the class into teams of two to four pupils. Provide each team with a dry cell, two short pieces of wire (20 to 40 centimeters long), and a 3-volt flashlight bulb. After they have the supplies ask the pupils to "get the bulb to light up."

Although the correct diagram is given in Fig. 6–7 do not show it to the pupils at this time. They will quickly learn the right way by trial and error. (*Caution:* Most pupils will probably "short out" the wires in their attempts to get the bulb to light up. Tell them that if a wire gets hot, to disconnect immediately and try another way.)

Fig. 6–7. **To light the bulb, one wire must touch the metal housing (side); the other must touch the metal tip (bottom).**

Pupil Investigations (may include the following processes):
1. Experimenting with wires connected in various ways
2. Discovering that some connections cause the wires to get hot
3. Discovering that when the bulb lights up the wires remain cool
4. Visualizing the path of electrons through the circuit

Event 6–G. Stop and Go Signals for Electricity (Switches). Distribute strips of flexible metal. You may get them by cutting up an aluminum can, but do so only *if you can be sure that all sharp edges have been filed smooth.* Otherwise acceptable strips can be made from folded layers of aluminum foil.

Ask students if they can find a way to make a switch that will automatically turn off the current if a person leaves it. Set up a simple current with bulb and battery and two wires. Ask them to place the strip between the wires so that they function as an automatic switch.

Pupil Investigations (may include the following processes):
1. Experimenting with different ways of turning the current on and off
2. Comparing ideas with one another to see if any plan will actually work out successfully
3. Inferring a relationship between the switch and the pathways of electricity

Event 6–H. Pop the Fuse. Cut a piece of foil from a used gum wrapper into the shape shown in Fig. 6–8. (Do not strip the paper backing from the foil.) Touch the wires from a 6-volt battery to the ends of the foil. Can you get the foil to melt?

Pupil Investigations (may include the following processes):
1. Experimenting with various sizes to see if they melt
2. Observing that the foil melts if it is thin enough
3. Generalizing that the foil acts as a fuse

Event 6–I. Series and Parallel Circuits. Divide the class into teams of two to four people. Provide each team with two dry cells, four short pieces of wire (20 to 40 centimeters long), and two 3-volt flashlight bulbs. (*Caution:* It is easy to connect wires so that there is a short created that will make the wires hot and quickly drain the batteries. Warn the pupils that if the wires get hot, disconnect and try another way.)

This event can be used in middle and upper grades. Ask the teams to do the following activities:

1. Light one bulb with two cells. Compare series wiring with parallel wiring. Put the diagram in Fig. 6–9 on the chalkboard.
2. Getting two bulbs to light up with one dry cell using series and parallel wiring. Put the diagram in Fig. 6–10 on the chalkboard.
3. Getting the brightest and dimmest arrangements using two bulbs and two cells. (Do not put Fig. 6–11 on the chalkboard at this time. If pupils understand the first two parts of the event, they will get it right without the diagram.)

Pupil Investigations (may include the following processes):
1. Comparing series with parallel wiring of cells
2. Comparing series with parallel wiring of bulbs
3. Discovering the brightest combinations of two cells and two bulbs

Events 6–F Through 6–I Explained in Context (Circuits)

WHAT IS A CIRCUIT? Before a current can travel anywhere, it must have a path to follow. A complete path, called a *circuit*, starts at the energy source, flows through a conductor, and returns to the energy source. *Event 6–F. Light the*

Fig. 6–8. **The gum-wrapper "fuse" melts when too much energy is sent through it.**

Fig. 6–9. **Top view of two cells connected in series and in parallel.**

Fig. 6–10. **The top bulbs are connected in series; the lower in parallel.**

Fig. 6–11. **Bulbs connected in parallel with batteries connected in series produce the most light.**

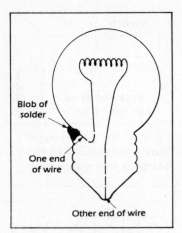

Fig. 6–12. **A bulb is a wire surrounded by glass. Connect the ends to a dry cell to get the bulb to light up.**

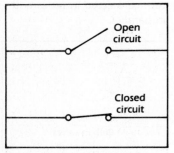

Fig. 6–13. **In which circuit is the electricity turned on?**

Fig. 6–14. **When the metal strip is pressed down, it turns the current on (closes the circuit). When released, it springs up and turns the current off (opens the circuit).**

Bulb is designed to help pupils understand a simple circuit. Encourage pupils to experiment and most will quickly get the bulb to light up. Then ask them to visualize, or mentally trace, the path taken by the current.

In their experiments pupils will undoubtedly make incorrect connections before finally getting it right. That is permissible, of course, but needs a word of caution. An incorrect connection will cause the wires to get hot and can burn out a dry cell if left on too long. A simple remedy is to tell pupils that if the wires get hot, disconnect at once and try another way.

It helps pupils to realize that a bulb is not much more than a piece of wire enclosed in glass. Look closely at a bulb and you will see a small blob of solder between the glass bulb and metal base. That is where one end of the wire is attached. The other is hidden in the very bottom tip of the base. (See Fig. 6–12.)

To get the bulb to light up, the two wires from the dry cell are connected to the two ends of the wire in the bulb. Refer back to Fig. 6–7 for the proper connections.

You can use a 1.5-volt bulb instead of a 3-volt bulb for this event. The bulb will burn quite brightly because it is matched with a 1.5-volt cell. However, you cannot use the 1.5-volt bulbs later in this chapter where two cells are connected in series. The 1.5-volt bulbs will burn out. Thus, it is probably better to use 3-volt bulbs for all activities in this chapter. They give a low, but acceptable light in this event, and a bright light in the later event.

OPEN AND CLOSED CIRCUITS. As stated earlier, a current can travel only if it has a complete path to follow. However, often that is not enough. For convenience, there should also be an easy way to disconnect the path. Otherwise a room light, for example, would stay on all the time.

How is the light turned off? By a *switch*, of course. When a switch is turned off, it is called an *open circuit*. When a switch is turned on it is called a *closed circuit*. (See Fig. 6–13.)

In *Event 6–G. Stop and Go Signals for Electricity* students are asked to make a switch that automatically opens the circuit when a person leaves the device. Unless you use such a switch, some pupils will leave wires hooked up to bulbs when they are finished with an activity. They forget to turn off the current, and the cells are dead in 15 to 30 minutes.

An automatic switch solves the problem, but students think it is too difficult to make. Yet the solution is simple. Just attach a metal strip to a board as shown in Fig. 6–14. It is similar to a key of a telegraph. To turn the current on, just push down the switch. When you leave, the strip springs back. Thus, pupils cannot ruin a battery by forgetting to turn off a switch.

SHORT CIRCUITS. An example of a typical circuit is an electric toaster that is plugged in. The current travels through the toaster's electrical plug-in cord (which stays cool) and through toaster wires (which become red hot). After going through the toaster the current returns through the plug-in cord to the wall outlet, completing the path.

We know that the wires inside the toaster become red hot. Why are those wires hot while the appliance cord remains cool? After all, the same amount of electricity is going through both. The effects are different because the wires are different. The appliance cord is made of relatively large copper wires that can carry the current easily. The toaster wires are small and made of a noncopper substance (nichrome) that cannot carry the current easily. As a result, the toaster wires get hot as the nichrome resists the current.

Suppose the plug-in cord is damaged so that the two wires within it touch each other. What will happen? The current will no longer go through the toaster. Instead, it will take the shorter path (making a *short circuit*) and jump across to the other wire of the cord.

As soon as the current jumps to the other wire of the appliance cord, it no longer meets the resistance that existed in the toaster wires. With less resistance the current increases greatly. Suddenly, instead of the toaster wires getting red hot, the plug-in cord becomes red hot! Can you guess what will happen to a house if the electric wires within its walls become red hot?

FUSES AND CIRCUIT BREAKERS. The scene just described would be a disaster unless protected by a safety device. Fortunately, such safety devices exist. They are called fuses and circuit breakers. A *fuse* is a protective device that cuts off the current when it is too great for the house wires. It acts like an automatic switch, turning off the current when a circuit is overloaded. Most new homes now use *circuit breakers* to perform the same function as fuses.

The operation of a fuse can be demonstrated by doing *Event 6–H. Pop the Fuse*. The center part of the fuse should be cut quite narrow to be sure that the event will work. When the current is large enough, the fuse burns out.

Foil from gum wrappers works better than kitchen foil. Gum wrapper foil is thinner and tends to melt quickly when a battery current goes through it. (It is not necessary to peel the paper backing from the foil.)

SERIES AND PARALLEL WIRING OF BATTERIES AND BULBS. If we wish to have more light in a room, we simply turn on another lamp. How surprising it would be to find that as we turn on another lamp the lights become *dimmer*. Both these results are possible in *Event 6–I. Series and Parallel Circuits*.

Refer back to Fig. 6–9 to check the correct way to get the brightest light from two cells and one bulb. It is a series arrangement of batteries. Refer back to Fig. 6–10 to check the correct way to get the brightest light from two bulbs and one cell. The parallel arrangement of bulbs gives a brighter light. In fact, the series arrangement actually gives *less* light than a single bulb.

Why does the series arrangement of bulbs cause a dimmer light? Think of the bulbs as resistances. As the current enters the bulb, it is resisted by the fine tungsten wire inside. If two bulbs are connected so that the same current has to go through both bulbs, then the current has twice as much resistance as it originally had. Thus, less of the current can get through, and it produces less light.

In a parallel arrangement, however, current that goes through one bulb *does not go through the other bulb*. The current has alternate paths that it can choose. Notice that in a parallel arrangement there are always two wires between any two objects. Refer back to the lower diagram in Fig. 6–10.

Suppose the current enters from the left in the lower line. The current reaches a branch where it can either go up through the first bulb or go on to the second bulb at the right. Once through either bulb, the current goes on its way back to the cell. No electron ever goes through more than one bulb in a parallel arrangement.

You will find that when working with bulbs, it is the parallel arrangement that gives the most light, and when working with cells, it is the series arrangement that gives the most light. Thus, the brightest possible combination of batteries and bulbs is with cells in series and bulbs in parallel. (Refer back to Fig. 6–11.)

Why does the series arrangement of cells produce a brighter light in bulbs? Because the energy of the two cells is combined. If the cells are 1.5 volts each, two cells connected in series produce 3 volts.

When two cells are connected in parallel, the voltage remains the same. It is as if you added another gas tank to your car. It does not make the engine stronger, but it will run twice as long before it uses up the gas. The parallel arrangement adds no brightness to the bulbs, but it doubles the time they will remain lit.

Sometimes it helps to compare electricity to water. The cells are like tanks of water. If you add one water tank on top of another, you increase the pressure. It is like connecting the cells in series. The added pressure can be compared to the added volts when batteries are connected in series. As stated earlier, two cells of 1.5 volts each produce 3 volts when connected in series.

If, instead, you place the second tank alongside the first and connect them with a pipe, the water pressure remains the same. However, it takes twice as long to use up the water supply. The increase in time can be compared to the action of cells connected in parallel. The combination still produces only 1.5 volts but will last twice as long.

In summary, cells connected in series produce a higher voltage but no greater life span. Cells connected in parallel produce a longer life span but no additional voltage.

USES OF ELECTRICITY (EVENTS 6–J AND 6–K)

Discrepant Events and Pupil Investigations

Event 6–J. Power-Packed Performer. Attach a length of bell wire to each terminal of a strong dry cell (6-volt if possible), and touch the ends to a batch of steel wool. What happens to the steel wool? (*Caution:* Do the activity as a demonstration. Avoid the hot wires, have a pan of water handy to extinguish glowing wires, and have good ventilation for possible fumes.)

Pupil Investigations (may include the following processes):
1. Observing that the steel wool becomes so hot that it burns
2. Inferring that the heat is caused by resistance in the thin strands of the steel wool
3. Generalizing that electricity can be used to produce heat and light

Event 6–K. Stop and Go Magnets. If you wrap an insulated wire around a nail and attach the ends of the wire to a dry cell, you will have made an electromagnet. See how many paper clips the electromagnet will pick up. Have pupils try arrangements of 10, 25, 50, and 100 turns of wire around the nail. Also, try arrangements of one and two cells connected in series. (See Fig. 6–15.)

Pupil Investigations (may include the following processes):
1. Observing that the magnetism starts and stops with the turning on and off of the electrical current
2. Inferring that electricity produces the magnetic field
3. Recording the results of the investigation in Table 6–3

Fig. 6–15. **When an insulated wire is wrapped around a nail and connected to a battery, it becomes an electromagnet.**

Table 6–3. **Electromagnets**

Trial	Turns of Wire	Number of Cells	Number of Clips
1.			
2.			
3.			
etc.			

Events 6–J and 6–K Explained in Context (Uses of Electricity)

Electricity is used to generate heat in toasters, ranges, and clothes irons; to generate light in bulbs; and to do work in electromagnets and motors. Pupils should be asked to look for examples of how electricity is used around the home and in school.

In *Event 6–J. Power–Packed Performer* electrical energy is used to burn the fine wire in steel wool. Remember to be careful. Avoid touching the red hot wires, have water handy to put out burning wires, and be sure that any possible fumes are removed by ventilation. (This activity can also be used in Chapter 2 in the section on fire. The fine wire allows so much oxygen to reach the steel that it can actually burn.)

A 6-volt battery will work better than a 1.5-volt cell. (There is no danger of shock from these cells because the voltage is too low to pass through the skin.)

Electricity and magnetism are related. Just place a compass next to an electric wire and you will see the compass needle jump when the current is turned on and off. It proves that an electric current produces a magnetic field around a conductor.

Another way to see the magnetic field is shown in Fig. 6–16. Cut a sheet of paper or cardboard halfway through. Center the sheet around the wire and sprinkle with iron filings. The iron filings will align themselves with the magnetic field. Thus, the field will be made visible.

Fig. 6–16. **Iron filings sprinkled on this sheet of paper are lined up in concentric circles. This indicates the existence of a magnetic field in a current-carrying wire.**

The magnetic field of a wire can be made stronger by merely wrapping the wire around a soft-iron core, such as a nail, as is done in *Event 6–K. Stop and Go Magnets*. At first each added turn adds to a magnet's strength. However, a point is reached when the added resistance of the additional wire reduces the current and makes the magnet weaker.

You can see if that point is reached in your class by recording the data in Table 6–3. Those points will vary greatly depending on the size of wire and on the condition and quality of the cells.

Some final notes: Be sure to use insulated wire because bare wire will not work. Be sure, also, that the wire is always turned around the nail in only one direction. It makes no difference which way you wrap the wire, but do not change directions once started.

THINGS TO MAKE

Fig. 6–17. **A three-way switch has three wires (or ways) for current to travel. The current can be turned on and off in two different places.**

Fig. 6–18. **When the wire is moved to the right, the resistance is decreased so more current can flow through the circuit.**

Fig. 6–19. **This tin-can timer regulates the lighting of the bulbs. The upright parts of the three wires touching the can must be bare, and the tin can must be part of the circuit.**

A THREE-WAY SWITCH. We have all seen lights that can be turned on at one end of a hallway and turned off at the other end. What kind of switch allows the lights to be controlled from two places? Such a device is called a *three-way switch* because it needs three wires or pathways for the current to travel. (See Fig. 6–17.)

RHEOSTAT (DIMMER SWITCH.) There are several ways of making a dimmer or rheostat. One method is shown in Fig. 6–18. The device works better with a 6-volt cell than with a 1.5-volt cell.

Another dimmer can be made by using saltwater in place of the pencil lead. Just bring the wires close together in the saltwater to make the light brighter and move the wires away to make the light dimmer. This activity works best with somewhat higher voltage than other events. You may need to wire two 6-volt cells together in series to make a 12-volt source. However, if you accidently touch the wires together, the bulb burns out. So, be careful.

AUTOMATIC TRAFFIC LIGHT. The automatic traffic light is nothing more than a glorified tin can. (See Fig. 6–19.) Be sure that the ends of the three upright wires are cleared of insulation. The bare wire must touch the can.

MODEL TELEGRAPH. There are many ways to make a model telegraph. One example is shown in Fig. 6–20. Attach an iron hinge to a wooden frame. Make an electromagnet using wire and a bolt. The bolt head must be close to the hinge but cannot touch it.

Sometimes a little latent magnetism remains in the bolt, so that the hinge will stick to the bolt even when the current is turned off. A single layer of adhesive tape across the bolt head is enough to keep the hinge from sticking. Unfortunately, the tape will also deaden the sound of the "click."

Fig. 6–20. **This is one example of a simple telegraph.**

7

Teaching Children about Sound

**WHAT IS SOUND?
(EVENTS 7–A
THROUGH 7–D)**

Discrepant Events and Pupil Investigations

Event 7–A. The Big Splash. Strike a tuning fork against the heel of your shoe, or hit it with a rubber mallet. Place the tips of the tines (the two vibrating ends of the tuning fork) into a beaker of water. What do you observe? What does this event show us about sound? (See Fig. 7–1.)

Fig. 7–1. **What happens when the tuning fork is dipped into the water?**

Pupil Investigations (may include the following processes):
1. Observing that the water splashes out of the beaker when the tuning fork touches the water
2. Experimenting with tuning forks of different sizes
3. Inferring (incorrectly) that the larger the tuning fork, the bigger the splash
4. Inferring (incorrectly) that the higher the frequency, the bigger the splash (Actually, the inference is correct up to a certain point, but then the splash decreases as the frequency increases.)
5. Generalizing that where there is sound there is vibration

Event 7–B. Ping-Pong Bounce. Strike a tuning fork and hold a tine against a suspended Ping-Pong ball. What happens to the ball when it is touched by the tine? (See Fig. 7–2.)

Pupil Investigations (may include the following processes):
1. Observing that the Ping-Pong ball bounces away when touched by a tine
2. Experimenting with tuning forks of various sizes
3. Forming a theory that the tuning fork had energy that was transferred to the ball
4. Inferring that the tuning fork was vibrating

Fig. 7–2. **What happens to the Ping-Pong ball when it touches a vibrating tuning fork?**

Event 7–C. Rubber-Band Riders. Fasten a rubber band between two nails and drape a few paper "riders" over the strand. Pluck the rubber band and observe.

Pupil Investigations (may include the following processes):
1. Observing that the paper riders are bounced and tossed about
2. Observing that the rubber band is vibrating

82

3. Comparing this activity to others in this section in which objects are disturbed by a tuning fork
4. Generalizing that sound is caused by vibrations

Event 7–D. Vibrating Voices. Ask students to hold one hand against the throat above the Adam's apple while talking or humming. What do they feel? What conclusions can be made about voice and vibrations?

Pupil Investigations (may include the following processes):
1. Feeling vibrations when talking or humming
2. Inferring that these vibrations cause the sounds
3. Comparing these vibrations to those produced in other events

Events 7–A Through 7–D Explained in Context (What Is Sound?)

This section is intended to establish the fact that *sound is a form of energy produced by the vibration of matter* or, to put it more simply, that *sound is caused by vibrations.*

There are many events that can be done to discover this principle. In *Event 7–A. The Big Splash,* for example, it is the vibrating motion of the tuning fork that causes the water to splash. When the tuning fork is struck, the tines move back and forth (or vibrate) rapidly.

When the fork is dipped into the water, this vibrating motion is strong enough to cause the splash. Pupils will find that a large tuning fork of about 126 vibrations per second has a large motion that can be seen fairly easily and will produce a good splashing action.

Smaller tuning forks of 256 and 512 vibrations per second cause even greater splashes, even though their vibrating motions are much shorter and harder to see. The splashes are larger because the tines travel faster.

Tuning forks of even smaller size, however, do not work well. Their vibrating motion becomes so small that they disturb the water less and less. By the time you use tuning forks of 2000 and 3000 vibrations per second, they do not cause any splash at all.

Event 7–B. Ping-Pong Bounce shows the effect of vibrations also. If the tuning fork is really vibrating, then perhaps its rapid movement will cause something to happen with the Ping-Pong ball. Suspend the ball by a thread and touch it with a tine of a vibrating tuning fork. The ball will bounce away with surprising energy. The best results are obtained with tuning forks of 256 to 512 vibrations per second.

Still another activity that shows the same result is simply to hold the end of a sheet of paper lightly against the tuning fork. The vibrating sound of the tine striking the paper will be easy to hear.

While the vibrations of a tuning fork are often hard to see, the vibrations of a rubber band are usually more visible. This visible evidence of motion is increased still more by placing folded bits of paper on the band as suggested in *Event 7–C. Rubber-Band Riders.*

Be sure to relate this activity to the earlier events. In each case the vibrating matter (the tuning forks and the rubber band) produced a visible response when some object touched it. Each event gave us evidence that an object that produced sound was actually vibrating.

Pupils may wonder if the sounds of talking, singing, and humming are also produced by vibrating matter. *Event 7–D. Vibrating Voices* should be of great interest to them. If the pupil holds a hand on the throat, the vibrations coming from the larynx (voice box) will be felt.

In all the events in this section there is evidence that sound is produced by vibrations. These events make it clear that vibrations actually exist.

HOW DOES SOUND TRAVEL? (EVENTS 7–E THROUGH 7–K)

Discrepant Events and Pupil Investigations

Event 7–E. Tabletop Messages. Hold your ear against a tabletop while someone taps and scratches lightly against the other end of the table. What is heard? How do the sounds coming through the table compare to the sounds coming through the air?

Pupil Investigations (may include the following processes):
1. Listening to the sounds coming through the tabletop
2. Controlling variables by making sure that sound is coming only through the table (plug the exposed ear)
3. Comparing the sounds through the table with those that come (from the same source) through the air
4. Inferring that sounds travel through solids

Event 7–F. Teeth: Sound Detectors. Anyone can listen to a watch by holding it against his or her ear. Find out if you can hear your watch with your *teeth*. Can you hear the watch with your ears plugged? (You need a watch that "ticks" for this event. A digital watch will not work.)

Pupil Investigations (may include the following processes):
1. Experimenting by holding the watch carefully with the lips and then with the teeth
2. Controlling variables to be sure that no sound comes through the ears (plug the ears)
3. Inferring that sound travels through the solids (of the head) to be detected

Event 7–G. Spoon Chimes. Tie two lengths of string to a spoon. Wrap one string around a finger of one hand and the other string around a finger of the other hand. Then plug the fingers into your ears. Lean forward so that the spoon strikes a desk or table. Listen to the sound. What do you hear? (See Fig. 7–3.)

Pupil Investigations (may include the following processes):
1. Comparing the sound heard through the string with the sound heard through the air

Fig. 7–3. **Did you ever listen to a spoon? Compare the sound as heard through the string with the sound as heard through the air.**

2. Experimenting with spoons of different sizes and with other objects
3. Inferring that sound travels through the string

Event 7–H. Tin-Can Telephone. Punch a tiny hole through the end of a tin can. Pull a string through the hole and fasten it to a button on the inside. (The button keeps the string from being pulled out of the can.) Do the same with the other end of the string and a second tin can. The string should be at least as long as the classroom.

Have one pupil on each end of the string, holding on to a tin can. Be sure that they pull the string tight. Then have one talk into the can while the other listens. What is heard? How does the tin can telephone transmit sounds?

Pupil Investigations (may include the following processes):
1. Discovering that sometimes sounds can be heard quite well but at other times there are no sounds at all
2. Experimenting to find out how the telephones must be held to produce the best results
3. Testing with different lengths and thicknesses of string
4. Inferring that sounds travel through the string

Event 7–I. The "Dancing" Salt. Stretch a rubber film (from a balloon) across the open end of a tin can and sprinkle some salt on the film. Strike a tuning

Fig. 7–4. **A vibrating tuning fork causes the salt to "dance" on the stretched rubber.**

fork and hold it about 1 centimeter over the film. What do you observe? What does this event show us about sound? (See Fig. 7–4.)

Pupil Investigations (may include the following processes):
1. Observing that the salt "dances" if the tuning fork is held a certain way
2. Experimenting with various ways of holding the tuning fork
3. Comparing tuning forks of different sizes
4. Formulating a rule to explain why the tuning fork causes the salt to dance

Event 7–J. Listening Tube. Attach a rubber hose to a funnel as is shown in Fig. 7–5. Place the funnel against a ticking clock. Can you hear the sounds coming through the tube? Is it louder or softer than the sounds coming through the air? Use the device to listen to your heart.

Pupil Investigations (may include the following processes):
1. Comparing the sounds heard through the tube with the sounds coming through the air
2. Experimenting with various lengths and sizes of tube
3. Forming a theory to explain why the sounds coming through the tube are louder

Fig. 7–5. **The ticking of the clock sounds louder through the tube than through the air.**

Event 7–K. Underwater Sounds. Fill a large bowl or fish tank with water. Then place your ear against one side of the tank while holding a ticking clock against the other side. Plug your exposed ear with a finger so that you are listening only with the ear held against the tank. This activity is commonly suggested to show that sounds travel through water. *What is wrong with it?* (See Fig. 7–6.)

Fig. 7–6. **Can you hear the sound of the clock through the water? Try it with an empty aquarium. Can you still hear the clock?**

Pupil Investigations (may include the following processes):
1. Listening to the ticking sounds that reach the ear
2. Inferring (incorrectly) that the event proves that sounds travel through the water
3. Experimenting to find out if the sounds can be heard with an *empty* fish tank
4. Devising a way to prove that sounds travel through the water

Events 7–E Through 7–K Explained in Context (How Does Sound Travel?)

SOUNDS TRAVEL IN WAVES. To understand how sounds travel, we need to have some background information about waves. Sounds are transmitted from one place to another in waves.

There are two types of waves: (1) transverse and (2) longitudinal. *Transverse waves* are common side-to-side waves similar to water waves. *Longitudinal waves* are push-pull waves of the type that can transmit sound.

The transverse wave can easily be shown by attaching one end of a rope to a door knob or other object and snapping the other end. The snakelike wave moves quickly from your hand to the other end of the rope. Both waves can be demonstrated with a wire coil (a Slinky). Stretch the coil across a table and have students hold each end. Then have one student make vigorous side-to-side motions with the coil. The snakelike waves travel across the table. (See Fig. 7–7.)

The longitudinal wave can also be shown with the coil. Instead of shaking the coil from side to side, just make vigorous push-pull motions. The waves can easily be seen as they travel along the coil.

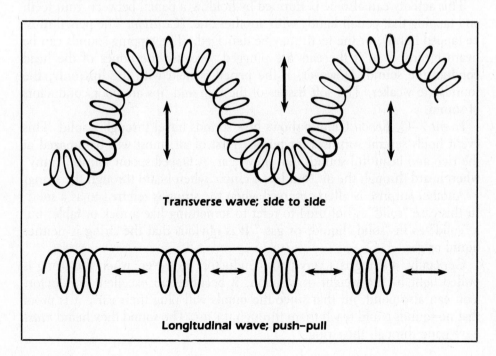

Transverse wave; side to side

Longitudinal wave; push–pull

Fig. 7–7. **The transverse and longitudinal waves can both be demonstrated with a *Slinky* coiled spring.**

SOUNDS TRAVEL THROUGH SOLIDS. In the days of the Old West, Indians often detected the presence of wagon trains or herds of buffalo by listening for them. They did not listen for them through the air; they listened for them through solids. By holding an ear against a boulder or hard ground, an Indian could detect the noises over a much greater distance than they could be detected through the air.

Today railroad workers do somewhat the same thing when they listen for a train. A worker holds an ear against a rail. If a train is heard, they know that it is not safe to take out a section of rail for repair. They wait until no train can be heard before they remove a rail.

Another version of this activity is performed by the auto mechanic who holds one end of a stick against parts of a car engine while holding his ear against the other end. If bearings are not functioning well, the grinding noises can be heard through the stick much better than through the air.

Each of the preceding examples pertains to one fundamental principle of sound: *sound travels through solids*. In fact, most of the time sounds travel through solids much better than through the air.

Many classroom activities show that sounds travel through solids. *Event 7–E. Tabletop Messages* is a miniature example of the buffalo detection described earlier. However, instead of detecting sounds that travel many kilometers, the sound travels only a few meters in the table. Pupils will notice that sounds are quite loud when heard through the table.

In *Event 7–F. Teeth: Sound Detectors* a ticking watch can be heard quite well if it is held between the teeth and if the ears are plugged with fingers. The ticking will have a deeper tone than when the watch is held to the ear. The sound travels through the bones of the head to the auditory center, again demonstrating that sounds travel through solids. (Use only a watch that ticks. Electronic watches make no sounds.)

This activity can also be performed by holding a pencil between your teeth and tapping that pencil lightly with another one. (*Caution:* The pencil must be tapped lightly, or the teeth may be damaged.) The tapping sounds can be heard clearly even if the ears are plugged, because the bones of the head conduct the sound. However, if the pencil is held with the lips only, the sounds are weaker. The soft tissues of the skin and lips are poor conductors of sound.

Event 7–G. Spoon Chimes shows how sounds travel through a solid. This event holds several surprises for pupils. First of all, most will be amazed at the rich and beautiful sounds that they hear. A tapped spoon sounds "tinny" when heard through the air, but like a chime when heard through the string.

Another surprise is often observed when the string is referred to as a solid. In this case "solid" is not used to refer to something like a rock or table, but a "solid" as in "solid, liquid, or gas." It is obvious that the string is neither liquid or gas.

Generally, a string is a very poor conductor. However, when the string is pulled tight by the weight of a spoon, it becomes an excellent conductor. You can also point out that since the pupils will plug their ears, it is proof that no sounds could reach them through the air. The sound they heard *must have* gone through the string.

You can use many other items such as forks, knives, and coat hangers in place of the spoon. Each will give a surprisingly rich sound when heard through the string.

Event 7-H. Tin-Can Telephone also shows that a string conducts sound. If done correctly, the sounds can be carried over a distance of 50 meters or more. For it to work the string must be tight. Otherwise it will carry no sounds. It is also important that the pupils place their hands on the sides of the can instead of the back. Holding the back will tend to smother the vibrations that are being transmitted.

SOUNDS TRAVEL THROUGH AIR. The fact that we can hear people talk is clear evidence that sound travels through the air. However, there is an event that shows this characteristic of sound in a more unusual way. In *Event 7-I. The "Dancing" Salt* a vibrating tuning fork causes the salt to dance and bounce. Since the tuning fork does not touch the salt, membrane, or tin can, it is obvious that the sound must travel through the air. (This event is also good to show that sound is related to vibrations, as was shown earlier in Events 7-A through 7-D.)

The salt will not dance if it is on another surface because most surfaces are far too massive to be affected by sound waves. However, a thin rubber membrane is so light that it works. The energy from a tuning fork is strong enough to cause the membrane to vibrate, which in turn causes the salt to dance.

Sound energy is not very great and loses its strength rapidly as the distance increases. Thus, the salt will dance only if you hold the vibrating tuning fork no more than 1 or 2 centimeters away.

Although sound weakens rapidly through free air, it remains quite strong if trapped inside a tube. *Event 7-J. The Listening Tube* provides this evidence. The ticking of a clock sounds much louder through the tube than through the air. It is even possible to detect your heartbeat with the tube and funnel as long as there is no background noise to interfere with your listening.

An interesting application of the listening tube is found on big ships. Of course, there are telephones on big ships. But what if the electricity is shut down by an accident? How can the captain talk to the engine room? By the listening tube, of course. Such tubes (called speaking tubes) are used as emergency lines of communication to all essential parts of the ship.

SOUNDS TRAVEL THROUGH LIQUIDS. How can you show that sounds travel through water? It is not very easy. *Event 7-K. Underwater Sounds* is sometimes suggested in some books. Unfortunately, there is a serious flaw in doing it as shown. Why? Just try the event with an empty container. It still works. You can still hear the ticking of the clock. Sound travels very well through the glass walls of the bowl.

The event can be modified so that it has at least a fair amount of accuracy. Just tap some rocks together under water or open and close a scissors under water. Even there, it is possible that the sound could travel up your arms and into the air. However, most of the sound you hear will have had to travel through some water to reach you.

Perhaps it may be best to simply ask pupils if they have ever heard sounds while swimming underwater in a pool. Many will verify that they have heard sounds such as the filter motor and other noises.

NO SOUNDS IN A VACUUM. We have seen that sound travels through solids, liquids, and gases. It does not travel through a *vacuum*. It must have some kind of material medium through which to travel. Since a vacuum is an absence of matter, it cannot conduct sound.

If sound cannot be transmitted through a vacuum, how do astronauts communicate with each other in the vacuum of the moon or space? They do so by visual signals or by radio. They cannot hear as they do on earth.

THE SPEED OF SOUND (EVENTS 7–L, 7–M, AND 7–N)

Discrepant Events and Pupil Investigations

Event 7–L. Speed Detector. Make a pendulum that has a period of half a second. Shortening the string speeds up the pendulum; lengthening the string slows it down. Hang the pendulum from a support and assign a student to keep it swinging.

Have another student strike together two pieces of wood at the exact moment that the pendulum weight is at a given point in its arc. The event works just as well if the wood is struck only at every second or third swing of the pendulum. Ask the students to determine how the speed of sound can be measured.

Pupil Investigations (may include the following processes):
1. Observing that moving away from the sound causes a time lag between the time you see the pieces struck and the time that the sound is heard
2. Inferring that sound travels more slowly than light
3. Measuring the distance from the listener to the source
4. Computing the speed of sound from the data gathered in the activity

Event 7–M. Echo Speed Computer. You can hear an echo if you hit two wooden sticks together in an open space in front of a large flat surface such as a building or even a line of trees.

Perhaps your school building is the only large surface nearby. If so, stand about 80 to 90 meters from the building and strike the sticks together. You should be able to hear an echo.

Then start walking toward the building, striking the sticks as you walk. (It is not necessary to strike the sticks in rhythm. You are merely listening for an echo.) As you approach the building, the echo will be harder and harder to detect because it moves closer to the original sound. How can the speed of sound be calculated by following the instructions? (*Hint:* The ear can hear an echo following the original sound by as little as one-tenth of a second.)

Pupil Investigations (may include the following processes):
1. Measuring the distance between the building and the point where the last echo was heard

2. Forming a theory that the sound travels twice the distance to the reflecting surface because it makes a round trip to it and back again
3. Computing the speed of sound from the information available in the activity

Event 7–N. Echo Range Finder. Stand in front of a large flat surface such as a building or even a line of trees. Clap your hands together repeatedly. Can you hear an echo? Clap so that your second clap is just in time with the echo from the first.

When you synchronize your claps in this way, count the number of claps in a given period of time, say, 10 seconds. How can the distance to the surface be measured using this method? (*Hint:* To get the answer, you need to know that sound travels 330 meters per second.)

Pupil Investigations (may include the following processes):
1. Recording the number of claps in a given period of time
2. Inferring a relationship among the number of claps, the speed of sound, and the distance to the surface
3. Computing the distance to the object with the information gained in the experiment

Events 7–L, 7–M, and 7–N Explained in Context (The Speed of Sound)

SPEED OF SOUND IN AIR. Scientists have discovered that sound travels at 330 meters per second at 0 degrees Celsius. The speed increases slightly when the air warms up and decreases slightly when it gets colder.

There are several ways of measuring the speed of sound that may be suitable for use in the upper grades. In *Event 7–L. Speed Detector* students must combine the factors of time and distance to compute the speed of sound.

After the pendulum weight is set in motion and the pieces of wood are struck in tempo with the pendulum's swing, students begin to move away. They will soon notice that the sound is no longer in rhythm. That is, what is heard lags behind what is seen.

Finally, the lag will be a full $\frac{1}{2}$ second and thus be exactly in tempo with the pendulum again. At this point all that needs to be done is to measure the distance. It should be 165 meters. Thus, the sound traveled 165 meters in $\frac{1}{2}$ second. That is equal to 330 meters per second, or 1200 kilometers per hour.

If there is no clear area of 165 meters on or near the school grounds, the pendulum can be set to a shorter time period. However, if the pendulum swings too fast, it becomes more difficult to time the pendulum accurately.

The speed of sound can also be found by using the method suggested in *Event 7–M. Echo Speed Computer.* Students should be able to pinpoint the distance from the last echo to the wall of the building fairly well. The point where the echo can no longer be detected should be about 16 or 17 meters from the reflecting surface.

Remember, however, that the sound makes a round trip to the wall and back, so that the sound actually travels a total of about 33 meters. Given the fact that the ear can distinguish an echo that is heard $\frac{1}{10}$ second after the original sound, it means that the sound traveled 33 meters in $\frac{1}{10}$ second. Again, that is 330 meters per second.

Once we know that sound travels 330 meters per second, that information can be used to measure distances, as stated in *Event 7–N. Echo Range Finder*. If you clap your hands in tempo with the returning echo, you can measure the distance to the reflecting surface.

Suppose that you clapped 15 times in 10 seconds and that each clap was in tempo with the preceding echo. Thus, a single clap would go to the surface and back in $\frac{2}{3}$ second ($\frac{2}{3}$ sec $\times$ 15 = 10 sec). Sound travels 220 meters in $\frac{2}{3}$ second. Since the sound made a round trip to the surface *and back*, the distance to the surface is one-half of 220 meters, or 110 meters.

You can also use the speed of sound to measure the distance to a lightning flash. Just count the number of seconds between the lightning and the thunder. Thus, a 3-second delay between lightning and thunder indicates that the lightning was 1 kilometer away.

SPEED OF SOUND IN DIFFERENT MEDIA. The speed of sound depends mostly on the elastic properties of a substance. Surprising as it may seem, at the molecular level, water and steel are far more elastic than air. Sound travels at 1450 meters per second in water and 4800 meters per second in steel as compared to 330 meters per second in air.

The density of a substance is also a factor in sound transmission. The more dense a substance, the worse it transmits sound. Concrete, for example, is a dense substance and a sound absorber. Although steel is also a dense substance, it is far more elastic than it is dense. Therefore, the net effect is to make steel an excellent conductor of sound.

VOLUME (LOUDNESS) (EVENTS 7–O THROUGH 7–T)

Discrepant Events and Pupil Investigations

Event 7–O. Tuning Fork Amplifier. Strike a tuning fork with a mallet and press the base against a tabletop or some other surface. What happens to the sound? Explain why this occurs. (*Caution:* Be sure to touch the *base* of the tuning fork to a surface, *not* the tines. The tines can damage surfaces. See Fig. 7–8.)

Fig. 7–8. **Place the base of a tuning fork against a solid surface and listen.**

Pupil Investigations (may include the following processes):
1. Observing that the sound becomes louder
2. Forming a theory that the object (table, desk, etc.) acts to increase the energy of the tuning fork
3. Inferring that the tuning fork forces the object to vibrate
4. Generalizing that there is a relationship between the size of the vibrating surface and the loudness of sound

Event 7–P. Wastebasket Megaphone. Hold up an empty wastebasket and talk into it. What does your voice sound like? Place a battery and a buzzer or bell into the wastepaper basket and listen to the bell ring. Is the sound louder?

Pupil Investigations (may include the following processes):
1. Observing that the sound becomes louder when talking into the wastebasket
2. Comparing the sound of the bell inside and outside the wastebasket
3. Inferring that the wastebasket is similar to a megaphone
4. Generalizing that there is a relationship between the size of the vibrating surface and the loudness of sound

Event 7–Q. Make the Lion Roar. Punch a tiny hole in the bottom of an empty milk carton and insert a string. Fasten the string to a button so that it will not pull out of the hole. Hold the string tightly and stroke it with a damp cloth or paper towel. What does it sound like? (You can try the same activity with a tin can to make "the rooster crow.")

Pupil Investigations (may include the following processes):
1. Experimenting with the device to determine the kinds of sounds that can be created
2. Observing that the sound caused by rubbing is very loud
3. Inferring a relationship between the size of the vibrating surface and the loudness of sound

Event 7–R. Vibrating Air. Hold a vibrating tuning fork of about 520 vibrations per second about 1 or 2 centimeters above the top of an open cylinder. Hold the cylinder upright, and lower it slowly into a deep container of water so that only about 12 to 14 centimeters of the cylinder remain above the water. Then move the cylinder up and down carefully at this height to find the point of greatest effect. What do you hear? (See Fig. 7–9.)

Fig. 7–9. **If the air column is made to resonate, the sound of the tuning fork will become much louder.**

Pupil Investigations (may include the following processes):
1. Listening to the sound and estimating its increase in intensity
2. Experimenting with tuning forks of different frequencies
3. Measuring the height of best effect for each tuning fork
4. Inferring that there is a relationship between the size of the tuning fork and the length of the vibrating air column

Event 7–S. Singing Wine Glasses. Wash your hands with soap and water. Then dampen a finger with vinegar and rub it gently on the rim of a wine glass. Keep doing this even if nothing happens immediately. (It takes practice, but it will work if you don't give up.) Vary the speed and pressure slightly. Eventually, a loud clear sound should be produced. How is the sound made? (See Fig. 7–10.)

Fig. 7–10. **Rub your finger gently along the edge of the glass goblet. Can you make it "sing"?**

Pupil Investigations (may include the following processes):
1. Experimenting to produce a loud clear sound
2. Comparing the sounds created with different levels of water in the glass
3. Comparing the sound made when the glass is rubbed with the sound made by tapping the glass with a pen or pencil
4. Generalizing that the sounds are natural vibrations of the glass

Fig. 7–11. **It would take a "hurricane holler" to blow the heavy book very far, unless the secret is known.**

Event 7–T. Hurricane Huff! Do we need the huff and puff with the force of a hurricane to blow away a heavy book? Find a way to move the book without too much puffing. (See Fig. 7–11.)

Pupil Investigations (may include the following processes):
1. Observing that the heavy book will swing slightly after it is blown
2. Observing that the swinging book has a natural rhythm
3. Experimenting with puffs that are timed to coincide with the natural swing of the book
4. Inferring a relationship between the swinging book and the loudness of sound

Events 7–O Through 7–T Explained in Context (Volume or Loudness)

There are a number of factors that affect the loudness of sound. Most of these factors are presented in the following list:

1. The *energy* expended to make the sound. (Strike a gong harder, for example, and it makes a louder sound.)
2. The *distance* from the source to the listener. The inverse square rule applies: If the distance increases by a factor of 2, the sound is only one-fourth as loud. If the distance is three times as far away, the sound is only one-ninth as loud. What fraction results if the distance is four times as great? (one-sixteenth)
3. The *surface area* that is vibrating. The greater the area, the louder the sound. This is an important factor in the discussion of forced vibrations to follow later in this chapter.
4. The *resonance* of an object. That is, the ability of anything to vibrate by absorbing energy at its own natural frequency.

The loudness of sound is measured in units called *decibels*. Common sound intensities are given in Table 7–1.

Table 7–1. **The Loudness of Sounds**

Level of Sound	Decibels
Threshold of hearing	0
Whisper	10–20
Classroom activity	20–40
Conversation	50–60
Heavy street traffic	70–80
Loud thunder	100–110
Threshold of pain	120

FORCED VIBRATIONS. A very common means of making sounds louder is to use forced vibrations. Radio or television speakers give off sounds because the speakers are forced to vibrate in step with the incoming source of energy.

Forced vibrations can be demonstrated with *Event 7–O. Tuning Fork Amplifier.*

Strike a tuning fork and hold its base against a table or almost any solid surface. As you touch the surface, the sound becomes louder. The vibrations of the tuning fork travel into the larger surface and cause that surface to vibrate. The larger the vibrating surface, the louder the sound.

Try a variety of surfaces. Tables, desks, chalkboards, and windows all work quite well. (But be sure to use the *stem*, or base, of the tuning fork, not the tines. Otherwise you will break the window.) Some wall surfaces will also work well if they are not built of concrete or brick. Concrete and brick absorb energy, and little if any sound will be heard.

Event 7–P. Wastebasket Megaphone is another example of how forced vibrations produce a louder sound. When speaking into the empty wastebasket, the sound of your voice causes the large surface to vibrate. The larger surface produces a louder sound.

The final example of forced vibration is *Event 7–Q. Make the Lion Roar.* The string has a very small surface. So, when you rub it with a damp cloth or paper, it gives off a feeble, squeaky sound. When the sound goes into the milk carton, however, a much larger surface is set in motion; and the sound is much louder. The carton will produce a lion's roar. If you use a tin can, it will produce the sound of a crowing rooster.

NATURAL VIBRATIONS: RESONANCE. The number of times an object vibrates per second is referred to as the object's *frequency*. An object will vibrate best at only one frequency—its *natural frequency*. You can hear the natural sound of any object by striking it.

Remember that a source of energy can cause an object to vibrate, even though the vibrations are not at the object's natural frequency. What happens when the object *is* vibrating at its natural frequency? The object is then *resonating*. When an object resonates, it becomes much louder than normal.

For example, if you sing a loud tone in front of a piano, you will hear the piano "reply" in the same tone. Only those strings with vibration rates identical to the singing tones will resonate. They will vibrate loud enough to be heard.

Resonance can be produced in an air column by doing *Event 7–R. Vibrating Air.* By raising and lowering the cylinder, we are, in effect, changing the length of the air column inside the cylinder. In this way we can locate the exact height of the air column that will resonate with the sound of a tuning fork.

For example, a tuning fork with a vibrating rate of 520 vibrations per second will resonate in an air column of about 12 to 14 centimeters. A tuning fork of 260 vibrations per second will require an air column twice as high.

In *Event 7–S. Singing Wine Glasses* the sound is produced by friction between the rim of the goblet and your finger. Actually, your finger does not move around the rim smoothly. Instead, it moves in a series of jerky motions. It slips, catches, slips, and catches, again and again. The motion is so fast that it sends out vibrations.

Those vibrations are not loud enough to produce much of a sound until the right frequency is reached. When the natural frequency of the glass is reached, the glass resonates. Pour some water into the glass and the natural frequency changes. Note that the sound made by the finger on the rim is identical to the sound made by the glass when it is tapped.

Perhaps it is easier to understand resonance if the vibrations are slowed down. We can use a child on a swing as an example. A swing also has its own natural frequency, but that frequency is very slow. If a child tries to "pump" in a random way, the swing will not go very high. Instead, it just moves in random, jerky wiggles.

Once the child learns to time the pump with the tempo of the swing, however, then each pump adds to the previous pump, and the arc of the swing builds up to go higher and higher. Thus, the same energy that earlier caused wiggles now produces a great motion.

This, in slow motion, is what happens in resonance. Input energy is reinforced so that the effect is cumulative. *Event 7–T. Hurricane Huff!* works the same way as the swing example. Blow on the book with random huffs and the book wiggles. Time the puffs correctly, in tempo with its natural swing pattern, and the book goes into a higher and higher arc.

PITCH (EVENTS 7–U, 7–V, AND 7–W)

Discrepant Events and Pupil Investigations

Event 7–U. Rubber-Band Paradox. Introduce the event by calling attention to the relationship between the size of an instrument and its tone. A big instrument has a low sound, a small instrument has a high sound. A big bass fiddle, for example, has a much lower sound than a violin. Pupils will agree that the longer the string on an instrument, the lower the sound.

Pull rubber band

Fig. 7–12. **In which position is the pitch of the rubber band higher? Lower?**

Use a rubber band to represent strings of different lengths. Pluck it when slightly stretched; then lengthen it and pluck again. In which position does the rubber band have the higher sound? Does the activity "agree" with the instruments? (See Fig. 7–12.)

Pupil Investigations (may include the following processes):
1. Testing to find that the higher pitched tones occur when the band is long instead of short
2. Observing that there is a slight change in diameter of the band as it is stretched
3. Inferring that the pitch of the rubber band depends on factors other than length

Movable bridge

Fig. 7–13. **How do thickness, tension, and length affect the pitch of a string?**

Event 7–V. Strained Strings. Set up a board with strings or wires of different sizes as shown in Fig. 7–13. Provide various weights and a movable triangular "bridge" under the strings. Ask students to find out what factors affect the pitch of the strings.

Pupil Investigations (may include the following processes):
1. Experimenting with different weights, diameters, and lengths
2. Recording the data in a table such as Table 7–2
3. Generalizing that the pitch of a wire depends on its length, diameter, and tension

Table 7–2. **Factors Affecting the Tone of a String**

	High Pitch	Medium Pitch	Low Pitch
Thin wire			
Medium wire			
Thick wire			

Event 7–W. The Baffling Bottles. Set up two bottles as shown in Fig. 7–14. Fill one about one-half to two-thirds full of water. Leave the other bottle empty. Blow across the tops of each and note the sounds. One bottle gives a high tone, the other a low tone. Then tap each with a pencil or pen and listen again. The tones are now reversed! What causes the paradox?

Fig. 7–14. **Blow across the top of each bottle and listen to the sounds; then strike the bottles with a pencil and compare. How do the sounds differ?**

Pupil Investigations (may include the following processes):
1. Verifying the sounds heard during the demonstration by repeating the activity
2. Experimenting with other bottles of varying sizes, shapes, and amounts of water
3. Inferring (incorrectly) that the paradox is caused by factors unrelated to the principles of pitch

Events 7–U, 7–V, and 7–W Explained in Context (Pitch)

WHAT IS PITCH? The effect of the frequency of sound on the ears is referred to as *pitch*. Put another way, it merely refers to the highness or lowness of a sound. The higher the frequency, the higher the pitch.

It is important to realize that pitch is different from volume. A sound can have a low pitch but a high volume; or, conversely, it can have a high pitch with a low volume. For example, a brass horn produces a low pitch, but it can be played loudly (high volume); and a flute has a high pitch but it can be played softly (low volume).

Not all frequencies are audible to the ear. Humans with perfect hearing can detect sounds ranging from 20 to 20,000 vibrations per second. Frequencies above or below that are beyond the range of human detection. Normal conversation takes place in a frequency range of 500 to 3000 vibrations per second.

In some respects children have an almost intuitive knowledge of pitch. They seem to know that large objects produce lower sounds than smaller objects. For example, they know that a bass drum gives a lower sound than a snare drum and that a tuba gives a lower sound than a trumpet. In all cases, the larger the object, the lower the sound.

THE PITCH OF A STRING. The pitch of an object depends on a variety of factors. For a stringed instrument the factors are (1) length, (2) diameter (or thickness), and (3) tension (or tightness). These factors can be demonstrated with *Event 7–U. Rubber-Band Paradox.*

The event may confuse students at first. It appears to contradict the principle of length. As the rubber band becomes longer, the pitch becomes *higher*, not lower. This is just the opposite of what should be expected. Close inspection should give the pupils some clues. They will often notice that other things happen to the rubber band when it is pulled. Not only does the rubber band get longer, but (1) it gets thinner and (2) it gets tighter.

Length, by itself, will lower the pitch, but length is *not* by itself in this activity. The increased tension and reduced size more than offset the effects of length.

This event will show the importance of controlling variables in an experiment. If there is more than one variable, it is impossible to know which variable affected the outcome of an experiment. *Event 7–V. Strained Strings* is a way of showing how strings can be tested correctly. Only one variable is tested at any one time.

THE PITCH OF OTHER OBJECTS. *Event 7–W. The Baffling Bottles* is another surprising activity when first presented. When blowing across the bottles to produce a tone, the bottle with water in it gives the high sound. The bottle that is empty gives the low sound. When struck with a stick or pencil, the sounds are reversed!

What is the principle that governs the sounds? Do they contradict? Not at all. Just remember that *the more there is of something, the lower the sound, and the less there is of something, the higher the sound.* When blowing, the air is vibrating, and the larger air column (empty bottle) gives the low sound. When struck, the bottle and contents are vibrating—and again the larger mass (bottle with water) gives the low sound.

In each case the larger mass produced the low sound and the smaller mass produced the high sound. It was only the mass that changed, not the principle of sound.

There are many more activities that show variations in pitch. These activities include:

1. *Stick-comb pitch-indicator.* Run a pencil or stick across the teeth of a comb. The faster the movement of the stick, the higher the pitch. You can get the same pitch differences by running your fingernail over the fibers of cloth.
2. *Saw pitch-indicator.* Use a handsaw to cut a board. The faster you saw the board (sawteeth hitting the wood), the higher the pitch. The slower you saw, the lower the pitch.
3. *Straw clarinets.* Make a straw sound maker by cutting away the sides of one end as shown in Fig. 7–15. Place that end into your mouth and blow to produce a sound. Cut a piece off the other end of the straw and notice that the sound becomes higher as the length is reduced. *Note:* A paper straw works better than a plastic straw.
4. *Variable air column.* Blow over a straw and note the pitch. Place the lower end of the straw into a beaker of water and blow again. As you lower the straw into the water, the air column becomes shorter and the pitch becomes higher.
5. *Plastic ruler pitch-indicator.* Place a plastic ruler so that it extends over the edge of your desk. Strum it and note the sound. Lengthen

15 cm to 25 cm

Fig. 7–15. **Cut one end of a paper straw as shown. Place it into your mouth and blow. It vibrates to produce a pitch that depends on the length of the straw.**

the part that extends over the desk and the sound becomes lower. Shorten the overhang and the sound becomes higher.

6. *Water-pouring pitch-indicator*. Pour water into a container. Notice that as the container fills up the pitch becomes higher. Also, if you pour liquid from a can with a single hole, the "glug" sounds become lower as the can empties.

MUSIC

In a strict scientific sense, a musical tone is any sound produced by *regular vibrations of matter*. In an informal sense, it is usually felt that music should contain some pleasing quality.

Generally, a musical composition has (1) *melody* (also called *tune*), the effect of single notes in sequence; (2) *rhythm*, a timing pattern; and (3) *harmony*, the pleasing effect of two or more notes sounded together. (The unpleasant effect of two or more notes sounded together is called *discord*.)

The notes that fit together best for a pleasing effect (harmony) are ratios, that is, simple whole number comparisons of 1 : 2, 1 : 3, 2 : 3, 3 : 4, or 4 : 5 : 6. For example, if one note has a frequency of 100 vibrations per second, it will give a pleasing sound when combined with another note of 200 vibrations per second, or of 300 vibrations per second. The frequency of the musical scale on a piano is shown in Fig. 7–16.

Fig. 7–16. **The musical scale is based on the frequencies shown.**

MUSICAL INSTRUMENTS. Musical instruments can be classified into three major groups: *percussion*, *string*, and *wind*. Percussion instruments produce sounds by being struck. Stringed instruments produce sounds by plucking or bowing. Wind instruments produce sound with vibrating air columns. It is subdivided into three more groups: flutes, horns, and reeds. See Table 7–3 for details.

MUSICAL QUALITY. Musical *quality* is the characteristic of music that makes it pleasing to the ear. The effect of quality in speech can be shown by asking a pupil to say "spring is coming." First of all, ask the pupil to say the words normally. Then have the child say the words while holding his or her nose. Is the quality affected?

Table 7–3. **Musical Instruments**

Type of Instrument	Source of Sound	Examples
Wind: Flute	Sound caused by blowing across a sharp edge, then air is amplified by the instrument	Flute Piccolo Whistle
Brass horn	Sound caused by vibrating lips and amplified by air columns within the instrument	Trumpet Trombone
Reeds	Sound caused by vibrating reeds and amplified by air columns within the instrument	Clarinet Saxophone Accordion
Percussion:	Sound caused by striking a membrane or other surface	Drum Cymbals
String:	Sound caused by plucking or bowing a string	Violin Banjo

Other ways of demonstrating the importance of the mouth, teeth, lips, tongue, and nose on the quality of speech include saying the alphabet (1) without opening one's mouth, (2) without closing one's mouth, and (3) without letting the tongue touch the teeth.

MUSICAL TUMBLERS. Fill four glasses with varying amounts of water. Place a little water in glass 1, twice as much in glass 2, three times as much in glass 3, and four times as much in glass 4. Play "Mary Had a Little Lamb" by striking the glasses with a pencil, pen, or long plastic spoon.

Strike them in the following sequence:

2,3,4,3,2,2,2,
3,3,3,2,1,1,
2,3,4,3,2,2,2,
2,3,3,2,3,4

Teaching Children about Light, Lenses, and Color

Discrepant Events and Pupil Investigations

Event 8–A. The Multiplying Lines. Cut a thin slit in a piece of foil with a sharp razor blade or knife. Look through the slit at the source of light. Start by holding it close to your eye and slowly moving it away, looking *through* the slit at the light at all times. If viewed correctly, you will see multiple fuzzy lines running the length of the slit. Where do they come from? (*Caution:* Look only at a safe light source such as a fluorescent light or other soft light.)

Pupil Investigations (may include the following processes):
1. Observing the dark bands of light in the slit
2. Measuring the distance between the foil and the eye at a point where the bands seem the clearest
3. Inferring (incorrectly) that the bands are caused by some obstructions in the slit
4. Generalizing that the bands are evidence of the wave characteristic of light

Event 8–B. The Invisible Light. Darken the inside of a shoebox or similar box with black paint or dark velvet. Cut holes on the ends (to shine a light through) and a hole on top (for viewing). Shine a beam from a flashlight through the box and observe. (See Fig. 8–1.) The beam is not visible even though it is right below your eye. Where did it go?

Pupil Investigations (may include the following processes):
1. Checking the opening to be sure that nothing is blocking the path of the light
2. Measuring to see if the viewing port is located directly in line with the beam of light (It should be.)
3. Inferring (incorrectly) that mirrors are used to divert the path around the viewing port

Event 8–C. See Through, Shine Through. Set up one or more observation posts around the room. Provide pupils a variety of materials to examine. Have them classify objects as transparent (see through), translucent (shine through), or opaque.

WHAT IS LIGHT? (EVENTS 8–A, 8–B, AND 8–C)

Fig. 8–1. **Look at the invisible light passing through a box a few inches below your eye. (This figure shows the box with the side removed.)**

Pupil Investigations (may include the following processes):
1. Identifying materials that permit you to see objects clearly through them
2. Identifying materials that permit light to pass through but do not allow clear images to be seen
3. Identifying materials that block all light
4. Classifying the materials according to light transmission

Events 8–A, 8–B, and 8–C Explained in Context (What Is Light?)

WAVES OR PARTICLES? Theories about the nature of light go back to ancient times. At one time it was believed that an object sent little images of itself to the eye, and thus, we were able to "see" it. However, the theory had a major flaw. It did not explain why those objects stopped sending those little images when it was dark.

In the fifteenth century scientists began forming a modern theory of light, but that theory had two branches that were not in agreement—Was light made of waves or particles? By 1655 Robert Hooke and Christian Huygens were the leading exponents of the wave theory, and by 1666 Isaac Newton was the leading advocate of the particle or "corpuscular" theory.

Newton supported the particle theory. He explained that light, consisting of particles, would travel in straight lines and produce shadows and images with sharp edges. If light traveled in waves, he said, the wiggly rays would blur those edges. He showed that the images were sharp, even when magnified with lenses.

Despite the evidence by Newton, the issue remained unresolved. In fact, shortly after the 1800s began, the weight of scientific evidence shifted toward the wave theory. Augustine Fresnel, with the aid of much stronger magnifying lenses, showed that the edges of shadows and images were *not* sharp. Instead, they had fringed edges—something that could only be explained by a wave theory.

The fringed edges limit the resolving power (useful magnification) of telescopes and microscopes. A typical telescope has a useful magnification of only about 50 times the diameter of its objective lens (the big lens). That is, if the objective lens is 2 inches in diameter (the calculations are based on the inch), the telescope has a useful power of 50 times 2, or one hundred times.

The metric equivalent of the rule is two times the size of the objective lens, as measured in millimeters. Thus, the same lens is about 50 millimeters in diameter, and when multiplied by 2 the useful maximum power of the telescope is again one hundred times. When lenses are arranged so that the power is increased beyond these limits, the image becomes blurred.

An example of what Fresnel studied can be seen by performing *Event 8–A. The Multiplying Lines.* When cutting a narrow slit in a piece of tinfoil and looking through the slit at a source of light, we are surprised to find that fuzzy or fringed lines appear in the opening. It takes some care and practice to be able to see these lines. They are caused by interference of light waves.

INTERFERENCE OF WAVES. When two waves reach an object at the same time, the effect can be greater or less than when the waves reach the object separately. It all depends on whether the crest of one wave is in step with the crest of another wave.

If the wave crests arrive at the spot together, they combine to form a larger crest. This wave action is called *constructive interference*. In the other instance, when the crest of one wave is in step with the trough of another wave, the two waves combine to cancel each other out. That wave action is called *destructive interference*. (See Fig. 8–2.)

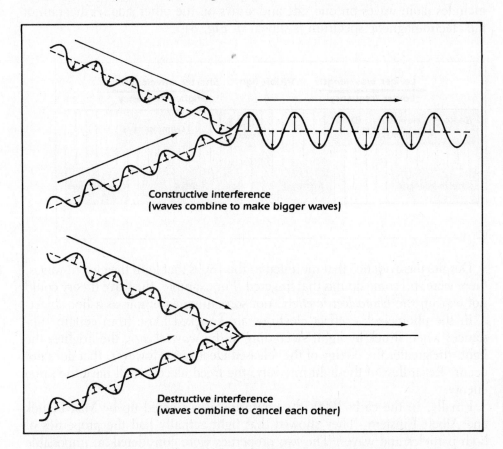

Constructive interference
(waves combine to make bigger waves)

Destructive interference
(waves combine to cancel each other)

Fig. 8–2. **Wave crests meet in the top diagram to make a bigger wave. Crest meets trough in the lower diagram to cancel the wave.**

It is destructive interference that accounts for the dark, fuzzy lines in the opening of the foil in Event 8–A. As the light passes through the slit, they are all more or less in step. However, they do not all arrive at the eye at quite the same time.

The light coming through at the edge of the slit travels farther than the light coming through the center. Thus, some waves arrive out of step with other waves and they cancel each other. Those areas show up as dark or fuzzy bands when viewing a light through the opening.

Destructive interference can be viewed in a pinhole as well as in a razor cut. Begin by holding the hole near your eye as you view a light through it. Then slowly move it away. If you do this right, you should see a fuzzy spot at the center of the hole or sometimes a fuzzy, triangular-shaped "donut."

The wave theory received a boost in 1801 when Thomas Young proved that light was the result of wave action. John Jonas Angstrom went a step further. He measured the length of waves and found that the length varied according to color. Today we use a unit of length called the angstrom to honor his work. The angstrom is 0.0000001 millimeter in length (ten million angstroms in one meter). The visible light spectrum is 4000 to 7000 angstroms in length.

By 1865 James Maxwell found that light was a part of the *electromagnetic spectrum*. Thus, light is just the visible part of a much longer spectrum that includes radio waves on one side and x-rays on the other side. A diagram of the electromagnetic spectrum is shown in Fig. 8–3.

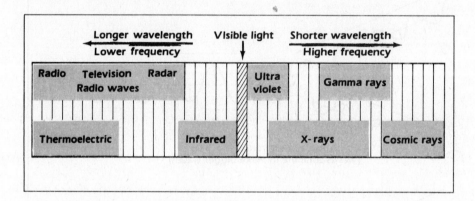

Fig. 8–3. **Visible light is only a tiny part of this electromagnetic spectrum.**

Despite the evidence that mounted in the 1800s that light traveled in waves, there were still some doubts that lingered. For example, the wave theory could not explain the *photoelectric effect*, nor something as simple as a hot object.

In the photoelectric effect electrons are knocked loose from certain substances when struck by light. According to the *wave theory*, the brighter the light, the greater the energy of the released electrons. However, that does not occur. Regardless of the light intensity, the freed electrons all have the same energy.

Finally, in the early 1900s the confusion was cleared up by Max Planck and Albert Einstein. They showed that light actually had the properties of both particles and waves. The two properties were considered an impossible contradiction. Yet those properties were combined after all. Light exists as discrete bundles of energy called *photons*. (These photons were reminiscent of Newton's corpuscles.) Photons are emitted and absorbed as particles, but they travel as waves. No wonder that it took hundreds of years to solve the puzzle.

As a particle, light is a real substance and falls of its own weight. In other words, light is attracted by gravity just like any other substance. Another property of light is that when it strikes an object, it exerts a force, just as if the object were hit by a ball.

For example, it has been estimated that the pressure of the sun's light is equal to about $\frac{1}{6}$ kilogram per square kilometer. This is not very much pressure, but it is enough to push a large tinfoil satellite out of its orbit by hundreds of kilometers per year.

LIGHT IS INVISIBLE. Light is visible in only two instances: (1) when it is the source of light (luminous object) and (2) when it is reflected off something (an illuminated object). Surprising as it may seem, light is invisible as it travels from the source to an object.

A good example of invisible light is to look into they sky on a clear night. The sun's light passes around the earth on all sides and fills the sky, but it is not visible unless it hits something (like the moon or a planet). The only other objects that are visible are stars, which are light sources.

Event 8–B. The Invisible Light shows that light is invisible as it travels. The source of light is visible (flashlight), and the reflected object is visible (your hand held in the beam); but light is invisible as it passes just a few centimeters below yours eyes. In fact, the box is not needed to show that light is invisible. Just lift both the flashlight and your hand up above the box and the beam is still invisible. (See Fig. 8–4.)

Fig. 8–4. **The box is not needed to show that light is invisible as it travels. Only the source and the object struck by light are visible.**

SPEED OF LIGHT. For a long time it was believed that light moved from its source to an object instantly; that there was no time lag at all. It was not until 1675 that Olaus Roemer discovered that the speed of light had limits after all.

Roemer timed the eclipses of Io, the innermost visible moon of Jupiter. Io disappeared routinely behind Jupiter every 42 hours and 28 minutes with a small, puzzling discrepancy: Io was always a little late at one time of the year and a little early 6 months later. The total difference during the 6 months was 22 minutes.

After 4 years of careful timing, he finally concluded that the difference in time was caused by a difference in distance. It took 22 minutes longer for the light to reach the earth at one time of year than the other time. Look at Fig. 8–5 to see the positions of the earth. When the earth was at point A, the light had to travel 300,000,000 kilometers more than when the earth was at point B.

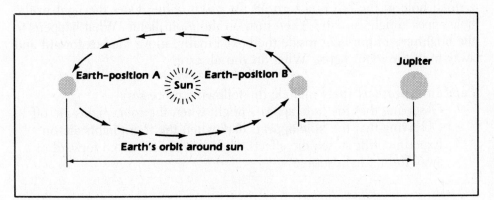

Fig. 8–5. **The earth in position A is 300 million kilometers farther away from Jupiter than when it is in position B. It takes 1000 seconds for light to travel this distance.**

Roemer took the distance of 300,000,000 kilometers and divided it by 1000 seconds (the 22 minutes of the time lag), and he concluded that light traveled about 300,000 kilometers per second. Roemer's calculations were remarkably accurate.

MATERIALS ARE TRANSPARENT, TRANSLUCENT, OR OPAQUE. Materials can be grouped into three categories depending on how well they permit light to pass through them. If light goes through a substance undistorted (as through a clear window), you can see images clearly through it. Such an object is *transparent* to light.

If a substance scatters light as it passes through, that substance is *translucent* to light. In other words, a translucent substance allows light to go through, but you cannot see images clearly through it. Frosted glass, stained glass, or wax paper are examples of translucent substances.

A classroom exercise such as *Event 8–C. See Through, Shine Through* is intended to show the differences between transparent (see through) and translucent (shine through) materials. If a substance blocks all light, that substance is *opaque*. Most pupils can classify according to the three groups without too much difficulty.

BRIGHTNESS OF LIGHT (EVENTS 8–D AND 8–E)

Discrepant Events and Pupil Investigations

Event 8–D. Changing Spots. Rub a bit of oil or butter into a piece of paper and hold it up to a light. Does the spot appear bright or dark? Now hold the paper down toward the floor. Does the spot still appear the same way, or has it changed? What do you observe? (See Fig. 8–6.)

Pupil Investigations (may include the following processes):
1. Observing that the spot appears bright when the light is behind it
2. Observing that the spot appears dark when the light is in front of it
3. Experimenting to find that at certain points the spot seems to disappear
4. Forming a theory about measuring the brightness of two light sources

Fig. 8–6. **A spot of oil or grease on a sheet of paper will appear light if the light is behind it or dark if the light strikes the front of it.**

Event 8–E. Changing Lights. Place a very weak light inside a small box. Cut a small hole in the box and turn off the room lights. Does the light in the hole appear bright or dark? Then turn on the room lights. What happens to the brightness of the light inside the box? Finally, move the box toward and away from the room lights. What do you observe?

Pupil Investigations (may include the following processes):
1. Observing that the hole appears bright when the room lights are off
2. Observing that the hole appears dark when the room lights are on
3. Experimenting to see the effects when the box is moved forward or away from a light source

Events 8–D and 8–E Explained in Context (Brightness of Light)

The brightness of a light depends on two main factors: first, the brightness of the light source itself and, second, the distance from the source to the observer. The farther away the object is, the dimmer it appears. For example, a small candle held near the eyes appears brighter than a distant star in the heavens.

These factors are examined in *Event 8–D. Changing Spots* and *Event 8–E. Changing Lights.* In each event the object being investigated is a kind of *photometer*—a device used to measure the brightness of light.

When the paper is held up to a light, the grease spot appears brighter than the surrounding paper. This means that the light is brighter behind the spot. When the paper is held down, the spot appears dark, indicating that the light is brighter in front of the spot. The spot will almost disappear when the light is equally bright on both sides of the paper.

To compare the brightness of two light sources, just move the paper with the grease spot back and forth between the two sources until the spot disappears.

The box with the hole works essentially the same way. If the room lights are on, the hole looks dark, but when the room lights are off the hole looks bright. If the box is moved toward and away from a light source, there is a point where the hole almost seems to disappear. At that point the brightness of the lights outside and inside the box are equal.

Another photometer can be made with a piece of foil between two blocks of wax (or paraffin) held together by string or a rubber band. The wax block that receives the most light appears bright when viewed from the side. (See Fig. 8–7.)

Fig. 8–7. **A paraffin (wax) photometer (side view) can be used to compare the brightness of two lights.**

Discrepant Events and Pupil Investigations

Event 8–F. Ghostly Candle. Set a mirror on a sheet of paper as shown in Fig. 8–8. Draw a line at right angles to the mirror, and place a candle to the left and a few centimeters in front of the mirror. Go to the right-hand side of the paper, and look just barely over the surface of the paper at the image of the candle.

Place a second candle behind the mirror to show where the image of the first candle appears to be. Measure the angles and distances from the mirror to the candle. Compare the angles and distances of the first candle with the angles and distances of the second candle.

Pupil Investigations (may include the following processes):
1. Measuring the distance between the first candle and mirror
2. Measuring the distance between the second candle and mirror
3. Measuring the angles involved with both candles
4. Making a rule about the reflection of light

Event 8–G. Watch That Wink. Look into a plane mirror and wink your right eye. Which eye does the image in the mirror wink? Set up an arrangement of two mirrors at right angles to each other, as shown in Fig. 8–9. Adjust the mirrors so that you see a single image on the split halves where the mirrors join. Then wink your right eye. Which eye does your image wink?

Pupil Investigations (may include the following processes):
1. Observing that when you wink your right eye the image in a plane mirror winks its left eye

LIGHT CAN BE REFLECTED (EVENTS 8–F THROUGH 8–I)

Fig. 8–8. **Place a second candle behind the mirror to measure the distance between the image and mirror.**

Fig. 8–9. **Look at a mirror and wink your right eye. Which eye does your image wink? Try two mirrors set at 90 degrees to each other.**

Fig. 8–10. **How does this special box allow a person to look through a book? The X indicates a spot on the wall.**

Fig. 8–11. **How does this special box change the picture?**

Smooth surface-even reflection

Rough surface-uneven reflection

Fig. 8–12. **Even reflection allows you to see images (as in a mirror). Uneven reflection shows only the surface from which the light is reflecting.**

2. Observing that when you wink your right eye the image in the arrangement of two mirrors winks its right eye too
3. Forming a theory (incorrectly) that the images in mirrors are totally reversed (They are only reversed from left to right, not top to bottom. Otherwise the image would stand on its head.)
4. Generalizing about the principles of reflected light

Event 8–H. The X-Ray Box. Set up a special box as shown in Fig. 8–10. (Details are given later in this section.) Look through the viewer and see the X taped to the wall. Place a book in the opening between the two tubes and look again. Can you look right through the book to see the X?

Pupil Investigations (may include the following processes):
1. Observing the X before and after placing the book between the two tubes
2. Inferring (incorrectly) that an X is located inside one of the tubes
3. Inferring that one does not *really* look through the book but that the view is possible because of some other principle.

Event 8–I. Get-the-Kid-to-Smile Box. Set up a special box as shown in Fig. 8–11. Tape a picture of a smiling child against the far wall under door A and a picture of a frowning child against the far wall under door B. Begin with door B open. Look through the viewing hole and you will see a picture of a frowning child. (Has he just been told that the school year is about to begin?) Then close door B and open door A to see the boy smile. (Has he just found out that *you* will be his teacher this year?) How can the opening and closing of the doors change the child's expression?

Pupil Investigations (may include the following processes):
1. Observing that the images change when the open doors change
2. Observing that the image seen with door A is brighter than the image seen with door B
3. Discovering that when both doors are open, the image of door A dominates
4. Inferring a relationship between the images and the reflection of light

Events 8–F Through 8–I Explained in Context (Light Can Be Reflected)

EVEN AND UNEVEN REFLECTIONS. One of the major properties of light is that it can be reflected. The light reflects off mirrors and off walls. In the case of mirrors you see images in it. In fact, if the mirror is really of good quality, you can hardly see the glass at all. You see only images that are reflected in it.

A wall also reflects the light, but there are no images visible in it; you see just the wall itself. The mirror and wall represent examples of the two ways that light can be reflected. The mirror represents *even reflection* and the wall *uneven reflection*. (See Fig. 8–12.)

Even reflections occur when a surface is so smooth that light rays all bounce off at the same angle. Uneven reflections occur when a surface is rough enough to scatter the rays that are striking it. Of course, the "roughness" can be so subtle that it does not appear rough to the touch, yet it scatters the light effectively. Most wall surfaces appear smooth, but when viewed through a microscope, they have a rough surface. That is why they scatter light rays.

In summary, in an even reflection we can see an image but no reflecting surface; in an uneven reflection we see the reflecting surface but no image.

ANGLE OF INCIDENCE IS EQUAL TO THE ANGLE OF REFLECTION. How will a light ray bounce off a smooth surface? It will bounce somewhat like a basketball on a floor. If you bounce the light ray straight down, it will come straight back. If bounced at a 45-degree angle, the ray will bounce away at a 45-degree angle, as shown in lines B–C in Fig. 8–13. Line A will bounce away as shown in Line D. The angle of the incoming ray (the *incidence*) is equal to the angle of the outgoing ray (the *reflection*).

Fig. 8–13. **The angle of incidence (incoming light) is equal to the angle of reflection (outgoing light).**

This principle can be demonstrated by darkening a room and shining a point source of light against a mirror. The light beam is invisible, of course, until you blow some chalk dust into the beam. Then the incident and reflecting beams become visible.

The *angles of incidence* and *reflection* can also be shown in *Event 8–F. Ghostly Candle*. If the lines are drawn carefully, the distances and angles should be identical.

Another trait of even reflection is that images are "folded over" from left to right. That is, if you stand in front of a plane mirror and wink your *right* eye, your image will wink its *left* eye. The same folding over characteristic can be seen in reflections of printed words. However, images are not folded over top to bottom.

When two mirrors are used at right angles to each other as in *Event 8–G. Watch That Wink*, the image is reflected once by one mirror and again by the other mirror. The double reflections make the image wink its right eye when you wink your right eye. The results are somewhat startling for most people.

The fact that light can be reflected also explains *Event 8–H. The X-Ray Box*. The box doesn't really allow us to look through a book. Instead, four mirrors are used, as shown in Fig. 8–14, to reflect the light around the book.

Fig. 8–14. **The inside view of the x-ray box shows the placement of mirrors and the viewing path. The X is on the wall.**

The x-ray box is not easy to build. It takes considerable patience and trial and error to position the mirrors correctly. Even a slight misalignment of one mirror will throw off the results by a wide margin. We have found that the job is made easier by attaching small wooden blocks inside the box so that each mirror fits very loosely in its approximate position. Then they can be secured and adjusted by wedging pieces of sponge between the mirror and block. Gradually the mirrors are aligned and held securely but gently.

Reflection also explains *Event 8–I. Get-the-Kid-to-Smile Box*. A clear piece of glass is placed at a 45-degree angle in front of the viewing hole. When door A is closed, the darkness allows the clear glass plate to act as a mirror. Thus, you can see the frowning face at B. When door A is opened, however, you look right through the glass and see a smiling face. (See Fig. 8–15.)

Fig. 8–15. **This top view of the box shows the clear glass and viewing paths to both trap doors.**

When A is open

B

When B is open and A is closed

A

Clear glass

Other activities used to demonstrate some of the principles of reflection include the following:

1. *Kaleidoscope.* Stand up two small mirrors at right angles to each other. Place bits of colored paper between them and adjust the mirrors. As the mirrors are adjusted slightly, the images are repeated many times to produce a bright kaleidoscopic effect. Then try it with three mirrors.
2. *Making money!* Stand up two small mirrors facing each other. Place a coin between the mirrors and see it multiplied endlessly in repeating images. Try various objects.

LIGHT CAN BE REFRACTED (EVENTS 8–J THROUGH 8–O)

Discrepant Events and Pupil Investigations

Event 8–J. Pinpointing the Bolt. Place a bolt upright in an aquarium or large bowl of water. Crouch down and look at the bolt *through the side of the*

Look at pencil through air

Look at bolt through water

Fig. 8–16. **Estimate the position of the bolt when looking through the side of the container.**

container. While holding this position, estimate how far away the bolt is and hold a pencil above the bolt. However, look at the pencil *through the air* and the bolt through the water. Then, holding the pencil steady, stand up and check your results. Did you get them lined up? (If you do the event right, you will get it wrong! (See Fig. 8–16.)

Pupil Investigations (may include the following processes):
1. Experimenting to verify results
2. Observing that the pencil is held closer to the observer than the bolt appears to be
3. Inferring that the water causes the light to alter the distance of the object
4. Generalizing about the altered views and the bending of light

Event 8–K. The Disappearing Coin. Place a coin under a beaker or clear glass tumbler. Ask pupils to view the coin *through the side of the glass.* Do not view from directly above or from desk level. Tell pupils that you have a "disappearing fluid" and pour it into the container. Watch the coin disappear. (See Fig. 8–17.)

Fig. 8–17. **Why does the coin "disappear" when water is poured into the beaker?**

Pupil Investigations (may include the following processes):
1. Observing that the coin disappears from view when the fluid is poured into the glass
2. Checking to see that the coin is still under the glass (It is.)
3. Verifying that water works the same as the "disappearing fluid"
4. Inferring that water makes the image of the coin disappear

Event 8–L. The Appearing Coin! After losing a coin in the preceding event, make it appear in this one. Place a penny at the bottom of a cup (inside the cup, not under it) and stand back far enough so that the penny is just out of sight. Then have someone fill the cup with water. Why does the penny lift into view?

Pupil Investigations (may include the following processes):
1. Observing that the coin becomes visible as the water is poured into the cup
2. Forming a theory that the water causes the light to bend
3. Generalizing that all the events in this section are related to the bending of light

Event 8–M. Looking at Lenses. Divide students into groups of two or three pupils each. Provide each group with a convex and concave lens. (Do not describe or identify the lenses at this time.) Give them a minute or two to find out as much as possible about the lenses.

Now distribute a candle to each group and ask them to set up the candle, lens, and screen as shown in Fig. 8–18. Ask the pupils to use a lens to project the candle flame onto a screen (of cardboard or notebook paper). Only one of the two lenses will work. Let them discover which one.

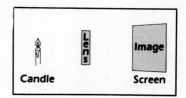

Fig. 8–18. **Which lens can be used as a projector? What happens to the image?**

Pupil Investigations (may include the following processes):
1. Discovering that one lens is thin in the middle and the other thick
2. Investigating to find that one lens makes images larger, the other makes them smaller
3. Experimenting to find that the convex lens can be used to project the candle flame
4. Discovering that the candle flame is inverted on the screen
5. Drawing diagrams to trace the path of light from the candle to the screen

Event 8–N. Reverse the Arrows. Place a row of many short arrows on a strip of paper. Then slowly pass the paper behind a full bottle of water. Make several passes with the paper touching the bottle. Then move the paper back about 10 to 20 centimeters, and make several more passes. What do you see? What direction do the arrows go in each case? (See Fig. 8–19.)

Fig. 8–19. **Why does the bottle reverse the arrows?**

Pupil Investigations (may include the following processes):
1. Observing that the arrows all appear to be moving in the same direction for the first several passes
2. Observing that the arrows viewed through the bottle reverse direction during the later passes
3. Inferring a relationship between the movement of the arrows and the distance the arrows are held behind the bottle
4. Generalizing from the observations that the bottle acts like a lens to invert an image

Event 8–O. Instant Eye Test. Look carefully at the pupils in the class who are wearing eyeglasses. Look carefully *through* a lens (of the eyeglasses) to observe the edge of a pupil's face. If you look carefully, you will be able to tell if the pupil is nearsighted or farsighted. (See the explanation for full details.) Tell each pupil what you observe. Ask the pupils to guess how you did it. (This event works only with those who wear eyeglasses, not contacts.)

Pupil Investigations (may include the following processes):

1. Observing that the eyes of some people appear smaller when viewed through their glasses
2. Observing that the eyes of others appear larger when viewed through their glasses
3. Discovering that the image through the lens is not in line with the image above and below the lens
4. Predicting that one kind of misalignment is caused by nearsightedness and the other by farsightedness

Events 8–J Through 8–O Explained in Context (Light Can Be Refracted)

REFRACTION CHANGES THE APPEARANCE OF THINGS. The events in this section are all related to the fact that light can be refracted. *Refraction* is the bending of light that occurs when it goes from one medium to another *at an angle*.

Refraction occurs because light travels at different speeds in different mediums. It travels fastest in a vacuum (300,000 kilometers per second). It travels more slowly through air, glass, or water. But for refraction to occur two conditions must be met: (1) Light must go from one medium to another and (2) light must enter or exit at an angle.

When light goes from one medium directly into another (not as an angle), as in *Event 8–J. Pinpointing the Bolt,* it does not bend. However, something else happens: An object appears to be closer than it really is. How much closer? Just look where you lined up the pencil. That is how close the bolt *appears* to be when viewed through the water.

Event 8–K. The Disappearing Coin is dramatic because the coin seems to disappear right in front of your eyes. Again, refraction is the cause of the effect. When water is added to the container, the light from the coin is bent upward so much that it goes out of the top of the glass. Thus, if light from the coin does not get out of the side of the glass, it is invisible when viewed from that angle.

Refraction also occurs in *Event 8–L. The Appearing Coin!* In this case, however, the coin appears instead of disappears. When water is added, the light is bent down so that the coin becomes visible. Again, the event shows that light is bent as it travels at an angle from one medium (air) into another (water).

LENSES. Any discussion of refraction would be incomplete without some emphasis on lenses. Lenses work because of refraction. In fact, since lenses are carefully shaped, the bending of the light is controlled. This controlled bending is shown in *Event 8–M. Looking at Lenses.*

As pupils examine the lenses, they should discover that one kind of lens is thicker in the middle than at the edges. That type is called a *convex* lens. Light that shines through a convex lens comes to a focus, or *converges*. When holding a convex lens close to an object, the object appears larger.

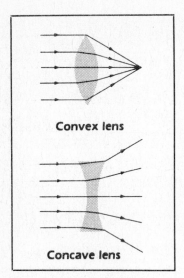

Fig. 8–20. **Light rays are brought together (converge) with a convex lens and spread apart (diverge) with a concave lens.**

Another type of lens is thinner in the middle than at the edges and is called a *concave* lens. Light that shines through a concave lens spreads out, or *diverges*. When held near an object, the object appears smaller. The converging and diverging rays of the two lenses are shown in Fig. 8–20.

Students should also discover that only the convex lens can be used to project the candle flame onto a screen. Pupils are usually surprised to find that the image of the flame is inverted. They can see why by just following the top and bottom rays in Fig. 8–21. The top ray is bent downward through the focal point and appears at the bottom of the screen. Conversely, the bottom ray is bent upward, passes through the focal point, and finally appears on the top of the screen. The result is an inverted image.

Pupils can also see the reversing effect of a convex lens by doing *Event 8–N. Reverse the Arrows.* The bottle of water acts as a very thick lens. If you hold the paper strip with arrows tight against the bottle, the arrows all point the same way. The arrows do not reverse until you hold the strip of paper back a few centimeters. You need to get back beyond the focal point for the image to reverse. *Note:* The focal point of a very thick lens (bottle) is very close to the lens (bottle).

A simple lens can be made by merely placing a drop of water on a pinhole in a piece of foil. The drop of water takes on a lenslike shape, and, as a result, it can actually be used to magnify images. It can only be used very close to an object, so place the foil on some pencils or straws. Put the object to be viewed under the lens and observe. (Printed matter works well.)

With this background in lenses we can understand how *Event 8–O. Instant Eye Test* works. Eyeglasses are really no more than very carefully made lenses. Thus, they will do just what the simple lenses did. The glasses will make objects appear larger or smaller.

Nearsighted people are those whose "near-sight" is relatively good. It is their distance vision that is bad. They wear concave lenses to correct their vision. Pupils often wonder how those lenses can help since, as stated earlier, concave lenses make objects appear smaller. The answer is that the lens corrects the

Fig. 8–21. **A convex lens projects an inverted image on the screen.**

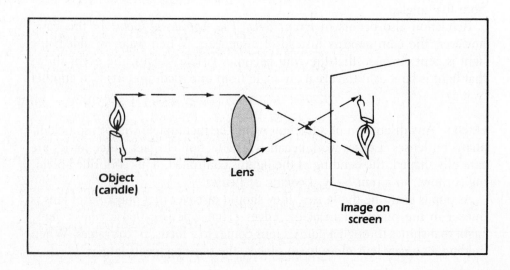

Object (candle)   Lens

Image on screen

user's vision by getting rid of the blur. It is not the size of the image, but how clear it is that makes for good vision.

Farsighted people have relatively good "far-sight." They wear convex lenses, which make objects appear larger. Again, it is not the change in size of the image that corrects the vision; it is the fact that the lens brings the light rays to a sharp focus on the retina.

Since lenses make objects appear smaller or larger, you can observe that change by lining up the edge of the face, *as viewed through the lens*, with the line of the face above and below the lens. If the image through the glasses is set inward, the correction is for nearsightedness. If the image is set outward, the correction is for farsightedness. (See Fig. 8–22.)

Fig. 8–22. **Look at the edge of the face through a lens. Compare it with the edge of the face above and below the lens. (This man is nearsighted.)**

There are a number of other activities that can be used to show that light can be refracted:

1. *The "broken" pencil.* Fill a glass tumbler with water and stick a pencil into it. When viewed from the side, the pencil looks broken at the water line. The light reaches your eyes through different mediums (air and water), and, as a result, the bending of the light is different for each. (See Fig. 8–23.)
2. *Pour light.* This works only in a darkened room. Also, it does not lend itself to large groups because of limited visibility. (The bottom of the sink is not easily seen by more than a few pupils.) However, where it can be used, the event is a surprise to students.

   Shine a flashlight into the top of a tall tin can about half full of water. Observe the water pour out of the hole into the sink. If the room is dark enough, the stream should be visible from the side, and the bottom of the sink should be slightly illuminated.
3. *Silver soot.* Hard boil an egg and cover it with a thick layer of black soot from a candle flame. When completely blackened, lower the egg into a glass of water. The egg appears silvery. Why? The answer is that soot captures some air and alters the bending of light so that those rays do not leave the water. The end result is that the egg looks somewhat like a curved silver mirror. *Note:* The layer of soot must be very thick for the silvery effect to appear.

Fig. 8–23. **Can you see the "broken" pencil. It is caused by refraction.**

COLOR (EVENTS 8–P THROUGH 8–V)

Fig. 8–24. **Make a color disc like this and spin it. The colors will blend to produce white.**

Discrepant Events and Pupil Investigations

Event 8–P. Color from White. Darken the room and turn on a strong light such as a projector. Hold a prism in the light beam and turn it slowly until a band of colors is visible. (*Caution:* Do not look directly into the strong light source.)

Pupil Investigations (may include the following processes):
1. Observing the formation of a band of colors on the wall
2. Recording in their notebooks the colors that are formed
3. Inferring that white light consists of colors

Event 8–Q. White from Color. Cut out a disk from 10 to 25 centimeters in diameter. Use stiff cardboard or tagboard. Carefully divide the disk into segments and paint or color them as indicated in Fig. 8–24. Devise a means of spinning the disk and observe. (Smaller disks can sometimes be spun "like a top" by inserting a short pencil through the middle. Or loop a string through two holes near the center of the disk to provide a means of spinning. Still another way is to attach the disk to the end of a hand drill.)

Pupil Investigations (may include the following processes):
1. Predicting what will happen when the disk is spun
2. Observing that the colors gradually blend to form white as the disk is spun
3. Inferring that white light consists of colors

Event 8–R. Mixed-Up Lights. (*Note:* This event is quite interesting if done with good quality color filters and projectors in a darkened room. However, flashlights do not work well, and the event should probably not be attempted with them.) Combine red and green lights so that they partially overlap on a white screen. What color results?

Pupil Investigations (may include the following processes):
1. Observing that when any two colors are combined, a lighter color is produced.
2. Recording the results in a simple table as follows:

   Red and green   = _____

   Red and blue   = _____

   Blue and yellow = _____

3. Forming a theory that the mixing of colors sometimes produces white, but never black

Event 8–S. Lingering Images. Stare intently for about 30 seconds at a brightly colored piece of paper. Then stare steadily at a blank white sheet of paper without letting your eyes wander. What image do you see appearing on the blank surface? (It helps to make a small dot in the middle of the colored paper, as well as on the white paper. The dots help to hold your gaze steady.)

Pupil Investigations (may include the following processes):
1. Observing a colored fringe forming around the original color being viewed
2. Discovering that a different color appears when the gaze is shifted to a white background
3. Forming a theory that the original color is subtracted from white when the gaze is shifted

Event 8–T. Two-Toned Fluid. Mix a few drops of red food coloring into a bottle of water. View the bottle with light shining at it from your viewing position. What color is the water? Then view the bottle with light shining from behind it. What color do you see now?

Pupil Investigations (may include the following processes):
1. Observing a red color when the light shines at the bottle from behind
2. Observing a green color with the light shining on the bottle from the front
3. Generalizing that the color changes are due to the transmission and reflection of light

Event 8-U. Mixing Pigments. Select chalk of various colors and grind them into powder, being careful to keep the colors separate. Mix water into the powders to produce a thin paste. Now carefully mix together various combinations of any two colors and note the results. (You can also use tempera paints, or even containers of water with food coloring added.)

Pupil Investigations (may include the following processes):
1. Observing that when two colors are mixed, a third color is formed
2. Recording the various trials to determine which colors produce the best results
3. Forming a theory about the fact that the colors often produce black mixtures but never white mixtures
4. Generalizing that when paints are mixed, they tend to absorb light

Event 8–V. Curious Colors. Select some objects such as colored samples of cloth and Christmas foil, and ask pupils to identify the colors when viewed in colored light. Darken the room and use a colored piece of plastic (as a filter) on an overhead projector. Do not let the students see the objects in natural light until later when they can check their observations.

Pupil Investigations (may include the following processes):
1. Identifying the color of objects as seen in colored light
2. Discovering that some of the objects have different colors when viewed in natural light
3. Forming a theory to explain the differences observed

Events 8–P Through 8–V Explained in Context (Color)

WHITE LIGHT CONTAINS ALL COLORS. As we look at surrounding objects, colors of all kinds can be seen. Where do the colors come from? It may be surprising to some pupils that all colors can be found in white light. If white light strikes an object, that object may absorb or reflect any or all parts of that light, resulting in anything from white to black.

The fact that white light consists of colors can be demonstrated with a prism in *Event 8–P. Color from White.* You will need to experiment with the correct position of the prism. Just hold the prism in the beam of the light and slowly

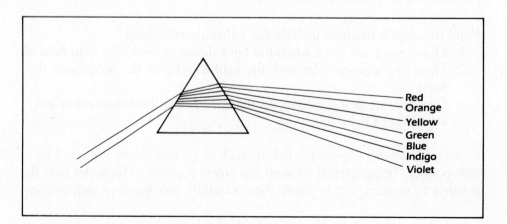

Fig. 8–25. **White light separates into the colors of the rainbow when it passes through a prism.**

Red
Orange
Yellow
Green
Blue
Indigo
Violet

turn it. The color bands will appear on the walls, ceiling, or floor, depending on how you hold the prism. You can also use sunlight as a light source if it is available in your room. Just open a curtain slightly to allow a thin ray of light to enter the room.

The colored band is formed by the prism because each color has a different wavelength, and each wavelength is bent differently as it passes into the prism and then out again. The result is to bend each color differently, forming a band. (See Fig. 8–25.)

ADDITIVE COLORS. We have seen that when white light shines through a prism, it is separated into a band of colors. Can we reverse the procedure? Can colors be added together to produce white? Yes.

Event 8–Q. White from Color shows one way to add colors to make white. When the disk is spun, each of the colors is "held" by the retina for a short time. This ability to retain an image is called *persistence of vision*. Thus, one color is seen and "persists" long enough for the next color to come into view. The colors combine, one after another, so that when they are all added together, they appear white to the viewer.

Another way of mixing colors to obtain white is shown in *Event 8–R. Mixed-Up Lights*. First of all, remember that the screen is white and can reflect all light. Thus, if a blue light strikes the screen, it will, of course, reflect blue. Then if a yellow light is also shown on the screen, it will also reflect yellow. Blue and yellow contain all the wavelengths of light, so when they overlap on the screen, they combine to produce white. See Fig. 8–26 for the results when various colors of light are combined.

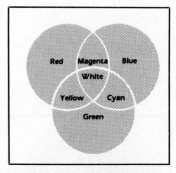

Fig. 8–26. **The primary colors of light are additive. When combined, they produce the colors shown in the overlapping areas of the circles.**

The mixing of colors is often attempted with flashlights and colored plastic films, but the results are usually disappointing. Unfortunately, it is necessary to have good quality light sources, such as projectors, and good quality filters to do this event with a reasonable chance of success.

If an object absorbs all the colors that strike it, then it can reflect light. As a result, it appears black. If it absorbs none of the colors and reflects all of them, the object appears white.

Most objects are somewhere in between. A red object, for example, absorbs all colors *except* red. It reflects red; therefore, red is the only color visible to a viewer.

COMPLEMENTARY COLORS. Most of us have seen many color combinations in homes and clothing. Often we hear that one color "complements" another. In everyday use *complementary colors* are those colors that seem to look nice together. In science, however, the definition is more precise.

Specifically, complementary colors are any two colors that when added to each other produce white. For example, the complementary color of blue light is yellow. Other complementary colors of light are green and magenta, and red and cyan.

Complementary colors are formed in *Event 8–S. Lingering Images*. After staring at a bright color for about 30 seconds, the eyes become tired of it. Thus, when you shift your gaze to a blank white surface (which, remember, reflects all colors), your eyes ignore the color they had just stared at. As a result, you see only the remaining or complementary color. In other words, you observe the color that is "left over" after the original color is subtracted from white.

For example, suppose that you stared at a blue object for a while. The eye becomes tired of that color. Then, when looking at a white surface, the blue (within the white) does not register until the eyes recover from their fatigue (15 to 30 seconds). Blue is subtracted from the colors that white reflects. The color that remains is yellow.

Complementary colors are also obtained by doing *Event 8–T. Two-Toned Fluid.* When the light shines through the fluid, only a reddish color is transmitted. Surprisingly, the balance of the colors (the complementary color) is often scattered and will appear as green.

It may take some trial and error to get just the right kind of mixture. Also, it is important that all other lights are turned off and that only a single light source is used. Sometimes a better effect can be achieved by using Mercurochrome instead of food coloring.

SUBTRACTIVE COLORS. Students can experiment with colors by performing *Event 8–U. Mixing Pigments.* When yellow and blue are mixed, for example, a green color is formed. The results of all trials should be summarized. Note that you will never get white when pigments are mixed. As more and more colors are combined, it is more and more likely that black will result.

This peculiarity can be explained by recalling that a colored object absorbs some colors and reflects other colors. Remember that a red pigment absorbs all other colors. Thus, if red is mixed with green, the red absorbs the green. The green, in turn, absorbs the red. As a result, the colors absorb each other and the mixture looks black.

When more than two pigments are mixed together, black is more likely to be produced than if only two are mixed. The primary colors of blue, red, and yellow will produce black. (See Fig. 8–27.)

In summary, when mixing pigments, many colors are absorbed, or *subtracted*, from the spectrum. This is why the mixing of pigments is sometimes referred to as the *subtractive rule of colors.*

Colors are also subtracted in *Event 8–V. Curious Colors.* If you look at a red object in a green light, it looks black because the red object reflects only red. It absorbs (or subtracts) the green light. Therefore, if no red light is available, red cannot be reflected. Students will find it difficult to determine the actual color of objects viewed in a colored light. (*Note:* It is important that the room be darkened very well. If stray light enters the room, it will be easy to detect the colors.)

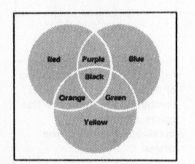

Fig. 8–27. The primary paints are subtractive. When combined, they produce the colors shown in the overlapping areas of the circles.

OPTICAL ILLUSIONS (EVENTS 8–W AND 8–X)

Discrepant Events and Pupil Investigations

Event 8–W. Tall Man, Short Man. Look at Fig. 8–28 and decide which man is taller. Then take a ruler and measure the height of each. How do you account for the big difference in the *appearance* of size?

Pupil Investigations (may include the following processes):
1. Observing that the man in back seems to be much taller than the man in the front
2. Measuring to find that they are both the same size
3. Experimenting with converging lines to see their effect on the appearance of size and distance

Fig. 8–28. **Measure the two men. Which one is larger?**

Event 8–X. Fish in the Bowl. Prepare a small card with a diagram of a fish on one side and a diagram of a bowl on the other. Insert strings into holes at each end of the card as shown in Fig. 8–29. Then twist the strings and let them unravel, causing the card to spin rapidly. What do you observe?

Pupil Investigations (may include the following processes):
1. Observing that the fish appears to be in the bowl when the card is spinning
2. Experimenting with other diagrams and cards to verify the observations
3. Forming a theory that both images blend together to produce the appearance of a fish in a bowl
4. Inferring that images persist on the retina

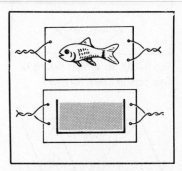

Fig. 8–29. **Put the fish into the bowl. Spin the card with the fish on one side and the bowl on the other side.**

Events 8–W and 8–X Explained in Context (Optical Illusions)

Since the days of the first magician it is likely that people had doubts about "seeing is believing." Pupils will surely doubt what they see in optical illusions. *Event 8–W. Tall Man, Short Man* is an example of how our eyes can be deceived.

Optical illusions work because our past experience helps us *most* of the time. For example, we know that an object in the distance looks smaller than the same object when it is closer. We make use of this experience by giving a simple two-dimensional picture the *appearance* of three dimensions by merely drawing the "distant" objects smaller.

Although the two figures in our picture take up the same height on the page, the figure on the right appears larger. Our eyes compensate for a "distance effect" by telling us that anything that far away must be quite large to appear so prominently in the scene.

Event 8–X. Fish in the Bowl is a simple example of another kind of optical illusion. The fish and bowl seem to merge into a single picture when the card is spun because the images linger a while in our vision. It is another case of *persistence of vision* discussed earlier with *Event 8–Q. White from Color.*

One image remains, or persists, for a fraction of a second after the picture is gone. If the card is spun rapidly, the new image appears before the old image is gone. Thus, they merge into a single image of a fish in a bowl.

The fact that images persist allows us to see "motion" in a series of still pictures. This is what happens in a motion picture film. In one common format 16 pictures are flashed on the screen every second. Each successive picture is slightly different so that the merged images appear to move.

Much the same thing occurs to permit us to see motion on television. On the television screen the picture is changed 30 times per second.

"Flip" pictures also produce motion. Draw a stick diagram on the last page of a note pad. Continue to make stick pictures on the pages before it, making only slight changes each time. Then flip the pages and the image appears to move!

There are many more optical illusions. Here are a few examples:

Fig. 8–30. **In which figure is the center stem longer?**

Fig. 8–31. **Is line A-B longer than line B-C?**

Fig. 8–32. **Is the top hat taller than it is wide?**

Fig. 8–33. **The floating finger illusion appears when two fingers are held close to each other while looking past them at a distant object.**

1. *Long and short lines–I.* Which line is longer in Fig. 8–30? Consider only the center stem of the figures, not the end lines. The upper figure appears to be longer because the outward-angled end lines seem to lengthen the figure. However, both center stems are of the same length.
2. *Long and short lines–II.* Which line is longer in Fig. 8–31, line A–B, or line B–C? Surprisingly, they are both the same length. The other lines of the parallelogram combine to make it appear that line A–B is longer.
3. *Top hat.* Look at the top hat in Fig. 8–32. Is it higher than it is wider? Surprisingly, no. Both dimensions are the same. The horizontal rim appears shorter because its length is divided between several vertical lines. The vertical lines, however, are unbroken, giving the appearance of greater height.
4. *The floating finger!* Touch your index fingers together, tip to tip. Hold them about ⅓ meter in front of you, and look just past them to an object on the far wall. As you look at the object, you can still see your fingers with peripheral vision. What do you see? Your fingertips should appear to be holding a suspended double-ended finger between them. Now pull your fingers apart slightly. The double-ended finger will appear to float. (See Fig. 8–33.)

    The illusion is caused by *parallax*. That is, when the eyes are focused on a distant object they do not, at the same time, focus on a near object. Actually, the left eye has one image, and the right eye has another. The two images overlap to produce the appearance of a two-pointed finger in the middle. The effect works only if you focus your eyes on a distant object, and you see the near object only with peripheral vision.
5. *Hole in the hand!* Roll up a sheet of paper into a tube and hold it alongside the open palm of your hand. Look through the tube with your left eye at an object at the end of the room. Hold your right hand alongside the tube, palm open and facing you, with fingers pointing up. Keep *both* eyes open. It appears as if you are looking through a hole in your hand. Here again, your eyes see two separate images, and your brain combines them to give the illusion.

    Sometimes a pupil will have difficulty seeing the illusion. If so, ask these questions: "What do you see with your left eye? What do you see with your right eye?" The reason they fail to see the illusion is that they allow one eye to dominate. By asking the two questions, you force them to use both eyes, one at a time. (Be sure to wait for an answer to each question.)

6. *Curving parallels!* Look at Fig. 8–34. Do the two horizontal lines appear to be straight or curved? Place a ruler or straight-edge along the horizontal lines and check. The lines are actually straight, but they appear curved because the crossed lines intersect at gradually different angles.

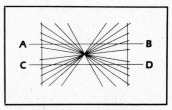

Fig. 8–34. **Hold a ruler or straight-edge alongside lines AB and CD. Are they curved or straight?**

9

Teaching Children about Air and Air Pressure

AIR IS A REAL SUBSTANCE AND OCCUPIES SPACE (EVENTS 9–A THROUGH 9–E)

Discrepant Events and Pupil Investigations

Event 9–A. Fill the Balloon with an Empty Bottle. This activity should be performed as a demonstration. Set up two large soft-drink bottles. Place a pencil or some other small object into one bottle but leave the other one empty. Ask a pupil to "pick the empty bottle." Let several pupils verify that one is "empty."

Now attach a small balloon over the top of the empty bottle. Be sure that it lies limp. Then set the bottle into a container of water. (The water must be hot, but pupils should not be told at this time that the water is hot.) As the pupils watch, the balloon slowly fills up. How can the balloon be filled with an "empty" bottle? (For best results use a large bottle and a small balloon. See Fig. 9–1.)

Pupil Investigations (may include the following processes):
1. Verifying that the bottle seems to be empty
2. Feeling that the water is warm
3. Experimenting to see if the reaction is reversible when the bottle is removed from the hot water (It is. The balloon goes limp.)
4. Concluding that the bottle was not really empty

Event 9–B. Squeeze-Box Candle Snuffer. Cut a 1-centimeter hole at the end of an empty shoe box. Hold up the open box so that all pupils can see it. Let them verify that the box is "empty." Cover the box with the lid and hold it so that the hole points to a candle flame. Now squeeze. The candle goes out! How did the "empty" box put out the flame? (Be sure to aim carefully. If the hole is not properly lined up, the event will not work.)

Pupil Investigations (may include the following processes):
1. Verifying that the box appears to be empty
2. Duplicating the experiment to check results
3. Concluding that the box was not really empty

Event 9–C. Pouring Air. Anyone can pour water from one beaker to another. But can you pour air? Provide two beakers and a large container of water. Ask pupils to find a way to pour air from one beaker to another. Tell them

Hot water

Fig. 9–1. **Can the balloon be filled with an "empty" bottle?**

that the event is not only possible, but that if they do it right, they will be *sure* that air is being poured. (Pupils will often make pouring motions in the air, but those motions prove nothing. Emphasize that we cannot see anything happening in such motions, so they give no evidence about anything being poured.)

Pupil Investigations (may include the following processes):
1. Performing the pouring motions in the air
2. Experimenting with the beakers in the water
3. Generalizing that air takes up space and can be seen under water

Event 9–D. Keep the Paper Dry Underwater. Fill a large container about two-thirds full of water and ask pupils to push a paper towel underwater without getting it wet. Have a small, empty beaker available, but do not call attention to it.

Pupil Investigations (may include the following processes):
1. Observing that the paper gets wet when an edge is touched to the water
2. Experimenting by pushing the paper into the bottom of a beaker, inverting the beaker, and lowering it into the water
3. Forming a theory that air keeps the water out of the beaker

Event 9–E. Pour Water into an "Empty" Bottle. Set up a bottle with a one-hole stopper and a funnel as shown in Fig. 9–2. Try to pour water into the empty bottle. Be sure to use a funnel that has a narrow tubelike stem that will fit into the one-hole stopper. Or use a short rubber hose to connect the funnel to a glass tube and (carefully) fit the tube into the stopper.

Fig. 9–2. **If the funnel and tube are fitted securely into a one-hole stopper, most of the water will not enter the bottle.**

Pupil Investigations (may include the following processes):
1. Observing that the water does not run into the bottle very well (It will sometimes dribble in a little. At other times it may "percolate" as alternately some water enters and some air bubbles leave.)
2. Verifying that the tube is not blocked
3. Forming a theory about the invisible substance that is keeping out the water (The pupils will likely know that it's air.)

Events 9–A Through 9–E Explained in Context (Air Is a Real Substance)

NEGATIVE PROPERTIES OF AIR. When discussing air, we need to consider a number of factors that are *not* there. For example, air has no color, odor, or taste and cannot be seen. In a sense, we are identifying air by describing what it is *not*. These are the negative properties of air.

We can focus on the negative properties by creating a verbal discrepancy for the pupils. Begin by saying that people often believe things that are not true. In fact, you might say that some people believe in superstitions. Cite examples of breaking a mirror causing 7 years of bad luck, of a black cat walking across your path, of having the luck of a four-leaf clover, horseshoe, or rabbit's foot.

Then tell them that some people still believe in misconceptions and superstitions, even today. "Do you realize that even here, in this very room, there are some people who believe that there is such a thing as air!"

There will be stunned silence.

"Oh, I can see that there are some students who really believe that air exists. Well, let's check it out scientifically. If there is such a thing, where is it? Look under your desks; behind the door. Check the hallway too. Can anyone see it? Of course not. Why not? Because it does not exist!

"Let's continue the investigation. Can you smell it?" Pupils will sniff the air but feel foolish. Then someone is likely to say, "I can smell Mother's cooking." Some pupils will nod in relief.

"Of course, you can smell Mother's cooking because it really exists. It is actually there. We can also smell vinegar, mothballs, perfume, onions, and many other things because *they are really there*. But what does *air* smell like? You cannot smell air because it does not exist. Let's investigate further. Maybe we can taste air. What does it taste like?" Pupils will stick out their tongues, again in a slightly embarrassed way because they know it will not do any good. Often someone will hold an imaginary mug, scoop up imaginary air, and drink it. Pupils will laugh, and soon they are all scooping up the air with their pretend mugs.

"At last we have discovered something. I see that you are drinking air, so air must be a liquid. Right?" Well, "no," the pupils will say. They were just pretending with the mugs.

"I see. You used pretend mugs to do pretend drinking because air is a pretend thing. The mugs aren't there and neither is the air. They are just pretend."

You may continue to ask about the shape of air, its color, or other possible properties. Finally, when you have completed the various tests for air, conclude by summarizing: "Air has no smell. It has no taste. It has no shape. It has no color. It has no texture, and it cannot be seen because *there is no such thing as air!*"

Pretend that the summary statement concludes the discussion. Tell them that tomorrow we will talk about another subject. Pupils will become quite disturbed. In the face of the so-called evidence they will be momentarily stopped. But they *know* that air really exists. It is not just a superstition. Let them simmer and stew for a while. Then say, "Okay, if you think air really exists, how can we prove it?"

Tell them that the topic will be discussed again tomorrow. Ask them to bring in evidence that air really exists. Pupils will be highly motivated to find proof. They will discuss the topic in school, at recess, and in the lunch line. They will lean into a strong wind on their way home saying, "There just *has* to be a way we can prove that air really exists."

By the next day it is quite likely that pupils will bring in much evidence: You can feel the wind; you can see that it moves trees. You can blow on your hand and feel the air. You can fill a balloon with air. Air fills tires and holds up cars. Air fills up footballs, basketballs, and volleyballs. Many more examples are likely to be presented.

The preceding discussion highlights the *negative* properties of air, namely, that air is colorless, odorless, tasteless, and invisible. But it *does* exist.

POSITIVE PROPERTIES OF AIR. Despite the preceding activities, air *is* a real substance and it occupies space. All the events in this section are designed to show that air truly exists.

For example, in *Event 9–A. Fill the Balloon with an Empty Bottle* the balloon begins to fill as soon as the air inside the bottle warms up. Obviously, if the balloon fills up, the bottle could not have been empty. (Be sure to use a large bottle and a small balloon because the expansion is not very great. The balloon will not do much more than "stand up.")

Similarly, *Event 9–B. Squeeze-Box Candle Snuffer* also shows that the box was not really empty. When squeezed, the box pushes out a puff of air that blows out the flame. We cannot see the air itself in these events, but we can see what the air does.

Event 9–C. Pouring Air can be achieved underwater. Use two beakers. Invert the first beaker and push it underwater. It is filled with air. Lower another beaker underwater in an upright position. After it fills with water invert it above the first beaker. Slowly tip the first beaker (filled with air) so that bubbles stream upward into the second beaker (filled with water). You are "pouring" air. (See Fig. 9–3.)

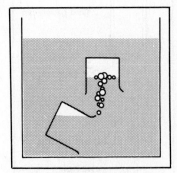

Fig. 9–3. **Pour air from one beaker to another, underwater.**

When doing this event, it is a good idea to refer to the air in a positive way. The beaker with air is "full of air." The beaker with water is "empty of air." (Not "full of water.")

Event 9–D. Keep the Paper Dry Underwater is somewhat similar to Event 9–C because in both cases the beakers trap air underwater. In Event 9–D the paper towel is wadded up inside the beaker. When the beaker is inverted and submerged, the air keeps the water out. As pupils often say, the water cannot get in "because air is already in there." (See Fig. 9–4.)

In performing *Event 9–E. Pour Water into the "Empty" Bottle* the pupils will find that the water will not enter the bottle, except for a few drops in the beginning. The reason is simply that the bottle is already full (of air). The few drops of water enter at the beginning because the air can be compressed somewhat by the weight of the water.

Fig. 9–4. **How can you keep paper dry "underwater"?**

If you use a tube that is too large, air will bubble out and water will come in, alternating back and forth until the bottle is filled with water. Even if your experiment works that way, it is still a success. It shows clear evidence that air is a real substance and that air occupies space. Point out that the water does not enter until air, a real substance, leaves.

The events in this section show that air is a real substance and occupies space. Additional activities may also be done to show the same property of air.

1. *Blow up a balloon.* When blowing up a balloon, we can see that "something" is going into it. That something is called air.

2. *Blow out a candle.* We see the effects of air when we blow out a candle, even though the air is invisible.
3. *Blow through a straw.* Blow through a straw into water. The bubbles are clear evidence that air is a real substance and occupies space.

AIR EXERTS PRESSURE (EVENTS 9–F THROUGH 9–L)

Discrepant Events and Pupil Investigations

Fig. 9–5. As water flows from the can through the tube into the catch basin, the outside air pressure crushes the can.

One gallon can

One-hole stopper

Glass tubing joined by one-hole stoppers

Catch basin

Event 9–F. Can Crusher Number 1. Fill a gallon can with water and insert a one-hole stopper. You will need a long tube. If you do not have one, you can make it by using one-hole stoppers to connect several shorter lengths. Make a holder of strong cord or wire so that you can hang the inverted can from a high support. Let the water run down the length of the tubing into a container on the floor. As the water empties, the can is slowly crushed. (See Fig. 9–5. It is somewhat awkward to hang up the can because of the long tubing, so one or more helpers may be needed to accomplish the task.)

Pupil Investigations (may include the following processes):
1. Observing that water runs out of the can through the tubes into the container
2. Observing that the can is slowly being crushed
3. Forming a theory about the unseen force that is crushing the can

Event 9–G. Can Crusher Number 2. Do this event as a demonstration. Cover the bottom of a gallon can with about a cup of water. Heat the water and let it boil for a minute or two. Remove the can from the heat and immediately seal the opening with a stopper. Set the can on a high platform for all to see. Observe.

Caution: If done incorrectly the event is dangerous! Do it only if you are *sure* you can do it right. Do not seal the can too quickly. The can must be removed from the heat before sealing it. Otherwise the steam quickly builds up pressure inside and the can might explode.

On the other hand, if you wait too long to seal the can, the event will not work, or work poorly. Once removed from the heat, place the stopper quickly. If done right, it is safe and exciting.

Pupil Investigations (may include the following processes):
1. Observing that the can is slowly crushed
2. Inferring that the can was full of steam when it was stoppered
3. Inferring that the steam condensed into a few drops of water when it cooled
4. Forming a theory that the condensing steam created a vacuum inside the can

Event 9–H. Is a Newspaper Stronger Than a Board? This event should be performed by the teacher as a demonstration. Obtain a thin board. (A cheap yardstick will do. A thin strip of plywood will *not* work.) Lay the board on a table so that one end extends over the edge by 15 to 30 centimeters.

Place sheets of newspaper over the remainder of the stick on the table. (This part should be at least 60 to 80 centimeters long.) Be sure to place extra sheets directly over the stick so that the stick does not cut through the paper when you perform the event.

Ask pupils to predict what will happen when you push slowly on the stick. Yes, the stick will push up the newspapers. Are the newspapers heavy enough to break the stick? No. After discussion hit the stick sharply. What happens? Why? (See Fig. 9–6.)

Fig. 9–6. **Air pressure on layers of newspaper is strong enough so that the stick breaks when struck.**

Pupil Investigations (may include the following processes):
1. Predicting that the board will lift up the newspapers when you push down on the exposed end of the stick
2. Observing that the stick breaks when it is hit sharply
3. Inferring that some form of pressure is exerted when the board is hit hard as compared to when it is pushed easily
4. Forming a theory about the form of pressure that holds down the newspaper

Event 9–I. Drinking Race. Ask two pupils to compete in a soft-drink race. See who can drink a small glass of the beverage fastest. See to it that one pupil has a normal straw, but give the other student a straw filled with pinholes. (Of course, the pupil should not be made aware of the pinholes. Also, the event works just as well with water as with a soft drink.)

At a given signal, they begin. The pupil with the good straw will easily win. Ask the class why there was such a difference.

Pupil Investigations (may include the following processes):
1. Inspecting the "losing" straw to see if it is defective
2. Inferring that the pinholes caused the pupil to lose the race
3. Experimenting by having the losing pupil try with another straw
4. Generalizing about the force that pushes fluids up a straw

Fig. 9–7. **Why does the water run uphill from container B to A?**

Event 9–J. Antigravity Fountain. Set up an arrangement of containers and tubes as shown in Fig. 9–7. Start with 5 to 10 centimeters of water in the inverted top bottle and then open the clamps. The fountain begins to flow in the top container. Why?

Pupil Investigations (may include the following processes):
1. Observing that container C fills with water
2. Observing that container B empties out
3. Recording with a diagram the path of the water from B, through A, and into C
4. Forming a theory to explain why water goes uphill from B to A

Event 9–K. Weightless Water. Fill a tumbler with water, cover it with an index card or sheet of paper, and invert it. Everyone expects the water to pour out. However, it will not pour out if you use weightless water! Show the class

Fig. 9–8. **The water does not spill out because air pressure pushes against the paper. The tumbler does not have to have an air space for this activity to work.**

Fig. 9–9. **Can you stop the leak in the can by plugging the *top* hole?**

that the paper holds the water inside the tumbler, even if the tumbler is turned upside down. (However, don't stretch your luck. Do it over a sink.) (See Fig. 9–8.)

Pupil Investigations (may include the following processes):
1. Observing that the card and water do not fall
2. Inspecting the card to see that sometimes there is a slight *upward* bulge at the center of the card
3. Experimenting with tumblers containing varying amounts of water and discovering that they all work
4. Forming a theory about the force that holds the water in the tumbler

Event 9–L. Stop the Leak. Punch a nail hole into the bottom and top of a tin can. Fill the container with water and securely seal the cover. The water, of course, runs out. Ask the pupils to stop the flow of water with a finger, but *without* getting it wet. *Note:* Be sure to use a can with a tight fitting cover. A loose cover will not work. (See Fig. 9–9).

Pupil Investigations (may include the following processes):
1. Experimenting by placing the finger on the top opening
2. Observing that the water stops running when the top opening is closed
3. Inferring that some unseen force holds the water in any time the top opening is closed

Events 9–F Through 9–L Explained in Context (Air Exerts Pressure)

The events in this section all pertain to an important principle of air: *air exerts pressure.* It will surprise most pupils to learn that air can crush a can, but that is what happens in *Events 9–F* and *9–G. Can Crushers Number 1* and *Number 2.* In *Event 9–F,* as the water runs out of the can, air from the outside tries to get in. However, since there is no opening for air to enter, the air tries to get in by pushing in the sides of the can. After a while the can is totally crushed.

Where does all the air pressure come from? It comes from the weight of air. At first impression it seems unlikely that air could be that heavy. However, if you have enough of it, air begins to become a powerful force. The pressure comes from the weight of hundreds of kilometers of air pushing down from above the earth.

At sea level the pressure of air is so great that it pushes with a force of 1 kilogram per square centimeter. The total force on the can may reach more than 1800 kilograms.

If air pressure is that great, why aren't we crushed by it? Not only does it leave us uncrushed, we can't even feel it! The reason is that the air pressure pushing down on us is equaled by the pressure within our bodies pushing outward.

Only in rare cases, when pressures are not equal, do we notice it. For example, you can sometimes feel your ears "popping" when going up or down a steep road or when going up or down in an airplane. Air pressure varies with elevation, so those changes can sometimes be noticed.

If you can create a situation where the normal pressure is removed, then the existing air pressure can exert itself. This is what is done with the can crusher events. In Event 9–F gravity removes the water from the can, leaving a vacuum. Air pressure crushes the can as it attempts to fill that vacuum.

It is important that the exit tubing be quite long. Otherwise the air will just get into the can by going up the tube. Even if the air cannot get in, the water will not get out and nothing happens.

It is also important that you use tubing with rigid or strong walls. Glass tubes are the strongest, but heavy plastic or rubber tubing might work as well. Just be careful that the pressure does not flatten the tube. Then the water cannot get out and the can will not be crushed.

Event 9–G. Can Crusher Number 2 is similar to Event 9–F. The only difference is the method used to create the vacuum. In this event the water is brought to a boil, which quickly fills the can with steam. The steam drives out all the air, especially if you let the water boil for a minute or so.

Then after the can is removed from the heat, quickly seal the opening. *Caution:* Do not seal the can too soon. You must wait until *after* it is removed from the heat. Otherwise the can could explode! If you are not *sure* how to do it right, *don't do it*. Perhaps you can ask a high school science teacher to show you how to do it safely.

Then when the can is removed from the heat, quickly seal the opening. What happens to the steam when it cools off? It condenses into a few drops of water, leaving a vacuum in its place. The air will crush the can as it tries to get inside. (See Fig. 9–10.)

The pressure of air is also responsible for the discrepancy in *Event 9–H. Is a Newspaper Stronger Than a Board?* The newspapers should be carefully flattened out over the stick and onto the table. When the end of the stick is hit, air pressure pushes down on the newspaper with such force that the stick is broken. If the stick is pushed down slowly, air can get in from the sides to equalize the pressure, and the paper is lifted easily.

Be sure to observe a note of caution when doing this event. First, if there are too few newspapers, instead of breaking, the stick will simply cut through the paper and fly up into the air (hitting your head, if you are not careful). Therefore, be sure to have enough layers of newspaper to keep the newspaper from being cut by the stick. Second, do not take chances. Keep your head out of the way in case the stick does not break.

Event 9–I. Drinking Race is also designed to show how air pressure exerts itself. When you sip on a straw, you lower the air pressure inside. As a result, the outside air pressure, which is greater, pushes down on the surface of the liquid, forcing it to move up the straw.

When you sip on the straw with the holes, however, the air pressure is pulled directly into the holes. The pressure does not exert itself on the liquid, and the liquid does not rise. (See Fig. 9–11.)

Event 9–J. Antigravity Fountain is quite baffling to pupils when they first see it. Let them observe the event carefully. First of all, they should determine

Fig. 9–10. **Does air exert pressure? It can easily crush a can.**

Fig. 9–11. **Why does air pressure push the liquid up straw A but not straw B?**

in which direction the water is going. Ask them to find out where the water is coming from and where it is going to.

Then have pupils find out why the water is going "uphill" into the top container. In fact, the water often enters with such force that it hits the top of the flask. If you use an ordinary glass tube in the flask, it will drain the water in container B rather quickly. If, however, you narrow the opening of the glass tube in the flame of a Bunsen burner, or even if you just use the glass part of an eye dropper, the event will run for quite a while before container B empties.

Point out that some outside force must be causing the water to go uphill from container B to the top of the flask. Gravity is obviously not that force because gravity would push the water "downhill," not up. What provides that force? Air does!

It may be easier to understand what happens by starting at the top flask and working backward. Open the clamp, and water flows out, leaving behind a partial vacuum in the flask. Air tries to get in to fill that vacuum but water is in the way. Since container B is higher than C, it takes less pressure to push the water in from B than from C. Thus, the path is set in which the water moves from container B to the top flask and down to the bottom container.

The force of the fountain can be increased by raising container B (so that the water does not have to be lifted as high) or by lowering container C (so that gravity pulls down with a greater force, to create a greater vacuum).

The activity is closely related to a siphon. The only difference is that the top part of a siphon does not contain a flask. Instead, the siphon is a closed tube going from one container, over an obstruction, to a lower container.

It is important to realize that water will flow in a siphon only as long as the outlet end of the hose is lower than the inlet. The net direction of the siphon has to be down. There is no way that a siphon can ever raise a liquid if the outlet is higher than the inlet.

Thus, the lifting of liquid takes place only in the middle part of a siphon or antigravity device. The outlet end is always lower than the inlet.

Event 9–K. Weightless Water again shows that air exerts pressure. It is especially good in showing that the pressure pushes in all directions, even upward. The reason that the water does not fall from the tumbler is that air pressure is pushing against the card, keeping the water inside.

If some air gets in along an edge, then the pressure inside the tumbler becomes equal to the pressure outside the tumbler and everything splashes down promptly. For obvious reasons this event should be done over a sink.

Anyone can stop the flow of water from the can in *Event 9–L. Stop the Leak* by just putting a finger on the lower hole. However, how can we stop the leak without getting a wet finger? Just place a finger over the *top* hole.

When water runs out of the lower hole, air enters the top hole. Thus, air gets inside and makes the pressure equal to the pressure outside the can. However, when the top hole is blocked, air pressure can no longer enter on top so it tries to enter through the lower hole. In its attempt to enter, air pushes against the water at the lower exit, keeping the water from running out.

By reviewing the seven events in this section, we clearly see that there are many ways to show that air exerts pressure.

Fig. 9–12. **After the fire goes out the air cools and shrinks (contracts). Outside air then pushes the egg into the bottle.**

Discrepant Events and Pupil Investigations

AIR EXPANDS AND CONTRACTS (EVENTS 9–M THROUGH 9–P)

Event 9–M. The Egg-in-the-Bottle Mystery. Take a hard-boiled egg and remove the shell. How can we put that egg into a milk bottle? Pushing it will not work.

Light a small strip of paper and drop it into the bottle. Quickly place the egg on the mouth of the bottle. It is important not to wait after dropping in the flaming paper. Put the egg on the mouth at once. Observe. (See Fig. 9–12.)

Pupil Investigations (may include the following processes):
1. Predicting what will happen to the fire (It will burn for a while and then go out.)
2. Predicting what will happen to the egg (It will be sucked into the bottle.)
3. Observing that the egg bounces up and down for a few seconds right after being placed on the bottle
4. Observing that the egg is pulled into the bottle after the fire goes out
5. Experimenting to find a way to get the egg out of the bottle

Fig. 9–13. **Do two candles use more oxygen than one? Why does the water rise higher in the bottle when more candles are lit?**

Fig. 9–14. **Push down on the cylinder and the diver goes down; pull up and the diver rises. Notice the air space *inside* the medicine dropper.**

Fig. 9–15. **Compressed air and a partial vacuum can inflate the balloon in this activity.**

Event 9–N. Oxygen in the Air. Set up an arrangement of candles on the bottom of a tray as shown in Fig. 9–13. Fill the tray with about 5 centimeters of water. Light one of the candles and place an inverted bottle over it. Observe and record the results. Repeat the activity, but this time with two candles. Repeat once more with three candles. What are the results?

Pupil Investigations (may include the following processes):
1. Predicting what will happen to the flame (It will go out after a short while.)
2. Predicting what will happen to the oxygen inside the bottle (It will be used up to support the flame.)
3. Predicting that water will enter the bottle to replace the oxygen
4. Recording the level of water that enters the bottle after each trial with one, two, and three candles
5. Making a rule to explain the increased water levels with each additional candle

Event 9–O. Diving Dropper. Fill a medicine dropper with enough water so that it will either just barely float or just barely sink. Either choice will be fine. Place the dropper into a full cylinder of water. Then place the palm of your hand over the top of the cylinder. Press down, and the dropper goes down. Then carefully pull up with your palm to form a suction, and the dropper comes up. Why? (See Fig. 9–14.)

Pupil Investigations (may include the following processes):
1. Predicting what will happen when you press down (or pull up) on the water with the palm of your hand
2. Observing that the dropper moves up or down in response to pressures exerted by the palm of your hand
3. Observing that the liquid *inside the dropper* responds to the pressures by your palm
4. Inferring that the dropper goes up (or down) because water goes out of (or into) the dropper making it lighter (or heavier)
5. Generalizing that air can be compressed and expanded

Event 9–P. Balloon Blowup. Set up an arrangement of bottle, tubes, and balloon as shown in Fig. 9–15. Blow into tube A and the balloon inflates. Release, and the balloon deflates. Now blow into A and release, but this time hold B shut. What happens?

Pupil Investigations (may include the following processes):
1. Predicting what will happen to the balloon if B is held shut
2. Observing that the balloon remains inflated as long as tube B is held shut
3. Verifying the activity—checking that air escapes from B while the balloon is being inflated
4. Experimenting to see if the balloon can be inflated by drawing air out of the bottle through tube B (It can.)

Events 9–M Through 9–P Explained in Context (Air Expands and Contracts)

We learned in the unit on heat energy that most substances expand when heated and contract when cooled. This principle, as it applies to air, is reviewed in this section.

Event 9–M. The Egg-in-the-Bottle Mystery is astounding to pupils who have never seen it before. Yet the explanation is fairly simple, even though the event is incorrectly presented in some textbooks.

To get the egg into the bottle, a fire has to be dropped into the bottle and the egg placed on top of it at once. After the fire goes out the egg is sucked in. (We repeat: for the event to work correctly, the egg must be placed on the bottle quickly after the fire is dropped inside. If you wait, it will be too late.)

Why does the egg go in? Some books mistakenly state that the fire uses up the oxygen, which creates a vacuum. The outside air pushes down in its attempt to get in. In reality, it is another principle that accounts for the activity: the expansion and contraction of air.

Air expands when heated and contracts when cooled. When the fire is dropped into the bottle, it heats the air inside. When the air is heated, it expands and goes out of the bottle. You will often see the egg bounce for a moment or two as the heated air escapes around it.

When the fire goes out, what happens to the hot air? It cools off. As it cools it contracts, leaving a partial vacuum inside. The air that was pushed out earlier tries to get back inside. Now, however, the egg is in the way, so it is pushed in.

There is another way to get the egg into the bottle. Instead of using fire, heat the bottle with water. Then put the egg on top. The air in the bottle slowly cools off and contracts. A vacuum is formed and the outside air gradually pushes the egg inside. Be patient, because it will take several minutes for all this to happen.

When the egg is inside, how do we get it out? Just reverse the situation. No, we do not build a fire in the room and expect the egg to pop into it. Reversing the situation means that instead of creating a vacuum inside the bottle (which brought the egg inside), we place pressure inside to force the egg out.

Of course, when the pressure is raised inside, the egg must be lodged in the opening of the bottle. Otherwise the pressure will just escape. Hold the bottle upside down so that the egg will naturally seal the opening.

You can put pressure inside by blowing past the egg into the bottle. Then when you stop blowing, the air will try to get out again. However, since the egg is in the way, it pushes the egg out instead.

Another way is to pour hot water over the inverted bottle and let the air warm up inside. As it expands, it puts enough pressure on the egg to push it out.

Event 9–N. Oxygen in the Air is also caused by the expansion and contraction of air. It is a common misconception to state that the water rises inside the bottle because it replaces the oxygen used by the candle flame.

Based on that false theory, it should make no difference how many candles are lit. The water should rise to the same level each time because all the oxygen is used up in each case.

However, the results are quite different from those expected in the false theory. The greater the fire, the higher the water level. It is obvious that the amount of oxygen in the bottle is not the critical factor.

The key factor is that air expands when heated and contracts when cooled. The candle flame heats the air inside the bottle, forcing it to bubble out. In fact, if you listen, you can hear the air bubble out during the first few seconds after the bottle is inverted. It happens so fast, however, that many people are not aware of what is happening.

Later, after the fire goes out, the air inside the bottle contracts and creates a partial vacuum. The air from the outside tries to get back inside. Since it cannot get in directly, the air pushes the water into the bottle to replace the air that was originally pushed out.

In summary, the greater the heat, the greater the expansion, and the greater the amount of air pushed out of the bottle. Then when the fire goes out, the greater is the influx of water into the bottle. Thus, the more candles you use, the higher the water level in the bottle.

Event 9–O. Diving Dropper also is caused by expansion and contraction of air. In this case, instead of using heat and cold to expand and contract it, you use pressure from your hand.

When you press down on the opening of the cylinder, be sure that you have an airtight fit between your palm and the rim of the cylinder. Otherwise the pressure will escape and nothing will happen. When you apply pressure, water is pushed into the dropper. With the added water the dropper is heavier and sinks to the bottom.

When you pull up on the cylinder with the palm of your hand, you pull water out of the dropper. Then the dropper weighs less and rises to the top.

Sometimes it is easier to cover the top of the cylinder with a rubber cover taken from a balloon. Hold it firmly in place with several rubber bands. Then pull or push on the rubber to move the dropper. Use of the rubber cover allows people with small hands an easier way to operate the system.

A final example of the compression of air can be seen in *Event 9–P. Balloon Blowup*. The air inside a balloon is slightly compressed. Normally, when the balloon is opened, the compressed air rushes out quickly.

However, when tube B is closed, the balloon does not deflate. Air would have to enter the bottle through tube B to fill the space taken by the deflating balloon. If the air cannot get into the bottle directly, then it gets in indirectly. It enters through the balloon, keeping the balloon inflated.

Teaching Children about Weather and Climate

Discrepant Event and Pupil Investigations

Event 10–A. Classifying Climates. List the following words and statements on the chalkboard: (1) calendar, (2) clock, (3) day, (4) month, (5) season, (6) storm, (7) it is hot today, (8) it was a hot summer, (9) it was a rainy day, (10) our summers are usually dry, (11) the wind is blowing hard, and (12) we have mild winters.

Ask pupils to classify the words and statements into two groups to represent *weather* and *climate*.

Pupil Investigations (may include the following processes):
1. Comparing the words and statements to find common traits
2. Classifying the 12 examples into two groups
3. Inferring that time is an important factor in defining the terms

Event 10–A Explained in Context (What Is Weather? What Is Climate?)

What is the difference between weather and climate? Time! The major factor that helps classify the terms is the time period of each example. If it is a relatively short time, the words and statements pertain to the *weather*. If it covers a long time, the words or statements pertain to *climate*.

The "weather" words and statements in the preceding list are clock, day, storm, it is hot today, it was a rainy day, and the wind is blowing hard. The climate words and statements are calendar, month, season, it was a hot summer, our summers are usually dry, and we have mild winters.

In summary, temporary or short-term conditions of the atmosphere pertain to weather. Long-term conditions of the atmosphere pertain to climate.

The event can be modified to fit a fairly wide range of class levels. Upper grades will find the lesson easy but still useful. Middle grades will find it within their abilities. Lower grades will find it somewhat challenging but still useful if the list is shortened.

Even pupils in primary grades and kindergarten can learn about weather and climate but by a different method. Ask them to help with a class weather calendar. Draw the calendar on a large piece of cardboard or make it out of

WHAT IS WEATHER?
WHAT IS CLIMATE?
(EVENT 10–A)

CALENDAR

SUN	MON	TUES	WED	THUR	FRI	SAT
			1 sun	2 sun	3 sun	4
5	6	7	8	9	10	11
12	13	14	15	16	17	18

Fig. 10–1. **This is an example of a weather calendar showing the weather for the first 7 days of a month.**

felt board or other material. Have available simple symbols representing the sun, clouds, wind, and rain.

Every day at a given time, perhaps an hour before dismissal, ask the class to decide which picture (symbol) best describes the "weather for today." As they focus on the daily weather for the entire month, not only do they focus on daily weather, but also a visual pattern unfolds that shows something about the long-term conditions of the atmosphere (climate). See Fig. 10–1 for an example of one week's weather.

CONVECTION CURRENTS (EVENTS 10–B AND 10–C)

Fig. 10–2. **Smoke goes down chimney A and up chimney B in this convection box, showing that warm air rises and cool air falls.**

Discrepant Events and Pupil Investigations

Event 10–B. Curious Currents. Set up a convection box as illustrated in Fig. 10–2. A convection box is essentially a metal box with two chimneys and a sliding glass front for viewing. Light the candle and close the glass cover. Hold a smoldering piece of cloth or string that gives off lots of smoke over the top of chimney A. Then hold it above chimney B. What do you observe?

Pupil Investigations (may include the following processes):
1. Observing that the smoke goes up at chimney B
2. Observing that the smoke goes down at chimney A
3. Recording data with a diagram showing the path of the air currents
4. Inferring that warm air rises and cold air descends

Event 10–C. Tornado Box. Select a cardboard box that is about 30 to 40 centimeters high and just slightly larger than a good square-shaped hot plate. Cut out large "windows" on two adjacent sides of the box and cover them with clear plastic. Paint the inside of the box black.

Cut a 10-centimeter hole in the ceiling and insert a 1-meter chimney into it. Seal all air leaks with tape. Finally, along the four corners of the box, cut

Fig. 10–3. **A specially prepared box and chimney can be used to make a miniature tornado.**

long, upright slots about 1 to 2 centimeters wide and extending to within 3 centimeters of the top and bottom. (See Fig. 10–3.)

Place a shallow square tray of water on the hot plate. (The tray should be about the same size as the hot plate.) Cover the tray and hot plate with the tornado box. Bring the water to a vigorous boil.

Shine a flashlight through one of the windows, and view the effect through the other window. What do you see?

Pupil Investigations (may include the following processes):
1. Observing that a cloud forms over the boiling water
2. Observing a whirlwind over the pan, similar to a miniature tornado
3. Generalizing that the tornado is formed because of rising air and swirling incoming air

Events 10–B and 10–C Explained in Context (Convection Currents)

The great weather patterns of the earth are caused by uneven heating and cooling of air. These air movements are called *convection currents*. Small-scale examples of those currents can be shown in the classroom. *Event 10–B. Curious Currents* is an excellent activity to show those air movements. You will see that air rises when it is heated and falls when it is cooled. The candle heats the air and sends it out of chimney B, as is expected by most pupils. However, pupils are often surprised to find that air goes *down* chimney A.

Let pupils diagram the path: down chimney A, across to the candle, and up chimney B. As stated earlier, those currents are a miniature sample of how winds are formed on the surface of the earth.

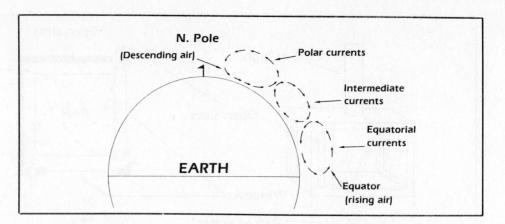

Fig. 10–4. **Rising hot air at the equator and descending cold air at the pole provide the power to move the air in great circular patterns.**

On the earth's surface we find that the equator is hot and the poles are cold. Thus, the equator acts like the candle in the box and is similar to chimney B. The poles, on the other hand, act like chimney A. Cold, heavy air often comes sweeping down from polar regions, especially during the winter, to cover much of the United States.

The comparison of the earth to the convection box is not exact. The air currents do not form a single large circulating pattern from the poles to the equator and back again to the poles. The distances are too great for the air masses to make the journey undisturbed. Instead, three subcycles are formed.

Polar air pushes one of the subcycles. The air sweeps south but warms up long before it reaches the equator. The equatorial air powers another subcycle. The hot air masses of the equator rise and move north but do not reach the poles; long before, the air masses get cold and descend. The polar and equatorial currents drive an intermediate cycle between the two major cycles. The United States is mostly under the influence of the intermediate cycle. (See Fig. 10–4).

In addition to the great global air patterns that cover thousands of kilometers, there are smaller cycles covering hundreds of kilometers. These smaller areas contain the familiar "highs" and "lows" shown on weather maps.

Even smaller versions of the circulation patterns, covering only a few kilometers, can form within the highs and lows. The smaller patterns can form whenever the larger systems become stagnant. An example of the small area system is the breeze that forms along a lake or seashore. The winds blowing in from the lake are called *sea breezes*.

The local sea breezes develop for the same reason that the currents formed in the convection box. Air is heated (over the land) and cooled (over the water). The cool air moves from the water to the land, just as the cooler air in the box moved to the candle. (See Fig. 10–5).

What happens in the middle of the night when the land cools off and is cooler than the water? (Land gains and loses heat much faster than water, so it gets hotter in daytime but colder at night.) At that time the cycle reverses. Since the water is warmer than the land, the cool air blows from the land to the water. Those breezes are called *land breezes*.

Just remember that regardless of which way the breezes blow, they are

Fig. 10–5. **A sea breeze is formed when warm air rises on the land and is replaced by cooler air from the lake. The paths are similar to the currents in a convection box.**

always relatively cool breezes blowing into relatively warm areas. In the daytime the cool breezes come from the water; at night they come from land.

The breezes form only when there is a temperature difference. Thus, the sea breeze is strongest at midafternoon, during the warmest part of the day. The land breezes are strongest just before sunrise during the coldest part of the night. By midmorning and late evening temperatures tend to equalize and the breezes stop.

Again, it bears repeating—the land and sea breezes form only when the major weather systems are weak or stagnant. When a major weather system is moving through an area, those winds overpower any local weather patterns that might otherwise develop.

WHAT ARE MONSOONS? *Monsoons* are special kinds of sea breezes that cover large areas of the world. Perhaps the most famous monsoons are those that visit India each year. The winds come loaded with moisture from the warm Indian Ocean. When they reach shore, they are lifted up to go over the land and later the foothills of the Himalaya Mountains.

As the air rises, it cools. As it cools, air loses its capacity to carry the moisture. Therefore, the moisture falls in great quantities. It should be noted that the monsoon winds are not caused by local differences in heating and cooling. They are driven by much larger air masses that tend to prevail at certain times of the year in that region. In other parts of the earth the prevailing winds will create deserts. Those drying winds will be discussed more fully later in this chapter.

COLD AND WARM FRONTS. You have often seen weather maps on television and in the newspapers. Different air masses and temperatures are commonly shown. What happens when air masses collide?

It is often not just a simple matter of air moving in a cycle covering hundreds of kilometers. Instead, when a mass of air that large begins to move, it is hard to stop. Thus, weather masses will sometimes come out of the frigid Arctic and sweep across the entire continent.

Such an air mass forms a *cold front* as it moves south. In winter the cold front brings with it bitter cold and strong winds. In summer a cold front brings

Cold Front
Thunder
showers
Movement
of cold air
Warmer
air

Warm Front
Movement of warm air
Stratus clouds
Gentle rains
Cooler
air

Fig. 10–6. **Heavy, cold air pushes away warmer air in a cold front (left). Warm air slides slowly over the cooler air in a warm front (right).**

thunderstorms as it enters warmer air. Sometimes a cold front brings with it hail, high winds, and tornadoes.

Event 10–C. Tornado Box can be used to show, in miniature, the formation of a tornadolike vortex (whirlwind). A tornado is formed from moisture and rapidly rising warm air plus clashing wind patterns. All three conditions exist inside the box. Sometimes it helps to blow some chalk dust into the box to make the swirling winds more visible.

(It should be noted that unless the box is made correctly, the tornado will not form. There is not much room for error. However, if everything is made right, a powerful twisting column of steam and air will be easy to see. The most important factors are strongly boiling water, the air slots, and the careful fitting of parts.)

As a general rule, cold air overpowers warm air because cold air is heavier. On occasion, however, a warm air mass will push into a colder area and form a *warm front*. This happens when the warm air is part of a larger weather system. Even then, the warm air does not push the heavier cold air away. Instead, the warm air slides up over the cooler air and slowly warms it. A warm front usually brings a long, gentle rain. Study the diagrams of the cold and warm fronts in Fig. 10–6.

THE WATER CYCLE (EVENTS 10–D THROUGH 10–H)

Discrepant Events and Pupil Investigations

Event 10–D. Evaporation Race. Form several teams of three or four pupils each. Give each team a small amount of water in a test tube. Hold a race to see which team can get the water to evaporate the fastest.

Rules should be set to permit any innovation as long as the team gets approval from the teacher first. (Throwing the water on the floor is not permitted, for example.) The teacher gives approval for any idea that does not cause a mess.

Another good rule is to permit only one team to use any idea. Then you can keep rules to the very minimum. Just approve or disapprove an idea when a team presents it. Otherwise it is too easy to give away solutions in the instructions (such as "be careful with the hot plate," which, of course, would give away the idea that heating the water speeds up the evaporation process). See which team wins the race and analyze the methods used.

Pupil Investigations (may include the following processes):
1. Experimenting by pouring the water from the test tube into a large tray

2. Experimenting by heating the water
3. Experimenting by using a fan to blow air across the water
4. Controlling variables
5. Generalizing that evaporation is increased by heat, surface area, and air movement.

Event 10–E. Two Temperatures. Set up the thermometers side by side. Wrap one end of a short cotton cloth on the bulb of one thermometer and dip the other end of the cloth into a dish of water. Check the two thermometers at periodic intervals.

Pupil Investigations (may include the following processes):
1. Observing the temperatures at periodic intervals
2. Recording the observations on a graph
3. Discovering that the wet-bulb thermometer is cooler
4. Inferring (incorrectly) that the cool temperature is due to cool water
5. Generalizing that evaporation has a cooling effect

Event 10–F. Discovering the Dew Point. Place a few cubes of ice into a beaker of water. Insert a thermometer in the water and carefully observe the temperature. At what point does dew form on the outside of the glass?

Pupil Investigations (may include the following processes):
1. Recording the temperature at which dew is first noticed on the outside of the beaker
2. Repeating the activity on different days
3. Discovering that the dew point is not at the same temperature every day

Event 10–G. The Convection Contradiction. Present a verbal discrepancy to the class: If warm air rises and cold air descends, why is it colder at high altitudes (where the warm air goes) than at low altitudes (where the cold air goes)? (See Fig. 10–7.)

Fig. 10–7. **If warm air rises, why is it cold on top of a mountain?**

Pupil Investigations (may include the following processes):
1. Checking references to be sure that higher altitudes are, indeed, cold (Find pictures of snow on top of mountains.)
2. Discovering that the sun's energy warms the earth's surface but not the air as it passes through it
3. Discovering that the air is warmed by the earth's surface
4. Generalizing that air is warm at the source (earth) and gets colder as it moves away
5. Forming a theory that something must be cooling the air as it rises and warming the air as it descends

Event 10–H. Water Cycle. Set up a miniature water cycle in a jar. Fill a large, wide-mouthed glass or plastic jar with 1 or 2 centimeters of hot water.

Fig. 10–8. **Can you identify the major parts of the water cycle?**

(Be sure to use heat-resistant glass or plastic. Otherwise there is danger of cracking when the hot water is added.)

Cover the top of the jar with a metal pie plate filled with crushed ice. From time to time add a small amount of smoke inside the container. See if pupils can identify miniature forms of clouds, air movement, and rain. (Allow plenty of time for the results to occur. (See Fig. 10–8.)

Pupil Investigations (may include the following processes):
1. Observing the formation of clouds, "rain," and "wind"
2. Comparing the events inside the jar with events in the atmosphere
3. Forming a theory on what causes rain

Events 10–D Through 10–H Explained in Context (The Water Cycle)

EVAPORATION. We have seen that air currents are essential to the formation of weather patterns. However, air does not move alone; it carries with it huge amounts of water.

Where does air get its water? It comes from oceans, lakes, and streams, as well as from plants. The process whereby water changes from a liquid to a gas and goes into the air is called *evaporation*.

The speed at which evaporation occurs depends on a number of conditions, most of which the pupils can discover for themselves by doing *Event 10–D. Evaporation Race.* Initially, the teams may be unsure about what to do. However, as they discuss it among themselves, ideas soon flow. Teams typically discover the following three factors that speed the evaporation of water:

1. *Increasing the surface area.* If the teams keep the water in the test tube, it could take days for it to evaporate. However, spreading the water out in a large pan reduces the time to minutes. Spreading it out over a counter or table could reduce the time even more. (If a cloth is used to spread the water, the cloth must be hung up to dry before the team can be considered finished.)
2. *Increasing the heat.* Again, it could take days for the water to evaporate from the test tube if the water is kept at room temperature.

However, heating the water will cause it to be boiled away in minutes.

(*Caution*: Do not overheat and always point the mouth of the test tube away from people. Overheating will cause steam and boiling water literally to explode from the test tube! Supervise closely. It is wise to allow only a mild heat source and to allow only one team to use heat.)

3. *Increasing the movement of air.* When air is saturated, it cannot accept any more moisture; evaporation cannot occur. Thus, evaporation can be increased if saturated air above the water is replaced by unsaturated air. This can be accomplished by using a fan.

Fig. 10–9. **If an air mass has a capacity of 10 liters and humidity of 5 liters, what is the relative humidity?**

There is only one factor missing: the relative humidity of the air. Thus, pupils will typically discover three of the four conditions that affect the rate of evaporation. The fourth factor (relative humidity), is too technical to discover in the classroom.

RELATIVE HUMIDITY, HUMIDITY, AND CAPACITY. *Relative humidity* is defined as "the amount of moisture in the air compared with the amount that the air can hold." It compares capacity with the actual amount of moisture in the air. The definition is somewhat abstract.

Often it is easier to understand what the term means by comparing an air mass to a "weather man" with a water bucket. In our comparison the weather man represents an air mass, the bucket represents capacity, and the water in the bucket is the humidity. (See Fig. 10–9).

Relative humidity is a comparison of capacity with *humidity.* For example, if a 10-liter bucket contains 5 liters of water, the bucket is 50 percent full. Similarly, if a mass of air is able to hold 10 liters of moisture but is actually only holding 5 liters, then the air is "50 percent full," or has a relative humidity of 50 percent.

Notice that (1) capacity and (2) humidity are physical quantities, but that (3) relative humidity is always a percentage. Relative humidity is a *comparison* of the first two factors.

The relative humidity of air can be found in the classroom by doing *Event 10–E. Two Temperatures.* The wet-bulb thermometer will show a cooler reading than the dry-bulb thermometer. The cooling action comes from the evaporation of water that is on the cloth on the wet-bulb thermometer.

The lower the relative humidity, the greater the rate of evaporation, and the cooler the temperature. Hence, the difference in the two readings can be used to find the relative humidity of the air. Some common relative humidity figures are shown in Table 10–1.

It is important to realize that the three factors of capacity, humidity, and relative humidity are not fixed. They are all variables and each can change in a given air mass.

For example, evaporation increases the amount of humidity in the air, but rain decreases it. A change in humidity, in turn, affects the relative humidity. Surprising to many pupils is the fact that the capacity changes too.

Table 10–1. **Difference Between Dry- and Wet-Bulb Thermometers**

Degrees—F	1	2	3	4	5	6	7	8	9	10	11	12	13	14	15
Reading of Dry-Bulb Thermometer (Degrees—F)							*Percentage Relative Humidity*								
63	95	89	84	79	74	69	64	60	55	51	46	42	38	33	29
64	95	89	84	79	74	70	65	60	56	51	47	43	38	34	30
65	95	90	85	80	75	70	65	61	56	52	48	44	39	35	31
66	95	90	85	80	75	71	66	61	57	53	49	45	40	36	32
67	95	90	85	80	76	71	66	62	58	53	49	45	41	37	33
68	95	90	85	81	76	71	67	63	58	54	50	46	42	38	34
69	95	90	86	81	76	72	67	63	59	55	51	47	43	39	35
70	95	90	86	81	77	72	68	64	60	55	52	48	44	41	36
71	95	91	86	81	77	72	68	64	60	56	52	48	45	41	37
72	95	91	86	82	77	73	69	65	61	57	53	49	45	42	38
73	95	91	86	82	78	73	69	65	61	57	53	50	46	42	39
74	95	91	86	82	78	74	70	66	62	58	54	50	47	43	40
75	95	91	87	82	78	74	70	66	62	58	55	51	47	44	40

Capacity is affected by temperature. The warmer the air, the greater its capacity; the colder the air, the lower its capacity. The effect of temperature on capacity can be seen by doing *Event 10–F. Discovering the Dew Point.* We often see moisture form on the outside of a cold glass of ice water. Why does it form? Because the cold surface reduces the capacity of the air to hold moisture. If the air can no longer hold the moisture, it condenses into visible dew on the cold surface.

To use our weather man analogy, his bucket can stretch and shrink, depending on the temperature. If it is warm, the bucket is large; if cold, the bucket is small. If it gets very cold, it is no larger than a thimble.

The analogy shows the tremendous variation in air's moisture-holding capacity. Hot summer air has a capacity hundred of times greater than frigid winter air. And to repeat, the capacity depends entirely on temperature, nothing else.

Actual figures from the weather bureau show the following capacities: 0.02 percent at 0 degrees Celsius, 2.0 percent at 27 degrees Celsius (one hundred times greater), and 6.0 percent at 43 degrees Celsius (300 times greater than at 0 degrees Celsius).

Perhaps we can see how the three factors interrelate by looking at the diagram of the weather man in Fig. 10–10. Notice that when the capacity decreases, the relative humidity increases. In the first diagram the relative humidity is 50 percent; that is, the bucket is 50 percent full. The air would *feel* dry at that level.

When the temperature drops, however, so does the capacity. In the second example the capacity is reduced to 10 liters (L), equal to the humidity. At that point the bucket is 100 percent full (meaning that the relative humidity is 100 percent). The air would feel quite muggy even though there is no actual change in the amount of moisture in the air. The feeling is caused because perspiration cannot be evaporated from our bodies when the air is already "full."

Fig. 10–10. **When air cools off, its moisture-holding capacity (the size of the bucket) decreases. How does this affect the humidity and relative humidity?**

In the third diagram of Fig. 10–10 the capacity shrinks (because the temperature drops) down to 5 liters. But remember that the air contains 10 liters of moisture in our example. How can a 5-liter bucket hold 10 liters of moisture? It cannot. The excess moisture overflows the bucket. We call that overflow "rain" in summer and "snow" in winter.

Study the diagrams carefully. They contain all the factors that affect the amount of moisture in the air.

It is interesting to note that most rainfall occurs because the capacity shrinks, not because of other factors. Air gains moisture fairly slowly but can lose it quickly. All it has to do is cool off. The cooling can be caused by another air mass, by cold land surfaces, or by being lifted higher into the air.

Let us see how the three factors of capacity, humidity, and relative humidity are applied to an air mass that comes from an ocean and moves across a shoreline and over some inland mountains. Study the diagrams in Fig. 10–11.

Fig. 10–11. **The moisture-holding capacity of air (the size of the little man's bucket) decreases as the temperature goes down. It tends to produce rain when it cools off (III) but not when it is warmer (II).**

See if you can fill in the blanks with the right answers. Is the relative humidity higher or lower in the second diagram? What happens to the humidity? Now look at the third diagram. What is the humidity? The relative humidity?

The capacity of the air mass increased in the second diagram because its temperature increased. Assuming no additional evaporation, the humidity remained the same at 9 liters. Thus, the relative humidity dropped to 50 percent. (The capacity increased to 18 liters, so that the 9 liters only filled the bucket half full.)

The third diagram, however, shows the capacity shrinking sharply (because the temperature is lower). The capacity shrinks down to 5 liters. Can you put 9 liters into a 5-liter bucket? No! The excess moisture comes down as rain.

The example shown in the diagrams is common to many areas of the earth. When the winds reach land, they produce a dry climate.

It is different from what people often believe. There is a common misconception that an air mass moving from the ocean to the land will always produce rain. That, indeed, does happen sometimes, but only if the air mass cools down so that its capacity shrinks.

In other places when the air warms up, the capacity increases and the air becomes drier. Some very dry lands are located right along some great oceans. Examples of such dry areas are the coastal areas of Southern California, Baja California (Mexico), Chile, and Peru. In each case the prevailing winds travel over relatively cool bodies of water but warm up when they reach shore.

In those areas there is little rain until the air masses are pushed up by hills and mountains to much colder heights. Then the capacity shrinks and the rain falls.

This brings us to *Event 10–G. The Convection Contradiction?* Why is it that the higher the altitude, the colder the temperature? Remember that earlier in this chapter we stressed that air goes up when it is heated and goes down when cooled. Why is it cold on top of a mountain (where, presumably, the warm air rises), and warm in the low lands (where, presumably, the cold air descends)?

The answer is twofold. First, although the source of the heat is the sun, the sunlight passes through the air without heating it. The sun's energy is turned into heat only when it hits something that is not transparent. Thus, the sun warms the surface of the earth. So, one reason that the land is warm is that the sun heats it.

There is another factor that is just as important. Sea level air is highly compressed by the weight of all the air above it. Increasing the pressure makes air warmer; decreasing the pressure makes air colder. When air rises, the pressure on it decreases. In turn, the air expands and cools. By the time the air gets into the stratosphere it is extremely cold. As a result, the cold air of high altitudes keeps the tops of mountains cold.

All the factors of evaporation, humidity, and precipitation occur in a *water cycle*. Water moves in an endless cycle. The cycle includes water (1) evaporating and rising into the sky, (2) condensing to form clouds, and (3) coming down as rain or snow. All three elements of the cycle can be shown in miniature by doing *Event 10–H. Water Cycle.*

A convection current is set up inside the jar. The hot water heats the air, so it rises. The cold metal plate cools the air, so it descends. The different temperatures power a continuous current inside the jar. If you put some smoke inside the jar, the currents become much more visible.

The moving air produces a water cycle. Warm air carries moisture up to the cold plate. The cold plate causes the water to condense into droplets. After a while enough water forms to fall down as "rain."

(For best results, be sure to have the water as hot as possible. It should be understood that the rain forms very slowly. It may take several minutes for the first drop to form and several more minutes for each succeeding drop.)

Discrepant Events and Pupil Investigations

THE SEASONS (EVENTS 10–I AND 10–J)

Event 10–I. The Four Seasons. Use a light bulb and globe to show why there are four seasons in a year. Set the light source on a table and move the globe in a path around it. Stop at four points in the path to show the four seasons. (See Fig. 10–12.)

Be sure to hold the globe at an angle showing the tilt of the earth on its axis. Tape two markers on the globe and label them A and B. Determine the season of the year at each of the two markers at each of the four locations.

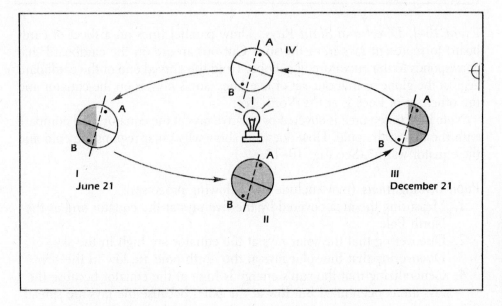

Fig. 10–12. **Use a light bulb to represent the sun. Move a globe around the sun to show the seasons of the year. Notice that the sun is more directly overhead during summer than during winter.**

Pupil Investigations (may include the following processes):
1. Experimenting with the globe and bulb to determine the effect of the tilt of the earth on the seasons
2. Discovering that in June the sun (bulb) is high in the sky (more directly overhead) in the Northern Hemisphere and low in the sky in the Southern Hemisphere
3. Observing that the sun's (bulb's) relative position changes as the globe moves around the sun
4. Generalizing that the combination of tilt and orbital motion combines to cause the seasons

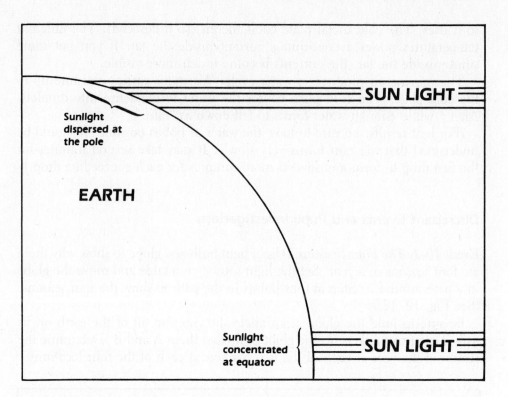

Fig. 10–13. **Can you see why sunlight at the equator produces more heat than sunlight at the poles?**

Event 10–J. Direct and Slant Rays. Draw parallel lines on a sheet of cardboard to represent rays from the sun. Cut out an arc on the cardboard that corresponds to the curvature of a globe. Hold the curved end of the cardboard against the globe so that one set of five lines (sun's rays) is on the equator and the other set of lines is at the North Pole.

Note how much area is covered by the five rays at the equator, and compare with the rays at the pole. How does this show why polar regions are cold and the equator warm? (See Fig. 10–13.)

Pupil Investigations (may include the following processes):
1. Measuring the area covered by the five rays at the equator and at the North Pole
2. Discovering that the solar rays at the equator are high in the sky
3. Discovering that the solar rays at the north pole are low in the sky
4. Generalizing that the sun's energy is high at the equator because the rays are concentrated but low at the poles because the rays are spread out

Events 10–I and 10–J Explained in Context (The Seasons)

Pupils may have observed that the sun is generally closer to the horizon during the winter than during the summer. However, they are often unaware of what causes this apparent seasonal movement of the sun.

The seasonal changes are not caused by an actual movement of the sun. The sun's change of position is caused, instead, by the movement of the

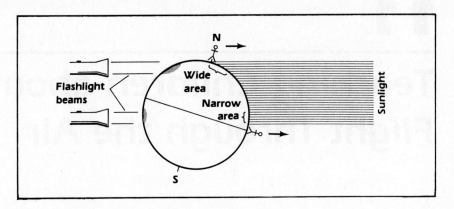

Fig. 10–14. Sunlight strikes the polar region at an angle. Solar energy is spread out over a larger area at the poles than at the equator. This effect can be demonstrated with a flashlight.

earth. Perform *Event 10–I. The Four Seasons.* Tape and label some markers (points A and B) on the globe. (Refer back to Fig. 10–12.)

If you start at position I, labeled June 21, you will find A, located in the Northern Hemisphere, at the start of its summer season. Point B, in the Southern Hemisphere, starts its winter season. Note that the sun is high overhead at point A and low in the sky at B.

At position III, labeled December 21, the situation is just reversed. In the points in between the fall and spring seasons trade places. In each case the sun is high overhead during its summer and low during its winter.

Point out that the earth is tilted on its axis. That is, the North and South poles are tilted at an angle. Otherwise the seasons would not change during the course of a full year. Experiment with a no-tilt earth in each of the positions. The angle of the sun does not change in any of those positions.

When the sun is low in the sky, a given amount of the sun's rays are spread out over a wider area of the earth than when the sun is high overhead. Perform *Event 10–J. Direct and Slant Rays.* Cut out the cardboard template and draw parallel lines on it to represent sunlight.

Pick four or five lines and see how much area is covered at the equator. Then measure the areas at the pole covered by the same number of lines. You will find that the rays are spread out and diluted at the poles, keeping the area from getting warm. (See Fig. 10–14.)

One final factor makes the problem even worse. The sunlight is not only diluted at the poles, but it is also filtered and weakened by the many hundreds of kilometers of atmosphere that it must pass through on its slanted path to the earth. At the equator the sun takes a much shorter and direct path to the earth.

These activities help pupils understand how some areas of the earth receive more heat energy than others. It also helps them understand why and how air currents circulate, especially if the events are related to the air movements in the convection box discussed early in the chapter.

CHAPTER

11

Teaching Children about Flight Through the Air

**FORCES OF FLIGHT
(EVENTS 11–A
THROUGH 11–E)**

Sheet of paper

Fig. 11–1. **Blow under the sheet (A) and the paper rises. What happens when you blow over the sheet (B)? (You must blow very hard.)**

Air stream

Ping Pong ball

Straw

Fig. 11–2. **Blow hard through a small straw and the Ping-Pong ball will be held in the air above it.**

Discrepant Events and Pupil Investigations

Event 11–A. Lifting Forces. Anyone can lift up a sheet of paper by blowing under it. However, can you lift the paper by blowing *over* it? Hold a sheet of paper as shown in Fig. 11–1. If you blow into it at position A, it goes up as expected. Then blow over the paper at point B so that the air column just touches the top of the paper. What happens? (You will need to blow forcefully.)

Pupil Investigations (may include the following processes):
1. Observing that the paper is lifted as expected by blowing against the paper in position A
2. Discovering that the paper is also lifted by blowing over it at position B
3. Inferring that a moving column of air attracts the paper upward
4. Comparing the lift on the paper with the lift on an airplane

Event 11–B. The "Floating" Ping-Pong Ball. Hold a paper or plastic straw upward and blow *very hard* through it. Carefully place a Ping-Pong ball into the moving stream of air. What happens? [(See Fig. 11–2.) Remember, you need to blow very hard.]

Pupil Investigations (may include the following processes):
1. Observing that the Ping-Pong ball seems trapped in the air column
2. Observing that the floating Ping-Pong ball seems to be held inside the air column by an invisible wall
3. Forming a theory to account for the wall-like effect
4. Generalizing that a moving air column has low internal pressure

Event 11–C. The Inviting Air. Can you blow away a pair of Ping-Pong balls? Suspend two Ping-Pong balls from a support so that they are about 1 to 2 centimeters apart. Blow through a straw between the two balls. Can you blow them away? (Be sure to blow forcefully.)

Pupil Investigations (may include the following processes):
1. Observing that the Ping-Pong balls seem to be pushed *into* the air column instead of away from it

2. Forming a theory about the invisible force that seems to push into the air column instead of away from it
3. Experimenting with other objects to check results

Event 11–D. Funnel Magic. Place a Ping-Pong ball into a funnel and ask pupils how high they can blow it into the air. Then see how far they can blow it horizontally across the room. Finally, see how forcefully they can blow the Ping-Pong ball straight down to the floor. In the horizontal and downward attempts be sure to have pupils hold the ball in the funnel until they are blowing . . . *hard!* Who can blow the ball the farthest? (See Fig. 11–3.)

Fig. 11–3. **Can you blow a Ping-Pong ball out of a funnel?**

Pupil Investigations (may include the following processes):
1. Observing that the ball cannot be blown out of the funnel in *any of the three positions*, if the pupil blows hard enough
2. Forming a theory about the invisible force that holds the ball in the funnel
3. Inferring correctly that the invisible force works best when the force of the flowing is strongest

Event 11–E. Straw Atomizer. Can you blow away the liquid? Or, does a good blow bring the liquid *into* your puff? Set up an arrangement of two straws as shown in Fig. 11–4. Hold the horizontal straw so it barely touches the upright straw and blow strongly. Be careful not to angle the horizontal straw downward. Keep it level or, better yet, angle it upward slightly. Observe what happens.

Fig. 11–4. **Blow through a straw directly across the opening of another straw in a container of water.**

Pupil Investigations (may include the following processes):
1. Observing the water rise in the upright straw and being lifted *into* the air column
2. Inferring that some unseen force is pushing the water into the moving air
3. Generalizing that a high-speed column of air has low internal pressure

Events 11–A Through 11–E Explained in Context (Forces of Flight)

There are four basic forces that act upon an airplane in flight: *lift*, *gravity*, *thrust*, and *drag*. Lift is the upward force, offsetting the downward force (gravity). Thrust is the force that moves the plane ahead, and drag is the force that holds it back. (See Fig. 11–5.)

Fig. 11–5. **Four forces affect the flight of an airplane.**

Fig. 11–6. **A high-speed column of air has low internal pressure.**

Fig. 11–7. **The upper part of an airplane wing is curved. Air flowing over the top travels farther and faster than air flowing under the wing.**

A number of good discrepant events can be done to show the effect of lift on an airplane. Most pupils believe that the lift on a plane is due to the "kite effect," that is, the upward push of air striking the underside of the wing. Such is not the case.

The kite effect produces only a small amount of lift. Instead, most of the lift comes from the air going *over* the wing, not under it. Ask pupils to do *Event 11–A. Lifting Forces.* Blow against the underside of the sheet of paper and it rises as expected. Then blow *over* the paper and, surprisingly, it rises again *into* the airstream.

It takes a little practice with the technique to do it right. Hold the paper by the top two edges and turn it so that it makes a rounded curve on top. Refer back to Fig. 11–1 and study the diagram carefully. Then blow sharply, touching the top rounded edge of the paper. The sheet should pop into the airstream.

The main principle of science that causes the action is *air pressure*. Remember that static air exerts pressure; and if a way can be found to reduce air pressure in one place (the air column), then the existing pressure around it (room air) exerts itself.

It comes as a big surprise to pupils that moving air has lower pressure than still air. So, if you can move air very fast, its pressure can be lowered greatly. That is why the static air *around it* can exert itself.

Keep the air column in mind when doing all the other events in this section. They all work the way they do because air columns have low internal pressure. (See Fig. 11–6.)

How does this effect work on an airplane? Air pressure pushes the wing upward just as the paper was pushed upward. The top surface of the wing is curved as shown in Fig. 11–7; the lower surface is fairly flat. Thus, the air going over the wing has to travel farther to get to the same place.

In traveling farther, the air speeds up. It forms, in effect, a high-speed column of air above the wing and produces the same kind of pressure that you got when blowing above the paper. The pressure pushes on the underside of the wing, lifting the airplane.

See *Event 11–B. The "Floating" Ping-Pong Ball.* The ball is suspended in the midst of a column of air above the straw. The direct pressure of the air pushes the ball up, as is expected; but why doesn't the ball go off to the side and fall down?

Again, the column of air, having low internal pressure, is surrounded by the higher pressure of the static air in the room. The static air forms a "wall" around the moving column, keeping the ball from escaping. It will help to refer back to the diagram of the air column shown in Fig. 11–6. Just turn it upright.

The activity works only if you blow hard enough. It takes a good strong effort to do the event successfully.

An effective demonstration is to use a vacuum cleaner and reverse its airflow. The air column is so strong that a beach ball will be held in the air above the outlet. Or, if you have a fan, aim it upward and see if you can suspend some weighted balloons in the column. Use paper clips or similar weights on the balloon. Otherwise they will be too light to stay close to the fan.

The inward push of static air is also shown in *Event 11–C. The Inviting Air.* By blowing between them, the static room air pushes the Ping-Pong balls *into* the air column. Similar results will be obtained by using apples, baseballs, bottles, books, or just about anything else in place of the Ping-Pong balls.

Event 11–D. Funnel Magic is also useful in showing the effects of a moving air column. The only problem, if any, is figuring out where the air column is. The air goes through the stem of the funnel and then around the ball. As it goes around the ball, the air has its greatest speed and the effect is strongest. As a result, the higher pressure of the still air in the room pushes the ball *into* the funnel.

Most pupils will expect to blow the ball up to the ceiling. However, they will find that if they blow hard enough, they cannot get the ball out of the funnel, *even if they aim it toward the floor.* When aiming toward the floor, do not release the ball until you are blowing quite hard, and it will stay in. The harder you blow, the better it works. (See Fig. 11–8.)

The last event in this section, *Event 11–E. Straw Atomizer,* also shows how static room pressure pushes into a moving column of air. In this event the column of air is located at the top of the upright straw, so that static room air pressure pushes the water up into the moving air column. When it reaches the airstream, the water is atomized (broken up into tiny droplets).

The event is a rough model of how sprayers and atomizers work. Thin straws will often give better results than larger straws because you can get higher air speeds with them.

Fig. 11–8. **High-speed air has low internal pressure, so the ball is held inside the funnel.**

Discrepant Event and Pupil Investigations

Event 11–F. Streamlining for Speed. How can a candle flame show us the value of streamlining? Light a candle and hold a flat card (index card is fine)

STREAMLINING FOR SPEED (EVENT 11–F)

Fig. 11–9. **What happens to the flame when you blow against the flat and round cards?**

a few inches in front of the flame. Then blow directly into the cardboard. Have others observe the flame. How does it act? Then try the activity by using a piece of paper bent into a teardrop shape. What happens to the flame when you blow? (See Fig. 11–9.)

Pupil Investigations (may include the following processes):
1. Observing that blowing against the teardrop paper causes the flame to move *away* from the source of the air
2. Discovering that blowing against the flat cardboard causes the flame to move *toward* the source of air
3. Recording the data on diagrams showing the path of air currents
4. Inferring that some form of pressure works against the blowing when a flat card is used

Event 11–F Explained in Context (Streamlining for Speed)

Since it is important for an airplane to travel fast, it is clear that planes need powerful engines that develop great thrust. What is not quite so clear is the need to reduce the drag on a plane or the force that tends to hold it back.

At the high speeds attained by aircraft drag is a far more serious problem than it is at the lower speeds involved in auto travel. As a result, aircraft engineers are constantly testing surfaces, shapes, and designs to reduce drag as much as possible.

Event 11–F. Streamlining for Speed shows two designs that affect drag. When the straight card is used, air goes around it and actually turns back, moving *toward* the person who is blowing. With some practice the candle flame can actually be blown out that way. When using the teardrop shape, however, the air goes around it and continues on its way. The candle flame moves in the same direction as the original air.

If you have a clear glass plate about the size of an index card, the person who does the blowing can see the results much better. An index card is very easy to use, but, unfortunately, the blower cannot see the effect very well. Likewise, instead of using a card in the teardrop shape, a round bottle or tumbler can also be used. If so, you can show pupils how to blow out a candle "through a bottle."

Ask pupils to diagram the airflow in the two trials. They will see that blunt shapes cause drag in two ways: (1) by pushing into the air column and (2) by producing the suction and turbulence of the air behind the card.

HOW AIRPLANES ARE CONTROLLED (EVENT 11–G)

Discrepant Event and Pupil Investigations

Event 11–G. Airplane Flying Contest. Have pupils make folded paper airplanes or cardboard models that are capable of flying when tossed into the air. Have them bend the back edges of the wings on the models up or down to see the effects on flight. Let them bend the upright stabilizer left or right to see if its position affects flight.

After testing their work, let the pupils hold a paper plane flying contest. See which plane can stay in the air for the longest time, which plane flies the greatest distance, and which one flies a circular path to return nearest to its launching point.

Pupil Investigations (may include the following processes):
1. Experimenting with different weights (paper clips) on the nose of the paper plane and the effect of different launching speeds
2. Experimenting with the control surfaces to see the effect on flight
3. Comparing the controls to those used on full-sized aircraft

Event 11–G Explained in Context (How Airplanes Are Controlled)

More controls are needed to fly an airplane that are needed to drive a car. A car has two sets of controls: (1) to move ahead and back and (2) to move left and right. A plane has controls to do the same things (except to move backward). A plane has additional controls: (3) to move up and down and (4) to tilt or roll clockwise and counterclockwise.

All the motions of a plane can be tested with paper airplanes as suggested in *Event 11–G. Airplane Flying Contest.* Your hand gives the airplane its forward motion, and adjustments on the wings and other surfaces can produce all other motions.

The major control surfaces of a plane are shown in Fig. 11–10. The *elevators* control the up and down motion of the plane. When the elevators are angled up, the tail is pushed down and the plane climbs. Conversely, when the elevators are angled down, the tail is pushed up and the plane heads down.

The *rudder* is located on the trailing edge of the vertical tail section. When the rudder is angled toward the left, the air pushes the tail to the right. Thus, the nose of the plane is pointed toward the left. When the angle of the rudder is reversed, the plane's flight path is also reversed.

Another important control surface is the *aileron*. The aileron is located on the trailing edge near the end of each wing. It is used to tilt the aircraft in a clockwise or counterclockwise roll. To tilt in one direction, the aileron on

Fig. 11–10. **The major control surfaces of an airplane are identified.**

one wing is angled up while the aileron on the other wing is angled down. To tilt or roll the plane in the other direction, the aileron angles are reversed.

The aircraft also has *flaps*. They are located on the trailing edge of each wing. Flaps are designed to increase lift during takeoff and landing when speeds are slow. When the flaps are extended and angled down, the air column going over the top of the wing must travel even farther than normal. This has the effect of increasing the speed of the airflow over the top of the wing, which, in turn, increases the lift. When the aircraft is flying at high speeds, the extra lift is not needed and the flaps are retracted.

Although the flaps and ailerons are both on the trailing edges of the wings, they do different things. The flaps are always used together and provide more lift when the plane is flying slowly (as in landing and taking off). The ailerons are much smaller and are always used as opposites to rotate the plane clockwise or counterclockwise.

When flying an airplane, a number of controls are often used at the same time. For example, when the pilot wants to turn the aircraft, the ailerons, elevators, and rudder are often all used at the same time.

Almost all the controls of an airplane can be tried with the paper airplanes. Pupils will find various combinations that will permit long flights or controlled turns. In the process of flying paper airplanes the pupils will gain a better understanding of control surfaces of real aircraft.

Upsweep

Fig. 11–11. **Notice how the wings angle upward. The upsweep makes the airplane more stable in flight.**

THE UPSWEEP OF THE WINGS. Have you ever looked carefully at the front view of an airplane? Notice that the wings are *not* level with the ground. The wings are angled upward from the fuselage. (See Fig. 11–11.)

The upsweep serves a very important function in the control of flight. It helps to keep the plane stable. If the plane is rolled by air currents so that one wing is pushed up, the other turns down. The wing that is turned up no longer gets as much lift as the one that is down. The added lift on the lowered wing corrects the rolling action.

The upsweep can also be tested with the paper models. It will help to produce planes that have very stable flights. Many kites are also built with the upswept design to provide more stable flight

SUPERSONIC FLIGHT (EVENTS 11–H, 11–I, AND 11–J)

Discrepant Events and Pupil Investigations

Event 11–H. Speed of Sound. Station a pupil at one end of the playground and take the rest of the class about 110 meters away. At a signal have the pupil strike together two sticks or hit a washtub or make some other loud sound. Ask the class to compare what it sees with what it hears.

Pupil Investigations (may include the following processes):
1. Observing the sticks being struck before the sound is actually heard
2. Inferring that the speed of sound is slower than the speed of light
3. Devising a system to time accurately the delay in order to measure the speed of sound

Event 11–I. Sonic Boom. Read the following description of a *supersonic* flight across the country: "The aircraft exceeded the speed of sound over the entire length of the country. But only the people near the start of the flight heard the sonic boom as the plane broke the sound barrier." Ask pupils to figure out what is wrong with the description.

Pupil Investigations (may include the following processes):
1. Forming a theory (incorrectly) that the boom is heard only once at the beginning of the flight when it breaks the sound barrier
2. Forming a theory (incorrectly) that the boom is heard twice: at the beginning and again when it slows to subsonic speeds at the end of the flight
3. Forming a theory that a sonic boom is created all the way across the country
4. Diagraming the sonic waves created by a supersonic aircraft

Event 11–J. Approaching Aircraft. Ask pupils to find the error in the following description about the approach of a supersonic aircraft: "As the plane approached, it had a high-pitched sound. After it passed by, the sound had a much lower pitch."

Pupil Investigations (may include the following processes):
1. Forming a theory (incorrectly) that the pitch should be the same both coming and going
2. Forming a theory that the listener could hear no sound at all before the plane passed by
3. Inferring a relationship between the speed of sound and the cause of sound

Events 11–H, 11–I, and 11–J Explained in Context (Supersonic Flight)

Many aircraft travel at or above the speed of sound. Just how fast is that? Find out by doing *Event 11–H. Speed of Sound.* If the class moves 110 meters from the source of the sound, it will hear the sound just $\frac{1}{3}$ second after the sound is made. That is, the class will see the object struck (to produce the sound) and then will hear it $\frac{1}{3}$ second later. (*Note:* The distance of 110 meters is about the length of a football field, plus both end zones.)

Pupils will be impressed to realize that an aircraft that flies at the speed of sound will travel as fast as the sound did in their experiment. They will be even more impressed to realize that many (military) aircraft travel two and three times the speed of sound.

We saw earlier in this chapter that most of the lift of an aircraft comes from the high-speed column of air that forms above the wing. Once the plane reaches the speed of sound, however, the principle of lift changes greatly. Instead of lift, it slowly changes to a down pressure.

The change occurs because the air going over the wing travels faster than the plane. (Remember that the air going over the upper curve of the wing speeds up.) As a result, the air column reaches the speed of sound before the plane does.

In effect, the high-speed air piles up on itself as soon as it reaches the top of the wing. This "piling up" forms a higher pressure that pushes downward, not the usual low pressure that lifts the plane up. Thus, the wings of supersonic planes do not have the upper curved surfaces. Also, they are made as thin as possible.

As the plane goes still faster, the pressure builds up even more on all its leading edges. When strong enough, this pressure reaches the ground and is called a *sonic boom*. The pressure trails behind the aircraft much like a water wave trails a moving boat.

The faster the plane goes, the louder the boom. Of course, if the plane flies very high (as it usually does), the sound is not very loud on the ground. In fact, sometimes the boom cannot even be heard.

What happens when the plane flies low enough for the boom to be heard clearly on the ground? Will it make a "boom" only when it breaks the sound barrier and then fly silently on? What is wrong with the description in *Event 11–I. Sonic Boom?*

Some pupils will think that the boom occurs only when the plane "breaks" the sound barrier. Others will think that the boom can be heard twice: once when it enters supersonic speed, and once again when it returns to subsonic speed. They think that the boom can be heard at both ends of the trip.

Unfortunately, the pressure wave that causes the boom is present any time the plane flies at supersonic speeds. Thus, the boom follows the plane all the way across the country.

Part of the reason for the misconception comes from a poor choice of words. For many years plane designers knew that great problems existed in attempting to reach the speed of sound. They knew that a new form of power would be needed to accomplish the task. As a result, it was regarded as a barrier. With the development of jet engines, there was finally enough power to accomplish the task. The speed of sound, which for so many years acted as a barrier, was finally "broken."

Because of the use of the terms *barrier* and *broken*, many people gained a false impression that "breaking" the sonic barrier was a single event and that once accomplished the plane would fly quietly at supersonic speed.

Pupils may question the explanation because many of them may have heard sonic booms, which *sound* like single events. Just keep in mind that the shock wave travels as fast as the plane and it passes by so fast that we hear only a single boom. The listener hears only a tiny instant of the continuous sound. That tiny instant is the "boom."

The boom is the only warning an observer would received in *Event 11–J. Approaching Aircraft*. An observer cannot hear the approach of a supersonic aircraft at all because it is traveling faster than the sound it makes. By the time the sound reaches the listener the plane *has already passed by*. Thus, all that the listener would hear is the boom and then the sound of the departing airplane. (See Fig. 11–12.)

Fig. 11–12. **Why is it that people at A and B cannot hear the approach of a supersonic airplane? The boom is heard at C.**

Supersonic aircraft are designed differently from subsonic aircraft. Because of the greater stress of supersonic flight, those planes are built stronger, have smaller wings, and are streamlined to offer a minimum of resistance to air.

One important design innovation is the "coke-bottle" shape of the fuselage. Designers discovered that when the fuselage is "pinched in" by an amount equal to the cross section of the wing, drag is reduced. Look for the coke-bottle shape in pictures of supersonic aircraft.

CHAPTER
12

Teaching Children about Space Science

FROM FIRECRACKERS TO SPACEFLIGHT

Rockets and space travel had their beginnings in ancient China. Some 750 years ago rockets were first used for displays of fireworks on holidays and special occasions. Not long after that they were used in warfare against Mongol invaders.

At about that time an attempt was also made to use rockets for space travel. According to legend, recorded by an unknown writer, a chieftain named Wang Hoo had designed a spaceship out of bamboo and fitted it with a propulsion system of 40 giant firecrackers. When everything was ready, Wang Hoo climbed aboard. At a given signal coolie technicians lit the fuses and rushed for cover. The firecrackers boomed!

After the smoke and debris cleared, the coolies looked for the space pioneer. He couldn't be found. Although the spaceship had not succeeded in escaping the earth, Wang Hoo, himself, had.

Thirty years after rockets were first used in China they were introduced in Europe. During the late 1200s and early 1300s rockets were often used in battles. After that time, however, the use of rockets declined because a better weapon was invented: the cannon. The cannon was superior to the rocket because it was far more accurate.

Rockets were seldom used again until the 1800s, when Sir William Congreve of England found ways to make them more effective. In fact, the British used rockets against the United States during the War of 1812. In a famous attack the British bombarded Fort McHenry throughout the night. Francis Scott Key immortalized his observations of that attack in our national anthem, "The Star-Spangled Banner."

Another great pioneer was the American scientist, Dr. Robert Hutchings Goddard, who conducted countless experiments from 1919 through the late 1930s. Goddard received many patents for inventions that improved the design and flight of rockets.

All his patents were purchased for a nominal fee by German scientists who later built the V-2 rockets that were used in World War II. By the end of the war, more than 1300 of the missiles had been launched against England.

During the closing days of the war 120 of the top V-2 scientists and technicians crossed war-torn Germany to surrender to advancing American troops. Another 4000, however, were captured by Russian armies. These personnel led the development of space vehicles for *both* countries.

The USSR launched the first satellite in 1957. The United States followed in January 1958. Since that time rockets and space vehicles have been used for weather prediction, communication, the exploration of the moon and planets, as well as for many other scientific purposes.

Discrepant Events and Pupil Investigations

Event 12–A. Jetting to the Moon. What does the future hold? Test the pupils with the following hypothetical statement made 100 years into the future: "These new jet aircraft are so powerful that we can fly all the way to the moon." What is wrong with that statement? What is the scientific error?

Pupil Investigations (may include the following processes):
1. Predicting (incorrectly) that the jet spacecraft could work
2. Predicting that jets could never be used in space
3. Generalizing about the kind of propulsion that must be used in space

Event 12–B. Balloon Rockets. Ask pupils to build rockets from balloons. If an inflated balloon is released, it flies in an uncontrolled way. Ask pupils to find ways of controlling the flight of balloon rockets.

Pupil Investigations (may include the following processes):
1. Discovering that attaching one or more straws to the mouth of a balloon tends to stabilize its flight
2. Experimenting with balloons attached to strings
3. Experimenting with balloons of different shapes and sizes
4. Comparing the flight of balloons with the flight of rockets

Fig. 12–1. **When the thread is cut, the toy is catapulted one way and the launching platform goes the opposite way.**

Event 12–C. Rubber-Band Catapult. Build an arrangement of board, straws, rubber bands, nails, and thread, as shown in Fig. 12–1. Place a weight in the catapult and cut the thread. Watch the weight go in one direction and the board go in the other. Make a mark on the table to show the position of the catapult before and after the launch. What do you find?

Pupil Investigations (may include the following processes):
1. Observing that as the weight is thrown one way, the catapult goes another way
2. Experimenting with larger weights and stronger rubber bands
3. Measuring the distance the catapult traveled and comparing it with the distance the weight was thrown
4. Generalizing about the principles of action and reaction

Event 12–D. Rocket-Launching Problem. Suppose that you have two large rockets ready for launching. Each has a mass of 10,000 kilograms. The rockets are alike in every respect except for the thrust that they can produce. Rocket A can produce 2000 kilograms of thrust for 300 seconds, whereas rocket B can produce 20,000 kilograms of thrust for only 10 seconds. The problem: Which rocket will travel farther?

Pupil Investigations (may include the following processes):
1. Calculating the total energy of each rocket by multiplying thrust by time
2. Predicting (incorrectly) on the basis of the calculations that rocket A will go farther
3. Inferring (correctly) that gravity (weight) is an important variable in this problem

Event 12–E. Man-in-the-Desert Problem. Assume that a man is stranded in the middle of a desert, 600 kilometers from the nearest oasis. Suppose, also, that he has a truck, a jeep, and a motorcycle, each capable of traveling only 200 kilometers. He cannot transfer gas from one tank to another. How can he reach the oasis? (See Fig. 12–2.)

Pupil Investigations (may include the following processes):
1. Comparing ideas with each other about how to solve the problem
2. Comparing the desert problem with space travel
3. Concluding that the distances that the individual vehicles can travel must be combined to reach the destination

Fig. 12–2. **How can this man go 600 kilometers through a desert to an oasis when each of the vehicles has a range of only 200 kilometers? (Fuel cannot be transferred in this problem.)**

Events 12–A Through 12–E Explained in Context (Power for Flight)

Power is one of the major ingredients of the space age. Just to place a satellite into orbit requires tremendous amounts of fuel and energy. To send a team of astronauts to the moon and back requires even more energy. For example, the Saturn moon rocket had a mass of 2.7 million kilograms. Almost all of the mass was used up in the mission. Only 4,500 kilograms remained to come back safely to earth.

What type of engine is needed to produce such great power? Only the rocket engine can do the job. Jet engines cannot be used in space because they *must fly through the air* to get the oxygen that is needed to burn the fuel. As a result, the error in *Event 12–A. Jetting to the Moon* is that jet aircraft cannot operate in the vacuum of space. Since there is no oxygen in space, jet aircraft cannot be used.

Rocket engines, however, carry with them everything that is needed to burn the fuel. With both fuel and oxidizer aboard, they can travel in the vacuum of space.

Event 12–B. Balloon Rockets should be useful in showing some of the effects of rocket engines. Pupils will find that a long, thin balloon tends to be more stable than a short, round balloon. Also, the flight will be more stable when straws are attached to the mouth of the balloon. Still another method of stabilizing the flight of a balloon is to tie a "tail" to it.

The purpose of the event with the balloons is to show pupils how hard it is to control the flight of a rocket. Pupils will find that unless some form of control is worked out, the balloons go every which way. Such flight would be a disaster for rockets.

THE THIRD LAW OF MOTION. One of the principles of rocket flight that is demonstrated by a balloon is the *third law of motion: An action produces an equal but opposite reaction.* Let us see how that law applies to the flight of a balloon.

The *action* is the escaping air; the *reaction* is the movement of the balloon. In other words, the escaping air goes one way, while the balloon goes the opposite way. The action-reaction principle works the same way in rockets. The burning gases go one way; the rocket goes the other way.

Event 12–C. Rubber-Band Catapult also shows the action-reaction principle. When the thread to the rubber band is cut, the weight is thrown one way; the catapult, on its roller platform (straws), goes another way. Experiment with different weights, bands, and platforms.

There are a number of additional activities that can be done in the classroom to demonstrate action-reaction. One method that can still be found in some books is actually dangerous. It suggests suspending a bottle horizontally with two strings. Then (the dangerous part) pour vinegar and baking soda into the bottle and quickly plug it with a cork.

The vinegar and baking soda quickly react to form a powerful pressure to blow off the cork. The "action" (the exploding cork) and the "reaction" (the bottle swinging away) are shown. The activity is quite exciting for pupils. *Unfortunately, it is also dangerous. The pressure can cause the bottle to explode!* Do *not* use a glass bottle with this activity.

The same instructional value can be achieved by using an iron pipe with a threaded cap, as shown in Fig. 12–3. The pressure of the vinegar and baking soda cannot possibly blow apart the pipe, regardless of how tightly the cork is pressed into the pipe. Of course, keep all pupils away from the exploding cork.

Fig. 12–3. **Baking soda and vinegar create energy to pop the cork from the pipe. The cork goes one way and the suspended pipe goes the other way.**

Getting a rocket off the launching pad requires tremendous force. As suggested in *Event 12–D. Rocket-Launching Problem*, it has a variable that is easy to overlook. The first impulse is to multiply the thrust with the time to get total energy. Unfortunately, you would get the wrong answer.

Rocket A produces three times as much thrust as rocket B. Yet B is the winner. Why? The thrust of rocket A is not equal to the weight of the vehicle, so, regardless of how long it burned, it could not even get off the launching pad.

Rocket B has the brute force to lift the vehicle off the pad and send it on its way. Even though rocket B burns for only 10 seconds, it sends the vehicle farther than rocket A.

It is apparent that brute force is needed to get a rocket off the ground. Once in orbit, however, the situation changes. There, any kind of thrust affects the flight of a rocket. Thus, if the two rockets were fired from a space station in orbit around the earth, then rocket A would be the clear winner. On the ground, however, only rocket B could get off the pad.

STAGING. Because of the great amount of energy needed in getting rockets into space, scientists have designed a system of "staging" to help get the job done. *Staging* is a process where one or more smaller vehicles hitch a ride, "piggyback" style, on a large rocket vehicle. The largest section, the first stage, is the base of the vehicle. On top of that the second stage is joined. Some vehicles have a still smaller third stage on top of the first two.

Upon launch the first stage lifts the entire vehicle off the pad and into the start of its journey. When the first stage burns out, it is simply discarded. Then the second stage ignites and pushes the rest of the vehicle on its way without the heavy weight of the empty first stage. In a similar way, the third stage takes over when the second stage burns out and is discarded.

The technique of staging is somewhat similar to the question posed in *Event 12–E. Man-in-the-Desert Problem.* How can the man get out of the desert? The answer is to carry the motorcycle in the jeep and the jeep in the truck. Then when the truck (first stage) runs out of fuel, switch to the jeep (second stage). After the jeep's fuel is gone, the motorcycle (third stage) brings the rider (the payload) to the destination.

Using the staging method is a very expensive way to make a trip because you abandon the truck and jeep along the way. Similarly, staging is an expensive way to travel in space, but it is sometimes the only way to get to the destination.

GRAVITY AND INERTIA (EVENTS 12–F THROUGH 12–M)

Fig. 12–4. **Tape together two funnels as shown and set them on a triangular-shaped ramp. The action may be surprising.**

Discrepant Events and Pupil Investigations

Event 12–F. The Ascending Cones. Attach two funnels or cones as shown in Fig. 12–4. Also, make a triangular ramp out of cardboard or wood similar to the one shown in the diagram. Set up the ramp and place the funnels at both the top and bottom ends. What happens?

Pupil Investigations (may include the following processes):
1. Observing that the funnels appear to roll uphill
2. Measuring the height to both ends of the ramp
3. Measuring the height of the cones (or funnels) at both ends of the ramp
4. Generalizing that the cones do *not* actually run "uphill"

Event 12–G. The Gripping Chair. Most people can get up from a chair with ease. However, by making a few rules, the task becomes impossible. Two general rules are enough: (1) Do not lean forward and (2) keep the feet in contact with the floor *in front* of the chair. Why is it impossible to get up when following those rules?

Pupil Investigations (may include the following processes):
1. Experimenting with the simple task of standing up from a chair to notice the position of the upper body and the feet
2. Recording data by making diagrams showing the body's center of gravity and its base of support (the feet)
3. Generalizing about the center of gravity and balance

Event 12–H. The Balancing Ruler. Normally when you balance a ruler on the edge of a table, you can place it so that about 6 inches extend over the edge before it falls off. (That is, if you use the old foot ruler. If you use a metric ruler of similar size, about 30 centimeters, you can push it to about the 15-centimeter point before it falls off.)

However, there is a way in which you can push the ruler so that only a few centimeters remain on the edge of the table and still keep it from falling off. Furthermore, you can even hang a hammer *on the long section that extends over the edge and still keep the ruler from falling off!* How is this seemingly impossible task done? (See Fig. 12–5.)

Fig. 12–5. **Hang a hammer on the end of a ruler as shown; you can suspend the ruler on the edge of a table.**

Pupil Investigations (may include the following processes):
1. Predicting (incorrectly) that the arrangement must surely fall
2. Checking to see if the ruler is attached to the table in any way (It is not.)
3. Experimenting with the position of the hammer on the ruler
4. Generalizing that when the center of gravity is below the point of support, an object is very stable

Event 12–I. Fast-Falling Paper. Hold up a discarded book in one hand and a single sheet of paper in the other hand. Ask pupils which of the two will fall faster when dropped. They will surely pick the book to drop faster than the sheet of paper.

Ask them to find a way to make the paper fall as fast as the book. It can be done; and they are not allowed to put the paper under the book, inside the book, or fasten it to the book in any way.

Pupil Investigations (may include the following processes):
1. Experimenting with the book and paper to see which drops faster
2. Observing that the paper drops slowly compared to the book
3. Experimenting by crushing the paper to see if it falls faster (It does, but still not so fast as the book.)
4. Discovering that when a sheet is placed on *top* of the book they both drop at the same speed

Event 12–J. Magic Tablecloth. Have you ever seen a magician pull a tablecloth out from under a complete setting of plates, tumblers, and dishes? We do not recommend that you try the stunt with your mother's best dishes.

Instead, a somewhat less ambitious task can be tried and still show the same principle. Use plastic or light wooden objects rather than glass and water. Even a single object on a sheet of paper will show the principle.

Pupil Investigations (may include the following processes):
1. Experimenting with many materials and techniques to see how well the activity can be performed
2. Predicting what will happen when the cloth or paper is moved slowly or when it is moved quickly

3. Observing that when the cloth or paper is pulled slowly, objects on it will move also
4. Making a rule to explain why objects remain stationary when the cloth or paper is pulled quickly

Event 12–K. Coin in the Cup. Place a small piece of cardboard (such as an index card) on top of a cup or tumbler, and place a coin on top of the card. Find a way to get the coin into the cup without touching the coin or without tipping over the card. Essentially, then, get the card out; but do not tip the card in any way to cause the coin to slide or drop into the cup.

Pupil Investigations (may include the following processes):
1. Experimenting with ways of moving the card to accomplish the task
2. Analyzing the action of the coin when the card is moved quickly
3. Generalizing about the effect of inertia on the coin

Event 12–L. Strong Pull, Weak Pull. Suspend a weight from a support with a stout string or rope. (See Fig. 12–6.) Attach a thin thread to the weight and pull gently to make the weight swing. Repeat, but this time pull sharply. What happens?

Pupil Investigations (may include the following processes):
1. Observing that when the thread is pulled gently, the weight begins to swing
2. Observing that when the thread is pulled sharply, the thread breaks
3. Experimenting with various weights
4. Forming a theory to explain why the weight does (or does not) move

Event 12–M. Antigravity Pail. Pour a few centimeters of water into a bucket. Then swing the bucket in a large upright circle. Does the water pour out? (If done correctly the water does not fall out. Perhaps you should practice outdoors.) *Note:* This event also works well if you tie a stout string on a tin can and then swing the can with the string.

Pupil Investigations (may include the following processes):
1. Discovering that the water remains in the pail when the pail is swung overhead
2. (If performed outdoors) experimenting with various speeds to see when the water begins to fall out
3. Making a rule that explains why the water stays inside the pail

Events 12–F Through 12–M Explained in Context (Gravity and Inertia)

To a large degree the information in this section seems self-evident. Everyone knows that objects have weight and that they fall when dropped. Yet the

Fig. 12–6. **Pull the thread slowly and you can move the weight. Pull the thread quickly and it breaks because the weight has inertia.**

concept must be studied in greater detail so that its scientific principles become clear.

In several events it seems that gravity reverses itself. How can the cones roll uphill in *Event 12–F. The Ascending Cones?* Are they really rolling uphill? It takes careful observation and measuring to see that the cones are, indeed, rolling downhill.

The key to the event is the triangular ramp. The narrow end is high, and the wide end is low. Start the cones on the narrow end; they *drop down* into the ramp and *actually go downhill*. Measure the center line of the cones as shown in Fig. 12–7, and you will see that the center of gravity is actually going down as the cones sink into the ramp.

To get the activity to work correctly requires care in building the ramp correctly. Practice with different angles and different inclines to get the best effect.

Fig. 12–7. **The funnels, or cones, appear to be rolling uphill, but they do not. The funnels sink downward into the opening of the ramp.**

Even such a simple task as standing up from a chair becomes impossible if done according to the rules set up in *Event 12–G. The Gripping Chair.* The action is so common that most people never think about the actions involved when getting up. However, to be able to do it, the body's center of gravity must be moved over the body's support (feet). There are two ways in which this is done. You can lean forward with the upper body so that the center of gravity moves over the feet. Another way is to just move the feet back. Most often, people use a combination of both actions. (See Fig. 12–8.)

Event 12–H. The Balancing Ruler is still another example of an event that seems to defy the law of gravity. If you push the ruler so that more than half of it extends over the edge, it surely must fall. It seems impossible to push the ruler past its midpoint, much less hang a weight on the end.

Again, careful observation will show that the arrangement is actually quite stable. The center of gravity of the hammer is located in its heaviest part, the head. The head comes to rest right under the point of balance, the table edge. Thus, the arrangement is no more than a weight resting under its point of support.

Any time the center of gravity is located *below* the point of support, it is stable. Conversely, if the center of gravity is *above* the point of support, it is less stable. In fact, the higher the center of gravity, the less stable is the object. For example, racing cars are built as low to the ground as possible to gain stability. Old cars had much higher center of gravity and tipped over at much slower speeds.

Fig. 12–8. **You cannot get out of a chair unless you move the weight of the body over the feet (by moving the upper body ahead or the feet back).**

To give another example, you are quite stable while lying down. You would find it difficult to fall or tip over from a flat position. If you were on stilts, however, where the center of gravity is much higher, you could fall much more easily.

Gravity causes all objects to fall at the same rate of speed as long as there is no air resistance. How can we prove the statement? We can see that gravity affects a book and sheet of paper the same way in *Event 12–I. Fast-Falling Paper.*

Normally a sheet of paper falls slowly because it is hindered by air resistance. The secret is to place the paper *on top* of the book. The book keeps the air from slowing the paper as it falls. Thus, the paper is affected only by gravity, not air, and it falls as fast as the book. It shows that gravity causes all things to fall at the same speed regardless of their weights as long as there is no air resistance.

In summary, the events that pertain to gravity confirm that gravity attracts objects to the earth. At first glance some of the events tend to contradict that principle, but when fully understood, they actually confirm the principle involved.

INERTIA. The first law of motion, as defined by Isaac Newton, states that *an object at rest tends to stay at rest* and *an object in motion tends to stay in motion*. The events that follow focus on that law.

No doubt, pupils have experienced the effects of inertia on the school bus. When the bus starts out, pupils, especially those who are standing, are swayed backward. The pupils tend to stay at rest, even when the bus begins to move. Later, when the bus stops, pupils tip forward because they tend to stay in motion.

The *first law of motion* is the scientific principle governing the final four events in this section. In *Event 12–J. Magic Tablecloth* many objects will stay at rest if the cloth or paper is pulled fast enough. That is, the cloth or paper can be pulled out without disturbing the objects resting on top.

Only if the cloth or paper is pulled slowly will gravity and friction have enough time to overcome the tendency to stay at rest. Thus, if pulled slowly, the objects move along with the cloth or paper. If pulled quickly, the objects stay at rest.

In *Event 12–K. Coin in the Cup* the coin remains at rest if the card is pulled quickly. In fact, you can snap the card out with your finger, as shown in Fig. 12–9. The card moves so fast that the coin "stays at rest." As soon as the card is gone, of course, the coin drops down into the cup.

Another example of inertia is shown in *Event 12–L. Strong Pull, Weak Pull*. The heavy weight has a tendency to stay at rest. Try to move the weight quickly and the thread breaks. If you pull gently, however, the inertia is overcome and the weight will move.

In *Event 12–M. Antigravity Pail* the effects of inertia are again evident. In this case the swinging of the bucket puts the water in motion. Once in motion the water has a tendency to keep moving in a straight line. Since the bucket is moving in a circle, the water pushes against the bottom of the bucket in its attempt to "stay in a straight line." This "push" is strong enough to overcome the force of gravity during the part of the swing in which the bucket is upside down.

GRAVITY AND INERTIA IN SPACEFLIGHT. At first glance it may not appear that these events relate closely to spaceflight. However, they do. Gravity and inertia are essential to flight through space.

We have all experienced the effects of gravity, but only on or near the surface of the earth. The force of gravity exists in space also, and affects rockets, satellites, and even the moon. If gravity did not extend away from earth, satellites and even the moon would fly off into distant space.

Fig. 12–9. Snap the card off the tumbler and the coin drops down. The card moves too quickly to overcome the coin's inertia.

Although gravity keeps a satellite in orbit, gravity could not do this alone. By itself, gravity would simply pull the satellite crashing into the earth.

Another force is needed: *inertia*, the force that tends to keep it moving in a straight line. The two forces act together and cause a satellite to move in a circular path around the earth.

Discrepant Events and Pupil Investigations

Event 12–N. Baseball Throw. Ask pupils to see how far they can throw a baseball or softball. After some warming up have them throw several times using high, medium, and low paths. Ask them to pay special attention to the flight path of each throw. (See Fig. 12–10.)

Pupil Investigations (may include the following processes):
1. Experimenting to see which angle gives the best results
2. Discovering that a ball thrown parallel to the ground does not travel as far as one thrown with an upward angle
3. Observing that the ball follows a curved path toward the ground
4. Generalizing that another force is acting upon the ball to bring it to the ground

Event 12–O. High and Low Orbits. Study Fig. 12–11 showing two satellites orbiting the earth. Satellite A is in high orbit; satellite B is in low orbit. Which satellite is traveling faster?

Pupil Investigations (may include the following processes):
1. Generalizing (incorrectly) that the satellite in high orbit must travel faster because it has farther to go per orbit
2. Generalizing (incorrectly) that both satellites may travel at the same rate of speed
3. Concluding (incorrectly) that there is not enough information available to solve the problem
4. Comparing the upward and downward forces acting on a satellite
5. Generalizing that the speed needed to balance gravity varies with the altitude of the satellite

Event 12–P. Fast Friction. Rub your hands together briskly and firmly. What do you feel?

Pupil Investigations (may include the following processes):
1. Feeling the hands become warm
2. Experimenting with different rubbing rates and speeds to see how it affects the production of heat
3. Comparing the activity to the heat formed on a returning spacecraft

Event 12–Q. Reentry Capsules. Study the diagrams of the blunt-nosed and sharp-nosed capsules in Fig. 12–12. They have different shapes but are iden-

TRAJECTORIES, ORBITS, AND REENTRY (EVENTS 12–N THROUGH 12–Q)

Fig. 12–10. **Throw a baseball in different arcs or trajectories. A very low or very high arc will produce less distance than an intermediate path.**

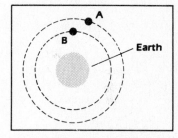

Fig. 12–11. **Does satellite A or satellite B travel faster?**

Fig. 12–12. **These space vehicles are the same weight, going at the same speed and in the same direction. Which will get hotter upon reentry to the earth's atmosphere?**

tical in weight, speed, and paths. Decide which capsule gets hotter when it returns from space and reenters the earth's atmosphere. Decide which capsule strikes the atmosphere with greater impact.

Pupil Investigations (may include the following processes):
1. Identifying what causes a reentering nose cone to get hot
2. Predicting that the blunt-nosed capsule strikes the atmosphere with the greater impact
3. Predicting (incorrectly) that the blunt-nosed capsule gets hotter upon reentry

Events 12–N Through 12–Q Explained in Context (Trajectories, Orbits, and Reentry)

Gravity and inertia are well-known forces on the surface of the earth. However, the forces are not limited to this planet but extend out into space.

Therefore, when a spaceship goes into space, it is constantly under the influence of those two forces. In addition, the force of friction becomes very important when the spaceship returns from a spaceflight and reenters the atmosphere of the earth.

TRAJECTORY. *Trajectory* means "path." It refers to the path of any object in flight, from a thrown baseball to a lunar spacecraft. In *Event 12–N. Baseball Throw* pupils can see the trajectory, or path, of a thrown object.

Each throw is affected by gravity (which pulls the ball to earth) and inertia (which keeps it going in a straight line). The two forces combine to form a curved path.

Even a rifle bullet is affected by gravity. Despite its speed, a shot fired parallel to the earth is pulled down to the ground. In fact, the bullet falls to the ground just as fast as one that is not fired but merely dropped.

The forces of gravity and inertia have to be calculated very carefully in spaceflight. Otherwise small errors will grow into huge misses in the great vastness of space.

The distances are so great that an error of only 1 or 2 kilometers in a 10,000 kilometer flight near earth expands to a miss of 100 kilometers in a flight to the moon. With the same degree of accuracy, the spacecraft would miss Venus or Mars by tens of *thousands* of kilometers.

To look at it another way, a spaceship needs to reach a speed of 41,600 kilometers per hour in order to reach Venus. If the takeoff speed is off by only 1 kilometer, the ship would miss its target by 40,000 kilometers.

ORBITS. Imagine placing a large cannon on a mountaintop 100 kilometers high. A cannonball fired level with the ground would be pulled to earth by the force of gravity.

If the cannon fires the ball at one speed, the ball takes the path identified as A in Fig. 12–13. If the cannon fires the ball at greater speed, the ball travels farther before it is pulled to earth by gravity (shown as path B).

If the cannon shoots the ball with enough force, the ball's inertia (tendency to go straight) is great enough to balance gravity (the force pulling it to earth). At that point the cannonball will be in *orbit*, shown as path C. Finally, a still greater speed will send the ball out into space away from the earth, shown as path D.

The minimum speed needed to get into orbit is 28,800 kilometers per hour. The lowest practical orbit is at about 150 kilometers above the earth. Orbits lower than 150 kilometers begin to run into the thin air of the upper atmosphere, which drags satellites down to earth.

Consider the problem posed in *Event 12–O. High and Low Orbits*. Which satellite will travel faster, the one in a high orbit or the one in the low orbit? The most common response by students is to claim that there is not enough information available to make a decision.

Yet, the information is there. Assuming a circular orbit, the speed of a satellite depends on its height above the earth. In any orbit the satellite is affected by gravity and inertia. So, if the orbit is a circle (instead of an oval), the speed must be just great enough to overcome the gravity. To put it another way, gravity pulls the satellite in, whereas inertia pushes the satellite out.

The force of gravity is greater as you get closer to the earth. Thus, a satellite *must* go faster to offset that gravity. As stated earlier, a satellite 150 kilometers from the earth must go 28,800 kilometers per hour to stay in orbit. On the other hand, the moon, 384,000 kilometers from the earth goes at only 3,500 kilometers per hour to stay in orbit. Thus, in answer to the problem in Event 12–O, satellite B travels faster than satellite A.

REENTRY. It is quite spectacular to send astronauts to the moon. Yet, as amazing as such a trip is, the mission is an obvious failure if the capsule does not return safely to earth. The return to earth, to reenter the earth's atmosphere, is a dangerous part of the trip.

One of the problems of reentry is the tremendous heat that is generated when the capsule returns to the earth's atmosphere. Much of that heat is caused by friction. Pupils can experience how friction forms heat by doing *Event 12–P. Fast Friction*. By rubbing your hands together firmly and quickly, you can feel the heat that is generated. The event also shows how one form of energy (muscular) is changed into another form of energy (heat).

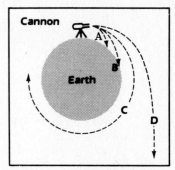

Fig. 12–13. **The imaginary cannon fires cannonballs at ever-increasing speeds, finally getting them into orbit.**

The amount of heat produced by a returning satellite is enormous. There is enough energy available to vaporize the capsule many times over. Therefore, engineers have found designs that overcome the heat problems.

The most obvious design that is used to avoid the extreme heat problem is shown in *Event 12–Q. Reentry Capsules*. One may think that the sharp-nosed capsule is preferred to the blunt-nosed capsule but . . . not so! The sharp nose slides through the air too easily, allowing the air to rub the sides of the capsule. The rubbing produces friction, and the friction produces heat. The sharp-nosed capsule would burn up too easily.

The blunt nose, however, hits the air and forms a shock wave. The shock wave extends out beyond the sides of the capsule and dumps off most of the heat that is formed upon reentry. The blunt-nosed capsule was the form used almost exclusively in all of our early spaceflights.

ASTRONAUTS IN SPACE (EVENT 12–R)

Discrepant Event and Student Investigations

Event 12–R. Soft-Drink Gases. Hold a bottle of a clear carbonated soft drink (one that fizzes when opened and poured). Look carefully when removing the cap. You should see bubbles form in the liquid.

If you get very poor results, shake the bottle gently once or twice after opening, not before. (*Caution:* It is dangerous to shake a closed bottle of pop because the pressure could cause it to explode.) How is the soft drink similar to an astronaut in space?

Pupil Investigations (may include the following processes):
1. Observing the bubbles rise to the top when the cap is removed
2. Observing that the bubbles seem to appear out of nowhere
3. Comparing the formation of the bubbles in the soft drink to some potential problems in the blood of the astronauts

Event 12–R Explained in Context (Astronauts in Space)

On earth you have an environment that is friendly to human life. In space the surroundings are hazardous to life. What are the hazards? There are two kinds: (1) danger from things that *are* there and (2) danger from things that are *not* there. For example, dangers that are there include radiation and meteors. Things that are not there are oxygen and air pressure, both vital for life.

Let us take a trip out into space. On the earth we have plenty of oxygen and air pressure. As we go up into the sky, we begin to lose both items. By the time we are 6000 meters high, there is so little oxygen that most people will lose consciousness.

At 9000 meters we run out of air pressure. Why is that a problem? Because the blood and body fluids begin to fill with bubbles from dissolved gases. It is similar to what happens in a bottle of pop when it is opened. See *Event 12–R. Soft-Drink Gases.* Gases that are dissolved in the liquid suddenly form visible bubbles when the pressure is lowered (by removing the cap).

When going from sea level up to 9000 meters, air pressure decreases quickly; and we face the same condition inside our bodies that occurs in the bottle of pop. Undersea divers who come to the surface too fast have the same problem. That condition is called "the bends."

The hazards of low pressure become still greater as the flight continues to go higher. At 19,000 meters the pressure is so low that body fluids begin to boil. The boiling point of water actually drops to 37 degrees Celsius, or normal body temperature.

Naturally, astronauts are protected from the absence of pressure. First of all, the capsules are usually pressurized. Second, their space suits are also pressurized. That is, the suits are filled with air, somewhat like air is pumped into a football or basketball to give it more pressure (but, of course, not that much).

By the time a spacecraft reaches a height of 150 kilometers, it faces danger from meteors and radiation. That is, the spacecraft might collide with meteors or be burned by excess radiation. However, these dangers are far less severe than was believed when the space age began. In fact, these dangers have proved to be so rare that today they are hardly ever mentioned.

13

Teaching Children about the Sun, Moon, and Stars

CONCEPTS OF NUMBER, SIZE, AND DISTANCE (EVENTS 13–A THROUGH 13–D)

Discrepant Events and Pupil Investigations

Event 13–A. Concept of Number. What is wrong with the following statement? "The observatory has finally completed a new star atlas that lists all the stars in the heavens."

Pupil Investigations (may include the following processes):
1. Forming a theory (incorrectly) that the stars have all been counted and listed
2. Inferring (incorrectly) that the number of stars can be counted
3. Generalizing that the number of stars is so great that they will never all be counted or listed

Event 13–B. Concept of Size. Draw a 12-millimeter circle on the chalkboard. Assuming that the circle represents the size of the earth, how large is the moon on that same scale? How large is the sun on that same scale?

Pupil Investigations (may include the following processes):
1. Estimating that the moon is smaller than the earth
2. Estimating that the sun is larger than the earth
3. Computing the correct ratio using the same scale that was used to draw the earth
4. Applying the ratio to the moon and sun

Event 13–C. Concept of Distance. Draw a 28-centimeter circle on the chalkboard to represent the sun. Based on that scale, how far away is the earth? Remember, for the moment, that we are not concerned with the *size* of the earth at this time but only *how far away* it is. On the same scale, how far is the moon from the earth?

Pupil Investigations (may include the following processes):
1. Estimating the scale distance between the sun and earth
2. Estimating the scale distance between the moon and earth
3. Computing the scale distances

Event 13–D. Playground Solar System. Combine the concepts of size and distance in a scale model of the solar system. An area larger than a football field is needed to do this exercise. Mark out the placement of planets on a playground, athletic field, or park. Use modeling clay to make the planets and a volley ball for the sun. Use a scale of 20 centimeters equals 1 million kilometers, and make a scale model of the solar system.

Pupil Investigations (may include the following processes):
1. Computing the scale distances from the sun to the planets
2. Computing the scale sizes of the planets
3. Applying the scale of size and distance to include our Milky Way galaxy

Events 13–A Through 13–D Explained in Context (Concepts of Number, Size, and Distance)

OUR EXPANDING NEIGHBORHOOD. In ancient times a neighbor was someone who was within easy walking distance. Today a neighbor is someone who is within easy rocket distance.

When our country was first settled, people were bound closely to their neighborhood. They seldom traveled more than a day's horseback ride from their homes. Going beyond their neighborhood was a difficult task.

As transportation improved, the distances that were traveled became greater. With the invention of cars and trains, the size of the "neighborhood" increased greatly. A day's travel covered a much greater area and was a far more comfortable journey than previously.

With the invention of the airplane, the "neighborhood" expanded again. Suddenly, whole countries and continents could be reached in a single day.

The final expansion of our neighborhood came with the space age. As a result of the gains in transportation, our concept of neighborhood has expanded to include the moon and planets and maybe someday even the stars.

CHANGING CONCEPT OF NUMBER. Look into the heavens on a clear night. How many stars can you see? How many stars are there? Have they all been counted yet?

The questions call attention to a concept of number that has new meaning in the study of stars. There are so many stars that they will never all be counted and listed. The statement in *Event 13–A. Concept of Number* is obviously false.

There are so many stars that the human mind cannot possibly comprehend the number. Perhaps a concept of number can be reached by pointing out that there are more stars in the universe than there are grains of sand on all the seashores of all the world.

Think about it the next time you are at the seashore. Look at all the sand. Then pick up a single grain and put it in the palm of your hand. That grain, according to our concept of number, represents our entire solar system of sun, planets, and moons. Would that grain of sand be missed if it were lost? So, be careful. Don't lose our solar system.

Another way to think about the concept of number is to consider the possibility of another planet, somewhere in the universe, with conditions favorable for life as we know it. Does another such planet exist? If we consider only mathematical possibilities, the answer is almost surely yes.

There are so many stars that even if only one star in a million had a set of planets, and if only one planet in a million of those sets had a planet like ours, then there would still be billions upon billions of planets with conditions just like ours.

CHANGING CONCEPT OF SIZE. How big are the planets, sun, moon, and stars? Their sizes vary so much that it is difficult for a person to comprehend their sizes by merely reading the figures in kilometers. Scale drawings give us a better idea of their sizes.

People who lived in ancient times could only guess at the sizes. When they gazed into the sky, they estimated the sun and moon were about the same size because they "looked" the same size. Obviously, the earth appeared gigantic in comparison to the sun and moon. It is easy to see why they thought that the earth was the center of the universe.

As early as 500 B.C., however, some Greek astronomers began to believe that the sun and moon were not of equal size. They had noticed that from time to time a shadow covered (or eclipsed) the moon. They reasoned that the shadow was that of the earth. It showed that the earth was round—a shocking discovery!

In 270 B.C. Aristarchus shook the foundations of astronomy by declaring that the *sun*, not the earth, was the center of the solar system. He reached this conclusion by using his knowledge of mathematics and by following some remarkably simple logic.

First of all, it was easy to see that the moon was smaller than the earth. During an eclipse you could see the earth's shadow on the moon's surface. The shadow showed that the earth was much larger. As a result, it was easy to conclude that the moon was a satellite of the earth.

Yet the sun looked no larger than the moon, and it, too, seemed to circle the earth. How did Aristarchus decide that the sun was so large and that the earth was merely the sun's satellite?

This is what he did. On a day when the moon was in a *quarter-moon* phase he made careful measurements of the angles between the earth, moon, and sun. Fig. 13–1 shows what he saw.

He had no difficulty with the angles from the moon because he chose the quarter moon phase to do his measuring. During the quarter moon the angle between lines MS and ME is exactly 90 degrees.

He had no difficulty in measuring the angles between EM and ES either because those lines originated on earth. To his astonishment that angle came to 90 degrees also!

All Aristarchus had to do was add together the angles to complete a triangle. Remember that the three angles of a triangle equal 180 degrees. He was amazed to find that he already had 180 degrees using only *two* of the three angles. Thus, according to his figure, there were no degrees left when figuring the third angle from the sun. In other words, a ray of sunlight reaching the moon was parallel to a ray of sunlight reaching the earth.

Those results could only mean that the sun is an incredible distance away.

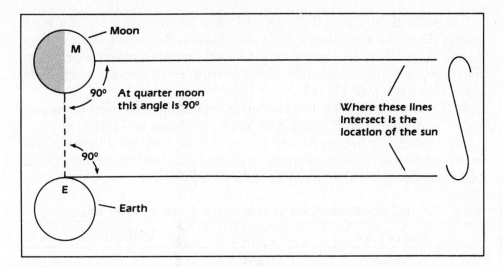

Fig. 13–1. **An early Greek astronomer, Aristarchus, found that the sun was a great distance from the earth by performing the observations as shown.**

And if the sun is that far away and still looks as large as the moon, it must actually be far bigger. In fact, it was easy for Aristarchus to infer that the sun was hundreds of times larger than the earth.

If the sun was so much larger than the earth, it was logical to conclude that the earth was a mere satellite and that the sun was the center of our solar system.

Despite the published work by Aristarchus, it was almost 2000 years before the sun-centered idea was widely accepted. In fact, it was not until the invention of the telescope in the early 1600s that the scientific world finally accepted the seemingly incredible facts.

Today the sun-centered solar system is universally accepted by all educated people. However, there are still some mistaken notions about size and distance. These ideas can be clarified by performing *Event 13–B. Concept of Size.* Using the scale of 12 millimeters to represent the size of the earth, the moon is only 4 millimeters in diameter. The sun, however, is gigantic. It is 1.382 meters in diameter. In fact, only a part of it will fit on a chalkboard or bulletin board.

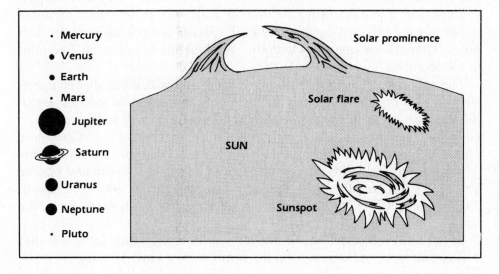

Fig. 13–2. **The sizes of the sun and solar system are drawn to scale. The distances between them are not shown because they would go far beyond the pages of a book.**

The scale of the sun and planets can make an interesting bulletin board display. Draw the sun, using a string and chalk on the surface of the bulletin board. Then fill the area inside the circle with red construction paper. Place the planets and our moon on the bulletin board, going over the image of the sun if necessary. (See Fig. 13–2.)

In that way pupils will gain an accurate impression of the sizes of the sun, moon, and planets. The scale for the display is shown in Table 13–1.

After impressing the pupils with the sun's huge size, see if they can gain an idea of the vast distances of space. In the bulletin board model there should be no attempt at showing distances; indicate only size.

Table 13–1. **Bulletin Board Solar System (Scale: 1 mm = 1,000 km)**

Heavenly Body	Size (km)	Scale on Board (mm)
Mercury	5,000	5
Venus	12,300	12
Earth	12,600	12
Mars	6,700	7
Jupiter	138,700	139
Saturn	114,600	115
Uranus	51,200	51
Neptune	49,600	50
Pluto	5,800	6
Sun	1,382,400	1,382
Moon	4,000	4

NOTE: Most educators recommend the use of metric figures. In fact, many states mandate it. However, teachers often wish to have comparisons given in inches: Mercury: $\frac{3}{16}$, Venus: $\frac{1}{2}$, Earth: $\frac{1}{2}$, Mars: $\frac{1}{4}$, Jupiter: $5\frac{1}{2}$, Saturn: $4\frac{1}{2}$, Uranus: 2, Neptune: 2, Pluto: $\frac{1}{4}$, Sun: 54, Moon: $\frac{1}{8}$.

CHANGING CONCEPT OF DISTANCE. Now let us clarify the concept of distance. Most people, young and old, have false impressions of distances in space. Part of the reason is that it is impossible to show the correct scale of both size and distance on the pages of a book, or even on the bulletin board. Yet in many books those scales are shown anyway. Unfortunately, they are incorrect!

Sometimes a footnote will state that the scale used to determine distances is different from the scale used for sizes. Pupils are not helped much by such notes. They are too impressed with the visual picture to notice the fine print in the footnotes.

The only scale that can be shown accurately in books is one that compares sizes only, or one that compares distances only. If the scale is reduced so that the distances fit on the page, the planets become too small to be seen.

To find out what impressions the pupils have, do *Event 13–C. Concept of Distance*. Sometimes the event can be made more interesting by drawing the 12-centimeter circle (the sun) on one side of a long chalkboard and placing several "x's" on the board with the last x being on the far side of the board. Ask the pupils which x represents the point where the earth would be on the scale.

Most pupils will select one of the "x's" on the chalkboard. Little will they realize that none of the points on the board is even close to being accurate. The accurate distance is 30 meters away. Most pupils will be astounded!

When the concepts of size and distance have been handled separately, it is time to put the two together. Since a page of a book is obviously too small to show both size and distance, what should be used? Surprisingly, even the classroom is too small to do the job. Use an athletic field, park, or long open area on the school grounds and do *Event 13–D. Playground Solar System.*

If you use a scale that makes the planets large enough to be seen, you will need a large outdoor area just to fit in the inner planets of the solar system. A convenient scale is 1 mm = 5,000 km (or, 1 m = 5,000,000 km). The sizes using that scale are given in Table 13–2.

Table 13–2. **Distances from the Sun**

Planet	Scale Size (mm)	Actual Distance (km)	Scale Distance (m)
Mercury	1	58,000	11.6
Venus	2.5	107,000	21.4
Earth	2.5	149,000	29.8
Mars	1	227,000	45.4
Jupiter	28	774,000	154.8
Saturn	23	1,419,000	283.8
Uranus	10	2,856,000	571.2
Neptune	10	4,475,000	895.0
Pluto	1	5,880,000	1,176.0
Sun	276		

Note: The comparable scale sizes (in inches) and distances (in feet) are Mercury: $\frac{1}{32}''$ and 39′, Venus: $\frac{1}{16}''$ and 70′, Earth: $\frac{1}{16}''$ and 98′, Mars: $\frac{1}{32}''$ and 149′, Jupiter: $1\frac{1}{8}''$ and 508′, Saturn: $\frac{7}{8}''$ and 931′, Uranus: $\frac{3}{8}''$ and 1,874′, Neptune: $\frac{3}{8}''$ and 2,936′, Pluto: $\frac{1}{32}''$ and 3,868′, Sun: 11″.

Even the playground scale is limited. It is unlikely that many playgrounds will be large enough to hold more than the first four planets. However, if you have room, build the scale out to Jupiter, 154.8 meters from the sun. The sun can be cut from construction paper and taped to a post or tree.

While standing at the outermost planet that you can fit on the playground, look back at the "sun." See how small it looks from way out there. Ask the pupils if they can understand why the outer planets are cold. Also, look at the earth, a tiny ball only 2.5 millimeters in size and see all the space between the planets.

Then place the earth's moon on the scale at its proper distance from the earth. On that scale the moon is only 1 millimeter ($\frac{1}{32}$ inch) in size and is located only 48 millimeters (1-$\frac{7}{8}$ inches) away. Thus, the earth with its moon will fit on the palm of your hand. Compare a space trip to Jupiter with a trip to the moon.

The distances are so astounding that it is worth emphasizing them in another way. Calculate the distances by using a measuring stick of time. Assume that you had a spaceship that could travel at a constant speed of 40,000 kilometers per hour. At that speed, how long will it take to make the following trips: (1) around the earth, (2) to the moon, (3) to the sun, and (4) to the nearest star (other than our sun)? The figures are given in Table 13–3.

Table 13–3. **Travel Times in Space**

Vehicle	Around Earth	To Moon	To Sun	To Nearest Star
Jet plane	40 h	16 days	17 yr	—
Rocket ship	1 h	9 h 36 min	$\frac{1}{2}$ yr	117,000 yr

Still another way to measure the vast distances of space is to use weight as a measuring stick. Suppose that a single strand of a spider's web, long enough to go around the earth, weighed only 1 gram. According to that scale, a length needed to reach the moon would weigh about 10 grams; to the sun, 3,720 grams (or 3.72 kilograms); and a length to the nearest star, an unbelievable 1,406,400 kilograms!

The human mind cannot fully grasp the sizes and distances in the solar system and universe. However, by using the scale models suggested in this section, pupils can begin to gain a truer impression of what space is like.

THE EARTH AND MOON (EVENTS 13–E THROUGH 13–H)

Discrepant Events and Pupil Investigations

Event 13–E. The Flat Earth. Common sense tells us that the earth is flat. There are hills and valleys, of course, but other than that the land certainly *looks* flat. Yet we know that the earth is really round. What evidence do we have to show that the earth is round when common sense tells us it is flat?

Pupil Investigations (may include the following processes):
1. Observing the shadow of the earth on the moon during an eclipse
2. Observing that televised pictures from space show that the earth is round
3. Inferring a round earth from observations of ships disappearing from view over the horizon

Event 13–F. Fingertip on the Globe. Blindfold a pupil and ask him or her to extend a finger. Guide the fingertip to touch a globe. (The student should not be told what the object is.) Ask the student to describe the object of which he or she is touching just a single spot.

Pupil Investigations (may include the following processes):
1. Sensing that the object is hard and smooth
2. Sensing (incorrectly) that the object is flat
3. Comparing the spot on the globe with a similar "spot" on the earth

Event 13–G. Earth-Moon Distance. This event works well at night with a full moon. However, it can also be done during the school day when the moon is in its first or third quarter. It will surprise many pupils to realize that even in the daytime the moon is often clearly visible.

Attach two strips of tape 1 centimeter apart on a window. Look between the tapes at the moon. If you place your eye between the tapes and look out, you have a full view. The tapes will not be in the way. However, as soon as you back away slightly, the space between the tapes presents a narrower and narrower view.

Back away until the moon just fills the space between the tapes. Mark the spot and measure the distance from the tape to the eye. If you know that the moon is 3500 kilometers in diameter, determine the distance to the moon. (See Fig. 13–3.)

Fig. 13–3. **Sight the moon so that it fits between two pieces of tape placed 1 centimeter apart. Measure the distance from the tape to your eye. If the moon is 3500 kilometers across, how far is it away?**

Pupil Investigations (may include the following processes):
1. Measuring the distance from the tape to the eye as 110 centimeters
2. Comparing the distance to the tape with the distance to the moon.
3. Comparing the distance between the tape with the size of the moon.
4. Concluding that the distance to the moon is 110 times its width

Event 13–H. Phases of the Moon. Demonstrate the phases of the moon as they appear to an observer on earth, and also as viewed from two points in space. Set up a projector or other strong light source in the back of the classroom as shown in Fig. 13–4. Observations are to be made at points A, B, and C. Hang a basketball from a support in positions 1, 2, 3, and 4 around point B. Determine the phases of the moon from each point.

Pupil Investigations (may include the following processes):
1. Observing that the phases of the moon change when viewed from point B
2. Inferring that point B represents the view from earth
3. Observing that the phases do not change when viewed from points A and C
4. Discovering the correct phases of the moon as determined by the moon's path around the earth

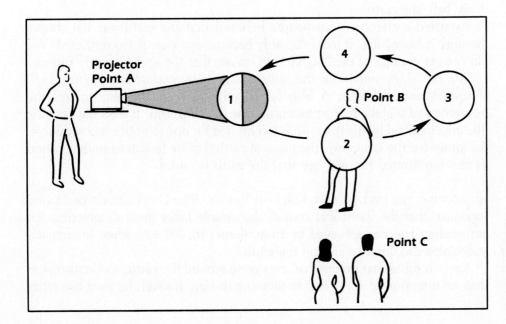

Fig. 13–4. **Gain an idea of the phases of the moon by performing the activity with a basketball and a projector. Point B is the earth and shows the moon at position 1 in the *new moon* phase.**

Events 13–E Through 13–H Explained in Context (The Earth and Moon)

Perhaps one of the most obvious discrepant events that confronted the early astronomers occurred when they observed an eclipse of the moon. They could see that the earth's shadow on the moon was slightly rounded. Could it be that the earth was actually round?

Although people had seen the eclipses for thousands of years, it was not until about 500 B.C. that some Greek astronomers realized that the shadow on the moon was actually cast by the earth. That discovery came as a great surprise because they thought the earth was flat.

Today the concept of a round earth is not surprising. Everyone knows that the earth is round. Nevertheless, when suddenly confronted with the question posed in *Event 13–E. The Flat Earth,* pupils are often at a loss to give any evidence for their beliefs.

The problem for early astronomers was much greater than for pupils. There was no equipment available in those ancient times for viewing or calculations. Everything had to be based on simple observations.

As soon as astronomers began to think in terms of a round earth, evidence became easier to find. For example, in making long journeys (of 500 kilometers or so) in northerly or southerly directions, there were unexplained changes in the star patterns in the sky.

Those changes were explained by the round earth theory. As one traveled south, some stars would slowly become visible over the southern horizon. Going north, the stars would rise in the northern sky and dip below the horizon in the south. If the earth were flat, the same stars would always be visible.

Another indication that the earth is round is the fact that ships seem to sink slowly below the horizon as they move away from the observer. The appearance of sinking is, in reality, just the ship going over the horizon of a huge ball (the earth).

As stated earlier, ancient people believed that the earth was flat simply because it *looked* flat. It looks flat only because our view is too restricted. We do not get enough of the "big picture" to see that the earth is really round.

We can show somewhat the same situation by performing *Event 13–F. Fingertip on the Globe.* A blindfolded pupil will not be able to feel the roundness of a globe by just touching it with a fingertip. It feels flat because the area touched by the fingertip is too limited for one to notice its roundness. In somewhat the same way, the piece of earth that we look at from the ground is also too limited for us to see that the earth is round.

MEASURING THE DISTANCE AROUND THE EARTH. After Greek astronomers found evidence that the earth was round, they made other great discoveries. An astounding feat was achieved by Eratosthenes in 200 B.C. when he actually calculated the distance around the earth.

Keep in mind that no one had ever gone around the earth, so Eratosthenes had no intention of doing that to measure its size. Instead, he used two cities in Egypt, Syene and Alexandria, as points in a gigantic triangle. Those cities were known to be 789 kilometers apart.

He also knew that at Syene a festival was held every year on the one day when the sun's light reached the bottom of a well 12 meters deep. At noon of that day upright buildings and posts cast no shadows at all. The sun was directly overhead.

In Alexandria, however, Eratosthenes noticed that at that same time (high noon) all objects *did* cast shadows (though small). What a surprise! Why were there small shadows at Alexandria but none at Syene? Why was the sun directly overhead at Syene but not at Alexandria? He realized that this was evidence that the earth was round.

Eratosthenes also realized that he had found a way to measure the size of the earth. How? By just completing the circle. The shadows showed that at high noon in Alexandria the sun was about 7 degrees off from being directly above. Remember that at that time the sun was directly above in Syene. Since a full circle is 360 degrees, the 7 degrees amounted to about one-fiftieth of a circle. (See Fig. 13–5.)

Thus, if the distance between Alexandria and Syene was about one-fiftieth of the distance around the earth, all that he needed to do was multiply by 50 the 789 kilometers between Alexandria and Syene. Eratosthenes obtained a figure of 39,440 kilometers—remarkably close to the 39,728 kilometers used today. Of course, the figure is often rounded to 40,000 kilometers.

By 150 B.C. Greek astronomers had made rough calculations of the distance from the earth to the moon. We can do the same by performing *Event 13– G. Earth-Moon Distance*.

Sight the moon through the 1-centimeter space between the tapes. Move back until the moon just fills the opening. The distance from the tapes to your eye should be about 110 centimeters. This means that the distance to the moon is 110 times greater than the moon's diameter. As long as the diameter is given (3,500 kilometers), it is easy to calculate the distance. Multiply 3,500 by 110 to get 385,000 kilometers—very close to the actual distance to the moon.

ECLIPSES. From time to time the earth gets directly between the sun and the moon. When it does, it blocks the sun's light to the moon. That is called a *lunar eclipse*.

An eclipse does not occur every time the moon makes a revolution around the earth. Most of the time the earth or moon are slightly off line so no eclipse occurs.

On rarer occasions the moon will get directly between the sun and the earth, causing an eclipse of the sun, called a *solar eclipse*. A solar eclipse is much less likely to occur than a lunar eclipse. Why? Because the moon is much smaller than the earth. As a result, the moon's shadow will cover only a small part of the earth.

During a solar eclipse the moon's shadow on the earth is often no more than 100 kilometers wide. On the other hand, in a lunar eclipse, the earth's shadow will often cover the entire surface of the moon.

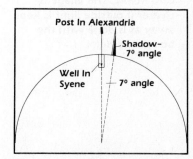

Fig. 13–5. **Eratosthenes saw that shadows at Syene and Alexandria differed by 7 degrees, or one-fiftieth of a circle. He multiplied the distance between the cities by 50 to obtain his estimate for the distance around the earth.**

Fig. 13–6. **A pinhole focuses the image of the sun on a card below. The image is clearer if outside light is kept away as is done with the box at the right.**

Since a solar eclipse is so rare, people who are in the viewing path will naturally want to observe it closely. Unfortunately, the event is associated with tragedy. Thousands of people damage their eyes when there is a solar eclipse. How? They look at the sun and are partially blinded. The sun can cause partial blindness very quickly.

You should never look directly at a solar eclipse. Even with the use of filters such as sunglasses, smoked glass, and colored glass, direct observation is very dangerous. In fact, even welders' glasses do not provide enough protection. The only safe way is to view the sun's *reflected image*.

The reflected image can easily be seen by using a sheet of cardboard or piece of foil with a pinhole in it. The pinhole acts as a lens and focuses the sun on a second sheet of cardboard held below the first. You view the image on the second sheet, not the sun itself.

If you wish to make a more sophisticated viewer, cut out the side of a box and use it as a viewing stage as shown in Fig. 13–6.

PHASES OF THE MOON. The moon is our most impressive heavenly body next to the sun itself. All pupils have seen the moon many times. Yet it is often surprising how little they know about how the *phases of the moon* are formed. They generally know that the moon changes its shape—that sometimes it is full, and sometimes half, and sometimes just a sliver—but they seldom understand how the phases are formed.

Event 13–H. Phases of the Moon is helpful in finding out what the phases are and how they are formed. Refer back to Fig. 13–4 to see how the event is set up. It is quickly apparent that when viewed from points A and C, no phases are visible at all. This means that the shadow on the moon does not change as the moon goes around point B.

Only the viewer at point B sees the changes. Point B represents how the moon appears when viewed from the surface of the earth. When the moon is at position 1, the viewer is looking toward the projector (the sun). (*Caution:* Be careful not to look directly into the projector's light.)

Anytime the moon is that near to the sun in the sky the moon is invisible. The blinding light of the sun makes it impossible to see the moon. That phase of the moon is called *new moon*.

Position 2 is the moon's location 7 days after the new moon. This phase is called *first quarter*. When looking at the basketball, only the right side is lit up, and it looks somewhat like the capital letter D. During the first quarter the moon is at right angles to the sun. Thus, at 6 P.M., for example, the sun is at the horizon and the moon is at 12 o'clock high.

Moving the moon to position 3 produces a *full moon*. The viewer must be careful not to block the light from the projector (causing an eclipse). At any rate, the sun is at the viewer's back. Thus, a full moon rises in the east when the sun sets in the west.

Finally, move the moon to position 4 to produce a *last quarter*. The lit part of the moon looks like a filled-in letter C. At this time the sun and moon are again at right angles to each other.

It takes 7 days to go from one position to another. The total trip of the moon around the earth takes 28 days. The 28 days were, at one time, called a "moonth." Today the length has been adjusted by a few days, and the period is now known as a "month."

Do you remember the order in which the moon phases appear? Fortunately, the moon spells out a word to help you. If the moon cannot be seen, it is in new moon; but in each of the other three positions the moon formed a letter of the alphabet.

The moon looks like a *D* in first quarter, an *O* at full moon, and a filled-in *C* in the last quarter. Put them together and the moon spells *DOC*, to show the order in which the phases appear.

WHY DO WE HAVE SEASONS? The subject of the seasons of the year is sometimes presented in a unit on the sun, moon, and stars. If you choose to do so, please refer back to the last section of Chapter 10 where it is presented.

14

Teaching Children about the Earth (Geology)

THE STRUCTURE OF THE EARTH

Fig. 14–1. **A cross section of the earth shows the mantle, core, and crust. At the scale shown, the crust is no thicker than the ink on the outer line.**

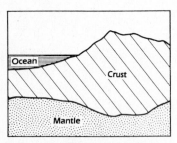

Fig. 14–2. **The earth's crust "floats" on the mantle and is thinnest under the ocean.**

To understand the structure of the earth, we should begin with its formation. Most authorities agree that the earth was at one time a huge ball of molten rock. A mass as large as the earth and hot enough to be molten rock was probably a churning, bubbling cauldron. Nevertheless, the lighter matter tended to float to the top and the heavier matter tended to settle downward.

After the rock cooled and hardened, the different rock densities were evident even on the crust of the earth. The rocks under the oceans are composed mostly of basalt, a heavy rock; the great landmasses and mountains are made mostly of granite, a relatively light rock.

Today the planet is still mostly molten or plastic. Only the crust is truly solid. The solid crust is from 8 to 64 kilometers in thickness. Under the crust is the *mantle*, a semisolid zone about 2900 kilometers thick. Finally, the center core is mostly molten and is about 3500 kilometers in diameter. The layers of the earth are shown in Fig. 14–1.

The crust is so thick that no one has ever gone below it, yet when compared to the rest of the earth, it is extremely thin. In comparison, the crust is thinner than the skin of a peach.

The crust "floats" on the mantle and is not of uniform thickness. It is thickest on landmasses and thinnest under oceans. In that respect it is like ice floating on water. A larger chunk of ice will sink deeper in water than a small chunk. Likewise, a large landmass extends deeper into the mantle than the thin ocean beds. (See Fig. 14–2.)

The deeper you go into the earth, the hotter it gets. The temperature increase is noticeable even in deep mines and oil wells. For example, a mine that is 1800 meters deep is about 55 Celsius degrees hotter than a mine near the surface. (The temperature increases about 1 degree Celsius every 33 meters.)

How do we know so much about the mantle and the core if we have never been there? Scientists have been able to make inferences by conducting experiments, making certain observations, and using logic.

For example, the boundary line between the crust and the mantle was detected by the bending of sound waves. Scientists produced the sound waves by setting off explosions on the surface. Sound travels through the solid crust at a different speed than through the somewhat plastic mantle. In addition, sound is refracted (or bent) when it enters the mantle at an angle. In fact, sound is bent somewhat like light is refracted when it goes from one medium into another. By studying the reflected echoes, scientists can tell how deep the various layers are.

We have already noted that the temperature increases as we go deeper into the earth. It is simple logic to suggest that if you keep on going deeper, the earth will keep on getting hotter. Finally, we know that pressure produces heat. The weight of the entire earth is concentrated in its core, making it very hot indeed.

Scientists have also studied earthquake shock waves. An earthquake sends out several types of waves. The first wave is called a *primary wave*. It is a push-pull wave (longitudinal wave)—a kind of wave that travels through solids, liquids, and gases. The primary wave goes through the mantle and liquid core of the earth to be detected all over the earth.

Another wave is a side-to-side, snakelike wave (called the *transverse wave*), which can travel only through solids, not liquids. As a result, the transverse wave does not go through the liquid core and cannot be detected in those parts of the earth that are blocked by the core. (See Fig. 14–3.)

By studying the places of the earth that do not receive the transverse wave of an earthquake, geologists have found that the liquid core is about 3500 kilometers in diameter.

Fig. 14–3. **The push-pull earthquake waves go through solids and liquids and can be detected in all parts of the earth. The snakelike waves of an earthquake do not go through the earth's liquid core. Thus, the part of the earth between A and B does not receive these waves.**

Discrepant Events and Pupil Investigations

Event 14–A. Geological Maps of Your Area. Obtain geological survey maps and/or aerial photos of your area. (They may be purchased from the Washington Distribution Section, U.S. Geological Survey, 1200 South Eads Street, Arlington, VA 22202—if you live east of the Mississippi River—or from the Geological Survey Distribution Section, Federal Center, Denver, CO 80225— for those living west of the Mississippi River.)

If you can get maps with scales of 1:24,000 to 1:63,000, it may be possible to take a walking or riding tour of your area and compare the maps with the actual surface features of the land.

Pupil Investigations (may include the following processes):
1. Discovering that contours on the map show land shapes and elevations
2. Analyzing the colors on the maps to distinguish among land, water, and other surface features of the earth
3. Interpreting the map and comparing it to on-the-spot inspections of the surface features

Event 14–B. Folded Mountains. Flatten out several layers of clay of different colors. Place these layers, one on top of another, on a board and put two boards on each end of the clay. Press inward on the two end boards. What happens to the layers of clay? How does this activity show us something of the structure of the earth? (Look ahead to Fig. 14–5 if necessary.)

SURFACE FEATURES OF THE EARTH (EVENTS 14–A, 14–B, AND 14–C)

Pupil Investigations (may include the following processes):
1. Observing that the pressure from the sides causes the layers of clay to form folds
2. Comparing the model to the formation of folded mountains
3. Generalizing that many landforms are caused by pressures that formed the folded mountains

Event 14–C. Isostatic Adjustment. Tie several strings from a thick wooden block to a thin wooden block. Arrange them so that about 15 or 20 centimeters separate the two. Float the blocks in a container of water.

Pour sand on the thick block so that it barely floats. Carefully observe the positions of the blocks in the water. (See Fig. 14–4.) Now take some of the sand from the thick block and place it on the thin block. What do you observe?

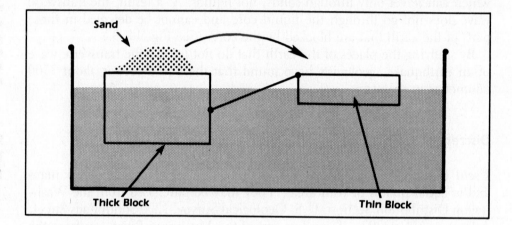

Fig. 14–4. **As the sand is transferred, the thick block rises and the thin block sinks. Thus, the elevations do not change much. This illustrates isostatic pressure.**

Pupil Investigations (may include the following processes):
1. Observing that the thick block settled deeper into the water when sand was added to it
2. Measuring the height above the water before and after some sand was removed
3. Discovering that the height above the water did not change much when sand was added or removed
4. Comparing the event to isostatic adjustment in mountains

Events 14–A, 14–B, and 14–C Explained in Context (Surface Features of the Earth)

Taking long trips by car or flying over expanses of land by air makes one aware of many surface features of the earth. Most land surfaces are topped with soils of various types, although bedrock is sometimes exposed in mountainous areas.

Students in the upper grades can become more familiar with their local surface features if they study geological survey maps as suggested in *Event 14–A. Geological Maps of Your Area.* Then the features on the maps can be identified by an on-the-spot tour.

By studying the maps, students will realize that a great deal of information can be placed on a flat surface. For example, the elevation of land is shown by contour lines. Certain surface features are identified by symbols, shadings, and lines called hachures.

Colors are also used on geological survey maps. Black is used to show boundary lines and the results of human effort such as roads and buildings. Blue is used for water features such as lakes, rivers, canals, and glaciers. Brown is used for land features. Red is used to emphasize built-up urban areas, boundary lines of public lands, and the importance of major roads.

Geological survey maps are usually printed in scales ranging from 1:24,000 (1 inch equals 2000 feet) to 1:1,000,000 (1 inch equals 16 miles). (Note that the dimensions are in inches and feet instead of metric units.)

How did the surface of the earth come to look as it does? Does it always stay the same? What are the forces acting on it? Actually, the surface is in a constant state of change. These changes are usually far too slow to be apparent to an observer during a lifetime, but over the span of geologic eras the changes are massive and constant.

Change is caused by both internal and external forces. The internal stresses are produced by the gradual shifting and possibly shrinking of the earth. These forces are very evident when volcanoes erupt or when strains deep below the surface are released as earthquakes.

In a more gradual way, the stresses and shifting crust form pressures that produce folded mountains. *Event 14–B. Folded Mountains* gives us an idea of how certain mountain ranges are formed. When pressed together, the layers are humped up in the middle.

If sufficient pressure is applied, the layers will finally break apart; and some layers will slide up over other layers. (See Fig. 14–5.) These features are called *block mountains.*

In addition to the mountains that are formed by the stresses of the earth, some mountains are formed by displacement. That is, light matter floats higher than heavy matter.

Displacement mountains do not tend to become smaller. Study *Event 14– C. Isostatic Adjustment.* Notice what happens to the level of the block when sand is taken from it: It floats higher in the water.

In a similar way, when erosion wears down a mountain, it becomes lighter and tends to rise up on the earth's crust. The net result is very little actual change in the height of the mountain.

Conversely, when sediment is washed down into the ocean, the extra weight will eventually cause the ocean floor to sink. In those places where *isostatic adjustment* is dominant the elevation of the land and the depth of the ocean tend to be more or less stable.

In addition to the internal forces discussed previously, other forces, external ones, are also important in causing changes on the surface of the earth. Glaciers are examples of a visible and dramatic force that causes changes.

Fig. 14–5. **When pushed together with movable blocks, layers of modeling clay become folded, representing folded mountains. If pushed still further, the layers may break and slide over one another to make block mountains.**

They carve out valleys and level off mountains in their relentless advance across the earth. Much of North America was covered by glaciers on four different occasions.

Other important external forces that cause changes in the surface of the earth are weathering and erosion. These forces will be discussed in greater detail later in this chapter.

ROCKS AND MINERALS (EVENTS 14–D THROUGH 14–G)

Discrepant Events and Pupil Investigations

Event 14–D. Classifying Rocks. Collect rocks from around your school and neighborhood. Place them in a big pile and ask pupils to identify and classify them into groups.

Pupil Investigations (may include the following processes):
1. Observing rocks for evidence of traits or characteristics
2. Classifying rocks according to the observed traits
3. Comparing the classification made by pupils with the official system used to identify rocks

Event 14–E. Crystal Formation. Dissolve as much alum in a container of hot water as you can. Keep adding alum and stirring until no more will dissolve. Then pour equal amounts of the solution into two beakers. Place one beaker in a bed of crushed ice and insulate the other. Observe the solutions from time to time during the next several hours.

Pupil Investigations (may include the following processes):
1. Observing that large crystals form in the insulated container and small crystals form in the cooled container
2. Inspecting the crystal formations with magnifying glasses
3. Inferring that the size of the crystals are related to the speed of cooling
4. Applying the results of the experiment to the size of crystals found in rock formations

Event 14–F. Layering Action of Water on Soils. Place enough sand, pebbles, loam, and clay into a jar to fill it half to three-fourths full. Add water to fill the jar and shake vigorously for a moment. Set the jar down and observe it for a few minutes.

Pupil Investigations (may include the following processes):
1. Observing that the pebbles and larger particles settle to the bottom of the jar quickly
2. Observing that the soil types settle according to the size of their grain structure (largest first)
3. Forming a theory that moving water causes some layering of soils and rocks

Event 14–G. Rock Sponges. Weigh pieces of rock such as granite, limestone, sandstone, and marble. Record the weights while dry and then soak them in water overnight. Weigh the rocks again the next day. What has happened to their weights?

Pupil Investigations (may include the following processes):
1. Measuring and recording the weight of the rocks before and after soaking
2. Discovering that some rocks are heavier after soaking but others do not change
3. Inferring that those rocks that gained weight have soaked up water

Events 14–D Through 14–G Explained in Context (Rocks and Minerals)

WHAT ARE ROCKS AND MINERALS? There are so many similarities between rocks and minerals that the terms are often used to mean the same thing. However, there are some differences that should be noted.

Rocks are fairly large units of the earth's crust. They may be of organic form (made from living matter such as coal) or of inorganic form (made of nonliving matter). Rocks may include consolidated or random matter and are usually composed of two or more minerals.

Minerals are different in that they are much more limited in definition. They contain specific elements, or combinations of elements, and are entirely inorganic in composition.

TYPES OF ROCKS. Rocks are divided into three groups: igneous, sedimentary, and metamorphic. There are many subgroups within each of the three general classes. Students should be given a chance to determine some traits and characteristics of rocks by doing *Event 14–D. Classifying Rocks.*

Let the students classify rocks according to traits that they think exist. It is unimportant at this stage of the lesson for the students to select the "correct" traits. Let them classify according to their best uninformed judgments.

After they have decided on their groupings, it is useful to bring in the official classification system for comparison. Students will want to know how closely they came to the system approved by geologists. After having tried it themselves, they can often see the value of a classification system.

CHARACTERISTICS OF ROCKS. There are eight major characteristics that are used to identify and classify rocks: (1) hardness, (2) color, (3) streak, (4) texture, (5) luster, (6) cleavage, (7) chemical, and (8) density.

Rocks vary greatly in *hardness*. Thus, it is a useful trait to help identify and classify rocks. An official scale that is used to measure the hardness of rocks is called *Moh's Scale of Hardness.*

The official scale is of limited value to the students until it is expanded to include examples that are more familiar to them. Table 14–1 shows Moh's scale, supplemented with many additional examples.

Table 14–1. **Scale of Hardness**

Scale Number	Scale Example	Other Examples	Explanations
1	Talc	Soft lead pencil	Greasy flakes of the substance will be left on fingers
1½		Ice near freezing	
2	Gypsum	Chalk Lead (metal)	Can be easily scratched with fingernail
2½		Fingernail	Can be scratched by silver and by copper wire
3	Calcite	Marble	Will scratch silver Can be scratched by copper penny Can be cut easily with knife
3½		Copper penny	
4	Flourite	Yellow brass	Can be easily scratched but not easily cut with knife
4½		Ordinary nail	
5	Apatite	Steel wool Nail file	Can be scratched with difficulty with a knife
5½		Knife blade Glass bottle	
6	Feldspar	Window glass	Can be scratched by a file but not a knife
6½		Steel file	
7	Quartz	Flint Sandpaper	Scratches glass easily
7½		Garnet paper	
8	Topaz		
8½		Emery paper	
9	Corundum	Silicon Carbide paper	
9½			
10½	Diamond		

A second factor used to classify rocks is *color*. The color observed is sometimes different from the color seen when the rock is rubbed against something. Thus, a third test, called the *streak test*, is used to check the color when rubbed.

Another test is called *texture* and refers to the size of the grains or crystals in the rock. The grains may be coarse, fine, or nonexistent.

Rocks can also be checked for *luster*—how the sample reflects light. If it reflects no light, it is dull. If it reflects light as a coin does, it has metallic luster; and if it reflects light as glass does, it has a glassy luster.

A sixth test is *cleavage*—the way a specimen breaks when struck by a hammer. A seventh check is the *chemical* test. For example, calcium carbonate (lime) will fizz and bubble if acid is dropped on it. If sulphur is present in a specimen, it will smell like rotten eggs.

Finally, students will find that rocks have different *densities*. Weigh each sample in the air and then while immersed in water. Record the difference in the weights. Divide the "air weight" by the *difference* to get a figure that is the *specific gravity* of the sample.

When the class has learned about the tests used to classify rocks, let them classify the same samples that they had worked with earlier. How did their first tries compare with the later attempts?

Igneous rocks are those that formed from molten matter. When a rock cools and hardens, it forms grains or crystals—the size of which depend on the speed of cooling. If the rock cools rapidly, it has little or no graininess. If it cools slowly, the crystals tend to be large.

The crystal formation can be seen by doing *Event 14–E. Crystal Formation.* As the containers cool, alum settles out of the solutions. If the alum cools slowly, the crystals are larger than when the alum cools quickly.

Sedimentary rocks are formed from materials carried by running water. Running water carries pebbles, rocks, and sand. As the matter is carried, pushed, and rolled, the sharp edges are ground down. As a result, most of the grains of sand, pebbles, and rocks are rounded.

The size of the grains that are deposited depends on the speed of the moving water. Fast currents move more matter than slow currents. When currents slow down, matter is dropped.

Since currents are often affected by seasonal changes, the deposited matter forms layers. Such layers are common to sedimentary rocks. To see how matter is deposited according to size and density, perform *Event 14–F. Layering Action of Water on Soils.*

Over eons of time hundreds and even thousands of meters of sediment may be deposited. The grains of these deposits become cemented by time and pressure to form rock. Examples of sedimentary rock are limestone, sandstone, and shale.

Metamorphic rock is really igneous or sedimentary rock that has been subjected to enough heat and pressure to alter its basic composition. For example, sandstone is changed to quartzite, limestone to marble, shale to slate, and bituminous coal to anthracite coal.

The location of rock layers is very important in finding water and petroleum. Sometimes water reservoirs are trapped far below the surface of the earth by a layer of impermeable rock above it. When the impermeable layer is pierced, the water below can rise to the surface.

Similarly, oil and gas deposits are often trapped deep below the surface in layers of *permeable* rock; that is rock that can "soak up" fluids. Such rock layers contain vast amounts of oil and gas. Perform *Event 14–G. Rock Sponges* to see how some stones can absorb water. Students should note that only the sedimentary rocks are capable of absorbing liquids.

WEATHERING AND EROSION (EVENTS 14–H THROUGH 14–L)

Discrepant Events and Pupil Investigations

Event 14–H. Dissolving Stones. Place a flat piece of limestone into a glass tray. Add a few drops of dilute hydrochloric acid to the stone. (*Caution*: Be careful not to get acid on hands or clothes.) After a moment or two add a few more drops. Continue to add more acid from time to time for several minutes. What do you observe?

Pupil Investigations (may include the following processes):
1. Observing that the acid "fizzes" on the rock
2. Discovering that a hole is slowly being formed in the rock
3. Inferring that the acid causes a chemical reaction
4. Generalizing that the formation of a limestone cave may be caused by chemical reaction

Fig. 14–6. **Tiny stalagmites and stalactites form between the two beakers containing a saturated solution of Epsom salt.**

Event 14–I. Building Stalactites and Stalagmites. Dissolve as much Epsom salt into a jar of water as you can. Fill two smaller jars with the dissolved saltwater and drape a thick string between them as shown in Fig. 14–6. Let the arrangement stand for a few days and observe.

Pupil Investigations (may include the following processes):
1. Observing that water soaks the string and slowly drips from its low point
2. Discovering that deposits slowly form on the string and on the surface below it
3. Forming a theory that the deposits are carried in solution to the point where they appear
4. Inferring that evaporation of the solution causes the deposits to form
5. Generalizing to compare the deposits of Epsom salt with the formation of stalactites and stalagmites in caves

Event 14–J. Rock Erosion. Fill a small jar half full of rock chips consisting mostly of sandstone, limestone, or shale. Shake vigorously for several minutes. Observe the chips carefully under a magnifying glass. Inspect the water and the bottom of the jar for any deposits.

Pupil Investigations (may include the following processes):
1. Comparing the appearance of the chips before and after shaking the jar
2. Observing that the chips are generally smaller and more rounded after shaking than before
3. Inferring that the shaking ground off tiny bits of rock that clouded the water and settled to the bottom
4. Generalizing to relate the activity to the mechanical erosion of rocks

Event 14–K. Pebble Pinnacles. Form a mound of some nonoily clay (not modeling clay) into a level mass, about 5 to 10 centimeters across. Place the mound into a tray or pan. Press some pebbles (or coins) into the top surface of clay. Take the mass outside and spray it with water from a hose. What happens?

Pupil Investigations (may include the following processes):
1. Observing that the spray slowly washes away the clay
2. Discovering that the pebbles stand on top of pinnacles after much of the clay is washed away
3. Inferring that the pebbles protect the clay from the erosion of water
4. Generalizing that hard surface rock formations protect softer rock formations below from erosion

Event 14–L. Force of Freezing. Fill a small jar brimful with water and tighten the cap securely. Place the jar into a plastic bag for safety and then, for even more safety, place it into a larger plastic tray. Put the tray into the freezer compartment of a refrigerator. Observe the jar after the water is frozen solidly.

Pupil Investigations (may include the following processes):
1. Discovering that the jar is broken. (*Caution*: Be careful of glass fragments, which will be inside the bag and tray.)
2. Forming a theory that water expands when it freezes
3. Inferring that ice can do to a rock what it did to the jar

Events 14–H Through 14–L Explained in Context (Weathering and Erosion)

WHAT IS MEANT BY WEATHERING AND EROSION? Weathering and erosion are terms often used interchangeably. However, there is a difference. *Weathering* refers to a gradual physical and chemical wearing away of rocks. Even hard rocks are slowly weathered and broken down into fine grains of sand by the action of wind, water, temperature changes, and chemical action.

Erosion is a somewhat broader term. It refers to the wearing away of the surface of the earth. Erosion is caused mostly by running water, and to a lesser degree, wind, glaciers, and temperature changes.

Chemical action affects certain rocks. Rainwater picks up oxygen and carbon dioxide as it falls through the air. Then by the time the rain seeps into the earth, the carbon dioxide has changed into a weak solution of carbonic acid.

Acids tend to dissolve limestone, as can be seen by doing *Event 14–H. Dissolving Stones.* When the dilute hydrochloric acid is dropped on the limestone, there is a bubbling and fizzing action as the limestone slowly dissolves. Eventually, a depression is formed in the rock where the acid has eaten away the stone.

The action of acids and other chemicals has carved out many large and beautiful caves such as Mammoth Cave in Kentucky and Carlsbad Caverns in New Mexico. The caves were formed over a period of millions of years by chemicals dissolved in groundwater.

Sometimes groundwater will deposit minerals instead of dissolve them. If the water is saturated with a mineral, some of it will change to a solid as the water evaporates. This action can be seen if water is left in a clear glass or plastic container to dry. After the water dries, a cloudy film of residue is left on the clear surface.

Another example of this depositing action can be seen by doing *Event 14–I. Building Stalactites and Stalagmites.* The Epsom salt solution travels along the string by capillary action until it reaches the low point between the two jars. There, it accumulates and drips off.

At the same time, however, air is evaporating the liquid, leaving a residue of Epsom salt on the string and on the surface below. The deposits on the string are similar to *stalactites* that hang down from the ceilings of caves. The deposits on the surface below the string are similar to *stalagmites* that build up from the floors of caves.

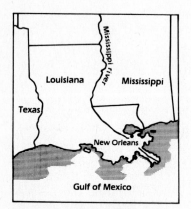

Fig. 14–7. **The Mississippi River has dropped millions of tons of soil at its mouth, extending the delta into the Gulf of Mexico.**

EROSION IS A CONTINUOUS PROCESS. Running water is the chief cause of erosion. The faster the water runs, the stronger its erosive force. When a stream doubles its speed, its capacity to carry suspended matter increases by an unbelievable 64 times! In addition, the slope of the land and the depth of the stream are factors that affect the force of water erosion.

The Mississippi River carries millions of tons of suspended matter to the Gulf of Mexico every year. Some of this matter piles up around the mouth of the river, forming a delta. Study maps that show major rivers emptying into the ocean. Many of those rivers have built deltas a hundred or more kilometers into the sea. (See Fig. 14–7.)

Some of the most striking examples of river erosion can be found by studying the causes of some of the greatest floods of history. For example, the great flood of China's Hwang Ho River (Yellow River) in 1887 is instructive.

The Hwang Ho, like all large rivers, carries enormous amounts of suspended matter, especially as the water flows quickly down the higher elevations. When the river reaches the fairly level lowlands, it slows down, dropping great amounts of matter into the riverbed.

Year after year the riverbed is built up. To protect themselves, people built up the banks (called levees) to keep the river in its channel. Time after time levees were raised higher and higher to keep ahead of the ever-rising riverbed. Finally, the river overflowed with disastrous results.

Sediment had built up the channel so much that even the bed of the river was higher than the surrounding valley. When the river finally overflowed the levees, it flooded 140,000 square kilometers of land and killed an estimated one million people.

Of course, the river did not return to its old, elevated channel. Instead, it simply cut a new channel through the lowlands and entered the ocean hundreds of kilometers from its previous mouth. Evidence shows that the Hwang Ho has changed its course in a similar manner many times during the passage of geological time. (See Fig. 14–8.)

Perform *Event 14–J. Rock Erosion* to see how mechanical action can grind and erode small rock chips. This event simulates the action of running water. As the rocks are tumbled and rolled in the running water, they slide and grind over each other. Slowly they take on round shapes and get smaller and smaller.

Fig. 14–8. **In 1887 the Hwang Ho (Yellow) River in China overflowed and cut a new channel to the sea. An estimated one million people died in the flood.**

Some of the same results can be noticed by shaking the chips in the jar. Be sure to use fairly soft sedimentary rocks for the activity. Hard samples will not show much change in any reasonable length of time.

A stream is not the only place in which water erosion takes place. Rainwater and the action of lakes and oceans also produce erosive forces.

In some of the western states there are unusual rock structures that look like tall spires or pinnacles. These were formed when relatively small layers of hard rock were deposited on top of softer rock. Over eons of time fractures developed through the top layer and the softer underlayer eroded away quickly. Now the remains of the harder rock serve as caps protecting the soft rock below it.

Event 14–K. Pebble Pinnacles is an activity that shows how the pinnacles were formed. A fairly gentle spray from above washes away the clay, leaving the pebbles (or coins) to serve as caps on top of mounds of clay.

Sometimes water seeps into the cracks of hard rocks. Later, if the water freezes, the ice expands to break the rock apart. A simple demonstration of the action of freezing water can be seen in *Event 14–L. Force of Freezing.* The ice breaks the jar easily as it expands.

Be sure to exercise caution by placing the jar inside a plastic bag and the bag into a larger tray or pan. In that way you protect yourself from broken glass as well as keep the broken glass out of the freezer.

Discrepant Events and Pupil Investigations

SOILS (EVENTS 14–M THROUGH 14–R)

Event 14–M. Permeability of Soils. Attach a screen to the bottom of a cylinder. [You can use an inverted plastic jug with the bottom removed. (See Fig. 14–9.)] Fill the container about three-fourths full of loam. Pour in some

Fig. 14–9. **Use an inverted clear plastic bottle to see how quickly a measured amount of water soaks through soils.**

water and keep the container brimful for a minute or two. Repeat with other jars containing other soil types such as sand and clay.

Pupil Investigations (may include the following processes):
1. Measuring the amount of water that seeps through each of the soil types in a given period of time
2. Observing that sandy soils allow a very large amount of water to pass through quickly
3. Observing that clay soils restrict the passage of water
4. Analyzing the function of a soil permeability test for a leach bed of a small home-sized septic system

Event 14–N. Water-Holding Capacity of Soils. Fill several containers three-fourths full of different soil types as described in Event 14–M. This time pour in a measured amount of water and no more. Allow sufficient time for the water to seep through the soils and measure again. Compare the before and after amounts for each soil type.

Pupil Investigations (may include the following processes):
1. Weighing the water before and after pouring
2. Comparing the water amounts to determine the amount held in the soil
3. Generalizing about the value of adding water-holding soils to croplands

Event 14–O. Erosion on Bare and Grassy Slopes. Fill two shallow boxes with soil. Place a layer of turf in one box and leave the other box bare. Lift the boxes so that they slope down, simulating a hillside. Then pour water on each from a sprinkler. Large basins should be used to collect the runoff. (Do not let the soil wash into the sink. It can clog the drain. If possible, perform the activity outdoors with a hose.)

Pupil Investigations (may include the following processes):
1. Discovering that the water runs off quickly from bare soil
2. Observing that the turf tends to "hold" the water and soil
3. Discovering that the bare soil is easily eroded
4. Measuring the runoff from the two boxes
5. Generalizing about the value of grasses to reduce soil erosion

Event 14–P. Check Dams. Select an area of ground in which a small gully has been cut by the action of running water. Build a dam in this gully using rocks, boards, and soil. Be sure that the rocks are piled on the downstream side of the dam to keep the overflowing water from washing away the dam.

Drive a stake into the streambed a meter or two on the upstream side of the dam. Measure the stake's height carefully and inspect the site after a hard rain.

Pupil Investigations (may include the following processes):
1. Discovering that the upstream side of the dam is filled with soil after a hard rain
2. Measuring the amount of soil deposited by the running water (by measuring the height of the stake before and after the rain)
3. Inferring that the soil was carried by rapidly moving water and then dropped as the water slowed in the lake

Fig. 14–10. **The layers of sand, charcoal, and pebbles are capable of filtering many impurities from muddy water.**

Event 14–Q. Cleaning Muddy Water. Use an inverted plastic bottle with the bottom removed. Make a filter by arranging pebbles, sand, and charcoal into layers as shown in Fig. 14–10. Pour in muddy water and observe it as it comes out below. (*Caution:* Sometimes this process cleans up the water so well that the water is crystal clear. This does *not* make the water suitable for drinking!)

Pupil Investigations (may include the following processes):
1. Observing that the water is clear as it emerges from the filter
2. Inferring that the contents of the filter have removed the muddy particles in the water
3. Comparing the demonstration with the filtering qualities of various natural soils

Event 14–R. Chemical Cleaning of Water. Pour some muddy water into a test tube. Let it stand for a few minutes. Note how muddy the water is at that time. Then shake the test tube and add some alum and shake again. After allowing the test tube to stand for the same length of time as earlier, compare the clarity of the water with the first sample. (*Caution:* Even though the water may clear up, it is *not* suitable for drinking.)

Pupil Investigations (may include the following processes):
1. Forming a standard for estimating the muddiness of water (perhaps by using different shadings on a sheet of paper)
2. Comparing the water before and after adding the chemical
3. Inferring that chemicals can help to purify water

Events 14–M Through 14–R Explained in Context (Soils)

Most of the land surfaces of the earth are covered with a layer of soil. Only the mountains have large exposed masses of rock without a soil covering. Mountain valleys, however, are filled with soil.

Fertile soils contain far more than just mineral matter. They contain organic matter as well as microscopic plant and animal life.

The size of soil particles varies greatly in different soils. Soils are classified according to the dimensions shown in Table 14–2. Good soils contain a proper blend of all sizes.

The size of the particles influences the *permeability of soils*, that is, the ability of soil to allow water to pass through it. By doing *Event 14–M. Permeability of Soils*, you will find that of the three types of soil listed in the

Table 14–2. **Soil Size and Type**

2.0 mm or larger	Gravel
0.05 to 2.0 mm	Sand
0.002 to 0.05 mm	Silt
0.002 mm or smaller	Clay

event, sandy soil is by far the best in allowing water to pass through it quickly. Loam, if it has a good blend of soils, is next; and clay is poorest. In many states permeability tests are required to determine the suitability of soils to drain away liquid wastes from home septic systems.

By continuing with *Event 14–N. Water-Holding Capacity of Soils,* we should find differences in how much water various soils can hold. As expected, sand does not hold much water. Clay holds more water than sand, but loam is the best "holder" of water. Loam is a soil rich in organic matter and can hold up to 200 percent of its own weight in water.

SOIL CONSERVATION. Only the top 5 to 10 centimeters of soil are suitable for growing crops in most parts of the world. Much of this thin covering can be blown or washed away if it is not protected. It is easy to see why topsoil must be conserved.

One method of protecting this thin layer of fertile soil is to keep the soil covered with plant growth as much as possible. (Even croplands can now be protected from erosion by using a "no-till" method of planting, instead of the plowing and seed-bed preparation that leaves soils entirely unprotected for weeks at a time.)

The effects of plant growth can be seen by performing *Event 14–O. Erosion on Bare and Grassy Slopes.* When water is sprinkled on both slopes, the water quickly carries away the bare soil. Small gullies are cut into the slope, and soil is washed down into the pan.

The grassy slope, on the other hand, holds much of the water and almost all of the soil. Plants provide excellent protection from the destructive effects of running water.

Once gullies are formed, pupils will see the value of building check dams to reduce erosion. When the check dam is built, as suggested in *Event 14–P. Check Dams,* pupils will find that after a hard rain a large amount of silt is dropped behind the dam.

When the running water reaches the "lake" of the dam, the water slows down and drops its silt. In fact, small check dams are often completely filled with silt after a few hard rains.

If the dams are located at strategic locations along a gully, the gully fills in with silt. Then the silt can be leveled and seeded with grasses to protect the waterway from further erosion.

Plants protect soils with their root systems. Their roots form a weblike mat that intertwines around soil particles to form a tightly knit web of soil holders. The length and number of roots and root hairs from a single plant is truly astounding.

According to a report by the U.S. Department of Agriculture, a single rye plant grown for 4 months in 1 cubic foot of loam soil developed a root system with the following statistics: 13.8 million roots, with a combined length of 616 kilometers, and a surface area of 232 square meters.

The soil also contained 14 billion root hairs with a combined length of 10,560 kilometers and a surface area in excess of 372 square meters. Figures such as these show why plants are so effective in holding soils in place.

CLEANING MUDDY WATER. We have seen that moving water picks up soil and dirt. It is quite surprising for pupils to learn that some soil particles are effective in getting rid of dirt. Sandy soils are a natural filter for underground water sources. They can be used to make a classroom filter in *Event 14–Q. Cleaning Muddy Water.*

Be sure that the sand is clean before using it in the filter. A classroom filter is too small to be very effective unless you use ground-up charcoal as one of the layers. It is hard for pupils to understand that charcoal, which is so messy to the touch, is so effective in cleaning up muddy water. If the filter is made correctly, muddy water can come out of the filter looking crystal clear.

Again, be sure to caution pupils *not* to drink it. The muddy particles are removed, but the system does not remove bacteria and harmful microscopic life.

Another way of purifying water is by using chemicals. One example of removing muddy particles is shown in *Event 14–R. Chemical Cleaning of Water.* When alum is added to the muddy water and then mixed, the muddy particles tend to settle to the bottom quickly. Alum is one of many chemicals that is used in water purification plants.

(*Caution*: As with our earlier warnings, the water is not safe to drink. The alum just takes out the muddy particles. Other chemicals, in addition to alum, are used in water purification plants to purify the water.)

15

Teaching Children about the Oceans

WHY TURN TO THE OCEANS? (EVENTS 15–A, 15–B, AND 15–C)

Discrepant Events and Pupil Investigations

Event 15–A. The Appearing Salt. Dissolve about 35 grams of table salt in a liter of water. After it is completely dissolved (you may need to wait a while for the water to become clear), pour the contents into a shallow pan. Allow the water to evaporate, or heat gently to hasten the process. When the water is gone, inspect the pan. What do you find?

Pupil Investigations (may include the following processes):
1. Observing that the water is clear before it evaporates
2. Discovering that a white residue forms as the liquid evaporates
3. Identifying the residue as table salt
4. Measuring the amount of salt that appears
5. Generalizing that evaporation is used to purify saltwater

Event 15–B. Seawater Gardening. Dissolve about 35 grams of table salt in a liter of water. Use this water to irrigate some young bean plants. Irrigate some additional bean plants with plain water. Compare the results after a few days.

Pupil Investigations (may include the following processes):
1. Conducting the experiment for several days (or more)
2. Recording the results of the experiment
3. Observing that the plants watered with saltwater wilt and finally die
4. Concluding that seawater is harmful to some plants

Event 15–C. Freeze-Fresh Water. Dissolve about 35 grams of table salt in a liter of water. After it is fully dissolved, pour the clear water into an ice cube tray and place it into a freezer. Check after a few hours or the next day. What happens to the saltwater?

Pupil Investigations (may include the following processes):
1. Recording the appearance of the water and ice in the ice cube tray at 30-minute intervals until the water is frozen
2. Analyzing, by melting and evaporation, the salt content of several sections of clear ice

3. Analyzing the unfrozen residue for its salt content
4. Measuring the temperature of the ice

Events 15–A, 15–B, and 15–C Explained in Context (Why Turn to the Oceans?)

Suppose that a spaceship from another galaxy happened to come upon a heavenly body that looked as though it could support life. Before trying to land, the spaceship aliens would have to make sure it was safe.

Suppose they sent down electronic probes to check the composition and environment of the unknown body. After gathering all the data they could obtain, they might give the following description of the planet:

The unknown planet consists mostly of a liquid that is seldom found anywhere else in the universe. The molecules of the liquid contain two atoms of hydrogen (which is plentiful in the universe) and one atom of oxygen (which is scarce).

This liquid, H_2O, covers over 70 percent of the surface of the planet. The rest of the surface is mostly granite, with a thin covering of organic and inorganic matter.

Careful collection of data shows that the temperature of the liquid ranges from a low of 0 degrees Celsius at the poles to a high of 33 degrees Celsius at the equator.

The land surfaces show much greater extremes of temperature, ranging from a low of −75 degrees Celsius to a high of 50 degrees Celsius. Not only do the temperatures vary from one place to another, but they vary even at a given spot from one day to the next.

All in all, the sharp temperature changes on land are likely to be quite hostile to life forms. Thus, it is our belief that the higher forms of life on this planet live in the abundant and favorable liquid, and the lower forms of life are forced to live on the scarcer, more hostile land areas.

This imaginary report describes our own planet, as seen by aliens from another galaxy. Even though humans do not live in the more "favorable" ocean, many of the other findings are correct. Certainly the oceans *are* important to this planet.

Highest mountain: 8800 m

Average height of land: 700 m

Average depth of ocean: 3600 m

Deepest part of the ocean: 10,900 m

Fig. 15–1. **A profile of the earth's surface is shown. It is clear that the oceans are a dominating feature of the globe.**

First of all, there is more water than there is land. The oceans cover most of the earth's surface. Secondly, the oceans are deeper than the land is high. If the highest mountain were placed in the deepest part of the ocean, the tip of the mountain would still be covered with 2 kilometers of water.

The average depth of the oceans is 3600 meters. The average elevation of land areas is only 700 meters. (See Fig. 15–1.) The sizes and depths of the oceans are listed in Table 15–1.

Table 15–1. **The Size and Depth of the Oceans**

	Area (sq km)	Average Depth (m)	Maximum Depth (m)
Pacific	166,000,000	4,300	10,900
Atlantic	83,000,000	3,900	9,200
Indian	73,000,000	3,960	8,000
Arctic	13,000,000	1,200	5,000

NOTE: The water areas around the Antarctic are not a separate ocean. Instead, they are parts of the Pacific, Atlantic, and Indian oceans.

RESOURCES OF THE OCEANS. The oceans are a great storehouse of resources. Furthermore, their resources are constantly increasing. How? By collecting those that are draining off land areas.

Every time it rains and water runs off into a river, the water carries with it some mineral resources from the land. Those resources finally reach the oceans. The oceans therefore contain all the minerals that have drained off the land since the beginning of time.

We can see that even clear water contains minerals by performing *Event 15–A. The Appearing Salt.* The amount of salt that is mixed into the water is equal to the salt found in seawater. Seawater contains about 3.5 percent salt, equal to 35 grams per liter. When the water sample evaporates, the salt is left behind to be seen again.

At first one might think that the ocean supplies only common salt. However, almost all minerals can be found as salts. Thus, just about any mineral that is found on land can also be found in the ocean.

How much does the ocean contain? The supply is almost limitless. See Table 15–2 to find how many resources are contained in a cubic kilometer of ocean water.

This is truly an impressive list of resources. Of course, a cubic kilometer is a very large quantity. It would cover an area 10 kilometers long and 10 kilometers wide to a depth of 10 meters. The total resources of the ocean become even more impressive when we realize that there are about 1.4 billion cubic kilometers of water in the oceans.

Most of the resources remain untapped because it is too expensive to extract the minerals from them. Only a few substances such as common table salt (sodium chloride), magnesium, bromine, iodine, and some phosphorites are taken at the present time.

The oceans also supply some important nonmineral resources, such as food. Fish have been harvested from the ocean for centuries. In the future the oceans are likely to take on greater and greater importance in supplying the world's supply of protein.

Table 15–2. **Resources in 1 Cubic Kilometer of Ocean**

Resource	Amount (metric tons)
Common salt	30,000,000.0
Magnesium	876,000.0
Calcium	432,000.0
Bromine	69,800.0
Carbon	28,000.0
Boron	4,752.0
Fluorine	1,296.0
Nitrogen	432.0
Gold	1.5

Another great nonmineral resource of the ocean is water—freshwater. Seawater is already being purified for use as drinking water in several parts of the world. However, it is still too costly to compete with most drinking water sources from the land. At present it is far too costly to convert seawater for use in agriculture.

Perform *Event 15–B. Seawater Gardening* to see the effect of seawater on plants. The salt content of seawater is far too high to be used with most plant life. The salt will actually pull water *out of* plants. As a result, seawater will kill most plant life.

One way of purifying water is to freeze it, as suggested in *Event 15–C. Freeze-Fresh Water.* When saltwater freezes, it tends to form crystals of fairly pure ice. Some salt may be trapped between the crystals, but most of the salt collects as brine in unfrozen pools. So, if ice is removed from the tray, melted, and evaporated, very little residue should remain. The brine, however, leaves lots of salt after it is evaporated.

Huge amounts of ice are found near the North and South poles of the earth. They represent vast quantities of freshwater. Many icebergs, several kilometers long and just as wide, float southward every year. A single iceberg—3 kilometers long, 2 kilometers wide, and 400 meters thick—contains enough pure water to supply the needs of 10 million people for a whole year.

The use of seawater for domestic and agricultural use will depend mostly on cost. At the present time large irrigation projects supply 30 liters of freshwater at a cost that will purify only 1 liter of seawater. There are only a few places on earth where pure water is so scarce that seawater is converted for domestic use.

Discrepant Events and Pupil Investigations

Event 15–D. Current Generator. Set up a fan so that it blows across a large container of water. Sprinkle some sawdust or pepper on the water and observe.

Pupil Investigations (may include the following processes):
1. Observing that the fan blows away the surface of the water
2. Diagraming the path of the water as traced by the sawdust or pepper (It is a large circular path.)
3. Comparing the currents in the pan with currents in the oceans

THE MOTIONS OF THE OCEANS (EVENTS 15–D THROUGH 15–L)

Event 15–E. Cold Currents. Mix some food coloring in water and freeze it in an ice cube tray. After the water is frozen, carefully lower a cube into a large clear container of still water. Observe.

Fig. 15–2. **Hot water rises and cold water descends.**

Pupil Investigations (may include the following processes):
1. Observing that colored bands flow down from the cube as it melts
2. Diagraming the path of the flowing currents
3. Inferring that cold water is heavier than warm water
4. Generalizing that ocean currents can be caused by differences in temperature

Event 15–F. Hot Water Chimney. Fill a small bottle with hot water and some food coloring. Cover it with a one-hole stopper and slowly submerge the bottle into a large container of cold water. (See Fig. 15–2.)

Pupil Investigations (may include the following processes):
1. Observing that water rises from the small bottle
2. Inferring that the warm water is lighter than the cold water
3. Diagraming the circulation of water that takes place in the container

Event 15–G. Floating Eggs. Lower an egg into a beaker of water. Does it sink or float? Now add several tablespoons of salt. Mix carefully and thoroughly. What happens?

Pupil Investigations (may include the following processes):
1. Observing that the egg floats after the salt is mixed into the water
2. Inferring that salt increases the density of water
3. Generalizing that the saltiness of ocean water is a factor in causing currents

Event 15–H. Deep Drafts. Assume that you are the captain of a ship steaming across an ocean. Suppose that you were asked to stop at a harbor located some distance upstream on a large river and that passage was safe only for ships with a draft of no more than 6 meters. Your ship is loaded so that its draft is exactly 5.9 meters. Could you make the trip up the river?

Fig. 15–3. **The colored water mixes in one pair of bottles but not in the other. How does the saltwater affect the circulation in the bottles?**

Pupil Investigations (may include the following processes):
1. Theorizing (incorrectly) that the ship's draft could clear the river bottom by 0.1 meter
2. Investigating with a hydrometer to see if it sinks to different levels in freshwater and in seawater
3. Inferring that ships float at different depths depending on the density of water

Event 15–I. Saline Currents. Set up an arrangement of four bottles as shown in Fig. 15–3. Mix food coloring into the two lower bottles. To invert a bottle without spilling, hold an index card or sheet of durable paper against the mouth of the bottle.

Be sure that the top bottle of one pair and the lower bottle of the other pair contain saltwater. After the bottles are inverted, carefully slip out the index cards from between the bottles. Observe.

Pupil Investigations (may include the following processes):
1. Observing that the colored water mixes with the clear water in one pair of bottles but not the other
2. Investigating and finding no temperature differences between bottles
3. Inferring that the mixing is caused by a difference in densities of the liquids

Event 15–J. Straw Hydrometer. Seal one end of a plastic straw with a lump of clay. Pour in enough sand so that the straw floats fairly low in a container of warm freshwater, as shown in Fig. 15–4. Mark the point on the straw that is exactly level with the surface of the water. Now float the straw in cold water. Try also warm and cold salt water. What do you find?

Fig. 15–4. **A plastic straw plugged with clay makes a simple hydrometer. Compare the densities of saltwater and pure water at different temperatures.**

Pupil Investigations (may include the following processes):
1. Observing that the hydrometer floats higher in the cold water and the saltwater than in the warm water and the freshwater
2. Inferring that water density increases when water becomes cold or more saline
3. Forming a theory about the effect of salinity and temperature on the formation of currents

Event 15–K. Penny in the Pool. Would the water level of a pool rise if you tossed a penny into it? Yes, ever so slightly. Would the level rise if you tossed the penny into a boat that was floating in the pool? Yes, again, ever so slightly.
   In which of the two ways would you cause the water to rise the most: (1) tossing the penny directly into the pool or (2) tossing the penny into a boat (which is floating in the pool)?

Pupil Investigations (may include the following processes):
1. Experimenting with floating objects and weights to compare the amounts of water displaced by each of the two methods described in the problem
2. Relating the problem to the principle of buoyancy and density
3. Comparing the amount of water displaced by (1) the volume of a penny and (2) the weight of a penny

Event 15–L. Tiny Tides. Go outside to do this event. Ask several pupils to carry a shallow tray filled with water. Ask them to carry it for 5 to 10 meters as carefully as possible without spilling. If the tray is shallow and about 30 centimeters by 20 centimeters (or more), it will be almost impossible to carry without spilling some water. How does this activity relate to the formation of tides in some parts of the world?

Pupil Investigations (may include the following processes):
1. Observing that a very small motion can produce a large effect with the water
2. Performing the activity to find how difficult it is to walk without spilling the water
3. Inferring a relationship between the water in the tray and the water in a tidal basin

Events 15–D Through 15–L Explained in Context (Motions of the Oceans)

It is doubtful that anyone has ever seen the surface of the ocean perfectly still. Even in ancient times when sailing ships were becalmed on windless days, the ocean was covered with gentle swells that rocked the ships from side to side. It is certainly true that the oceans are in constant motion.

There are at least three types of motions: (1) currents, (2) tides, and (3) waves. In addition, a fourth type, a *tsunami* (or tidal wave), also occurs from time to time. We will look at these types of motion separately.

OCEAN CURRENTS. Look at a map showing the major ocean currents. You will see that almost the entire ocean surface is affected by currents of one kind or another. (See Fig. 15–5.)

As early as 1770 Benjamin Franklin drew charts of the Gulf Stream, which flows from the Gulf of Mexico to the northern tip of Norway. It is a broad stream that flows at speeds up to 5 and 6 kilometers per hour in some places and carries a volume of water that is probably a thousand times greater than the Mississippi River.

Why is there such a current in the ocean? One of the causes is wind. A prevailing wind will tend to drive water ahead of it; and if it blows over a long enough area for a long enough time, a *current* will be created. A miniature wind-driven current can be seen by performing *Event 15–D. Current Generator.*

When the fan is set up to blow across the large tray, it pushes water ahead of it. The moving water begins to circulate. The current can be seen better if sawdust or pepper is sprinkled on the water.

In addition to wind, there are some other factors that cause ocean currents. Differences in temperature, for example, will cause a movement of water. *Event 15–E. Cold Currents* and *Event 15–F. Hot Water Chimney* both show the effects of temperature differences. The events show that cold water descends and warm water rises. The temperature difference starts the water moving, and it gains a momentum that sets up a circulation pattern.

Temperatures vary widely in the oceans. The hottest water in the seas or oceans is in Elphinstone Inlet in the Persian Gulf, where surface temperatures reach 32 degrees Celsius. On the other extreme, the coldest temperatures are found at the poles where the saline water reaches 3 degrees Celsius below zero before it freezes. (*Note:* Pure water freezes at 0 degrees Celsius, but saltwater does not.)

Fig. 15–5. **The major currents of the oceans.**

Given these temperature differences, in what parts of the world would you expect the water to rise and where would you expect it to descend? Since cold water descends, you can expect that the icy polar waters flow slowly along the ocean floor toward the equator. Even at the equator the water at the ocean floor is no more than 4 degrees Celsius.

The warm equatorial waters, by contrast, constantly move along the surface toward the poles. As the icy waters settle, they are replaced by the warmer currents slowly moving toward the poles.

A third important factor affects an ocean current. That factor is *salinity*. When water evaporates, it leaves behind water that is saltier than normal. If everything else is equal, the saltier the water, and the heavier it is.

The saltiest water is located near the equator and at the poles. At the equator hot weather speeds up evaporation so that the waters become more saline. The Red Sea has a salt content of 4 percent instead of the 3½ percent that is common in the oceans.

The ocean at the poles is also more salty than average. That is because when ice freezes, it takes freshwater from the ocean and leaves the salt behind. The high salt content plus the cold produces the densest waters in all the oceans.

The effect of salt on water density can be shown by doing the next three events. *Event 15–G. Floating Eggs* shows that when salt is added to the water, its density increases to a point where it will make the egg float.

Event 15–H. Deep Drafts is somewhat similar to the floating egg event. However, instead of the egg we have a ship. In which case will the object sink lower, in freshwater or in saltwater? Even though the ship rides high enough in the saltwater, the ship would sink too low in the freshwater of the river. The captain cannot take the ship up the river.

Event 15–I. Saline Currents is the best of the activities to show how saltwater can cause currents. When the index card is pulled from between the bottles, the saltwater and pure water mix on one side but not the other.

The mixing occurs on the side where the saltwater is placed in the top bottle. The saltwater descends because it is heavier. The water does not mix in the other pair of bottles because *the heavier saltwater is already on the bottom.*

In a small way *Event 15–J. Straw Hydrometer* is somewhat like two earlier events. A *hydrometer* is actually an instrument that measures the density of water. However, it works just like the ship and egg. It floats high in the water when the water is salty and lower when the water is fresh.

In discussing the density of water and the floating level of a ship, we are really talking about *buoyancy.* Buoyancy refers to the upward, or lifting force, exerted on an object in the water. If the object floats, the lifting force is obviously greater than the downward force of gravity.

In the events with the hydrometer, ship, and egg we see that freshwater has less of an upward, or lifting, force than saltwater. In other words, freshwater is less buoyant than saltwater.

Think about buoyancy in *Event 15–K. Penny in the Pool.* Is there a difference in the water level depending on whether the penny is tossed directly into the pool or into the boat (floating in the pool)? The answer is yes, there is a difference. The water rises more if the penny is tossed into the boat.

Why the difference? The penny displaces very little water. It goes right to the bottom. The downward force is not offset by water. If the penny goes into the boat, however, its entire weight (spread out along the bottom of the boat) is offset by water that is pushed aside, thus raising the level of the water in the pool.

A way to summarize the problem is to state that when tossed into the pool, the penny displaces very little of its weight (only its volume), but when tossed into the boat, the penny displaces its entire weight. (See Fig. 15–6.)

Fig. 15–6. **Toss a penny into a pool and a penny into a boat (in the pool). Which coin causes the water level to rise the most?**

TIDES. A second form of motion in the ocean is caused by the influence of the sun and moon. The gravity of the sun and moon attract the water, which is pulled up by as much as a meter in the wide expanses of the ocean. This attraction or pulling of the water is called a *tide*.

If the tidal action is no greater in the middle of the ocean than 1 meter, what causes the far greater tides that are so often seen along the shorelines of the great oceans? The answer to that question is somewhat more complex but can be partially explained by performing *Event 15–L. Tiny Tides*.

There is no tide that affects the water in the tray, but it is still hard to keep the water from spilling. What happens is that a small motion is started in the tray, and once going, the water is not easy to stop. It moves against the rim and sloshes up and over.

In somewhat the same way, a rather gentle motion of $\frac{1}{2}$ to 1 meter in the vast expanse of ocean starts something that does not stop abruptly when it hits the shoreline. Instead, the water "sloshes" ashore in tides that often reach 2 to 4 meters, and in the Bay of Fundy (between New Brunswick and Nova Scotia) they reach an incredible 15 meters.

Tides are greatest when the sun and moon are in line and "pull together" with their combined gravity. Those tides are called *spring tides*. When the moon and sun are at right angles, their effects are divided to produce comparatively low *neap tides*.

Air pressure also influences tides. When air pressure is low, as in a storm, water rushes in to "fill the vacuum." Tides will sometimes rise as much as a meter because of extreme changes in air pressure.

The greatest storm ever recorded in this country occurred in 1969, when Hurricane Camille hit the mainland from the Gulf of Mexico. The low pressure and 300-kilometer winds drove the water of the Gulf 10 meters above its normal level, destroying several coastal cities in the state of Mississippi.

WAVE MOTION. Waves are caused by the action of winds. When there is a wind, the first waves are very short, steep-angled, and choppy. If the wind keeps blowing, the waves get bigger. If there is an expanse of ocean that is long enough, and if the wind keeps on blowing, the waves can keep on growing for days. During storms ocean waves sometimes reach a height of 15 meters.

Time and distance are the two factors that influence the size of waves. As a result, waves on small lakes are almost always small and choppy. As the lake gets larger, so do the waves.

Ocean waves, once formed, keep on going for thousands of kilometers. They fan out from storms and travel far across the ocean to hit distant coastlines days later.

As the waves move across the ocean, they gradually change. The crests become smoother and the waves move farther apart from each other.

We can actually determine how far away the waves originated by measuring the time between crests as they pass a given point. For example, when waves come ashore every 5 to 7 seconds, the storm that caused them was quite close. When they arrive every 7 to 10 seconds, the source was 300 to 400 kilometers away. At 11 to 15 seconds the storm was 1500 to 3000 kilometers away, and at 13 to 20 seconds the storm that caused them was 5000 to 7000 kilometers away.

TSUNAMI (TIDAL WAVE). A fourth motion of the ocean is called *tsunami* or tidal wave. (The name *tidal wave* is somewhat misleading because the motion has nothing to do with the tides.)

The tsunami, or tidal wave, is a great water wave caused by a major underwater disturbance such as an earthquake. The wave will travel across thousands of kilometers of ocean with little effect until it hits a coastline. There, it can crash ashore and cause millions of dollars of damage.

On the high seas the wave cannot even be detected except with the most sensitive of equipment. Even though the wave travels at speeds of 600 to 900 kilometers per hour, the crests are often about 500 to 600 kilometers apart. The size of the wave is only about 20 to 30 centimeters. This means that it will take almost an hour for the wave to lift and lower a ship by only 20 to 30 centimeters.

When the wave reaches the coast, however, it can form a breaker of gigantic proportions. Remember the activity in which you tried to walk with a shallow pan? Once the water in the pan began to move, it tended to slosh over the sides. The same is true of a tsunami, only more so. Once the water is in motion, it keeps on moving. A tsunami can cause great damage to a shoreline when it hits.

LIVING UNDER THE SEA (EVENTS 15–M AND 15–N)

Discrepant Events and Pupil Investigations

Event 15–M. Underwater Distances. Tie a weight to each of several corks to hold them underwater in an aquarium. Arrange them near the side of the aquarium at various depths, as shown in Fig. 15–7. Be sure that all the corks are completely underwater. In fact, the corks should all be well below the surface.

Now look straight down from the top through the water at the cork. Then, without moving your head, make a mark on the glass with a grease pencil to indicate the height of the corks. To review: Look at the cork *through the water*, and make a mark on the glass by looking at the pencil *through the air*.

When completed, step to the side and compare the corks with the marks. Were they accurate?

Fig. 15–7. **Look straight down into the aquarium and mark the glass where the corks appear to be. Why is the view different from the side?**

Pupil Investigations (may include the following processes):
1. Observing that the pencil marks are always above the actual heights of the corks
2. Observing that the discrepancies are greater as the depth increases
3. Inferring that water affects our perception of distance

Event 15–N. Fading Colors. Suppose a diver wearing a white swimsuit dives to a depth of 80 meters and notices that the color of his suit has changed from white to blue. How do you account for the change in color?

Pupil Investigations (may include the following processes):
1. Inferring (incorrectly) that the algae had stained the diving suit
2. Inferring that color balances are different at that depth from those on the surface

3. Relating the color change to the changes observed in the unit on light

Events 15–M and 15–N Explained in Context (Living Under the Sea)

Humans became interested in the underwater world many years ago. It is believed that as early as 300 B.C. Alexander the Great viewed the wonders of

Table 15–3. **Underwater Pressures**

Depth (m)	Pressure (atm)	Comments
	1	
	2	No bends above 10 m; red light limit
		Orange light limit
	3	Oxygen poisoning begins at 20 m
30	4	
	5	Blue light limit
	6	Normal skindiving limit (50 m)
		"Nitrogen narcosis" begins (55 m)
60	7	Sea Lab II (62 m)
		Yellow light limit
	8	
	9	Green light limit
90	10	Maximum momentary depth for air-breathing skindivers (100 m)
	11	
	12	Maximum depth for hard-hat divers (125 m)
120	13	Oxygen is only 2 percent of breathing mixture
	14	
	15	Depth limit for successful swim away from crippled submarine (145 m)
150	16	
	17	
	18	
180	19	Average depth of continental shelf
	20	
	21	
210	22	
	23	
	24	
240	25	
	26	
	27	
270	28	
	29	
	30	$\frac{2}{3}$ of 1 percent of breathing mixture is oxygen
300	31	Keller and Small set scuba diving record (Keller died)

the marine world from a large submerged diving bell. It was not until recent times, however, that serious attempts were made to actually live in underwater stations for days and weeks at a time.

One of the problems of diving under the ocean's surface is the pressure that builds up as you go down. It takes only a depth of 10 meters to equal the pressure of all the air pushing down on the earth.

At sea level the air pressure is referred to as *1 atmosphere*. At 10 meters the pressure is 2 atmospheres; at 20 meters, 3 atmospheres; and so on.

Because of the extreme pressures, humans are restricted mostly to fairly shallow depths. In some unusual cases, however, long-term labs have been set up at depths of 60 meters, where divers lived inside (and outside) open pressurized living quarters for weeks at a time.

In general, the deeper the depth, the shorter the time that one can survive. Table 15–3 shows pressures, depths, and related information.

In addition to the great pressures, there are a number of other problems that must be met when trying to function in deep water. Lack of visibility is often a major concern.

Even in clear water vision is distorted because objects seem closer than they really are. Even using the very shallow depth of *Event 15–M. Underwater Distances*, it should be obvious that the objects seem closer when viewed through the water than when viewed through the air.

Another factor that impairs vision is the filtering effect of water on color. If you go deep enough, no light gets there at all, so everything is totally black. But even where the light is still visible, the view becomes color-distorted.

Sunlight that enters the water has light that contains all the colors of the spectrum. However, the water soon filters out the colors, one color at a time. Red light is gone within the first 5 to 10 meters. Orange light goes no deeper than 18 meters; yellow, 60 meters; and blue, 75 meters.

Thus, the problem posed in *Event 15–N. Fading Colors* is answered by the fact that no other light reached down to the depth of the diver. Even though the diving suit was white (which reflects all colors), it could reflect only the color that it received: blue.

In many cases light will penetrate even less if water is not crystal clear. Most waters are clouded with microscopic plants and animals, which blot out the sunlight at much shallower depths.

Teaching Children about the Plant Kingdom

Discrepant Events and Pupil Investigations

Event 16–A. Soaking Seeds. Soak lima beans in water overnight. After soaking, the tough outer covering can be easily removed. Carefully separate the seed halves and study them. What are the major parts of the seed? Compare seeds with some that were not soaked.

Pupil Investigations (may include the following processes):
1. Observing that the seeds expand when soaked
2. Discovering that the seed coating is tough when dry but easy to remove when wet
3. Examining the three main parts of a seed: the covering, the "baby" plant (embryo), and the food supply
4. Diagraming the parts of the seed
5. Generalizing about the functions of seed parts in germinating plants

Event 16–B. Seed Depth. Plant several types of seeds in each of several sets. Make all conditions the same except for the planting depths. Select large seeds such as lima beans and small seeds such as radishes.

Pupil Investigations (may include the following processes):
1. Recording growth rates of emerging seeds for 2 weeks
2. Comparing the size of seeds with their planting depths
3. Examining the seeds after 1 week to study their development
4. Forming a theory about the relationship between the depth of the soil and the size of the seed

Event 16–C. Bean Power. Plant a handful of bean seeds in several containers. As the bean germinates, the roots and stem develop and push the original bean seed up through the ground into the air.

When the beans begin to emerge, divide the seedlings into three groups. In one group carefully remove one of the halves of the original seed. In the second group remove both halves of the seed. Leave the third group as a control. (See Fig. 16–1.)

Fig. 16–1. **The developing bean plant pushes the original seed halves out of the ground.**

Pupil Investigations (may include the following processes):
1. Recording the growth rates of the beans
2. Observing that the beans with no seed halves do poorly, those with one-half do better, and the control group does best
3. Inferring that the seed halves contain the energy needed to support the early growth of the plant.

Event 16–D. Upside-Down Seeds. Place several layers of blotting paper against the sides of a drinking glass. Push some lima beans between the glass and blotting papers. (The blotters draw up water from the bottom of the tumbler to keep the seeds moist.)

Position the seeds so that they face various directions—up, down, and toward both sides. How does the position of the seed affect the germination and growth of the plants?

Pupil Investigations (may include the following processes):
1. Experimenting with seeds planted in various positions
2. Observing that the leaves always go up and roots always go down
3. Generalizing about the factors that control growth

Event 16–E. Water for Seeds. Plant radishes in five pots and lima beans in five additional pots. Use potting soil, and plant the seeds to the depth recommended on the packages. Carefully arrange a watering program in which one pot of each gets no water, and move in increments to a point where the last pot in each is almost always standing underwater.

To achieve the last condition, seal the drain hole in the bottom of the pot, or set it, rim deep, into a large container of water.

Pupil Investigations (may include the following processes):
1. Recording the amounts and frequency of watering
2. Observing and keeping a record of the growth of seeds
3. Inspecting some ungerminated seeds after a week
4. Generalizing about the best watering program for seeds

Event 16–F. Growth in Light and Dark. Plant some radishes and bean seeds in two drinking glass "gardens" made of blotting paper and drinking glasses. Cover one drinking glass with dark construction paper so that the seeds are in total darkness; leave another tumbler exposed to light. What happens in the two settings?

Pupil Investigations (may include the following processes):
1. Recording the germination of seeds and the rate of growth over a period of 1 or 2 weeks
2. Discovering that seeds grow faster in the dark than those exposed to light
3. Forming a theory to account for the growth differences in daylight and darkness

Event 16–G. How Do Seeds Travel? This event is best done in the autumn when a wide variety of seeds are available. Have pupils collect seeds of all kinds. Ask pupils to examine and classify them and to determine how they travel.

Pupil Investigations (may include the following processes):
1. Collecting some common seeds
2. Inspecting the outward appearances of seeds
3. Classifying seeds into groups according to how they travel

Events 16–A Through 16–G Explained in Context (Seeds)

There are many plants that reproduce from seeds. Seeds are divided into two main groups: the flowering plants, *angiosperms*; and the nonflowering plants, *gymnosperms*. Most seed plants are of the flowering kind. In fact, there are some 250,000 species of flowering plants and only about 600 of the nonflowering species.

HOW SEEDS GERMINATE AND GROW. In *Event 16–A. Soaking Seeds* students will have a chance to study a number of seeds. Lima beans are excellent for use in this event. They are large and fast growing. Other large seeds such as sunflower, corn, pea, pumpkin, and even peanut seeds can be used in these activities.

Seed germination can be observed in a variety of ways. Small seeds, such as the radish, carrot, and onion, can be sprinkled on moist cloth or blotting paper and observed. Just be sure that the cloth or paper is kept wet at all times. (See Fig. 16–2 for an example of how seeds may be germinated.)

The three main parts of a seed can be seen clearly in the lima bean: (1) the embryo (the "baby" plant), (2) the food supply, and (3) the protective seed coat. (See Fig. 16–3.)

The three parts can be studied if the seed is soaked overnight in water. The seed cover becomes soft and is easy to remove, thus making the other parts easy to inspect. Pupils will find that toothpicks are helpful in separating the seed parts.

After a number of observations pupils should be able to notice that there are two major groups of seeds: some with two halves (*dicotyledons*) and those with single units (*monocotyledons*). (Of course, pupils in lower grades do not have to refer to them by their scientific names.)

Let the seeds germinate for several days and have pupils study the seeds and new plants carefully. Repeated observations at periodic intervals will show that each baby plant has a growing system of leaves, stems, and roots. As it germinates, the food supply of the seed is slowly used up in the new plant's growth.

Pupils can study the germination of seeds by performing Events 12–B through 16–F. In *Event 16–B. Seed Depth* the pupils will notice that large seeds, like lima beans, will do well when planted fairly deep in the soil. If it

Fig. 16–2. **Small seeds can be germinated on a thick piece of absorbent cloth. Drape the cloth over a container and dip the ends in water. Moisture moves up the cloth to keep the seeds wet.**

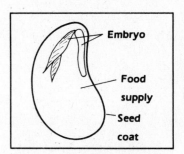

Fig. 16–3. **The lima bean has a "baby" plant (embryo), a protective seed coat (a thin outer covering), and a food supply for the new plant.**

is good soil, a depth of 5 centimeters is recommended. Small seeds, however, should be planted at more shallow depths. Radish, onion, and carrot seeds should go no more than about 5 or 6 millimeters deep.

After working with seeds for a while, pupils should be able to discover a relationship between size and planting depth. Small seeds are planted "shallow"; large seeds are planted "deep."

Plants grow entirely from stored energy until they reach sunlight. As a result, large seeds, with more stored energy, can push the new growth through more soil than small seeds. The greater depth also protects the seed from drying out.

The growth energy of the bean seed's stored food can be studied by performing *Event 16–C. Bean Power*. The beans without the two seed halves will grow poorly, if at all. The seed with one-half removed will grow better, but the seed with both halves in place will do best of all.

The growing beans use up the energy in the seeds after about 2 weeks. By that time the plant will have developed to the point where it can manufacture its own food supply.

By studying the development of the embryo of a seed, pupils can see that the leaves and stems always grow upward and the roots always grow downward. Even when the seedling is turned around, the plant will right itself again. This up-and-down seeking of the plant parts can be seen by doing *Event 16–D. Upside-Down Seeds*.

All the beans in this event have an equal chance of germinating. Regardless of the position of the seeds, the roots will always turn down and the stem will always move up. The up-and-down growth is governed by cells that are sensitive to gravity.

Another factor necessary for the proper germination of seeds is water. However, there should not be too much water. If pupils perform *Event 16–E. Water for Seeds* they may be surprised to note that seeds that get *too much* water will not even germinate.

This event shows that while water is needed for growth, too much is harmful. The roots need oxygen as well as water, and too much water blocks the oxygen that is needed for growth. The same is true for plantings as for seeds. If there is too much water, the plants will die.

Event 16–F. Growth in Light and Dark may also turn out to be a surprise to pupils. Most pupils believe that seeds need light to permit them to grow. Yet the seeds in this event will germinate very well in the dark. In fact, after germination the seeds left in darkness will often grow faster than the seeds exposed to light.

Although the results will be surprising to pupils, the explanation is really quite simple: *Seeds* do not need light to grow, but *plants* do. After all, seeds are planted underground where it is dark. It is only after they reach the sunlight that the seeds develop into little plants. At that point they begin to manufacture their own food and need the sunlight to survive.

During the first few days of germination the seed grows because it uses its own stored energy. During those days the seed is in underground darkness. If a seed is kept in darkness after it germinates, it will grow a long "leggy" stem "searching" for the sun. Often the plant's stem will be longer than one grown in sunlight.

Some of the best examples of plants with large amounts of stored energy are potatoes, parsnips, beets, and carrots. There is so much stored energy in each of these plants that they can grow stems of amazing length in the darkness. These examples are not seeds, however. They are either roots or stems that can develop into plants. They will be discussed in more detail later.

Minerals are also needed for plant growth. These are generally obtained from the soils in which they grow. Thus, plants growing in sand or other sterile surroundings will die even when the sunlight and water conditions are ideal.

If the plant gets its minerals, sunlight, and water, it can grow even if there is no soil. In fact, there is a type of soilless gardening called hydroponics where the correct nutrients are supplied in the water. This type of gardening may be of interest to some advanced pupils. Details about the correct mixture of chemical nutrients can be found in some encyclopedias and secondary science textbooks.

HOW SEEDS TRAVEL. Seeds travel in many ways. A partial list can be made after performing *Event 16–G. How Do Seeds Travel?* The list may include the three types detailed as follows:

1. *Seeds that fly.* Dandelion and milkweed seeds are "fliers." Individual seeds are attached to light "parachutelike" puffs of growth that are easily carried by the wind. Such seeds are scattered over a very wide area.

   Modified fliers, such as the seeds of the maple and box elder trees, have winglike attachments that permit the seeds to drift on wind currents or "helicopter" down for some distance before they land.
2. *Seeds that stick.* Have you ever seen a dog returning from a burdock thicket? The dog is covered with burrlike seeds. These seeds have hooks and barbs that attach themselves to the fur of animals. As a result, the animals disperse the seeds over a fairly wide area.
3. *Seeds that are eaten.* There are many seeds that are eaten. Some of them (such as nuts) are eaten for food. They are destroyed in the process and cannot germinate.

Other seeds are located inside a fruit and are discarded after the fruit is eaten. Those may germinate. Examples of such fruits are apples, oranges, avocados, pears, grapes, apricots, and peaches.

Still other seeds are eaten along with the fruit and survive the trip through the digestive tract. They can also germinate. For example, many types of berries eaten by birds survive and grow into plants. Just look at what happens along a farmer's fence line. Those fence lines become rows of berry bushes. Birds sit on the fences and excrete seeds. The seeds germinate and grow into plants.

SEEDLESS REPRODUCTION OF PLANTS (EVENTS 16–H, 16–I, AND 16–J)

Discrepant Events and Pupil Investigations

Event 16–H. Carrot Plantings. Take several carrots and plant them in potting soil. Plant them at various depths and keep the soil moist.

Pupil Investigations (may include the following processes):
1. Observing that a carrot grows as long as it receives enough oxygen and water (Too much water will kill the carrots.)
2. Inferring that the new plant obtains its energy from the carrot itself
3. Observing that the carrot begins to shrivel as the new plant grows

Event 16–I. Grass Growing. Plant some grass in a small box of potting soil. Be sure to plant the grass sparsely. Observe the grass over a period of a month or more.

Pupil Investigations (may include the following processes):
1. Observing that the grass is thinly spaced when it emerges
2. Discovering that new shoots keep developing, making the grass more and more dense
3. Devising a system for measuring grass density per unit area
4. Inferring that grass develops in other ways than from seeds

Event 16–J. Begonia Beginnings. Cut a section of stem with leaf attached from a rex begonia plant. Place the stem in water and set it in sunlight. Observe it for several weeks.

Pupil Investigations (may include the following processes):
1. Observing that roots form on the stem after a few days
2. Comparing this form of propagation to other forms
3. Generalizing about the propagation of plants by cuttings

Events 16–H, 16–I, and 16–J Explained in Context (Seedless Reproduction of Plants)

Seeds are extremely important in plant reproduction. However, pupils may be surprised to discover that many types of plants can be grown without seeds. In fact, there are a number of nonseed methods of plant reproduction.

Certain plants can reproduce from especially adapted roots and stems. Such plants have large amounts of stored energy that nourish the new plant. An example can be seen by performing *Event 16–H. Carrot Plantings.* The new growth of a carrot plant will receive great amounts of stored energy from the planted carrot itself. Only after a set of green leaves have developed will the plant manufacture its own food.

Similar results can be achieved by planting sweet potatoes, white potatoes, parsnips, onions, and numerous flower bulbs. (Be sure to point out that these plants can also be grown from seeds.)

It is important to stress again that a new planting needs oxygen to grow. Therefore, a carrot will grow best if it is placed only about halfway into the moist soil so that part of it will be exposed to air. A carrot will rot if it is completely buried in waterlogged soil.

Another means of plant propagation is by the formation of *runners*. Runners are special growths that develop on the stems of some plants. These runners grow away from the main stem, take root, and then form new plants.

Many common grasses reproduce this way. That is why a newly seeded area looks so thin when the seeds emerge but soon thickens into a lush lawn. The grass can be observed in *Event 16–I. Grass Growing*.

Since the thickening process is gradual, it may be difficult to notice the process. As a result, pupils should find a way to measure grass density. This can be done by actually counting the blades in a sample area of, say, 1 centimeter by 1 centimeter.

Another way of measurement is to compare photographs taken at periodic intervals. Care must be taken that the measurements are not distorted by changes in the length of the grass from one period to another. Other plants that propagate by sending out runners include strawberries and some forms of ivy.

A third form of seedless reproduction is achieved with *cuttings*. This is a process in which a leaf or leaf stalk is cut from a plant and placed into moist soil where the cutting takes root. Another option is to place the leaf stalk into a container of water where it forms roots. It can then be planted in soil.

Pupils can observe this form of growth by doing *Event 16–J. Begonia Beginnings*. The rex begonia, African violet, coleus, geranium, and echeveria, among others, can be propagated in this manner.

A more complex form of reproduction is *grafting*, a process in which cuttings are joined to other plants. Usually a branch or stem is cut from one plant and grafted to the stem of another plant. This practice is fairly common in nurseries. For example, the seedless orange tree can only be propagated in this way. Since the tree is seedless, it is obvious that it cannot grow from seeds. Instead, branches of the seedless trees are grafted to hardy roots and stems of a seed variety. Grafting is used to improve many other varieties of trees.

Discrepant Events and Pupil Investigations

THE PARTS OF A PLANT (EVENTS 16–K THROUGH 16–P)

Event 16–K. Roaming Roots. Plant a few radish seeds in a mixture of sand and humus near the outer walls of a glass container. Give the seeds enough moisture to germinate. Then water only one end of the container and observe the growth of roots.

Pupil Investigations (may include the following processes):
1. Observing that the root hairs grow toward the water supply
2. Comparing the root development with the roots' distance from the watered spot
3. Concluding that seeds need water

Fig. 16–4. **Moisture from the plant condenses on the inside of a clear plastic sheet that covers it.**

Event 16–L. Carnation Water Pumps. Mix some food coloring into a bottle of water; then insert the stem of a carnation into it. Observe the carnation after several hours.

Pupil Investigations (may include the following processes):
  1. Observing that the flower takes on the color of the water
  2. Inspecting the stem to find that a cut section has colored spots around the outer edge
  3. Inferring that the plant has a method of pulling liquid up the stem into the leaves and flowers

Event 16–M. Moisture Makers. Enclose the leaves and branches of a plant with some clear plastic as shown in Fig. 16–4. Gather the plastic together at the base of the stem. Set the plant in the sunlight and observe it for several hours.

Pupil Investigations (may include the following processes):
  1. Observing that water condenses on the inside of the plastic cover
  2. Inferring that the plant releases moisture into the air
  3. Forming a theory that plants contribute to the water cycle

Event 16–N. Solar Power Plant. See the effect of solar power on plants. Enclose a leaf in a cardboard or tinfoil envelope so that no light gets through. Remove the cover after 3 or 4 days and observe the results. Check to see if the leaf contains any starch. Compare it with a leaf that was not covered.

Pupil Investigations (may include the following processes):
  1. Observing that the covered leaf has lost most of its green color
  2. Testing with an iodine solution to see if the leaf contains starch
  3. Comparing the covered leaf with an uncovered leaf
  4. Generalizing that sunlight is essential to the food manufacturing process of a leaf

Fig. 16–5. **A plant will grow around obstructions to a source of light.**

Event 16–O. Light-Seekers. Place a bean plant into a shoebox arranged with dividers similar to those shown in Fig. 16–5. Keep the box covered for about a week (except for brief observations and for watering).

Pupil Investigations (may include the following processes):
  1. Observing that the plant grows rapidly while enclosed in the box
  2. Discovering that the green color of the leaves begins to fade
  3. Observing that the plant moves around the dividers in the box toward the light
  4. Inferring that plants have a mechanism that causes them to seek light

Event 16–Q. Parts of a Flower. Study the parts of a simple flower, such as a tulip or a sweet pea. Identify the parts and their functions.

Pupil Investigations (may include the following processes):
1. Identifying, with the aid of references, the main parts of a flower
2. Inferring a relationship between the pollen and ovule
3. Relating the function of plant parts to wind, insects, and gravity in the distribution of pollen

Events 16–K Through 16–P Explained in Context (Parts of a Plant)

What are the major parts of a plant and their functions? Pupils can usually identify these parts. Even at a very early age they seem to know that most plants have roots, a stem (or trunk), a system of leaves, and flowers. In this section these parts will be studied more carefully.

ROOTS. Roots serve at least two important functions: (1) They anchor the plant and (2) they gather raw materials such as water and minerals. The water-gathering function of roots can be observed in *Event 16–K. Roaming Roots.*

The roots need moisture so they grow only on the side of the container that is watered. They do not grow into the dry soil on the other side of the container. Radish seeds work well in this event (as in many others) because they germinate so quickly. Results will be seen in several days to a week.

Roots also serve to anchor the plant to the ground (which is well known to those who have tried to pull out weeds from a garden). The root systems of some weeds are so extensive that it is almost impossible to kill the weeds by pulling them from the ground. There always seems to be enough of the root system remaining to permit them to grow back.

Study the root system with a magnifying glass. Place the roots on some black paper so that the fine white root hairs are seen more easily. Note the extensive network of root hairs.

STEMS (TRUNKS). The stem of a plant carries the water and nutrients to the leaves where they are used in the manufacture of food. Much of the manufactured food is then transported through the stem back to the roots as well as to all other parts of the plant.

By performing *Event 16–L. Carnation Water Pumps,* we can see that liquids actually travel up the stems of a plant. It takes only a few hours for the plant to draw up the colored water and appear on the flower. Thus, if a white carnation is placed in red-colored water, a red fringe forms on the flower.

The movement of liquid observed in the carnation also takes place in trees. Some large trees must pump hundreds of liters of water to the leaves daily. The returning flow of sap is often seen dripping from breaks or wounds in trees, especially during the spring of the year. In some trees V-shaped notches are cut into the bark for the purpose of collecting the sap and making it into syrup and sugar.

The cross section of a tree trunk is fascinating. The rings in the trunk are formed by variations in growth patterns during the course of each year. A tree will generally have a vigorous growth spurt during the spring and summer of each year but will slow down and go dormant in the fall and winter.

The dark rings represent dormant or slow-growth periods. By counting the rings in the trunk of a tree, we can obtain a good estimate of the tree's age.

LEAVES. What happens to water that goes through the stem to the leaves? The water is given off by the leaves. Evidence of this water loss can be seen in *Event 16–M. Moisture Makers.* The moisture that is given off by the leaves condenses on the plastic that surrounds the plant. The plastic is soon covered with a fine film of water droplets.

Caution: Watch the plant closely for signs of overheating. Sunlight speeds up the water-emitting process, but it also heats the air and plant inside the plastic cover. Too much heat will damage the plant. In that case, set the plant near a window to get plenty of light but keep it out of the direct rays of the sun.

Pupils may be able to see how a leaf is structured by studying it under a microscope. Tear a leaf into two parts. If you look closely along the tear, a thin filmlike layer can be seen on the underside of the leaf. Remove a small section of that layer and observe it under a microscope.

Tiny openings, called *stoma*, should be visible as shown in Fig. 16–6. These are generally located on the underside of a leaf. If a leaf's top surface is studied, the openings cannot be seen.

The leaf is the manufacturing center of a plant. It takes carbon dioxide from the air and chemically combines it with water to produce a simple sugar that is quickly changed to starch. Starch is used as energy for growth or is stored for later use. Oxygen is a by-product of the manufacturing process and is released into the air.

The manufacturing process cannot take place without sunlight, which supplies the energy to "run the factory." Plants that use the sunlight have green-colored leaves. Any time the process stops, as in the fall of the year, the leaves lose their green color.

The effects of sunlight can be seen by doing *Event 16–N. Solar Power Plant.* When a leaf is covered, blocking out all light, it loses its green color in about 3 or 4 days. In the covered area the starch-making process stops. As a result, the iodine test will verify that starch is absent.

In the starch test iodine will turn deep purple if starch is present. If starch is not present, iodine does not change color.

It is somewhat more difficult to test the starch in green leaves than in foods because the green color masks the results. Therefore, the color should be removed prior to the test.

The green color can be removed by boiling the leaf in alcohol for about 15 to 20 minutes. Then the colorless leaf can be easily tested. (*Caution:* Alcohol is quite flammable. Do *not* boil alcohol over an open flame. Heat it in a double boiler, with water in the bottom section and alcohol in the top.)

Because leaves need light, a plant is quite sensitive to its light source. House plants will often lean toward the light of a nearby window. The leaves all seem to turn so that each gets the maximum amount of light.

Fig. 16–6. **Under a microscope the openings, or stoma, of the underside of a leaf are visible.**

An exaggerated example of this attraction is seen in *Event 16–O. Light-Seekers*. A plant left for several days in the specially designed box will grow around the dividers and finally grow right through the small opening. A bean plant is good to use in this event because it grows so quickly.

In the manufacturing process a leaf uses carbon dioxide and gives off oxygen. If the supply of carbon dioxide is cut off, the leaf will die. You can test this statement by coating the leaf with petroleum jelly, cold cream, or some other greasy substance. The substance will clog the tiny openings of the leaf so that carbon dioxide cannot be obtained from the air. In a few days the leaf will turn yellow.

What happens when the opposite is done, when plants get an enriched supply of carbon dioxide? It encourages rapid growth. In fact, for this reason greenhouse operators often add carbon dioxide to the greenhouse air.

STRUCTURE OF A FLOWER. To study the structure of a flower as suggested in *Event 16–P. Parts of a Flower*, we recommend that a simple plant be used such as a tulip or sweet pea. Do not use a compound flower, such as the sunflower, that has hundreds of duplicate parts all crowded together.

A simple flower will generally have a number of petals, several stamens, and a pistil. (See Fig. 16–7.) Pollen is produced on the upper knobs of the stamen and falls down to fertilize the ovules at the base of the pistil. The base of the pistil can be opened carefully with a toothpick or other sharp object. Inside are the small round objects that later turn into seeds.

Some flowers are self-pollinating; that is, the pollen produced by a flower will fertilize the ovules of that same flower. Other flowers depend on insects and wind to carry the pollen from one plant to another.

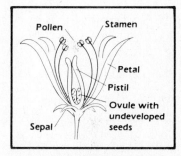

Fig. 16–7. **The major parts of a flower are shown.**

Discrepant Events and Pupil Investigations

MICROSCOPIC PLANTS (EVENTS 16–Q THROUGH 16–T)

Event 16–Q. What Sours the Milk? Pour some milk into a beaker and let it stand in a warm location. Leave it for a day or two. Observe it from time to time.

Pupil Investigations (may include the following processes):
1. Observing the milk at regular intervals and noting that it slowly changes from a liquid to a semisolid
2. Testing the milk with litmus paper to check on the acid-base content
3. Detecting a change in the odor of the milk
4. Inferring that there is a fundamental change occurring in the milk

Event 16–R. Fruit-Jar Cultures. Boil several uncovered fruit jars with a thin wedge of potato in each for 20 minutes. Boil the lids as well. Remove the jars and cover them loosely with the lids. After they cool, remove all but one cover and expose each to a different condition.

For example, touch the potato of one jar with your finger, let another jar stand in open air for several minutes, and cough into a third jar. Loosely cover the jars and set them in a dark place at room temperature. Observe the samples from time to time for about a week. (*Caution:* Gases might form in some of the jars, so the covers should be loose enough for the gases to escape. Otherwise a jar might explode.)

Pupil Investigations (may include the following processes):
1. Discovering the formation of growths on the potatoes inside the jars
2. Observing (if lucky) that the one jar that was not opened is free from any growth
3. Inferring that there are many sources of contamination

Event 16–S. Mold Farming. Find the best conditions in which molds will grow. Use several slices of bread and vary the conditions. Set one in a moist warm place; another in a dry warm place; a third in a cold dry place; and so on. Observe from time to time for several days.

Pupil Investigations (may include the following processes):
1. Observing the different slices of bread at periodic intervals
2. Recording the data found by the observations
3. Generalizing about conditions that are most favorable for the growth of mold on bread

Event 16–T. Yeast Plants. Mix some yeast and sugar in warm water. Let the mixture stand for several hours. Examine a drop under a microscope about every 30 minutes.

Pupil Investigations (may include the following processes):
1. Observing yeast plants under a microscope
2. Drawing diagrams of yeast plants, especially showing the formation of buds
3. Discovering that yeast plants grow rapidly

Events 16–Q Through 16–T Explained in Context (Microscopic Plants)

Pupils are familiar with the visible plant world that is all around them: the trees, grasses, garden plants, weeds, and farm grains, which cover the earth. However, there are many smaller plants that are also there but are not so apparent, including bacteria, fungi, yeasts, molds, and algae.

Some of the plants are so small that individual samples cannot be seen without a microscope. Others, such as fungi, are actually visible but can be studied far better with a microscope than without it.

Visible or not, the *effects* of these organisms are often far easier to observe than the plants themselves. For example, *Event 16–Q. What Sours the Milk?* shows the effects of a plant organism. If left in a warm place, milk will turn sour and after a day or two will form a semisolid mass, floating on a watery liquid.

Among the changes that occur is a chemical change when lactose (a sugar) is changed to lactic acid by the action of bacteria. The change can be detected by using litmus paper. Sour milk is acidic and turns litmus paper red.

You can simulate the souring of milk by pouring some vinegar into milk. The milk will curdle (form semisolid chunks) almost at once. The acid in this mixture will turn litmus paper red, just as the acid did in the sour milk.

Microscopic plants form colonies (or heavy growths) in which organisms are clustered together by the thousands or millions. In *Event 16–R. Fruit-Jar Cultures* it is likely that each of the exposed cultures will develop colonies of microorganisms in a fairly short time.

In fact, even the control sample may form colonies because it is quite difficult to get a perfectly sterile environment inside a jar and to keep it that way before it is sealed. At any rate, the control bottle should at least show that the growths are not so dense as in the other jars.

Be sure to exercise caution with the boiling water and jars. Also, attach the lids loosely so that excess pressure inside the jars can escape. That pressure could form from gases given off by the growths on the cultures. Too much pressure could cause a jar to explode.

The effects of bacteria on our food supply have been greatly reduced during the past several decades. Food spoilage still occurs, of course, but it is not so severe a problem as formerly because there are now better ways of preserving foods. Some of the methods used to prevent spoilage are listed here.

1. *Refrigeration and freezing.* Bacteria do not grow well if it is too cold. Thus, refrigerated foods are safe from spoilage far longer than foods kept at room temperature. If foods are frozen, they are safe from spoilage for years.
2. *Canning.* The high temperatures used in canning kill all bacteria. If the jars are sealed, then no bacteria exist inside to spoil the foods.
3. *Salting.* Salt inhibits the growth of bacteria. Salting was a popular method of preserving food before the use of freezing and canning.
4. *Drying.* Since bacteria cannot grow without moisture, foods can be preserved by drying them. Some forms of dried meat, such as *jerky,* were popular in the Old West and are still found as snacks today.
5. *Chemical preservatives.* Certain chemicals inhibit or stop the growth of harmful bacteria. Many foods contain these chemicals, and thus a wide range of low cost foods are made possible.
6. *Smoking.* Certain meats, when subjected to dense smoke, become permeated with it, preventing the growth of bacteria. This method of preservation was widely used along with salting before the use of refrigerators.
7. *Radiation.* High-energy radiation can kill all forms of bacteria without leaving any radiation danger in the food itself. It appears that radiation may prove to be the cheapest and safest way to preserve foods.

FUNGI. *Fungi* are another form of plant life. There are many varieties, such as molds, yeasts, mushrooms, lichens, and the organisms that cause athlete's foot. They are all alike in one fundamental way: They do not produce their food with the aid of sunlight. That is, they can grow in the dark. In fact, many fungi grow best in the dark.

Some of the conditions in which molds thrive can be explored by doing

Event 16–S. Mold Farming. The bread mold will grow best if it is kept warm, moist, and in a dark place. The bread that is allowed to dry out, is placed in direct sunlight, or is kept too cold will not produce a mold.

Mildew is another form of fungi. It is sometimes referred to as a mold that grows on nonfood items. Again, it needs warm, dark, and moist conditions. Mildew can grow rapidly in a pile of damp clothing during hot summer months.

It is important to realize that not all fungi are harmful. In fact, many are quite beneficial. They serve a useful function in speeding the decomposition of dead plant matter, breaking it down to become useful nutrients in the soil. Other useful fungi are used to produce life-saving drugs such as penicillin, streptomycin, and aureomycin.

Yeast is another useful fungus. It produces a chemical reaction that breaks down sugars and starches into simpler compounds, such as carbon dioxide or alcohol. Yeasts are used in breadmaking and in the production of alcohol. The growth of yeasts is shown in *Event 16–T. Yeast Plants.*

Yeasts grow rapidly in dark surroundings, with plenty of warmth and sugar. When viewing yeast through a microscope, the budding process of reproduction should be clearly visible. Buds, which form on a yeast stalk, develop into new plants.

Teaching Children about the Animal Kingdom

Discrepant Events and Pupil Investigations

Event 17–A. Classifying Animals. Display about 20 to 30 pictures of animals. Ask children to classify them into groups of their own choosing.

Pupil Investigations (may include the following processes):
1. Grouping animals according to such traits as size, how they move, where they live, what they eat, their coats (hair, feathers, scales), and which make good pets
2. Checking references as an aid to classifying animals
3. Analyzing the usefulness of the groupings
4. Comparing the groups selected by children with those selected by biologists

Event 17–B. What Am I (Number 1)? Ask pupils to classify the following mystery animal into one of five groups—mammal, reptile, bird, fish, or amphibian: "I have a backbone and lay eggs. My skin is covered with hair, and I cannot fly. What am I?"

Pupil Investigations (may include the following processes):
1. Classifying on the basis of the backbone that the animal could belong to any of the five groups
2. Inferring (incorrectly) that because it lays eggs, the animal could not be a mammal
3. Inferring (incorrectly) that its lack of flying ability is a key to the correct placement of the animal
4. Generalizing on the basis of having hair that the animal is a mammal

Event 17–C. What Am I (Number 2)? Ask pupils to classify this mystery animal into one of five classes—mammal, reptile, bird, fish, or amphibian: "I live in the water. I cannot survive on land. I have a backbone, and hair on my skin. My body temperature does not change very much."

Pupil Investigations (may include the following processes):
1. Classifying the animal (incorrectly) as a fish because it lives in water and cannot survive on land

2. Classifying the animal (incorrectly) as a reptile or amphibian because it lives in water
3. Classifying the animal on the basis of its hair

Event 17–D. What Am I (Number 3)? Ask pupils to classify the following mystery animal into one of five classes—mammal, reptile, bird, fish, or amphibian: "I have a backbone and walk on two legs. I cannot fly. I am warm-blooded and have no teeth. I grow to 8-feet tall and have feathers. I lay eggs."

Pupil Investigations (may include the following processes):
1. Predicting that the animal could be either a bird or mammal because it has two legs and is warm-blooded
2. Analyzing that factors of size, egg-laying, and lack of teeth are not valid traits used to classify animals
3. Inferring (incorrectly) that since it cannot fly, it could not be a bird (thinking that all birds can fly)
4. Classifying the animal as a bird because it has feathers

Event 17–E. What Am I (Number 4)? Ask pupils to classify the following mystery animal into one of five classes—mammal, reptile, bird, fish, or amphibian—"I have a backbone and eat meat. I live in the water and on land. I lay eggs and am cold-blooded. I have an armored skin."

Pupil Investigations (may include the following processes):
1. Classifying the animal (incorrectly) as a fish because it can live in the water
2. Classifying the animal (incorrectly) as a mammal because it can eat meat
3. Classifying the animal as a reptile because it is cold-blooded and has an armored skin

Event 17–F. What Am I (Number 5)? Ask pupils to classify the following mystery animal into one of five classes—mammal, reptile, bird, fish, or amphibian: "I have a backbone and lay eggs. I live on land and in the water. I have smooth skin and am cold-blooded."

Pupil Investigations (may include the following processes):
1. Classifying the animal (incorrectly) as a reptile
2. Concluding that because it is cold-blooded it has to be a reptile, fish, or amphibian
3. Generalizing that only amphibians meet all the characteristics of the mystery animal

Event 17–G. What Am I (Number 6)? Ask pupils to classify the following mystery animal into one of five classes—mammal, reptile, bird, fish, or amphibian: "I have a backbone and a lung. I live in water and breathe with gills. I am cold-blooded and have a scaly skin."

Pupil Investigations (may include the following processes):
1. Concluding (incorrectly) on the basis of its having a lung that the animal would have to be a bird, mammal, or amphibian
2. Classifying the animal as either fish, amphibian, or reptile because it has gills
3. Deciding that the animal could only be a fish or reptile because it has a scaly skin
4. Classifying the animal as either amphibian or reptile because it is cold-blooded
5. Concluding that a lung is not a valid factor for classification

Events 17–A Through 17–G Explained in Context (Animals with Backbones)

There are thousands of different forms of animal life. One of the best ways to understand the animal kingdom is to classify animals into related groups. In that way we can understand the characteristics of a group instead of trying to memorize the animals one at a time.

Before going into any classroom exercises that focus on animal groupings, it may be helpful to see how biologists have classified the animals. They have grouped animals into levels of greater and greater specialization. These groupings are presented briefly, beginning with the most general and ending with the most specific.

1. *The animal kingdom.* All living things are divided into two main groups. Except for a few classes of microscopic organisms, all living things are either plants or animals.

    Animals have the following characteristics: (a) They are capable of independent movement; (b) they contain no cellulose (or woody) material; (c) their cells contain no chlorophyll (the substance that colors plants green); and (d) they are capable of feeling and sensation.
2. *Phylum.* The animal kingdom is divided into a number of large divisions or phyla. These phyla, for example, include *Protozoa* (the one-celled animals) and *Chordata* (animals with a backbone).
3. *Class.* The phyla are further divided into classes. For example, the phylum *Chordata* is divided into mammals, reptiles, birds, fish, and amphibians.
4. *Order.* Each class is divided into orders. The class of mammals, for example, is divided into 16 orders that include *Carnivora* (the meat-eating animals), *Marsupialia* (the pouched animals), and *Proboscidea* (the long-nosed animals).
5. *Family.* Each order is divided into families. The order *Carnivora*, for example, is divided into families that include felines (the cats) and canines (the dogs).
6. *Genus.* Each family is divided into genera. For example, the family of felines is divided into a number of genera that includes lions and tigers.

7. *Species.* Each genus is divided into species. For example, the lions are divided into a number of species that include *Felis concolor* (the mountain lion)
8. *Subspecies.* Sometimes the species are divided still further into subspecies.

It is impossible to present all these groups in elementary school science lessons. Instead, relatively few animals should be presented to help children understand how the classification system works.

In this chapter we will focus on the five classes of *Chordata.* In other words, we will study the five groups of animals that have backbones. They include the mammals, reptiles, birds, fish, and amphibians. In addition, insects will also be discussed.

Placing pictures of animals into groups will help pupils to become familiar with factors that distinguish one group of animals from another group. Gather a group of 20 to 30 familiar animal pictures. Be sure that you have examples of all the groups that you want to teach about. Display them on a bulletin board or in any way that makes them all visible at the same time.

Ask pupils to classify the animals according to any system that seems to make sense to them, as suggested in *Event 17–A. Classifying Animals.* In the beginning of this exercise it is not important if the pupils follow any guidelines about official grouping systems. Let them select characteristics on their own. They may choose groupings based on size or even "animals that make good pets."

After they have worked with their groups for some time, go back over the traits that the students have chosen with a more critical eye. Ask, "Why is the trait good or weak?" Do all people agree about the animals that are listed as "pets"? If a dog is grouped as a pet, ask if a vicious dog is a pet? If size is selected, does a puppy change its classification just by growing up?

The pupils should be led to realize that any characteristic that is too vague is not of much help in classifying. Neither is a system helpful if it means different things to different people.

It is quite likely that the pupils will select at least some characteristics that are used in the official classification system. For example, "animals with feathers" or "animals with hair" is not too uncommon.

Some of the basic factors in the classification system can be highlighted by presenting a series of "What am I?" exercises from Events 17–B through 17–G. These six events focus on the five classes of animals that have backbones.

MAMMALS. *Mammals* are a class of warm-blooded animals that possess hair at some stage of their development and nourish their young by means of milk glands. Most, but not all, mammals give live birth to their young (instead of incubating an egg).

Event 17–B. What Am I (Number 1)? describes one of the rare egg-laying mammals: the duck-billed platypus. After the eggs hatch, they are nourished by milk glands just like other mammals.

Of course, the children are not expected to be able to identify the animal by name. The purpose of the exercise is to focus on the characteristics that are relevant in selecting a group. Egg-laying is not a relevant consideration among animal classes. It does not help because there are egg-layers among all five groups.

Event 17–C. What Am I (Number 2)? is somewhat easier for most pupils. In this event pupils can often name the correct animal. Examples of the mystery animal are the whale, dolphin, sea lion, and porpoise. All of these are mammals that must live in water. Each is a lung-breather, has hair on its skin, has a constant body temperature, and gives milk to its young. Those characteristics are quite different from fish, which are cold-blooded, lay eggs, obtain oxygen with gills, and have a scaly skin.

Animals are referred to as warm-blooded or cold-blooded. By this reference we mean that some animals have a near constant body temperature, whereas others have temperatures that vary with the environment. Humans, for example, have a normal body temperature of 37 degrees Celsius. This value changes only slightly depending on the rate of body activity and conditions of health. Even hibernating animals do not have a big change in their body temperature.

Cold-blooded animals are quite different. They generally undergo wide swings in temperature, depending on the temperature of their surroundings. A fish, for example, has a body temperature that is identical to the water in which it swims.

When the temperature warms up, cold-blooded animals become more active; when it cools down, they become less active. If it gets too cold, they cease activities altogether. Many such animals will remain inactive all winter.

Cold-blooded animals survive long winters because they use no energy to maintain body temperature. Furthermore, if it is cold, they do nothing, so no energy is used. Thus, they wait for the return of warm weather to become active again.

Warm-blooded animals, by contrast, use a great amount of energy just to maintain body temperature. Therefore, warm-blooded animals must eat much more food than cold-blooded animals.

BIRDS. Birds are distinguished by their feathers. The most common misconception people have is that all birds can fly. That is not true. There are several kinds of flightless birds, including the ostrich, penguin, kiwi, emu, and cassowary.

In *Event 17–D. What Am I (Number 3)?* the characteristic of feathers is what identifies the animal as a bird. The event describes an ostrich. In addition, all birds are warm-blooded and have two legs. (All birds also have two wings, but that does not necessarily mean that the birds can fly.)

Birds have huge appetites. Many smaller birds eat their weight in food every day. They need these great amounts of food because flying uses up a lot of energy. In addition, much food is needed just to maintain body temperature.

A smaller bird needs more energy per gram to keep warm than does a larger bird. The smaller the bird, the greater the relative skin area through which heat is lost. This statement may seem vague, at first, but should become clear by doing a simple experiment.

Compare the surface of one milk carton of $\frac{1}{2}$-gallon size, with two cartons, each of 1-quart size. Their volumes are the same; but the surface area of the two smaller cartons, when added together, is greater than that of the larger carton.

Just cut the three cartons apart carefully at the seams so that they can be laid flat. Then measure the surface area and compare. The same figures can be gained by simply measuring the boxes and doing the calculations. The two smaller cartons, when combined, should have 57 percent more surface area than the large carton.

In like manner, large animals have less surface area per unit of volume than small animals have. As a result, the larger animals need less energy per unit of volume to maintain body temperature than do smaller animals.

Can you guess the diet of birds that live in cold, snowy climates in the winter? Are they likely to be those that live on insects? Not likely, because there are no insects available when it gets cold. Only birds that can survive on seeds live in cold winter climates.

Those that need insects fly south. Some winter birds eat both insects and seeds, but in the winter they eat only the seeds that are available.

One easy way to observe birds is to build a birdfeeder. (See Fig. 17–1 to see how to make a birdfeeder from a tin can and pie plate.)

Fig. 17–1. **A simple birdfeeder can be built with a tin can and a pie plate. A wire can be attached to hang the feeder on the limb of a tree.**

HATCHING EGGS. One activity that is a real hit in the classroom is the incubation and hatching of eggs. Fertilized eggs will hatch if they are properly cared for in an incubator.

The temperature and humidity must be carefully controlled for the incubation to be a success. As a result, it is not likely that a "homemade" incubator will be successful. Most homemade incubators will either broil or freeze the eggs.

If it is well made, however, a homemade incubator might work. It must have a source of heat (usually a light bulb) and a thermostat wired into the electrical circuit to maintain an even temperature. If a light bulb is used, the eggs should be protected from the direct rays of the bulb (otherwise the eggs will be cooked by radiation even if the air temperature is correct). Finally, a shallow pan of water is needed to keep a high moisture content in the air. (See Fig. 17–2.)

It is unlikely that many teachers will be able to build a homemade incubator that will work satisfactorily. It is therefore recommended that a commercial incubator be used. Under no circumstances should someone who is not fully competent to work safely with electrical wiring attempt the project. It is far more complicated than just plugging in a light.

Fig. 17–2. **A cross section of an egg incubator. A thermostat is needed to keep the temperature accurate.**

Properly incubated eggs can be checked periodically to examine the stage of development of the growing embryos. Break open the eggs and carefully separate the developing embryo from the rest of the egg. After about one week of growth the embryo will be large enough for the eyes, wings, and legs to be visible.

After about 21 or 22 days of incubation the chick hatches from its egg. It uses a small ridge on the upper tip of its beak (the *egg tooth*) to break open the shell. The ridge drops off shortly after the chick hatches. Several hours are usually needed for the chick to pick its way out of the shell. The chick emerges wet and bedraggled, but soon the downlike feathers dry and the chick becomes a soft ball of fluff.

Once the chicks are hatched, they can survive a more varied environment than the incubator. As a result, the homemade chickbrooder is likely to be more successful than the homemade incubator.

A brooder must provide a warm place for the chicks and some freedom of movement so that they can run and eat. A two-part box, as shown in Fig. 17–3, is useful. The inside half can provide warmth if heated with a small light bulb carefully shielded against fire and electrical danger. Be sure that the bulb is out of reach of the chicks.

The other half of the box (the outside half) should be an open screened area to permit free circulation of air and allow easy viewing. Chicks should have food and water available at all times.

If you decide to have chicks in your class, it is important to realize that they require a lot of care in feeding and in keeping them clean. Any neglect in cleaning will quickly attract flies, mites, and other pests. Therefore, it is probably wise to give them away after a week.

Also, any neglect in heating and feeding will result in death for at least some of the chicks. So let the children enjoy the event and learn about the eggs and chicks. Then give the chicks away to someone who has the time and ability to care for them.

Fig. 17–3. **A chickbrooder can be made from a box divided into two parts. Chicks should be able to move freely from the heated half to the open half.**

REPTILES. *Reptiles* are a class of animals that are cold-blooded. They have a backbone and an armored (or scaly) skin. Reptiles breathe air with lungs and usually lay hard- or soft-shelled eggs. There are over 6000 species. Snakes, turtles, lizards, alligators, and crocodiles are some examples.

Event 17–E. What Am I (Number 4)? highlights the characteristics of reptiles. The mystery animal of this event is the turtle. Many types of reptiles spend most of their lives in the water. Nevertheless, they must breathe air with lungs to survive.

Some sea turtles spend most of their lives in the water and seldom come on land. They have flippers, which help them swim well, but which are poor for walking on land. Other turtles, more properly called tortoises, live mostly on land and occasionally go into the water. Accordingly, they have feet with toes and claws instead of flippers.

Because reptiles are cold-blooded, they depend on their surroundings for body heat. If the weather gets cold, they slow down and become sluggish. Warm weather is needed for them to function at their best. As a result, there are no turtles in very frigid climates. By contrast, reptiles abound in the tropics.

Turtles can usually survive fairly well if properly cared for. A habitat for a turtle should include some water, a gradual incline from the water to some sand or soil, and perhaps a flat rock. (See Fig. 17–4.) It should also be moderately warm and have some sunlight, but shade should always be available if the turtle wants it.

Turtles can be fed bits of lettuce if they are vegetarians. If they are not, they can be fed bits of hamburger or some insects. Commercial turtle food is generally available in pet shops.

There certainly are benefits with having a turtle in the classroom. However,

Fig. 17–4. **A habitat for a turtle should include water and a gradual slope to sand or soil. Include also a flat rock and a shelter from the sun.**

there are also problems. According to reports from zoo authorities who present educational programs to schools, many turtles are mishandled in the classroom and die.

Some starve to death because meat-eaters are fed plant food, and vice versa. Even more likely, however, is too much food. The excess food rots and contaminates the container. Still others die from drowning because there is no land to rest on. They are good swimmers, but they cannot swim forever.

The teacher should be fully aware of the benefits and problems in deciding whether to have a turtle in the classroom. Perhaps the best solution for a teacher who would like to have one is to keep it for a limited period of time. Most of the educational value is gained in several weeks. After that time it is often more humane to release the animal than to keep it.

AMPHIBIANS. *Amphibians* are a class of animals that are somewhat similar to reptiles. Each type is cold-blooded, lives on both land and water, and lays eggs. There is only one major difference. Amphibians have unarmored skin, which may be smooth or bumpy; reptiles have armored, or scaly skins.

The different between amphibians and reptiles is highlighted in *Event 17–F. What Am I (Number 5)?* The animal in the riddle is a frog, and the correct class is amphibian.

One additional difference between the reptile and amphibian is that the latter depends on gills during the early stages of its life cycle. However, the adult members of the amphibians are lung-breathers.

The frog is a good example of an animal that goes through a series of major changes in its life cycle. It starts out as an egg that hatches into a tiny tadpole, or polliwog. The tadpole has gills and gets its oxygen just as fish do. It does not breathe air with lungs at this point in its development. Slowly, the tadpole grows legs and loses its tail. Finally, the legs are fully grown, the tail is gone, and the frog breathes with lungs. (See Fig. 17–5.)

Frogs are able to obtain some oxygen from the water through their skins. This allows them to survive the winter months buried in the mud at the bottom of lakes and streams. When the ground and water warm up in the spring, they return to the surface.

FISH. Fish are a class of animals that are cold-blooded, live in water, and are usually covered with scales. There is no known exception to the trait that all fish use gills to extract oxygen.

However, there are several kinds of fish, among the thousands of species, that have two methods of getting oxygen. In addition to using gills, they also breathe with a lung.

One of the fish that uses two methods of obtaining oxygen is the lung fish, referred to in *Event 17–G. What Am I (Number 6)?* (Again, the children should not be expected to identify the specific animal by name.) Children should be able to identify the animal as a fish because only fish use gills to get oxygen from the water during their entire life cycle.

Contrary to some other animals, fish are often fairly easy to keep in the classroom. They do not require as much care as most other animals. Fish

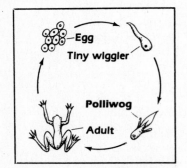

Fig. 17–5. **The life cycle of a frog includes the egg, tiny wiggler, polliwog, and adult.**

such as guppies are ideal for a classroom aquarium. They are inexpensive, reproduce quickly, tolerate a fairly wide range of temperatures, endure crowded conditions well, and are easy to feed.

By adding a few sea snails, the amount of care can be reduced even further. The snails are scavengers, or "garbage collectors." They help keep the aquarium clean; they also eat the algae that often grows in the water even if the aquarium is kept out of direct sunlight. If kept in the sunlight, the algae growth will get out of control.

A few sea plants can improve the aquarium still further. They supply the water with oxygen and remove carbon dioxide. With the right combination of fish, plants, and snails, the aquarium is said to be balanced. That is, the plants and animals work in harmony to balance each other's needs. Such an aquarium seldom needs cleaning. If it has a filter, it may go all year without cleaning.

Discrepant Events and Pupil Investigations

Event 17–H. Adaptations of Nature: Feet. What can you tell about animals by just looking at their feet? Ask pupils to determine the characteristics of birds that are represented by the feet in Fig. 17–6.

Pupil Investigations (may include the following processes):
1. Comparing the webbing, talons, and placement of toes in the three examples
2. Inferring that the feet with toes in front and back belong to a perching bird
3. Inferring that the foot with the sharp talons belongs to a predator such as an owl or hawk
4. Inferring that the webbed foot belongs to a bird that lives on or near water

Event 17–I. Adaptations of Nature: Beaks. What can you tell about animals by just looking at their beaks? Ask pupils to determine the characteristics of the birds shown in Fig. 17–7.

Pupil Investigations (may include the following processes):
1. Inferring that the short, pointed beak is adapted for cracking seeds and nuts
2. Inferring that the large, powerful hooked beak is designed for tearing
3. Inferring that the long, rounded beak is designed for scooping food out of watery places

Event 17–J. Adaptations of Nature: Eyes. What can you tell about animals by just looking at their eyes? Ask pupils to determine the characteristics of the animals that are represented by the eyes in Fig. 17–8.

ADAPTATIONS OF NATURE (EVENTS 17–H, 17–I, AND 17–J)

Fig. 17–6. **Decide what each of these birds does with its feet.**

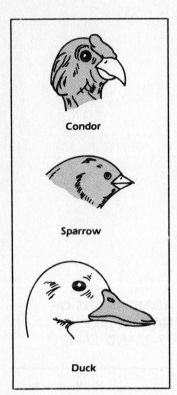

Fig. 17–7. **Decide what each of these birds does with its beak.**

Pupil Investigations (may include the following processes):

1. Observing that two animals have eyes located in the front of the head—designed for looking ahead
2. Observing that two animals have eyes located at the sides of the head—situated to see in all directions at the same time
3. Inferring that the position of the eyes is related to the animal's need to gather food and to survive
4. Generalizing that predators have eyes in front to pursue their food and that the intended victims have eyes on the sides of the head designed to detect the pursuer

Events 17–H, 17–I, and 17–J Explained in Context (Adaptations of Nature)

The earlier exercises in which pupils classified animals were to some degree exercises that focused on the various structural differences among animals. Those differences are the end result of millions of years of adaptations and changes to their surroundings.

Fish, which live in water, have adapted breathing organs that allow them to extract oxygen directly from water. Mammals, who maintain a constant body temperature, have hair that helps to insulate them from the effects of extreme cold weather.

In this section we will point, not to the gross adaptations that are the basis of the classification system, but rather, to the lesser adaptations that are not so obvious. Nevertheless, the adaptations are quite useful in teaching children about how animals cope with their surroundings.

In *Event 17–H. Adaptations of Nature: Feet* we see three types of feet. Each type is designed for special purposes. One type is designed to perch on branches. It has toes in front and back. The sparrow, parakeet, bluejay, and woodpecker are such birds.

Another type is designed for grasping and holding smaller animals. The hawk, owl, and eagle are examples of such birds. The third example is the webbed foot of a marsh or water bird. The webbed foot allows the bird to walk on the muddy bottoms of shallow lakes and marshes.

Some specialized types of beaks are shown in *Event 17–I. Adaptations of*

Fig. 17–8. **Decide by looking at the eyes which animals do the pursuing and which are the pursued.**

Nature: Beaks. The predator has a beak that can rip and tear its food. Examples are the eagle, hawk, and condor.

The seed-eating bird has a short pointed beak that can crack open seeds. The sparrow, parakeet, and nuthatch are examples of such birds. The third example is of a water bird such as the duck or goose, which strains seawater through its spoonlike bill or scoops up vegetation from shallow lake bottoms.

Another example of specialized adaptation is shown in *Event 17–J. Adaptation of Nature: Eyes.* Notice that the owl and lion have eyes in the front of the head. Those eyes are designed to look ahead. Both of these animals are predators. Their eyes are suited best for pursuing, for looking at something that they are chasing.

The other two animals, however, are the ones being pursued. Their eyes are located on the sides of the head, so that they can detect an enemy that might sneak up from any direction.

It is a form of defense that gives them a chance to spot a predator at the earliest possible instant. An instant is sometimes the difference between capture and escape.

There are many more adaptations of nature that have developed in animals. Here is a list of a few of them:

1. The camel's feet are big and flat so that it can walk on sand without sinking in. In similar surroundings a horse would sink in and have more difficulty walking.
2. The camel, which survives well in arid regions, has nostrils that permit the breathing of air but keep out blowing sand. It also has very long eyelashes to keep blowing sand out of its eyes.
3. Polar bears are adapted to their environment in a number of ways. They are colored white so that they blend into the background. They have thick fur to protect them from the cold. They even have fur pads on their feet to keep them warm and to give them better traction on the ice.
4. The tiger and giraffe are good examples of animals with protective coloration. (See Fig. 17–9.) The stripes of the tiger and the patches of the giraffe help the animals blend into their surroundings.
5. The mouth of the hippopotamus is designed for big meals. It uses its scoop-shovel mouth to gather vegetation from the bottom of ponds and rivers. It is a large animal that eats only plant life so it requires huge quantities of food to survive. Its mouth is built for the task.
6. The elephant is a huge animal. Yet it can walk through moderately wet and soft ground without getting stuck. Its foot is designed to spread out when stepping down on the ground. When pulling up, however, the foot shrinks, permitting it to be lifted up without getting stuck.
7. An African elephant lives in a very hot climate. Its ears are extremely large and are used for more than hearing: The big, floppy ears are also used like radiators to get rid of excess heat (to cool off). (See Fig. 17–10.)

Fig. 17–9. **The giraffe's coat of patches allows the giraffe to blend into its natural surroundings.**

Fig. 17–10. **The African elephant uses its ears like radiators to rid itself of excess heat.**

INSECTS (EVENTS 17–K, 17–L, AND 17–M)

Discrepant Events and Pupil Investigations

Event 17–K. Classifying Insects and Other Animals. Display a dozen or more pictures of various insects and other animals. Include some spiders and worms. Ask pupils to classify them.

Pupil Investigations (may include the following processes):
1. Analyzing the pictures to find certain traits that are similar in various animals
2. Comparing groups prepared by the pupils with the official classification system

Event 17–L. Fruit Fly Metamorphosis. Allow some fruit flies to gather on some very ripe fruit, such as bananas, in an open jar. Then cover the jar with very fine wire or some cotton. Keep the jar in a warm place (room temperature is okay) but out of direct sunlight. Observe for 1 to 2 weeks.

Pupil Investigations (may include the following processes):
1. Observing the fruit fly colony for a period of 1 to 2 weeks
2. Recording data by drawing diagrams of the stages of development
3. Predicting the size of the colony for future dates if growth is unhampered

Event 17–M. Ant Farms. Dig out the center of an anthill and drop the contents into a tall, narrow, glass-walled container. Cover one wall of the container with a sheet of dark construction paper. Observe for several weeks.

Pupil Investigations (may include the following processes):
1. Observing that the ants tunnel into the soil
2. Discovering that the tunnels are more visible behind the covered side than the uncovered side
3. Inferring that ants prefer to work in dark areas
4. Identifying different tasks performed by ants and by different parts of the colony

Events 17–K, 17–L, and 17–M Explained in Context (Insects)

Earlier we discussed several classes of animals with backbones. There are also many types of animals without backbones, with insects being the most predominant among that group. In fact, insects have the greatest number of species of all animal groups.

It is estimated that there are between 600,000 and 800,000 species of insects. (A *species* is a group of related plants or animals who can generally reproduce only with other members of that group.) Insects make up about 70 percent of all the animal species in the world.

There are several characteristics of insects that help us identify them: They have six jointed legs, a three-segment body (head, thorax, and abdomen), and an exoskeleton (a hard outer coat or covering that serves the same purpose as our inner skeleton). (See Fig. 17–11.)

These characteristics can be observed in *Event 17–K. Classifying Insects and Other Animals.* If there are good pictures of insects available for display, the distinguishing features should be quite visible.

In the beginning of the lesson let the pupils group the animals according to any system that seems to make sense to them. After the pupils have finished their original groupings, compare their work with the official classification system. Common examples of insects are flies, moths, butterflies, grasshoppers, mosquitoes, bees, and ants.

Be sure to include animals other than insects, such as spiders and worms. Worms differ from insects in exoskeleton, legs, and body parts. Spiders look much like insects and have jointed legs. However, they are different because they have eight legs, two body parts, and no exoskeleton.

Insects have many adaptations suited to their particular needs. For example, they have a good sense of smell and are attracted to food from long distances. You have, no doubt, noticed that they generally can find the food at a picnic.

Their sense of smell is quickly confirmed any time food is left outside a refrigerator or food scraps are discarded into a garbage can. If left uncovered, flies and other insects quickly swarm around a can.

Insects go through great changes, called a *metamorphosis*, during their life cycles. Most insects begin as eggs until the larvae hatch. After a period of time in which the larvae constantly eat, a covering such as *chrysalis* or *cocoon* is formed. Eventually, the adult insects emerge.

These four stages of the life cycle are included in *Event 17–L. Fruit Fly Metamorphosis.* Fruit flies are often used in classroom exercises because they grow to full adults in only 8 days. Other insects take much longer.

The only real problem with fruit flies is that they are so small. Be sure that pupils have magnifying glasses available so that they can study the four stages of development inside the jar. The eggs will be especially difficult to see.

Not all insects go through all four stages of development. A grasshopper, for example, has only three stages in its development. It starts as an egg, and hatches into a nymph (which looks like a miniature adult), and grows to an adult.

Some insects live in highly organized societies. Bees, for example, have a society in which some workers are assigned to feed the young, some to gather honey and pollen, others to make wax for the hives, some to tend the queen, some to help regulate the temperature of the hive, and others to guard the hive from intruders.

Ants are somewhat similar to bees. They also live in organized colonies. The ant colony can be observed very easily by placing it into a sealed display frame as suggested in *Event 17–L. Ant Farms.* Gather ants and soil for the ant farm from an anthill.

After gently placing the ants and soil into the display frame, commonly referred to as an "ant farm," seal it tightly so that none of them escape into the classroom. A typical ant farm is made with two glass panes about 20 to 30 centimeters wide and 15 to 20 centimeters high. The panes are held in a wooden frame that keeps the glass panes about 3 to 4 centimeters apart.

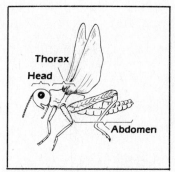

Fig. 17–11. **An insect such as a grasshopper, bee, or ant has six legs, an outer covering, and a three-part body. (A spider has eight legs and two body parts.)**

Be sure to keep the soil slightly moist. Otherwise the ants will not be able to tunnel effectively. If the soil is too dry, the tunnels tend to collapse and crumble. On the other hand, do not make the soil too wet. It speeds up the growth of molds and the ants could drown.

Place a small container of sugar water inside. That should satisfy their need for food. Ants recognize their own hive members and attack any intruders that might also go for the food.

If you cover one side of the display frame with black construction paper or other opaque material, the ants will build their tunnels right against the face of the glass. Ants avoid daylight, so you will seldom see tunnels in an uncovered part of the ant farm.

The covering can be removed from time to time to observe the ants at work. Often the tunnels and inner chambers of the colony will be revealed.

Pupils often think that all insects are harmful. This is not true. Children should realize that many insects are beneficial. Honey bees, for example, are extremely beneficial because they produce honey and pollinate flowers and fruits. Without pollination, many flowers, fruits, and crops would disappear from the face of the earth.

If insects should disappear, so would many types of birds. The only birds that could survive would be seed-eaters and plant-eaters. Even those birds might be endangered because many seeds and plants depend on pollination to reproduce.

INSECT CAGES AND COLLECTIONS

Some insects, such as moths and butterflies, may be collected and mounted for display purposes. Care must be taken so that the brittle parts of the insect are not destroyed.

Insects can be killed in a killing jar. A wide-mouthed jar can be used for this purpose. Soak some cotton with carbon tetrachloride or fingernail polish remover (ethyl acetate) and place it at the bottom of the jar. Cover the cotton with a sheet of perforated tinfoil or cardboard. Drop the insect into the jar and cover it for about 20 to 30 minutes.

The insects should be carefully spread out after removal from the jar. Do not attempt to change the positions of the wings and legs after the specimen has dried out. In a day or two they become so brittle that the parts will break if you try to bend or adjust them.

The insects can be pin-mounted on a sheet of styrofoam or other suitable material. After mounting, be sure to label the specimens. Finally, a frame should be built to hold the mounting board, and then a glass or plastic cover should be installed. In that way the specimens will be protected from damage, yet be easy to view.

Insect cages can be made from wide-mouthed jars with holes punched in the cover. Larger cages can be made with wire screen and aluminum pie plates.

Such cages are good observatories. For example, a caterpillar can be placed inside a wire cage along with the leaves and twigs on which it was found. Fresh leaves should be added to satisfy the caterpillar's food requirements. Eventually, it may spin a cocoon from which a moth or butterfly emerges in the spring.

18

Teaching Children about Nutrition and Health

Discrepant Event and Pupil Investigations

Event 18–A. See Cells. An onion is a bulb consisting of many layers. Some of the layers are extremely thin. Remove a piece of this filmlike layer and place it under a microscope to observe the cells.

Obtain a sample of another type of cell by gently scraping your cheek (inside your mouth) with the blunt end of a toothpick. Place the whitish smear on a slide and cover it with a cover plate. Observe it under a microscope. Finally, place a drop of pond water under a microscope and observe.

Pupil Investigations (may include the following processes):
1. Observing that the onion skin is composed of cells
2. Discovering that the material from inside the mouth also consists of cells
3. Comparing and finding that an onion cell has a more defined cell wall than does a cell of the mouth
4. Comparing one-celled plants and animals found in the sample of pond water
5. Drawing the cells

Event 18–A Explained in Context (Cell Growth)

Growth in living things takes place in the cell, the smallest unit of life. Most cells are too small to be seen without the aid of a good hand lens or a microscope.

Robert Hooke, an English scientist, was the first person to observe cells. He viewed the cells of cork, wood, and other plant specimens. Shortly thereafter a Dutch scientist, Anton van Leeuwenhoek (*Lay*-venhook), discovered that pond water contained one-celled animal life.

Pupils should be given a chance to observe the structure of several types of cells. They may recall the cell structure of leaves discussed in Chapter 16. For this chapter the pupils should review that information if necessary and perform *Event 18–A. See Cells.*

The onion skin is suggested because its skin is thin enough to give a fairly clear image of the cell's structure. However, be sure to use the very thin film from between the layers. Everything else is too thick to use.

Fig. 18–1. **A microscopic view of onion cells. Note their relatively uniform structure.**

Fig. 18–2. **A microscopic view of cells scraped from inside the cheek.**

A microscope of "100 X" magnification will give a view of the cells somewhat like those shown in Fig. 18–1. Any greater magnification tends to blur the image. Sometimes a clearer picture can be obtained if the cells are stained with a dilute iodine solution.

The cheek cells scraped from inside the mouth look different. They look like those cells shown in Fig. 18–2. Again, 100-power should be the maximum power used to study the cells.

In general, the cheek cell will appear transparent and be hard to see. The cell walls are made of thin nonrigid membranes. Pupils should be led to the conclusion that plant cells have thicker and more rigid cell walls than cells from human tissue. (That is why wood, for example, can be used for building purposes.) Upon close examination you should be able to see the nucleus (the darker spot) at the center of the cell.

GROWTH RATES (EVENTS 18–B AND 18–C)

Discrepant Events and Pupil Investigations

Event 18–B. Weight Table. Check the weights of males and females in Table 18–1. What conclusions can you draw from the data in the table?

Table 18–1. **Weight Table**

Ages	0–1	1–3	3–6	6–9	9–12	12–15	15–18	18–35	35–55	55–75
Male	18	29	40	53	72	98	134	154	154	154
Female	18	29	40	53	72	103	117	128	128	128

Pupil Investigations (may include the following processes):
1. Observing that up to age 12 boys and girls have the same average weights
2. Discovering that at the 12 to 15 age period girls weigh more than boys
3. Discovering that beyond 15 years of age males weigh more than females
4. Inferring that girls mature earlier than boys

Event 18–C. Height Table. Check the heights of males and females in Table 18–2. What conclusions can you draw from the data in the table?

Table 18–2. **Height Table**

Ages	1–3	3–6	6–9	9–12	12–15	15–18	18–35	35–55	55–75
Male	34	42	49	55	61	68	69	69	69
Female	34	42	49	55	62	64	64	64	64

Pupil Investigations (may include the following processes):
1. Observing that up to age 12 boys and girls have the same average heights
2. Discovering that at the 12 to 15 age period girls are taller than boys

3. Discovering that adult males are taller than adult females
4. Inferring that girls mature earlier than boys

Events 18–B and 18–C Explained in Context (Growth Rates)

Children are interested in the average growth rate of boys and girls. These are shown in *Event 18–B. Weight Table*. Pupils will see that up until 12 years of age boys and girls are of the same average weights.

Then the girls move ahead of the boys during the next 3 years. The gains by the girls are due mostly to the growth spurt that seems to affect girls earlier than boys. Boys, too, tend to start their growth spurt, but for a few years they lag behind the girls.

The height data, shown in *Event 18–C. Height Table*, confirms the pattern found in the weight table. Again, girls grow taller than boys during the 12- to 15-year-age period.

We must realize that the figures are for people of slight to medium build. People with different body builds will have weights and heights that vary from the average. A more complete set of height and weight tables is given in Table 18–3.

Another factor that should be emphasized is that some people tend to mature earlier than others. Thus, one person may be at his or her adult height at age 12, whereas a classmate may not even have started his or her growth spurt. Even members of the same family will often vary in their rates of development.

Table 18–3. **Heights and Weights**

	Men				Women		
Height	Small (lb)	Medium (lb)	Large (lb)	Height	Small (lb)	Medium (lb)	Large (lb)
5 ft 2 in.	128–134	131–141	138–150	4 ft 10 in.	102–111	109–121	118–131
5 ft 3 in.	130–136	133–143	140–153	4 ft 11 in.	103–113	111–123	120–134
5 ft 4 in.	132–138	135–145	142–156	5 ft 0 in.	104–115	113–126	122–137
5 ft 5 in.	134–140	137–148	144–160	5 ft 1 in.	106–118	115–129	125–140
5 ft 6 in.	136–142	139–151	146–164	5 ft 2 in.	108–121	118–132	128–143
5 ft 7 in.	138–145	142–154	149–168	5 ft 3 in.	111–124	121–135	131–147
5 ft 8 in.	140–148	145–157	152–172	5 ft 4 in.	114–127	124–138	134–151
5 ft 9 in.	142–151	148–160	155–176	5 ft 5 in.	117–130	127–141	137–155
5 ft 10 in.	144–154	151–163	158–180	5 ft 6 in.	120–133	130–144	140–159
5 ft 11 in.	146–157	154–166	161–184	5 ft 7 in.	123–136	133–147	143–163
6 ft 0 in.	149–160	157–170	164–188	5 ft 8 in.	126–139	136–150	146–167
6 ft 1 in.	152–164	160–174	168–192	5 ft 9 in.	129–142	139–153	149–170
6 ft 2 in.	155–168	164–178	172–197	5 ft 10 in.	132–145	142–156	152–173
6 ft 3 in.	158–172	167–182	176–202	5 ft 11 in.	135–148	145–159	155–176
6 ft 4 in.	162–176	171–187	181–207	6 ft 0 in.	138–151	148–162	158–179

SOURCE: Metropolitan Life Insurance Company height and weight tables for ages 25 to 29. Heights include shoes with 1-inch heels. Weights include clothes weighing 5 pounds for men and 3 pounds for women.

One final factor that affects the figures shown in the tables is that they change from generation to generation. About 1 inch has been added to the average height of adults every 25 years for the past 100 years. The average weights have increased also. Discuss what may have influenced those figures. Undoubtedly, better nutrition in recent generations has been an important factor.

FOOD TESTS AND TASTES (EVENTS 18–D THROUGH 18–H)

Discrepant Events and Pupil Investigations

Event 18–D. Testing for Starches. Gather together a variety of food samples. Include such items as rice, oatmeal, honey, puffed wheat, soda crackers, grape juice, meat, peanuts, potatoes, white bread, butter, corn syrup, and fruits. Let the pupils determine which of these foods contain starch.

Pupil Investigations (may include the following processes):
  1. Reading to find out how to test for starch
  2. Testing samples with drops of diluted iodine
  3. Classifying the foods according to their starch content

Event 18–E. Testing for Fats. Use the same group of food samples as was used in Event 18–D and determine if any of them contain fat.

Pupil Investigations (may include the following processes):
  1. Reading to find out how to test for fats
  2. Testing samples by rubbing them against paper
  3. Classifying the foods according to their fat content

Event 18–F. Testing for Sugars. Use the same group of food samples as those used in Event 18–D and determine if they contain sugar.

Pupil Investigations (may include the following processes):
  1. Reading to find out how to test for sugar
  2. Testing each food sample with Benedict's solution
  3. Classifying the foods according to their sugar content

Event 18–G. Testing for Taste. Prepare containers of sugar water, saltwater, diluted unsweetened lemon juice, and bitter chocolate. Take a cotton-tipped swab and dip it into one container; then apply it to the tongue. Be sure to move the swab along the front, sides, and back of the tongue. Let the taste linger on your tongue and decide which part seems to be most sensitive to each taste.

After each taste test it is advisable to drink a small amount of water and swish it around your mouth before swallowing. This tends to clear out the old taste and makes it possible to do each new taste test afresh. (Even so, tastes from a previous test will sometimes interfere.)

(*Caution:* Be sanitary. Each pupil should have a personal set of tiny paper-cup samples. Pupils should not dip their swabs into "community" containers.)

Pupil Investigations (may include the following processes):
1. Testing to see which part of the tongue is most sensitive to each of the tastes
2. Tabulating the results of the class investigations
3. Generalizing that different parts of the tongue are sensitive to different tastes

Event 18–H. Mixed-up Tastes. Prepare small slices or cubes of apples, pears, onions, and potatoes. Select several volunteers to be "tasters." The subject must taste the foods with eyes closed and, even more important, *with nose held tightly shut.*

Pick up a sample with a toothpick and place it into the subject's hand. The subject then tastes the food *while continuing to hold the nose tightly shut.* The subject should try to identify the four samples. (Remember, if the nose is released, even for an instant, the event will not work.)

Pupil Investigations (may include the following processes):
1. Observing and recording the taste tests of the subjects
2. Inferring that the sense of sight affects the sense of taste
3. Inferring that the sense of smell affects the sense of taste

Events 18–D Through 18–H Explained in Context (Foods Tests and Tastes)

TESTING FOODS. Several common ingredients of foods can be detected by performing rather simple tests.

Event 18–D. Testing for Starches is done by placing drops of dilute iodine on the foods to be tested. If the food contains starch, the iodine turns a deep purple or almost a totally black color. If starch is not present, the iodine will not change color.

The fat test, as suggested in *Event 18–E. Testing for Fats*, is even easier to do. All you need to do is rub the sample on paper. For example, what happens if you rub a peanut against some paper? A mark appears: a grease spot. It represents the fat in the peanut. Any food with a substantial fat content will leave a similar mark.

The sugar test, as suggested in *Event 18–F. Testing for Sugars*, is somewhat more complex. It requires the use of an *indicator* solution. An indicator solution is a substance that changes color to "indicate" the presence of the test food. The indicator solution for sugar is Benedict's solution and is usually available in drugstores.

If the test sample is a liquid, just add a few drops of the solution and heat it. If simple sugars are present, the sample turns red. If the food sample is a solid, it will have to be ground up and mixed with water before testing.

Surprising as it may seem, Benedict's solution will not detect table sugar because it is a complex sugar. Only simple sugars can be identified by this method.

The sample foods listed in the events are shown in Table 18–4.

Table 18–4. **Starches, Sugars, and Fats**

Starch	Sugar	Fat
Potato	Corn syrup	Peanut
White bread	Honey	Meat
Oatmeal	Grape juice	Butter
Puffed wheat	Many fruits	
Soda cracker		
Rice		

Proteins can be detected also, but the process is the most complex of the tests. First, mix about a teaspoonful of copper sulfate into a half full glass of water. Then take several drops of this solution and several drops of household ammonia and mix them in a glass containing the food to be tested. If the food contains protein, the mixture turns purple.

It is easy to test liquid proteins such as milk, but solids must be crushed or ground and then mixed with water. The liquid mixture can then be tested.

Fig. 18–3. **The tongue is sensitive to different tastes.**

THE SENSE OF TASTE. Pupils will find that different parts of the tongue are sensitive to different tastes by performing *Event 18–G. Testing for Taste*. In general, the tastes that can best be detected on the parts of the tongue are shown in Fig. 18–3.

Record the data for the class on the chalkboard to see which tastes tend to be most noticeable on various parts of the tongue. The majority will likely agree with the data in Fig. 18–3, but some members of the class will probably get different results.

Results are affected by the fact that some people actually do have different taste sensations. However, even with people who have "normal" tongues, it is sometimes difficult to keep the various samples from mixing inside the mouth. As a result, some pupils may not be sure where the sample taste is focused.

After pupils have decided that the tongue is useful for detecting tastes, they may be surprised to discover in *Event 18–H. Mixed-up Tastes* that the sense of smell is very important to the sense of taste.

The most important aspect of this taste test is that the subject *must* hold the nose shut. If even a small whiff of onion, for example, gets through, the test is lost. If you can get the pupils to hold their noses, they will have great difficulty detecting the differences between the four samples. It is often the texture or consistency, not the taste, that gives the only clue.

It is almost impossible to do the entire set of four foods without at least a slight lapse in nose-holding. As a result, the subjects will often be able to tell what the samples are. If so, ask them if it was easier to tell when not holding the nose. Invariably, they will admit that it was much easier that way. Thus, the event is successful even if some subjects cannot do the entire activity completely right.

One variation of the smell and taste test is to blindfold the subjects, but this time allow them to smell. Give them a sample food (using toothpicks to hold the food) while holding another sample under their noses. Often the smell of the sample under the nose is strong enough to confuse and overpower the taste being sensed on the tongue.

This event works best if the food on the tongue has a weak smell while the one under the nose has a strong smell (perhaps a potato on the tongue and an onion or an apple under the nose).

Discrepant Events and Pupil Investigations

FOODS AND DIETS (EVENTS 18–I THROUGH 18–O)

Event 18–I. Favorite Foods: Helpful or Harmful? Ask pupils to list all the foods they would eat for one full day if they could select anything they wanted. The list should include food for meals and any between-meal snacks. When they have finished their lists, analyze them to see if they meet the needs of good nutrition.

Pupil Investigations (may include the following processes):
1. Selecting the foods for a day
2. Comparing the list with good nutrition standards (Compare with the four food groups given later in this chapter.)
3. Computing the calorie totals for each pupil if a calorie reference can be obtained
4. Generalizing that taste is not a reliable guide to good nutrition

Event 18–J. Classifying Foods (Number 1). Display a wide variety of food pictures on the bulletin board. Let pupils select foods that fit the four food groups of (1) milk, (2) meat, (3) bread-cereal, and (4) vegetable-fruit.

An alternative method is to classify the foods without regard to the four groups listed here. Just ask the children to fit the foods into any groups that they think might be appropriate.

Pupil Investigations (may include the following processes):
1. Analyzing the types of foods to see where they fit the best
2. Comparing the selections with the four food groups
3. Gaining an awareness of the importance of good nutrition

Event 18–K. Classifying Foods (Number 2). Use the same display of food pictures as was used in the last event. This time ask the pupils to place the foods into the following three groups: (1) fats, (2) carbohydrates, and (3) proteins.

If some foods do not fit very well into any one group, just delete those pictures from the display. Ask the pupils to place the foods into the groups where they fit the best. (*Note:* You will need a nutrition book or some other reference that can supply the information to make the proper classifications. There are far too many possible selections to include them here.)

Pupil Investigations (may include the following processes):
1. Analyzing the types of foods to see where they fit best
2. Comparing the selections with the three food groups
3. Gaining an awareness of the importance of good nutrition

Event 18–L. Sugar: Good or Bad? The cells in our bodies use glucose for energy. They use nothing else. Every food that your body uses as energy cannot be used until it is changed to glucose. It may enter the body as fat, carbohydrate, or protein; but if it winds up as energy inside the cells, it has been changed to glucose. Glucose is sugar.

Here is a question for the class: If sugar is the only thing that the body can use for energy, why not eat it directly—in candies, desserts, and other "goodies"?

Pupil Investigations (may include the following processes):
1. Analyzing the way the body uses sugar
2. Forming a theory (incorrectly) that perhaps taking lots of sugar is good
3. Generalizing that too much sugar may be harmful

Event 18–M. Calorie Counting. How many calories do you need for daily living? Your calorie needs can be found by using the following rule of thumb: Multiply your weight by 12 if you are inactive, by 16 if you are moderately active, and by 20 if you are very active.

Pupil Investigations (may include the following processes):
1. Analyzing to decide what level of activity is the correct one to use in the calculations
2. Calculating the figures
3. Comparing the needs with the intake selected in Event 18–D
4. Analyzing one's personal weight to see if intake has exceeded use

Event 18–N. Overweight or Overfat? Solve the following two puzzles: Suppose two men are both 6 feet tall. One man weighs 220 pounds and the other 175 pounds, but the *lighter* of the two is too fat. How can that be possible?

Suppose a woman is 5 feet 6 inches tall and weighs 130 pounds at two different times. When weighed the first time, she was at a recommended weight; but the second time she was "too fat." How can that be possible?

Pupil Investigations (may include the following processes):
1. Forming a theory that the proper weight may depend on factors other than height
2. Inferring that the proper weight changes for a given individual with the passage of time
3. Inferring that "weight" does not necessarily mean "fat"

Event 18–O. Supermarket Diets. Collect headlines about diets from the tabloids that line the checkout stands of supermarkets. What are four themes that are found most often in those headlines? How valid are the diets?

Pupil Investigations (may include the following processes):
1. Collecting data on supermarket diets
2. Classifying the claims according to standards selected by the class
3. Analyzing whether the claims are extravagant

Events 18–I Through 18–O Explained in Context (Foods and Diets)

We know that food is necessary for health and energy. But do all foods serve these functions equally well, or are some better than others? If there are differences, how can we find those that are better than others from the hundreds that are available?

FOOD GROUPS (MILK, MEAT, BREAD-CEREAL, AND VEGETABLE-FRUIT). How can we follow a well-balanced diet? Do we depend only on taste? Find out how reliable your sense of taste is in selecting a good diet. Ask children to do *Event 18–I. Favorite Foods: Helpful or Harmful?*

Most pupils will, no doubt, show a strong preference for sweets. Conversely, they will avoid vegetables, grains, and possibly meats. It is not likely that many pupils will select a well-balanced diet on the basis of their favorite foods. The activity should make it clear that diets based on taste alone may have serious deficiencies.

What foods should we eat to meet our daily needs? The body requires food for three general purposes: (1) to provide energy, (2) to build and repair cells, and (3) to regulate body processes.

All these needs will be provided if foods are selected carefully. To make food selection easier, foods have been grouped into four categories by nutrition experts. The four *food groups* are listed here. Compare these four groups with the groups selected by pupils in *Event 18–J. Classifying Foods (Number 1)*.

The Four Food Groups

1. Milk Group

   Children: 3 to 4 cups
   Teenagers: 4 or more cups
   Adults: 2 or more cups
   Cheese, yogurt, and other milk products may be substituted

2. Meat Group

   (two or more servings daily)
   Beef, lamb, pork, veal, chicken, turkey, fish, and shellfish
   Eggs are good substitutes but should be limited to four per week
   Dry beans, dry peas, lentils, and nuts may serve as occasional
      substitutes
   Vegetarians should get expert dietary advice if meats are not eaten

3. Bread-Cereal Group

   (four or more servings)
   Breads of whole grain (preferred over white bread)
   Breakfast cereals of wheat, oats, corn, and rice

4. Vegetable-Fruit Group

   (four or more servings)
   At least one from this subgroup: citrus fruit, tomato, broccoli, raw
      cabbage, peppers, melons, or berries

A dark green or deep yellow vegetable
Other vegetables and fruits, including potatoes

After pupils have had a chance to study these groups, let them prepare sample meals for a day, using selections as suggested in the outline. Such an exercise should help pupils gain an understanding of good nutrition.

FOOD GROUPS (PROTEIN, FAT, AND CARBOHYDRATE). The four food groups in the preceding list have been widely used for many years. However, another way of classifying foods can also be highly beneficial. All foods can be divided into proteins, fats, and carbohydrates. Demonstrating this fact was the purpose of *Event 18–K. Classifying Foods (Number 2)*. A summary of data related to the three groups is given in Table 18–5.

Table 18–5. **Proteins, Fats, and Carbohydrates**

	Proteins	*Fats*	*Carbohydrates*
Calories per gram	4	9	4
Will build tissue	Yes	No	No
Will provide energy	Yes	Yes	Yes
Toxic residue	Ammonia	Ketone	None
Excess calories stored as	Fat	Fat	Fat

Protein is absolutely essential for good health. It is the *only* food that can be used to build muscle tissue. Protein is broken down into amino acids, which are the basic building blocks of muscles and connective tissue.

How much protein is needed? Probably less than most people eat. A person needs about 1 to 2 grams of protein per kilogram of body weight. Thus, a person of 60 kilograms (132 pounds) can use a maximum of 120 grams of protein (or 480 calories) per day. That amount is about 20 percent of a normal diet. What happens when someone eats more than is used for tissue-building? It does *not* go into additional muscle. It is used for energy.

Protein is not a particularly good source of energy. One of the main problems with protein is that when broken down for energy, ammonia is formed as a toxic by-product. Ammonia needs to be flushed out of the body.

High-protein diets will often show weight loss during the first few days (giving the dieter a false sense of success) because fluids are lost when the body gets rid of the ammonia. Unfortunately, the initial weight loss is not fat, just fluid.

Fats are high-energy foods, packing 9 calories per gram. That is more than twice the calories of proteins and carbohydrates.

A small amount of fat is needed in the diet, but that amount is far less than is actually consumed by most people. The amount of fat consumed daily should be limited to 30 percent of all calories taken in. The percentages of fat in some typical foods are listed in Tables 18–6 and 18–7.

When fat is used for energy, toxic by-products called *ketones* are formed and must be flushed out of the body. Thus, a high-fat diet can actually produce

Table 18–6. **Percentage of Fat in Foods**

100%	*60–70%*	*20–30%*
Butter	Eggs	Tomato soup
Corn oil	Potato chips	Crackers
Mayonnaise	Steak	Ice milk
	Chicken thigh	Lowfat yogurt
90–100%		
Cheese dressings	*50–60%*	*10–20%*
Olives	Hamburger	Broccoli
Bacon	Skim cheeses	Corn
Some nuts	Salmon	Egg noodles
	Trout	Cottage cheese
80–90%		Split-pea soup
Avocado	*40–50%*	Red snapper
Some nuts	Biscuits	Lobster
Sour cream	Doughnuts	
Bologna	Whole milk	*0–10%*
	Ice cream	Skim milk
70–80%	Sirloin	Many fruits
Many cheeses		Many vegetables
Some nuts	*30–40%*	Potato
Pork	Granola	Many fish
Hot dogs	Cheese pizza	
	Corn bread	
	Lowfat milk	

a short-term weight loss. That weight loss, however, is only water loss caused by the flushing-out process.

Too much fat harms the body. The most obvious harm is excess weight. In addition, fat clogs the arteries and circulatory system. Fat may also "teach" the body to "desire" excess weight. Once deposited as fat, it does *not* want to leave (as most dieters know only too well).

How does fat teach the body to desire excess weight? There is evidence to support the theory that fat upsets the *appistat*, or "set point"—the body's mechanism for regulating its percentage of body fat.

Once the set point (or percentage of body fat) is raised, it seldom comes down again regardless of diets. Thus, as people age, there is a slow but gradual increase in body fat that resists all attempts at reversal. Only one factor causes an exception: exercise.

Exercise seems to be the sole way of reversing the set point. It has to be sustained for at least 20 to 30 minutes at a time, and it must be done a minimum of three or four times a week to be effective. Exercise will be discussed in greater detail later in this chapter.

The third type of food shown in Table 18–5 is called *carbohydrate*. At one time the carbohydrates were considered undesirable foods, often being blamed as the cause of overweight. However, recent evidence shows just the opposite.

Carbohydrates do not produce an excess of calories per gram, and they have many benefits not found in other foods.

First of all, many carbohydrates are rich in vitamins that are needed to regulate body processes.

Table 18–7. **Percentage of Fat in Foods (by groups)**

Fruits	*Grains*
Olive—90%	Biscuits—40–50%
Avocado—80–90%	Doughnuts—40–50%
Most fruits—0%	Granola—30–40%
	Corn bread—30–40%
Vegetables	Crackers—20–30%
Nuts—70–90%	
Tomato soup—20–30%	*Fish*
Broccoli—10–20%	Salmon—50–60%
Corn—10–20%	Trout—50–60%
Split-pea soup—10–20%	Red snapper—10–20%
Potato—0–10%	Lobster—10–20%
Most other vegetables—0%	Most other fish—0–10%
Meats	*Oils*
Bacon—90%	Butter—100%
Bologna—80–90%	Cooking oils—100%
Pork—70–80%	Mayonnaise—100%
Hot dogs—70–80%	
Steak—60–70%	*Other*
Chicken thigh—60–70%	Potato chips—60–70%
Hamburger—50–70%	Eggs—60–70%
Sirloin—40–50%	Egg noodles—10–20%
Dairy	
Sour cream—80–90%	
Cheeses—70–80%	
Skim cheeses—50–60%	
Whole milk—40–50%	
Ice cream—40–50%	
Cheese pizza—30–40%	
Lowfat milk—30–40%	
Ice milk—20–30%	
Lowfat yogurt—20–30%	
Cottage cheese—10–20%	
Skim milk—0–10%	

Second, many carbohydrates, especially the vegetable-fruit group, provide fiber that seems to aid digestion without adding calories. (One medium potato of 100 grams contains only 98 calories; 100 grams of butter, on the other hand, contain 716 calories).

Third, carbohydrates are excellent energy foods. When digested, they produce no harmful toxins that inhibit bodily functions. In fact, it is well known that carbohydrates are now preferred by endurance athletes, such as marathon runners, who "carbo load" for several days prior to a race.

SUGAR. *Event 18–L. Sugar: Good or Bad?* poses a real discrepancy, at least at first glance. Most pupils know that too much sugar is "bad for you" and that too many sweets should be avoided. Yet they now find out that nothing else can be used in the cells to produce energy. If that is true, why should sugar be bad for you?

The answer is somewhat like saying that water is essential for life, but if you are a nonswimmer and fall into a pool, it could kill you. The big problem with too many sweets is that they overload the system with sugar.

To understand the danger of too much sugar, let us look first at how the body uses sugar from nonsugary foods. When nonsugars are consumed, they are converted to glucose in a slow, orderly manner. Glucose is released into the bloodstream for an extended period of time. A potato, for example, can release its energy for hours.

Look at Fig. 18–4. Normal blood sugar levels are between 60 and 120 milligrams per deciliter of blood. After eating a meal, the levels go up to the 120 milligrams mark. It provides the person with lots of energy. Gradually the glucose (and energy) levels decline. After some hours the glucose level reaches 60 milligrams. This makes one tired (to slow down and preserve energy) and hungry (to replenish energy).

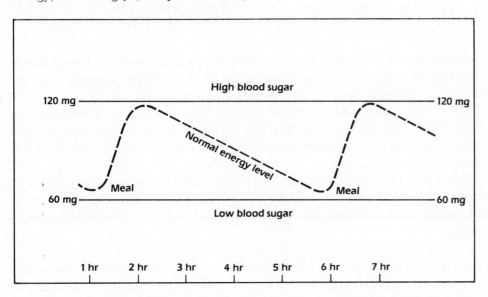

Fig. 18–4. **Normal blood sugar ranges from 60 to 120 milligrams per deciliter of blood.**

Now let us see what happens when too much sugar is consumed directly. The sugar enters the bloodstream immediately (even complex sugars are quickly changed to glucose). This quickly raises the blood sugar levels in the body. If the glucose level goes above 120 milligrams, it is toxic and the body's natural defenses quickly go to work to get rid of the excess sugar.

The pancreas dumps insulin into the bloodstream, which purges the excess sugar. But the body is so stressed by the excess sugar that it overcompensates and purges too much sugar from the bloodstream. Thus, after consuming sugar, it is entirely possible that within a short time the bloodstream will have a *shortage* of sugar in it. In other words, sugar may be an energy "pick up," but it is followed by an energy "let down." (See Fig. 18–5.)

Overeating sugar is harmful in four ways: (1) it makes you fat; (2) it makes you hungry; (3) it makes you tired; and (4) it makes you sick. Now the details.

How does sugar make you fat? What happens to all those calories that are swept out by the insulin? Most are stored as fat. Thus, the fastest way to convert food to fat is to eat too much sugar.

How does sugar make you hungry? When the body overcompensates and

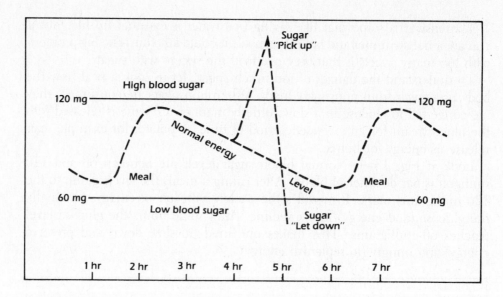

Fig. 18–5. What happens when too much sugar is eaten? The blood sugar level jumps, then crashes.

removes too much sugar from the bloodstream, the body suddenly has a shortage of energy. A natural response by the body to this shortage is to try to replace the shortage . . . by making you hungry.

How does sugar make you tired? When blood sugar is low, your energy is low. When you have no energy, you get tired. In turn, you tend to slow down, burning fewer calories than normal. As a result, you can actually gain weight while eating less.

How does too much sugar make you sick? There is evidence that too much sugar produces dental caries (cavities) and that excess sugar may be a cause of hypoglycemia (chronic low blood sugar) and diabetes (chronic high blood sugar).

CALORIE NEEDS. *Event 18–M. Calorie Counting* is a good exercise for pupils to gain an understanding of their calorie needs. It is important for them to realize that calorie needs are based on several factors. Most pupils will know that one factor is weight: A big person needs more calories than a small person.

What many do not realize, however, is the effect of activity. They may have some concept that if you work hard or play hard it takes more energy. But often they are amazed that a small active person needs more calories than a larger sedentary person. Check Table 18–8 for some sample figures.

As can be seen in the table, a very active 80-pound child will use more energy than an inactive person who is 50 percent heavier (120 pounds), and a very active 100-pound person will burn more energy than the inactive person of 160 pounds.

Table 18–8. **Calorie Use by Weight and Activity**

Type	Multiply by	80 lb	100 lb	120 lb	140 lb	160 lb
Inactive	12	960	1200	1440	1680	1920
Moderate	16	1280	1600	1920	2240	2560
Very active	20	1600	2000	2400	2800	3200

Table 18–9. **Calorie Use per Activity**

Form of Activity	Calories per Hour	
	Man (per lb)	Women (per lb)
Sleeping	0.4	0.4
Sitting quietly	0.6	0.6
Standing	0.7	0.6
Light exercise	1.1	1.0
Walking slowly	1.3	1.2
Walking moderately fast	2.0	1.8
Swimming	3.3	3.0
Jogging	3.7	3.4
Walking very fast	4.2	3.9

Another way to determine calorie needs is to check on the kinds of activities that are performed in a typical day. Let pupils use Table 18–9 to calculate their energy needs during a typical day.

It is likely that by using Table 18–9 pupils will get higher values than those shown in Table 18–8. Pupils tend to evaluate their activity levels higher than they really are.

Pupils may be amused by changes in the meaning of the terms *active* and *sedentary* during the past 90 to 100 years. In 1900 a nutrition textbook described a sedentary male as one who worked in an office for 10 hours a day, 6 days a week. He did not sit down but worked at a stand-up desk and walked much of the time.

In addition, he walked an hour each way, to and from work, and spent from 1 to 2 more hours daily doing chores around his home. These chores included splitting wood and shoveling coal. There are few "active" men today who expend as much energy as the "sedendary" man of 1900.

Another factor that affects the consumption of energy is the weather. During cold weather more energy is burned to maintain body temperature than when the weather is warm.

DIETS. Counting calories will often lead to a discussion of diets. Even some grade school pupils will have been on a diet, and almost all will have parents or older family members who have been on them.

Who should go on a diet? Someone who is overweight is the quick answer. Who is overweight? Just check the height and weight tables. Refer back to Table 18–3 to see typical values for adult ages 25 to 29.

The figures are of people fully clothed and wearing shoes with 1-inch heels. To find your place on the table, weigh yourself fully clothed. If you measured your height in bare or stocking feet, add 1 inch to find your proper place on the chart.

The table is a good approximation. However, there are many exceptions that pupils should be aware of. Normally, "overweight" means "overfat," but not always. Two exceptions are highlighted in *Event 18–N. Overweight or Overfat?* If two men are both 6 feet tall, how can the 175-pound man be overweight instead of the one who weighs 220 pounds? The answer: When the 220-pound man happens to be an all-star fullback in the National Football League. His extra weight is all muscle.

Athletes who are involved in strength sports like football often engage in intense training to build strength. As a result, many professional athletes gain considerable muscle mass and weight. However, that kind of weight (added muscle) is good, because it allows one to accomplish more work with less fatigue. It is fat that is harmful.

The 175-pound man, however, could be of very slight build and have a percentage of body fat in excess of good health. So, although the tables are a good approximation, there are exceptions to the figures. In summary, being overfat is a greater problem than being overweight.

The second example in Event 18–N is of a woman whose weight did not change from one time to the next. Yet she was at a proper weight the first time, but too fat the next time. How can that be? Simple! The weighings were 30 years apart.

Assume that at age 20 the woman was in good health and active in sports. Her weight would include a goodly amount of muscle tissue but very little fat. However, if she was inactive for the next 30 years, she would surely lose muscle tissue. Remember that muscles must be exercised to maintain them. Thus, if she is the same weight as originally, the loss of muscle is made up by an increase in fat. As a result, it is quite likely that at the second weighing, she is overfat.

It is quite common for people to lose strength as they grow older. The reason for the loss of strength is lack of the kinds of activity that developed that strength in the first place. Inactivity causes muscles to shrink.

Even if a person maintains the same weight as he or she grows older, the percentage of body fat tends to increase. Unfortunately, the situation is made even worse by the fact that there is often an increase in weight, over and above the shift toward more fat.

How can you tell if you are too fat? In addition to using the weight-height table, there are several other methods that can be used.

1. *Check your belt.* When a person reaches full maturity, the waist size does not change except for fat. Thus, if an adult gains an inch at the waist, it is an inch of fat. (Of course, this method does not work for children who are still growing.)
2. *Use skin-fold calipers.* "Pinch an inch" to see if you are too fat. Fat is deposited just below the skin on many sites of the body. Measuring the thickness of a fold of skin gives an indication of the percentage of body fat. Fairly accurate measurements can be taken using skin-fold calipers, available from many science supply houses.
3. *Water displacement method.* It is a method in which a person is weighed twice: once underwater and again out of water. Then the amount of displaced water is compared to the difference in weight to give an accurate body fat measurement. This method is generally available only at research centers.

The final activity, *Event 18–O. Supermarket Diets*, is useful to call attention to many fad diets that people often try. It is amazing how often a new, spectacular diet is proclaimed in the headlines of the magazines that line the checkout counters of supermarkets.

If the front pages are observed for a month or more, pupils are likely to find at least four major claims promoted in the headlines:

1. It is quick ("Lose a pound a day").
2. It is easy ("Fat melts away" . . . sometimes "while you sleep").
3. You can "eat all you want" ("including candy, cake, steaks, snacks").
4. Be like a television or movie star.

Why do the magazine publishers make such claims? Probably because those claims help sell the magazines. Why do people fall for those claims? Because they *want* to believe. Unfortunately, many (probably most) of the fad diets that are so highly promoted are worthless. Some may even be harmful.

First of all, look back at Table 18–8 to see how many calories you use per day. Then compare that figure with 3500 calories, the amount in 1 pound of fat. Thus, unless you actually need 3500 calories a day, it is quite impossible to "lose a pound a day." In fact, if you are an inactive person of 145 pounds and eat nothing at all, it will take 2 days to lose a pound of fat . . . assuming that only fat is lost!

Unfortunately, fat is often *not* the only thing that is lost. If a person goes on a crash diet, the body often "protects the fat" and burns muscle tissue for fuel. (Remember, muscles must be exercised. Otherwise muscle tissue is lost.) Some details are shown in Table 18–10.

Table 18–10. **Composition of Lost Pounds in Various Diets**

Type Diet	Fat (%)	Muscle (%)	Fluid (%)
"Sensible" diet, alone	75	10	15
Crash, or starvation diet	50	50	0
Slow diet with exercise	98	− 10 (gain)	2

The best hope of losing weight is to follow a sensible diet, combined with an exercise program. You should not expect to lose more than 1 or 2 pounds a week. Obviously, the diet and exercise program must be maintained for a long time for it to do any good.

AEROBIC AND ANAEROBIC EXERCISE. There are two types of exercise: *aerobic* and *anaerobic*.

Aerobic means "with oxygen." It is the kind of exercise in which the oxygen needs of the body are met by breathing. As a result, aerobic exercises can be maintained for a long time.

Aerobic exercise is excellent for the heart and lungs. It develops endurance (a measure of fitness) but not much strength. A distance runner is a prime example of a person who does aerobic exercise.

Much less strenuous, but just as good for most people, is easy jogging, brisk walking, easy swimming, biking, "jazzercise," or any other activity that keeps the heart beat elevated for 20 to 30 minutes.

Anaerobic means "without oxygen." It means that a muscle performs at a level in which oxygen needs are greater than can be supplied by breathing. The muscle cells can operate that way for a short while.

An example of anaerobic activity is the 100-meter dash. It is much more strenuous than jogging but can be performed for only a very short time. Track experts claim that even in the 100-meter dash, most sprinters cannot maintain their maximum speed for the full distance.

Other examples of anaerobic activity include hitting a golf ball, kicking a football, lifting a heavy weight, jumping, swinging an axe, throwing a discus, and hitting a baseball. Anaerobic exercise develops strength and is the kind of exercise performed by weight lifters and body builders.

Teaching Children about Fitness: The Heart, Lungs, and Muscles

WHAT IS FITNESS? Not too many years ago a typical dictionary did not contain an entry on *fitness*; and under the word *fit* the definitions pertained mostly to an agreement, say, between the size of the shoe and the size of the foot.

In recent years the term has taken on a new meaning—being of sound mind and body. Specifically, fitness means to be able to endure vigorous physical activity for a long period of time.

Discrepant Events and Pupil Investigations

Event 19–A. Step Test. (You will need to use a metronome—or an instrument that keeps exact time with a ticking sound—or play a ticking sound on a tape recorder.) Step up and down from a sturdy stand or platform for 5 full minutes. Use a pace and a step height that will elevate the heartbeat during the 5 minutes. A common pace is two steps per second, and a common height is 12 to 14 inches.

You can keep in step with the metronome if you do the moves in counts of four: (1) place one foot on the platform, (2) place the other foot on the platform, (3) place one foot down on the floor, and (4) place the other foot down on the floor.

Pupil Investigations (may include the following processes):
1. Recording data very carefully during the length of the test
2. Measuring the pulse rate
3. Interpreting charts and tables to find the correct data

Event 19–B. The 1-Mile Run-Walk. This is a strenuous test for most pupils. (Any pupil who has been cleared by a doctor to participate in any school sport is normally cleared for this test.) In this test the pupils run-walk a mile as fast as they can.

Those in good condition can probably run the entire mile. Others will probably have to do some walking. Let pupils run or walk according to how they feel. Acceptable times are listed in Table 19–1.

MEASURING FITNESS
(EVENTS 19–A, 19–B, AND 19–C)

Table 19–1. **One Mile Run-Walk: Acceptable Times (in minutes)**

Age	Male	Female
5	16:00	17:00
6	15:00	16:00
7	14:00	15:00
8	13:00	14:00
9	12:00	13:00
10	11:00	12:00
11	11:00	12:00
12	10:00	12:00
13	9:30	11:30
14 and older	8:30	10:30

SOURCE: Taken from **FITNESSGRAM Health Fitness Standards,** developed by the Institute for Aerobics Research, 12330 Preston Road, Dallas, Texas 75230, and sponsored by the Campbell Soup Company.

Pupil Investigations (may include the following processes):
1. Measuring the time needed to cover 1 mile
2. Interpreting the figures given in Table 19–1
3. Generalizing about the level of fitness

Event 19–C. The Sit-up Test. This is a test of strength. Pupils try to do as many sit-ups as possible in 1 minute. These sit-ups are done with bent knees, with arms crossed in front of the body, hands on the shoulders. Another person may hold down the ankles during the test.

Pupil Investigations (may include the following processes):
1. Measuring the number of sit-ups done in 1 minute
2. Interpreting the figures given in Table 19–2
3. Generalizing about the level of fitness

Table 19–2. **Sit-ups: Acceptable Number in 1 Minute**

Age	Boys	Girls
5, 6, 7	20	20
8	25	25
9	25	25
10	30	30
11	30	30
12	35	30
13	35	30
14 and older	40	35

SOURCE: Taken from the **FITNESSGRAM Health Fitness Standards,** developed by the Institute for Aerobics Research, 12330 Preston Road, Dallas, Texas 75230, and sponsored by the Campbell Soup Company.

Events 19-A, 19-B, and 19-C Explained in Context (Measuring Fitness)

Fitness is achieved by fairly vigorous exercise that is performed at least three times a week for about 25 to 30 minutes each time. Such a program produces a sound heart and lungs (the cardiovascular system) as well as strong muscles and bones.

A person who is fit has a cardiovascular system that can process oxygen very well. Those who are not fit cannot process nearly as much. By measuring the body's ability to process oxygen, a person's general fitness can be measured. In a lab a person can be hooked up to monitoring equipment to check how the heart and lung function while engaging in strenuous exercise. Such testing produces sophisticated data.

In the absence of such equipment, which is the case in most schools, there are a number of relatively simple tests that can be used to measure the degree of fitness. One test can be used by those who are not in good physical condition. It is presented in *Event 19–A. The Step Test*.

The step test is called a *sub-max* test. It means that it does not require a *maximum* physical effort; it requires only a *sub-maximum* effort. After doing the test for 5 minutes, the fitness level can be calculated.

First of all, the step height and step speed are calculated to find a "work factor." The work factor is then adjusted for age and is compared to the heart rate (taken immediately after finishing the 5 minutes of steps) to determine fitness. Fitness is given in *aerobic capacity* of "ml O_2/kg/min." This means "milliliters of oxygen per kilogram (of body weight) per minute."

The sub-max test requires the use of several tables to find the fitness level. (These tables are too lengthy to include in this book. One source that can provide all the information is The Submax Calculator, West Mountain Scientific, 19 Laurel Avenue, Summit, NJ 07901. Most science supply houses are also likely to carry this item.)

A person who is very fit will process lots of oxygen, but a person who is not fit will process much less. The highest figures ever reported are those of marathon runners—some of whom are able to process up to 80 milliliters of oxygen per kilogram of body weight per minute. In comparison, someone who is in poor physical condition will have a reading in the 20s. Someone who is able to run 5 miles in 1 hour will have a reading of about 45.

In contrast to the sub-max test, *Events 19–B. The 1-Mile Run-Walk* and *19–C. The Sit-up Test* are both "max" tests. That is, they are maximum efforts. What is an acceptable time? It depends on the age and sex of the pupil. Acceptable times are shown in Table 19–1.

Another measure of fitness is muscle strength. An especially good test of strength is the sit-up. It measures the strength of the stomach muscles and those muscles involved in keeping the body upright. Weakness there can lead to back problems. How many sit-ups should a pupil be able to do? Again, the answer depends on the age and sex of the pupil. Acceptable fitness levels are given in Table 19–2.

The 1-mile test and the sit-up test are good measures of fitness. However, they do not cover all areas of fitness. A complete assessment of fitness is beyond the scope of this book.

Readers who wish to have a complete program that is easy to administer and understand should contact the Institute for Aerobics Research, 12330 Preston Road, Dallas, TX 75230. In a program sponsored by the Campbell Soup Company, the Institute has developed, in addition to the mile run-walk and the sit-up test, standards for the pull-up (strength), sit and reach (flexibility), percent bodyfat, body mass index, and the flexed-arm hang (strength).

Another feature of the program is a report called the FITNESS-GRAM, which is personalized for each pupil and is very easy to understand.

THE HEART AND CIRCULATORY SYSTEM (EVENTS 19–D THROUGH 19–G)

Fig. 19–1. **What makes the thumbtack-toothpick device sway when placed on the correct spot of the wrist?**

Discrepant Events and Pupil Investigations

Event 19–D. Teetering Toothpick. Carefully place a toothpick into the end of a thumbtack and set the thumbtack on the wrist as shown in Fig. 19–1. Observe carefully. Adjust the position of the thumbtack several times until you can see it moving with your pulse. (*Note:* Rest the hand on a table or desk to keep it as steady as possible. If the hand is really steady, any movement caused by the heartbeat is more likely to be noticed.)

Pupil Investigations (may include the following processes):
1. Discovering that when placed in the right spot, the thumbtack-toothpick device wobbles
2. Observing a rhythmic movement
3. Inferring that the movement is caused by the heartbeat

Event 19–E. Pulse and Exercise. Teach the pupils to take their own pulse. If you tell them to place their fingers on the wrist, they will grab the front, the sides, the back, just about anywhere on the wrist, with very little success. Here is a way that works quite well: Have them make a fist and hold it so that the cords pop up on the wrist. Then ask them to place two or three fingers into the *hollow* along *the thumb side* of the cord. That is where the pulse can be found.

Have each pupil take his or her pulse. Then have them do a few minutes of brisk exercise and then take the pulse again. Finally, have the pulse taken once more after 5 minutes of rest. (*Caution:* Some teachers like to have pupils climb stairs. That may be acceptable if supervised. However, never let pupils run *down* stairs. It is very dangerous. If you fall while going up, you don't fall very far. If you fall going down, it may be a long tumble before hitting bottom.)

Pupil Investigations (may include the following processes):
1. Recording the pulse rates in each of the instances described previously
2. Charting the pulse rates of the class and averaging the figures for each of the instances
3. Analyzing the relationship between exercise and pulse rates

Event 19–F. Maximum and Exercise Heart Rates. The maximum heart rate for a newborn infant is 220 beats per minute. The maximum declines by one beat for every year of age. The safe sustained exercise rate for a person beginning an exercise program (assuming that there are no medical problems) is about 70 percent of the maximum.

Have the pupils figure out their maximum and safe exercise rates. Ask them also to figure those rates for a person 40 years old and another 60 years old.

Pupil Investigations (may include the following processes):
1. Recording their maximum and safe exercise levels
2. Inferring that the declining maximum rates reduce physical capacities in older people
3. Inferring a relationship between the declining maximum heart rates and the process of aging

Event 19–G. Hands Up and Down. Look carefully at the back of your hands as you hold them down low. Can you find the raised veins in the back of the hands? Leave the hands down for a minute or two. Is there any change in the veins? Now raise the hands overhead and observe. What happens to the veins?

Pupil Investigations (may include the following processes):
1. Observing that the veins are visible on the back of the hands when they are held low
2. Discovering that the veins disappear quickly when the hands are held overhead
3. Inferring that there is a relationship between gravity and the movement of blood in the veins

Events 19–D Through 19–G Explained in Context (The Heart and Circulatory System)

No mechanical pump has ever been devised that is even close to the efficiency of the human heart. Consider the job that it does. For the average person at rest it pumps about 70 times per minute. At that rate it pumps 4,200 times per hour, 100,000 times per day, and over 37 million times per year.

At rest, the heart pumps about 140 grams of blood per stroke. This figure is equal to 10 kilograms of blood per minute, 600 kilograms per hour, and over 4.5 million kilograms per year.

In volume, the heart pumps about 8 liters every minute, 480 liters per hour, 11,500 liters per day and 4 million liters per year.

The stream of blood that leaves the heart travels at about 100 meters per minute. As the blood branches out into smaller and smaller vessels, the speed decreases. It makes its trip to the lungs, back to the heart again, then out to other body tissues, and finally returns to the heart—all in about 23 seconds.

The figures are given so that pupils can gain an appreciation of the truly astounding job that the heart does. The children should not be expected to memorize the figures.

Blood flows through passages called *arteries* as it moves from the heart to the tissues. While the blood is in the main arteries the beat of the heart can be detected by fingers as well as instruments. A good place to locate the pulse is along the tendon that runs lengthwise near the surface of the wrist. Place two or three fingers into the hollow along the tendon on the *thumb* side of the wrist.

If the right spot is found, the pulse will be strong enough to make the toothpick pulsate with the beat of the heart, as suggested in *Event 19–D. Teetering Toothpick*. It will actually be possible to count the heart rate by looking at the toothpick.

The movement can also be detected if a tiny mirror is used and a strong light is reflected onto a wall. The light will flicker as the mirror moves slightly in response to the pulse beat.

After the pupils have had some practice in taking a pulse, they will be ready for *Event 19–E. Pulse and Exercise*. Pupils will find that there is a great increase in the pulse rate taken right after exercise.

Exercise causes large muscle groups to work. As soon as work is begun, the muscle cells need a greatly increased volume of oxygen. That is why people begin to pant and gasp for air when engaged in very strenuous exercise. The oxygen is carried to the muscles where it is used to burn fuel for energy. The muscle cells also produce waste products, which are carried away from the cells by the blood.

When exercise ends, the muscles soon return to normal. Thus, after 5 minutes of rest the pulse rate should be back to normal.

Pupils will find that there are many differences in the pulse rates among various members of the class. The differences can be caused by many factors. Some pupils will have worked much harder than others and, as a result, will show higher post-exercise pulse rates.

However, even if all pupils had exercised at exactly the same rate, there would still be differences. One of the major factors affecting the pulse rate is a person's physical condition.

Athletes who are in top physical condition will show a resting heart rate much lower than normal and an exercise rate also much below normal. They have developed such a strong heart that it can do its job at a much slower pace than the normal heart.

Some world-class marathon runners have resting heart rates as low as 35 to 40 beats per minute. Then when they are running a marathon (of more than 26 miles) at a pace of close to 5 minutes per mile, the heart rate is often only about 120 beats per minute. A sedentary person can reach that rate by climbing a single flight of stairs.

One of the key indicators of fitness is the resting heart rate. To gain an impression of its real benefits, it helps to look at some examples of typical heart rates. As stated in *Event 19–F. Maximum and Exercise Heart Rates*, the maximum heart rate decreases at a rate of one beat per year from the 220 rate of a newborn infant. The safe exercise rate is about 70 percent of the maximum (assuming no medical problems).

Some values for several age groups are shown in Table 19–3.

Look closely at the figures for the three age groups. As the person grows

Table 19–3. **Heart Rates**

Age	20	40	60
Maximum rate	200	180	160
Safe exercise rate (70% of max)	140	126	112
Resting heart rate	70	75	80

older, the safe range is lower and lower. At the same time, because of a lack of exercise, the resting rate tends to go up slightly. Can you see the narrowing of the safe range as the person grows older? At age 20 the resting rate can double before it exceeds the safe range. At age 60, however, it can only increase by 40 percent.

Can you see one reason why heart problems tend to occur more in older people than in the young? Of course, there are many other factors that tend to endanger the heart as a person grows older. The safe exercise rate is only one factor.

What happens if a person regularly engages in vigorous exercise? One of the major effects is a *lowering* of the resting heart rate. Look at the effect that it might have on a 60-year-old person. It is not unusual to lower the resting heart rate to 60 within 3 months. In rare cases the resting rate can be lowered to 40 beats per minute.

How much of a reserve does the 60-year-old person have after becoming fit? Instead of a reserve of only 40 percent (the difference between 80 and 112 in Table 19–3), it now changes to a reserve of 87 percent if the resting rate is 60 and to a whopping 180 percent if the resting rate is 40.

Even those figures are understated, because exercise not only *lowers* the resting heart rate, it *raises* the safe heart rate. A person who is very fit can exercise safely at a level at or near the maximum heart rate. Thus, the safe margin jumps to 167 percent for the 60-year-old who has a resting heart rate of 60 and to an astounding 300 percent safety margin if the resting rate is 40.

In recent years thousands of older people have become active and have gained the benefits of a strong heart. Instead of sitting in a rocking chair on the porch, many oldsters now go for a 5-mile jog.

During exercise the flow of blood increases to the muscles used in the activity. Thus, a runner will have a great increase in the flow of blood to the leg muscles. In fact, in a race of 5-minutes duration the blood flow to the leg muscles increases an amazing 15 times (1500 percent).

At the same time the flow of blood to the stomach is sharply reduced. What do you suppose happens to a big meal if you run vigorously right after eating? The meal just *sits* there! It is obviously not a good idea to eat just before vigorous exercise.

Have you ever noticed the veins on the back of your hands when you hold them down low? The veins are much easier to see than if you hold your hands high. The veins are especially visible on middle-aged and older people, but even children can notice them.

If the veins are so clearly visible, why not take the pulse there? Try it? You will feel nothing. There is no pulse in the veins because the blood has made its journey through the tissues and is no longer directly pushed by the pumping heart. The blood is pushed along by the blood that follows and also by the action of muscles.

Therefore, veins in the lower part of the body, the legs, and hands that are held low will fill up with blood. The force of gravity will tend to cause the blood to fill up the veins so that they bulge and are easy to see on the back of the hands.

This is what happens in *Event 19–G. Hands Up and Down.* When the hands are held low, gravity causes the blood to fill up the veins before it makes its way back to the heart. When the hands are raised, however, gravity helps push the blood down. The pressure on the veins is reduced and the veins disappear.

The buildup of blood in the veins sometimes causes problems for people who stand for long periods of time. They get swollen legs and feet. The swollen and painful legs are a result of standing, not of walking. During walking the muscles of the legs gently massage and push the blood back to the heart.

When the heart beats, it sends blood to all parts of the body. Sometimes the arteries become filled with obstructions so that it becomes more and more difficult for the blood to reach the tissues. The heart tries harder and harder to do its job and gradually increases the pressure at which it sends out the blood.

If the pressure gets too high, it becomes dangerous. It can stress the blood vessels just as too much air can stress a balloon. A "normal" safe blood pressure reading is 120/70.

There are two figures in that reading. The high value (called *systolic*) is the maximum pressure during the stroke of the heart. The low value (called *diastolic*) is the value to which the pressure drops between heartbeats. A reading of 140/90 is considered to be "high," and a reading of 160/95 is labeled *hypertension* and should receive medical treatment.

Health authorities have found that aerobic exercise tends to reduce high blood pressure. Aerobic exercise is any activity that is continuous and that pushes the heartbeat to its safe exercise level. Thus, someone who is in poor physical shape can reach his or her exercise level with a brisk walk, but an athlete must run or jog to achieve the same value. Jogging, swimming, aerobic dancing, and biking are examples of aerobic exercises. This topic was discussed in more detail at the end of Chapter 18.

LUNGS AND RESPIRATION (EVENTS 19–H, 19–I, AND 19–J)

Discrepant Events and Pupil Investigations

Event 19–H. Cloudy Water. Prepare four or five glasses, each containing a liquid that appears to be water. Unknown to the pupils, however, two of the tumblers should contain limewater instead of tapwater. Ask a pupil to stand in front of each glass and blow through a straw into the liquid. Let them blow through the straws for about a minute. What is observed?

Pupil Investigations (may include the following processes):
1. Observing that the water becomes cloudy in two of the containers
2. Discovering that with further blowing a chalky precipitate forms in the cloudy water
3. Inferring that the cloudy water must be different from tapwater
4. Inferring that there is something in exhaled breath that causes the water to turn cloudy

Event 19–I. Measuring Lung Capacity: Inverted Jar. Arrange a jar, water, and tube as shown in Fig. 19–2. Be sure to start with the inverted jar com-

Fig. 19–2. **Measure your lung capacity by blowing through a tube into an inverted water-filled bottle.**

pletely filled with water; then exhale through the tube and see how much air you can exhale.

A jar of about 4 liters is big enough for elementary school pupils and will be sufficient for most older persons. However, adults may need a larger container as will some bigger student athletes. A container of 6 liters will be large enough for everyone.

Pupil Investigations (may include the following processes):
1. Measuring the lung capacity of all pupils in class
2. Comparing the lung-volume figures with physical size
3. Comparing the lung-volume figures with athletic training

Event 19–J. Measuring Lung Capacity: Lung-Volume Bag. Obtain some lung-volume bags from a science supply house (Hubbard Scientific, Cenco, Science Kit, etc.), and measure lung volumes by having pupils exhale into them. (These are more convenient to use than the inverted jar.)

Pupil Investigations (may include the following processes):
1. Measuring the lung capacity of all pupils in class
2. Comparing the lung-volume figures with physical size
3. Comparing the lung-volume figures with physical fitness

Events 19–H, 19–I, and 19–J Explained in Context (Lungs and Respiration)

Respiration means breathing, that is, inhaling and exhaling air. We inhale oxygen and exhale carbon dioxide and excess water. Remember the path that blood takes in its trip through the body's circulatory system? The blood picks up oxygen from the lungs and sends it to the cells where it is burned for energy.

The waste products of the cells (mostly carbon dioxide) are collected, carried to the lungs, and exhaled. The cycle is repeated endlessly.

Air that is inhaled contains 79.02 percent nitrogen, 20.94 percent oxygen, and 0.04 percent carbon dioxide. Air that is exhaled contains about 79.2

percent nitrogen, 16.3 percent oxygen, and 4.5 percent carbon dioxide. You will notice that the respiration process removes about 4 percent of the oxygen, but adds 4 percent to carbon dioxide.

The exchange of oxygen-carbon dioxide in the body is similar to the exchange that occurs during any kind of oxidation. The oxygen is needed to support the "combustion" or "burning of fuel" that takes place. A simplified, *unbalanced* equation shows the process:

$$CH + O \quad \rightarrow \quad H_2O + CO_2$$

<table>
<tr><td>carbohydrate</td><td>water</td></tr>
<tr><td>and</td><td>and</td></tr>
<tr><td>oxygen</td><td>carbon dioxide</td></tr>
</table>

We can detect the carbon dioxide in exhaled air by blowing into a bottle of limewater as suggested in *Event 19–H. Cloudy Water*. Limewater is used as an indicator to detect carbon dioxide.

The normal breathing rate is about 16 to 24 times per minute. The total air exchange is about 9 to 10 liters per minute. However, the rate of air exchanged increases sharply during exercise because only about one-tenth of the lungs are used when resting.

Smoking reduces the effective air space of the lungs and reduces the efficiency of the oxygen-carbon dioxide exchange process. The lost space and efficiency is generally unnoticed at rest but becomes quickly apparent during exertion.

The physical lung capacity can be measured in several ways. A measuring device called a *spirometer* is used to measure lung volume. However, such a device is not likely to be available in a typical elementary school. As a result, two other methods are described that can be used.

Event 19–I. Measuring Lung Capacity: Inverted Jar and *Event 19–J. Measuring Lung Capacity: Lung-Volume Bag* are two methods that can be used in a classroom. The inverted jar is probably the least expensive, assuming that there is a large glass bowl or aquarium available in the classroom. With a gallon jar and a rubber hose, it is possible to measure lung volumes for all pupils.

A number of precautions should be observed. First of all, be sure to keep the mouthpiece of the hose clean. It can be wiped with an alcohol solution after each pupil has used it. Secondly, use a hose clamp or some other method of holding the air inside the jar. Otherwise the air will escape as soon as a pupil takes the hose from his or her mouth.

Finally, the measurements will be far more accurate if you mark the jar ahead of time with a grease pencil or marker to show liters and fractions of liters.

The lung-volume bags are even more convenient. They come with disposable mouthpieces, so that it is easy to keep them clean for all pupils. Just inhale as much as possible and then exhale into the bag. When finished, gather up the bag, starting from the mouthpiece, until the trapped air fills up the bag. Read the volume directly from the values marked on the bag. (See Fig. 19–3.)

Fig. 19–3. **A lung-volume bag. Exhale into the bag and measure your lung volume.**

Table 19–4. **Lung Volumes**

Age	Male (cc)	Female (cc)	Age	Male (cc)	Female (cc)
4	700	600	18	4200	2800
5	850	800	19	4300	2800
6	1070	980	20	4320	2800
7	1300	1150	21	4320	2800
8	1500	1350	22	4300	2800
9	1700	1550	23	4280	2790
10	1950	1740	24	4250	2780
11	2200	1950	25	4220	2770
12	2540	2150	26–30	4150	2720
13	2900	2350	31–35	3990	2640
14	3250	2480	36–40	3800	2520
15	3600	2700	41–45	3600	2390
16	3900	2700	46–50	3410	2250
17	4100	2750	51–55	3240	2160

What kind of volumes can you expect from pupils or adults? The averages (in cubic centimeters) are shown in Table 19–4.

A muscle, the diaphragm, controls the action of the lungs. When the muscle pulls down, it creates a partial vacuum in the lungs. Air rushes in to fill that vacuum. To exhale, the muscles merely squeeze the lungs together forcing the air out. The way the lungs work can be demonstrated with a device such as that shown in Fig. 19–4.

For best results cut off the bottom of a heavy plastic jug, or use an open glass cylinder fitted with a wide one-hole stopper. Securely attach a rubber diaphragm across the big opening with rubber bands or tape.

As you push in on the diaphragm, the balloon (the lung) squeezes together to push out the air (exhales). When you pull out on the diaphragm, the "lung" fills with air (inhales).

Fig. 19–4. **Pull on the rubber diaphragm and the balloon fills; push in and the balloon empties. This shows the action of the lungs.**

Discrepant Events and Pupil Investigations

MUSCLES, BONES, AND SKIN (EVENTS 19–K, 19–L, AND 19–M)

Event 19–K. Posture Strains. Stand, leaning forward at the waist. Hold this position for a minute or two. How do you feel?

Pupil Investigations (may include the following processes):
1. Observing that it becomes very tiring to stand this way
2. Comparing this activity with the strains placed on muscles as a result of bad posture
3. Inferring that good posture is less tiring than poor posture

Event 19–L. Touch Test. Have pupils work in pairs. Find out if they can tell by touch if one or two points of a hairpin are touching the skin. One pupil is the experimenter; the other is the subject.

The experimenter takes a hairpin and gently presses one or both points down on the skin of the subject. The subject does not look but tries to tell by touch how many points are touching the skin. Try with the points close together and also farther apart. Touch the back of the hand, the fingertip, the neck, and the arm.

Pupil Investigations (may include the following processes):
1. Observing that there are differences in how well the points can be detected on the body.
2. Experimenting to find out how far apart the points of the hairpin can be placed before they can be sensed as separate points
3. Inferring that those places where the points can be felt the best are areas with the most nerve endings

Event 19–M. One Nose or Two? Cross your fingers and close your eyes. Then touch your nose with your crossed fingers. Hold them there for a while and move them around. What do you feel?

Pupil Investigations (may include the following processes):
1. Feeling the sensation of two noses
2. Comparing the sensation of the fingers uncrossed and crossed

Events 19–K, 19–L, and 19–M Explained in Context (Muscles, Bones, and Skin)

The human body is supported by a framework of bones called the skeleton. The skeleton, in turn, is held together by a network of cartilage, ligaments, tendons, and muscles.

Look at pictures of skeletons and bones and note especially how the joints are attached to each other. Examine some chicken bones, observing the hinge joint of the knee and the ball-and-socket joint of the hip.

Perhaps some of the most interesting bones are those of the spine. Each segment is capable of limited movement, so that we can bend and twist; yet strain can damage these bones. It is particularly dangerous to try to lift heavy loads the wrong way. Lift incorrectly, and the back goes "b-o-i-n-g!"

You should lift by bending your knees, not your back. If you lift by bending the back, two dangerous things happen: The inner edges of the vertebrae are pinched together and the outer edges are pulled apart. (See Fig. 19–5.) The result can be a serious back injury. In Fig. 19–6 the model is shown in the correct lifting position. Notice that the spine is straight, not bent, and that the lifting is done with the legs, not the back.

Almost one-fourth of all disabilities suffered by American workers are caused by improper handling of materials. Correct lifting procedures will help avoid the many assorted strains, sprains, and other injuries that can otherwise occur.

Muscles work in pairs. When you lift your leg and bring the foot forward to take a step, it is the large muscle group in front of the leg (quadricep) that is contracting. Then when the foot is planted, the muscle group in the back of the leg (hamstring) contracts to push the body ahead.

Fig. 19–5. **Lift the wrong way and the spine goes "b-o-i-n-g!"** (Thanks to Rubber Products Division of Dayco Corporation.)

It is important to realize that muscles can only contract or pull. They cannot push. Thus, when you bring your hand up and bend your elbow, your biceps (in front of your upper arm) is contracting while the muscle in back of your upper arm (the triceps) is relaxing.

If one muscle contracts, the other must relax. Otherwise the muscles will be working against each other. Normally, in relaxed use the muscles work together very well. However, if muscles are overloaded, they will not relax properly. That condition greatly increases the work load of the active muscle and reduces its efficiency.

Where might such overloading occur? One common place to find examples of muscle overloading and inefficiency is at a track meet by runners who have overextended themselves. Have you ever seen a runner "tie up" while straining to finish a race?

The muscles become loaded with waste products and no longer respond. The muscle that should be relaxing remains tense, and the runner struggles along with a bent-knee stride that greatly inhibits the running motion.

One way in which athletes try to avoid "tying up" is to keep muscles limber and flexible with careful stretching exercises. Flexible muscles allow a greater range of motion and are more resistant to the tensions of extreme effort.

Good posture is important in good health and is often a clue to a person's physical condition. It is unlikely that a good athlete will have poor posture. When muscles are strong and in good condition, posture is usually good. In turn, good posture causes very little strain.

Poor posture, however, causes much greater strain. *Event 19–K. Posture Strains* is a good activity to show the effects of poor posture. It takes only a minute or two for strains to become evident if you try to assume an obviously poor posture. Leaning out of position for even a short time will quickly fatigue muscles that are stressed by the out-of-position body. The event should help pupils realize the benefits of good posture.

SKIN. The skin that covers your body is sensitive to touch. The degree of sensitivity varies from one place on the body to the next. This sensitivity can be explored by performing *Event 19–L. Touch Test*. Both points of the hairpin can usually be detected by touch in places that have many nerve endings, such as the fingertips.

However, on the back of the hand, the neck, and other parts of the body there are fewer nerve endings. As a result, it is impossible to tell if one or two points are touching the skin, unless those points are fairly wide apart.

You can try another activity that shows how the sense of touch varies among different sites of the body. For example, pinch the skin at your elbow. Then pinch the skin on the back of your wrist. Where does it hurt more? For most people the back of the wrist is far more sensitive.

Another activity that shows how we obtain messages from our sense of touch is demonstrated in *Event 19–M. One Nose or Two?* When you cross your fingers and then touch them to the tip of your nose, you will feel a strange sensation. It almost feels as if you have two noses! The left side of the first finger and the right side of the second finger both feel something, and it gives the impression of two objects.

Fig. 19–6. **Lift correctly and the strain is placed on the legs instead of the back. (Thanks to Rubber Products Division of Dayco Corporation.)**

Four different kinds of sensation can be felt by the skin: pain, pressure, heat, and cold. The events in this section all pertain to the effects of slight pressure on the skin and to how well those pressures can be detected.

EFFECTS OF TOBACCO ON THE BODY (EVENTS 19–N THROUGH 19–Q)

One cannot discuss fitness and health without a look at the effects of tobacco on the human body. It is important that this discussion be presented in the elementary school because many pupils begin to smoke during the elementary grades.

One preliminary caution: Be sure to present this topic in such a way that it does not ridicule or degrade adults who smoke. After all, many of the parents of your children are likely to be smokers. The evidence against smoking is quite strong, and the case can be made without ridiculing adults.

One way to proceed is obvious. Simply tell them "Be sure *not* to ridicule adults who smoke." Another way is to pretend that you have several sets of "smoking" parents sitting in the back of the room. How would they feel about your presentation? If the lesson is presented correctly, parents who smoke will be your strongest supporters.

Discrepant Events and Pupil Investigations

Event 19–N. Why Adults Smoke. Ask pupils to think of reasons why adults smoke. They always hear reasons why people should *not* smoke, but in this case ask them to think of reasons why adults *do* smoke. Write the reasons on the chalkboard.

Pupil Investigations (may include the following processes):
1. Expressing their perceptions about why adults smoke
2. Asking their parents and other adults about the reasons for smoking
3. Inferring from the responses that parents who smoke seem to prefer that their children do *not* smoke

Event 19–O. Why Children Smoke. After completing the list of reasons of why adults smoke, ask, "Why do children smoke?" Go over the list of responses given for adults. Do any of them apply to children ("Something to do"; "It tastes good"; "It is relaxing after dinner"; etc.)

The class will likely erupt in laughter when looking at those reasons for smoking. They know that children do not smoke because "it tastes good" or because "it is something to do after dinner"! None of the adult reasons applies. Ask them to think about the real reason why children smoke.

Pupil Investigations (may include the following processes):
1. Evaluating the adult reasons to see how they might apply to children
2. Predicting the real reason why children smoke
3. Becoming committed to resisting peer pressure to smoke

Event 19–P. Why Adults Quit. Studies have shown that adults quit smoking for three main reasons. Ask children to predict (to vote on) which of the following reasons they think is the most effective: (1) health, (2) example-giving, or (3) mastery (to gain control over the habit).

Pupil Investigations (may include the following processes):
1. Predicting the reason they believe to be most important
2. Tabulating the results for the class
3. Comparing their votes with evidence from health authorities
4. Inferring that some reasons will be effective and others not

Event 19–Q. Cigarette Money. Ask the class to spend some cigarette money. However, instead of spending it on cigarettes, how much would there be if it were saved for a year? Assume the cost of cigarettes is $2.50 per pack and a smoker used one pack a day. How much would be saved in a year?

Then ask them to take that figure, go to a favorite catalog, and place an order for anything they want, equal to the cigarette money that they would save during the year. Let them spend the cigarette money on something else.

Pupil Investigations (may include the following processes):
1. Calculating the cost of a pack of cigarettes each day for a year
2. Calculating the cost of goods selected from a catalog that is equal to the cost of the cigarettes
3. Inferring that cigarette money goes up in smoke but that the same money could buy something more useful

Events 19–N through 19–Q Explained in Context (Effects of Tobacco on the Body)

Event 19–N asks *Why do adults smoke?* Most pupils will not have given that question much thought. When you ask it, they will say, "I guess they must like it" or "I suppose it tastes good." Ask children to think of as many reasons as possible and then list the reasons on the chalkboard. The reasons most likely to be given include:

1. It tastes good.
2. It is something to do.
3. It is a habit.
4. They like it.
5. It is relaxing.
6. It keeps them from overeating.

After the pupils have given all the reasons that they can think of, focus on the real reason: Adults smoke because *it is too hard to quit!* Add that reason to the list on the chalkboard.

According to a national survey by a major television network, about 70 percent of all adult smokers have made at least one serious attempt to quit! That means that *most* adult smokers do so because *it is too hard to quit.* Children have a right to know that information.

Follow up by exploring when most adults *started* to smoke. They started before they were adults! Children have a right to know that information also. Surprisingly, the decision to smoke is usually not made by adults. It is made by children. By the time they become adults, most smokers are addicted. Practices and attitudes of adult smokers can be summarized as follows:

1. They began smoking before they were mature adults.
2. They would now prefer to quit.
3. They would feel just as mature if they did not smoke.
4. They strongly prefer that their own children do not smoke.

Have pupils ask their parents (who smoke) about the preceding attitudes. It is likely that the parents will confirm the findings. Of course, it is again important to present the information and to ask the questions in a way that does not disparage or ridicule adults. If the topic is handled carefully, parents who smoke will be your strongest allies.

Most parents will admit that they started to smoke at an age when they were not yet fully mature. They will admit that it has become a strong habit and that it is too hard to quit. Many pupils will bring back reports that their parents have seriously tried to quit.

Once pupils know the details of why adults smoke, they will be in a better position to resist the peer pressures that so many of them face. However, the next event is even more important.

Event 19–O. Why Children Smoke is a vital follow up. Ask pupils why children begin to smoke. Then turn to the list about adult smokers that should still be on the chalkboard.

You can say that we already have a list of reasons why people smoke. Are these the reasons why children smoke? The class will likely burst into laughter. They *know* that schoolchildren do not smoke because "it tastes good," or "it's something to do," or any other reason on the adult list.

They will almost always give the right reason. In one form or other they will say, "Those kids think they're more grown up"; "they think that they are more important than others"; "they think that they are big shots!" Teachers call it peer pressure; children call it "being cool" or being a "big shot"!

Discuss the reason with the class and then add it to the chalkboard. Use the term "big shot" in discussing the reason. It is important to blunt the attitude of superiority that the child-smoker uses in trying to get others to smoke. Use the term and explore the attitude.

Ask the pupils if they have ever seen one of their classmates smoke. Of course, do not ask for names. If that question is asked in the fourth, fifth, or sixth grade, the answer is almost always "yes." Ask them to analyze the situation. Did the smoker act proud? Did the smoker act as if he or she were superior? Like a big shot? Did the person act as if he or she were more mature or "grown-up?"

The beginning smoker is most likely driven to smoking by peer pressure and a feeling of prestige. Peers use this feeling as a powerful lever to make a nonsmoking child feel like a "baby" or immature. It is important that this pressure be blunted.

Ask if a child who sneaks a smoke is really a big shot. Is that child really mature? Do adults try to prove their maturity that way? Children can easily see that only immature children will try to pressure others to smoke. Adults do not act that way.

At this point we should mention that health dangers are *not* very effective in keeping children from smoking. Why not? Just observe how a child might be confronted with the temptation to smoke. Suppose a boy is walking home from school and comes across several of his classmates sneaking a smoke behind some bushes. They call to him to "come on over." They push a lit cigarette toward him and say, "Here, have a smoke." Suppose the child does not want to smoke. How does he avoid the pressure? He might say, "No, thanks. I don't care to smoke."

"What's the matter? Are you a baby?"

One cannot expect the boy to respond, "I am worried about emphysema and hardening of the arteries."

So, what can the victim say to blunt that powerful question: "What's the matter? Are you a baby?"

The victim can say, "What's the matter? Are you a *big shot?*" "Do you think you are *superior?*" "I don't need to smoke to act grown-up."

It is important that a teacher go over the pressures presented to children. Once the topic is fully explored in the classroom, it is quite likely that those who *do* already smoke will tend to avoid the tactic with other pupils in the class.

WHY DO ADULTS QUIT? *Event 19–P. Why Adults Quit* presents three reasons why adults have quit smoking. Surprisingly, health is not the main reason. True, most adults realize the health dangers, but the dangers seem far away. They rationalize: "I'm too young to get cancer or emphysema"; or "I don't inhale much"; or "I use filter tips."

One of the most important reasons is that of "example-setting." This is why parents have quit—to set an example for their children; why teachers have quit—to set an example for their pupils; and why doctors have quit—to set an example for their patients.

In 1950 more than 60 percent of all doctors smoked, but by 1965 only about 30 percent smoked. The trend is even more dramatic among newly graduated doctors. By 1990 only 4 percent of newly graduated medical doctors smoked.

Another major reason for quitting is "mastery." Many people have come to realize that smoking has taken over their lives. They decide that they will become the master of the smoking urge, not its victim.

THE COST OF SMOKING. Children are likely to have heard about "cigarette money." Ask them how much that money can amount to in a year or more. Perform *Event 19–Q. Cigarette Money* and see how much money is used in a year if a smoker buys one pack of cigarettes a day.

Assume that cigarettes cost $2.50 a pack. That amounts to $912.50 a year. Let the pupils do the calculations themselves. The figure will astound them. Then let them look through a catalog to see what they could buy with the "cigarette money."

To continue with the exercise, you may ask the pupils to figure the cost of smoking during an entire lifetime. Assume that a person begins smoking at age 15 and continues to age 75. How much is spent during the 60 years, assuming there is no increase in price? The figure is $54,750. Ask them how they would spend that amount of money.

If the money is deposited in a bank at the end of every year to gain compound interest at 6 percent a year, the total grows to more than $147,000 in 40 years, $282,000 in 50 years, and $530,000 in 60 years. Those are truly astounding figures. In addition to showing the cost of smoking, the figures are quite effective in showing the power of compound interest.

Teaching Children about Energy, Environment, and Pollution

In this chapter we look at some issues that are often discussed in the classroom. As issues they are more than just a collection of science facts. They also affect opinions and attitudes. As a result, special care should be taken to assure an unbiased presentation.

Yet, how can an unbiased presentation be accomplished? Frankly, it is difficult, especially considering the importance that is given to some of these issues in the news. Nevertheless, we will try to present some suggestions for handling the topics objectively.

One effective technique is to have students answer short surveys about some of the issues. Their responses can be compared with national figures, and the items become a basis for classroom discussion.

WHAT IS ENERGY? Most books give a definition of *energy* as "the ability to do work." Often the topic is broken down into such subtopics as heat energy, sound energy, light energy, and so on. In this chapter, however, we talk about the energy needed to produce our goods and services.

In fact, the first step is to define energy. What is energy?

Energy is *food*.
Energy is *clothing*.
Energy is *shelter*.
Energy is *heat*.
Energy is *transportation*.

Let us look at each of the benefits of energy in more detail.

HOW CAN ENERGY BE DEFINED AS FOOD? Have you ever tried to raise some vegetables in your garden? Did you do the weeding, watering, fertilizing, and debugging of the plants? Did you dig up the soil with a shovel? How big a garden can you maintain using only muscle energy?

It is unlikely that many schoolchildren have ever tilled a garden of substantial size. However, many may have grown a few carrots or radishes. They may also have dug into the turf enough times to learn that it is almost impossible to dig up an entire garden using only muscle energy.

Ask the children to check their neighborhoods. They will find that those who used only muscle energy have *very* small gardens—often no larger than the size of a table or two. Ask the children how long they could survive if they depended entirely on their own muscles for growing food. Not very long.

With a Rototiller, however, the energy of gasoline makes the tilling much faster and easier. With even larger equipment, a farmer tills an area that is enormous in comparison. In the United States each farmer grows enough food to feed 50 or more people.

U.S. farmers are such good producers of food that only 3 percent of the working population is involved in growing food. This means that 97 percent of the population can be busy producing other things.

The situation elsewhere is quite different. Worldwide, two-thirds of the population is engaged in the full-time production of food. Thus, only one-third of the world's population is free to produce other things. As a general rule, the greater the percentage of people who produce food, the poorer the country.

Refer to references such as the almanacs commonly sold in supermarkets. They list summary facts for each country of the world. You will find that the greater the percentage of people who work in agriculture, the poorer is the country. For example, in a recent edition of the World Almanac the 20 countries with the largest work force in agriculture had an average income of less than $324.60 per year. In contrast, the 20 countries with the smallest percentage of the work force in agriculture had an average income of more than $16,038.

If we depended on our muscle energy alone to produce food, many of us would starve. With the use of energy and machines, however, food is plentiful.

That is why we can say that energy is food.

HOW CAN ENERGY BE DEFINED AS CLOTHING? How many people are wearing clothes made entirely by muscle energy? How many sheared the sheep, cleaned the wool, carded it, spun it into yarn, and then knitted the clothing . . . all by hand? Very few.

If you wear cotton clothing, did you plant it, tend it, pick it, clean it, spin it into yarn, and weave the cloth? Did you then make the clothes you wear? Even those who do their own sewing are using electrical energy for running the sewing machine and are using cloth spun and woven on big machines in factories. Thus, the handwork is really mostly machine work, and covers only the final "assembly" of the product, not the production of the basic materials that are needed.

That is why we can say that energy is clothing.

HOW CAN ENERGY BE DEFINED AS SHELTER? How many people live in homes built entirely with muscle energy? How many went into the woods to chop down trees, hauled them to the building site, and built a home? It is unlikely anyone in this country is living in a home built entirely with muscle energy.

How many people would have shelter if they needed to depend only on their muscles? Very few.

That is why we can say energy is shelter.

HOW CAN ENERGY BE DEFINED AS HEAT? Can you imagine what winter would be like without heat? Most of the heat for homes is provided by fuel oil and natural gas. Before those resources were available, people used mostly coal; and prior to coal, wood. Without heat much of the world would be too cold to live in during the winter months.

That is why we can say energy is heat.

HOW CAN ENERGY BE DEFINED AS TRANSPORTATION? Have you ever made a trip across the state or across the country? Would that trip have been possible if you had to rely on your own muscles to get you there? Not likely.

That is why we can say energy is transportation.

In a unit on energy the pupils should realize that muscle energy is too weak to produce many of the necessities of life. If we depended entirely on our muscles to produce food, most of us would starve. Likewise, if we depended on our muscles for clothing or shelter, most of us would freeze.

Energy is needed for the production of goods. If energy is expensive, then food, clothing, and shelter will be expensive. If energy is scarce, then food, clothing, and shelter will be scarce.

What are the major sources of energy? They are (1) petroleum (oil), (2) natural gas, (3) coal, (4) nuclear, and (5) waterpower. (All other sources combined, such as wind, solar, geothermal, and others, produce less than 1 percent of the energy used in this country.)

Discrepant Events and Pupil Investigations

HOW OPINIONS CHANGE (EVENTS 20–A AND 20–B)

Event 20–A. Opinion Survey. Give the following quiz to the pupils.
Directions: The exercises in this survey (Table 20–1) are followed by several suggested answers. Mark the space representing your choice.
Source: Some items are taken from *Energy: Knowledge and Attitudes*, 1978, by the National Assessment of Educational Progress (NAEP), a project of the Education Commission of the States.

Pupil Investigations (may include the following processes):
In this event the processes are inherent in taking the survey and include comparing, analyzing, interpreting, concluding, predicting, and perhaps also suspending judgment while awaiting further data.

Event 20–B. Build a Power Plant. Ask pupils to take the role of directors of a power company. They will need to build a new power plant. What energy source should they use? Assume that the five sources (coal, natural gas, nuclear, oil, and waterpower) are equally available and that they should

Table 20–1. **How Much Do You Agree or Disagree with Each of the Following Statements?**

	Strongly Agree	Moderately Agree	Moderately Disagree	Strongly Disagree
1. Coal mining should be limited to the underground to protect the environment from strip mining.				
2. More dams should be built to generate electricity even if they will cover scenic wonderlands and wildlife areas.				
3. To save gasoline, the government should tax cars that do not get good gas mileage.				
4. The government should offer tax incentives to people who make their homes energy-efficient (weatherizing, insulating, etc.).				
5. You should be forced to help pay to insulate your neighbor's house.				

SOURCE: Some items are taken from *Energy: Knowledge and Attitudes*, 1978, by the National Assessment of Education Progress [NAEP], a project of the Education Commission of the States.

evaluate the environmental problems in making their choices. Place Table 20–2 on the chalkboard and fill in responses from the class.

When the energy sources are thoroughly discussed, ask pupils to rank their choices from 1 to 5 (with 1 being their first choice). Tabulate the votes on the chalkboard using a form such as Table 20–3.

Pupil Investigations (may include the following processes):
In this event the processes are inherent in responding to Tables 20–2 and 20–3. The processes include comparing, analyzing, interpreting, concluding, predicting, and perhaps also suspending judgment while awaiting further data.

Table 20–2. **Energy for a Power Plant**

Pollution Problems	Coal	Natural Gas	Nuclear	Oil	Waterpower
Smoke	Yes	No	No	No	No
Noxious gases	Yes	Yes	No	Yes	No
Carbon dioxide	Yes	Yes	No	Yes	No
Thermal	Yes	Yes	Yes	Yes	No
Radiation	No	No	?	No	No
To obtain	Strip mines	Pipe lines	—	Pipe lines	Lake
Other					

Table 20–3. **Responses to Power Plant Event**

Rank	Coal	Natural Gas	Nuclear	Oil	Waterpower
1	0	1	1	0	28
2	0	15	11	2	2
3	1	10	10	9	0
4	6	4	2	18	0
5	23	0	6	1	0

NOTE: The responses shown in Table 20–3 are typical of most classes. Your class may be different.

Events 20–A and 20–B Explained in Context (How Opinions Change)

Most elementary pupils like to "vote" on things. Thus, they are likely to enjoy the opinion survey on energy, environment, and pollution.

How should teachers treat topics like these? It is obvious that energy, environment, and pollution are not just abstract scientific concepts. They also involve opinions and attitudes. How can we respect opinions and still strive for facts?

One of the most important lessons to be taught is that opinions are surprisingly fragile. As a matter of fact, in *Event 20–A. Opinion Survey* it is likely that pupils will contradict themselves. Their responses will often depend not so much on the issue but on how the item is worded. Thus, the phrasing of items or questions will often *form* and *shape* opinions, instead of just gathering opinions.

Here are results found in typical college classes involving hundreds of prospective teachers. The items are presented with an alternative form. The first three are essentially similar except for the endings, which give a sharply different "feel" to them. Item 4 is an alternative form of item 5.

Item 1. Coal mining should be limited to the underground . . .
- to protect the environment from strip mining. (53% favored)
- even if thousands of miners will die of black-lung disease. (92% opposed)

Item 2. More dams should be built to generate electricity . . .
- even if they cover scenic wonderlands and wildlife areas. (69.9% opposed)
- especially if they will create scenic wonderlands and wildlife areas. (72% favored)

Item 3. To save gasoline, the government should tax cars . . .
- that do not get good gas mileage. (65% favored)
- designed for use by large families. (96% opposed)

Item 4. The government should offer tax incentives to people who make their homes energy-efficient (weatherizing, insulating, etc.). (85% favored)

Item 5. You should be forced to help pay to insulate your neighbor's house. (91% opposed)

Compare items 4 and 5. They are really alike, although at first glance they do not appear to be. Note that the word "incentives" in item 4 gives the impression of voluntary action. However, it refers to taxes that are not voluntary payments and can be described as the "force" used in item 5.

Look further at item 2 of *Event 20–A*. *Opinion Survey* pertaining to waterpower. Compare the responses of that item to those obtained in *Event 20–B*. *Build a Power Plant*. Typical college classes voted overwhelmingly in favor of waterpower as the *first* choice. Your class will probably do the same. You can then ask them, "If you really liked waterpower that much, why didn't you vote for it in item 2 of Event 20–A?" Students will often not realize until that moment that they have contradicted themselves.

In any lessons on energy, environment, and pollution biases can easily creep in. It is important for pupils to know how easily their opinions can be affected by the words used in the survey items. That knowledge is likely to help them reserve judgment when these issues are discussed and helps them guard against jumping to conclusions.

ENERGY USE IN THE UNITED STATES (EVENTS 20–C, 20–D, AND 20–E)

Discrepant Events and Pupil Investigations

Event 20–C. Total Energy Use. There are five sources of energy that provide more than 99 percent of all the energy used in the United States. Those sources are coal, natural gas, nuclear energy, oil, and waterpower. Ask the pupils to rank them in the order of their use.

Pupil Investigations (may include the following processes):
1. Estimating the energy sources and their use
2. Analyzing how and where energy is used
3. Comparing their estimates with official figures

Event 20–D. Energy for Electrical Power. List the same five energy sources that were used in Event 20–C. This time ask pupils to think only of the energy used to generate electrical power and to rank the sources again.

Pupil Investigations (may include the following processes):
1. Estimating the energy sources used in electrical power
2. Analyzing how and where the energy is used
3. Comparing their estimates with official figures

Event 20–E. Where Is Energy Used? All the energy used in this country can be divided among four groups: industry, commercial, home (including the family car), and transportation (trains, planes, trucks, etc.). Ask pupils to rank the groups according to how much energy each group uses.

Pupil Investigations (may include the following processes):
1. Estimating the use of energy by groups
2. Analyzing how and where energy is used
3. Comparing their estimates with official figures

Events 20–C, 20–D, and 20–E Explained in Context (Energy Use in the United States)

The three events in this section focus on the three main questions of energy use: (1) What are the total energy sources used in this country? (2) What are the energy sources used to generate electric power? (3) Where is the energy used? The answer to the first question is shown in Table 20–4. (The table also represents the response to *Event 20–C. Total Energy Use.*)

Table 20–4. **Total Energy Used in the United States**

Source	Percentage
Oil (refined into gasoline and heating oils)	48.5
Coal	21.6
Natural gas	17.9
Nuclear	8.1
Waterpower (hydroelectric)	3.9

You will see that by far the greatest amount of energy comes from petroleum (oil). Coal and natural gas are close together at second and third, respectively, and nuclear and hydroelectric energy are far behind. Most of the energy is used for two purposes—driving and heating.

Coal was widely used to heat homes a generation or two ago. Gradually, coal was replaced by oil, natural gas, and electricity. The trend away from coal is shown in the U.S. coal consumption figures. Coal consumption reached a peak in 1929 and declined steadily for 40 years. Coal use began to increase again in the mid-1970s because of a sharp increase in the number of coal-fired electric power plants. Oil, natural gas, and nuclear energy were either banned or restricted as energy sources for new power plants.

Coal is now used mostly in very large installations that can afford the cost of air pollution equipment and where coal can be burned efficiently. By far the greatest amount of coal is used to generate electrical power. Nuclear energy and waterpower are used exclusively for generating electrical power.

ENERGY FOR ELECTRICAL POWER *Event 20–D. Energy for Electrical Power* may show that students sometimes get confused when comparing *all* the energy used in the United States with that portion used to generate electrical power. Be sure to point out that most of the energy in this country is used, not to generate electricity, but for motor fuel and for heating purposes.

Different energy sources are used for electrical power. It is obvious that coal, nuclear energy, and waterpower cannot be used directly as motor fuel or (except for coal) to heat homes. Those sources, however, are important in the production of electricity. The figures for a recent year are given in Table 20–5.

There is some value in going back to an earlier event (Event 20–B) in which the five sources of energy were evaluated and ranked by the students

Table 20–5. **Energy Used to Generate Electricity**

Source	Percentage
Coal	55.3
Nuclear	20.6
Waterpower (hydroelectric)	10.1
Natural gas	9.4
Oil	4.2
Other	0.4

in "building a power plant." For the sake of that event we assumed that all sources were equally available.

Unfortunately, in the real world they are *not* all equally available. Oil and natural gas cannot be used in new power plants. They were banned by Congress because it was feared that we would run out of those fuels for use in motor vehicles and heating homes.

Waterpower is not widely available either. Hydroelectric plants can only be built in mountainous river canyons. They cannot be built in the flatlands. The best waterpower sites have already been used.

That leaves only coal and nuclear power. Almost all of our future power plants will use these two sources of energy. Nothing else is available. (Sources such as wind, solar, geothermal, tides, etc., are experimental and are not likely to make an impact in our lifetimes.)

We have seen where our energy comes from. Now let us look at the answer to *Event 20–E. Where Is Energy Used?* The figures for a recent year are given in Table 20–6.

Table 20–6. **Where Energy Is Used**

Place	Percentage
Home and family including family transportation	39
Industry	37
Commercial	16
Transportation (bus, truck, train, and airplane)	11

NUCLEAR ENERGY (EVENT 20–F)

Discrepant Event and Pupil Investigations

Event 20–F. Nuclear Power Survey. Potential hazards of nuclear energy were surveyed by the National Assessment of Educational Progress. Table 20–7 lists the potential hazards in that survey. Ask the class to take the survey and then compare their results with the national figures.

Pupil Investigations (may include the following processes):
In this event the processes are inherent in taking the survey and include comparing, analyzing, interpreting, concluding, predicting, and perhaps also suspending judgment while awaiting further data.

Table 20–7. **How Serious Do You Consider Each of the Following Potential Hazards Associated with Nuclear Energy?**

	Very Serious	Moderately Serious	Not Serious
1. Thermal pollution			
2. Radiation exposure from normal operation			
3. Explosion			
4. Theft of plutonium			
5. Disposal of radioactive waste			

Would You Be Willing to Have Each of the Following Energy Producers Built Within 25 Miles of Your Home?

	Yes	Maybe	No
6. Coal-burning power plant			
7. Nuclear power plant			
8. Dam with hydroelectric plant			
9. Geothermal power plant			

SOURCE: Taken from survey by the National Assessment of Educational Progress.

Event 20–F Explained in Context (Nuclear Energy)

The first commercial nuclear power plant was built in the United States in 1957. By 1990 there were more than 110 nuclear power plants in operation. They generated more than 20 percent of the electricity used in this country. By 1990 hundreds of additional plants were in operation throughout the rest of the world. In some countries, including France, Belgium, Hungary, South Korea, and Sweden, nuclear energy provided more than half of all generated electricity.

Despite the wide use of nuclear power throughout the country and the world, there is still much confusion about the topic. Let us explore this confusion by checking the responses to the survey items. The response to the items are shown in Table 20–8.

At this point the opinions can be compared, and the items can serve as a good base for classroom discussion. But that does not guarantee that the opinions are based on sound information. One way to proceed is to compare the opinions of scientists with those of the general public.

Students may be surprised by the results. In a study jointly sponsored by Columbia University, Smith College, and George Washington University, scientists were asked if they would be willing to have a nuclear power plant in *their* city. The results are shown in Table 20–9.

Table 20–8. **Survey Responses**

How Serious Do You Consider Each of the Following Potential Hazards Associated with Nuclear Energy?

			Very Serious %	Moderately Serious %	Not Serious %
1.	Thermal pollution	College sample	37	56	7
		National sample	34	48	17
2.	Radiation exposure from normal operation	College sample	56	31	13
		National sample	42	36	21
3.	Explosion	College sample	69	21	10
		National sample	57	26	16
4.	Theft of plutonium	College sample	41	42	17
		National sample	43	37	13
5.	Disposal of radioactive waste	College sample	91	8	1
		National sample	76	19	4

Would You Be Willing to Have Each of the Following Energy Producers Built Within 25 Miles of Your Home?

			Yes %	Maybe %	No %
6.	Coal-burning power plant	College sample	9	39	52
		National sample	14	37	48
7.	Nuclear power plant	College sample	3	20	77
		National sample	20	25	54
8.	Dam with hydroelectric plant	College sample	57	30	13
		National sample	34	32	33
9.	Geothermal power plant	College sample	22	57	22
		National sample	21	46	32

SOURCE: Taken from data reported by the National Assessment of Educational Progress and from 276 elementary teacher training students at Kent State University, Kent, Ohio.

Table 20–9. **Opinions of Scientists**

Scientists	Percent Responding Yes
Random sample of all scientists	69
Energy experts	80
Nuclear experts	98

SOURCE: Taken from study sponsored by Columbia University, Smith College, and George Washington University.

Compare these figures with those obtained in the national and class surveys. It is apparent that the more people know about nuclear energy, the more they tend to support it.

Ask children to ponder why scientists favor nuclear energy so much more than nonscientists. Do they favor it because they know it is dangerous? Or, do they favor it because they know it is safe?

Sometimes a pupil will say that a scientist is willing to take risks because he or she may be employed at a nuclear power plant. However, if there is real danger, scientists probably do not want to be exposed to it any more than anyone else. Just remember that if there is a danger of cancer, for example, the scientist will be the first to get it. If there is a danger to his or her life, the scientist will be the first to die. It is not likely that many scientists will accept those risks.

Secondly, even if scientists were willing to accept hazards for themselves at their workplace, very few would be willing to accept that risk for their families where they live. That is precisely what was asked. Would they be willing to *live* near a nuclear power plant?

In any event point out that many of the energy experts in the survey are *not* employed by power companies. Instead, they work in universities and research labs.

What is it that scientists know that leads them to their opinions? Perhaps we can find out by looking more closely at radiation and other hazards in the following sections.

Discrepant Events and Pupil Investigations

RADIATION (EVENTS 20–G, 20–H, AND 20–I)

Event 20–G. What Is Radiation? Ask students to classify into two groups the following sources of radiation: (1) cosmic rays, (2) electric heater, (3) fire, (4) fluorescent bulb, (5) incandescent bulb, (6) luminous watch dial, (7) medical x-ray, (8) nuclear power plant.

Pupil Investigations (may include the following processes):
1. Classifying the examples into two groups
2. Analyzing the examples to determine possible dangers
3. Comparing their choices with scientific evidence about ionizing and nonionizing radiation

Event 20–H. Ionizing Radiation. Ask students to rank the following sources of ionizing radiation according to amount: (1) fallout from bomb testing, (2) medical uses, (3) natural background, (4) nuclear industry, (5) occupational exposure (by miners, handlers, etc.), (6) all other sources.

Pupil Investigations (may include the following processes):
1. Ranking the sources according to amount of exposure
2. Analyzing the sources to determine possible dangers
3. Comparing their choices with scientific evidence

Event 20–I. Average Radiation Doses. Everyone is exposed to some radiation. Where does that radiation come from? Ask pupils to rank the following sources: (1) eating food, (2) breathing air, (3) watching television, (4) getting medical diagnosis and treatment, (5) living in homes, (6) flying in airplanes.

Pupil Investigations (may include the following processes):
1. Ranking the sources according to the amount of exposure
2. Analyzing the sources to determine possible dangers
3. Comparing their ranking with scientific evidence

Events 20–G, 20–H, and 20–I Explained in Context (Radiation)

HOW DO WE KNOW? Before we look at the scientific evidence, let us look at the problem of selecting the sources. Who knows about the effects of radiation? What sources are likely to be most accurate? To place the question in perspective, consider the history of radiation.

Radiation was first discovered by William Roentgen in 1895. It was soon realized that this mysterious ray could be used to take a picture *of the bones inside the body!* X-ray pictures were used to help set broken bones—a truly amazing achievement! X-ray machines were easy to build and were soon used by hospitals and doctors around the world.

Considering the poor level of medical practice at the beginning of the 1900s, it is no surprise that the x-ray became a medical "wonder." The x-ray was so valuable for setting broken bones that people soon regarded the x-ray as a "cure-all" for everything else.

Massive doses of radiation were used to treat many kinds of ailments. In England, for example, it was widely used to treat a severe form of arthritis called ankylosing spontelitis.

Were people afraid of radiation? Not at all. They would not believe that it could do any harm. When it became known that a place in Czechoslovakia had unusually high levels of radiation in its water, people were not scared at all. In fact, people from all over Europe flocked to the site to bathe in "the healing waters" and to drink "the healing liquids." For decades the radioactive liquid was bottled and sold as drinking water all over Europe.

X-ray machines became so popular that they were even installed in shoe stores in this country. Many older people still remember the late 1940s when they could go to a shoe store to see the x-ray view of the bones of their feet.

Nevertheless, it became more and more apparent to scientists that uncontrolled exposure to radiation could have harmful side effects. By the 1920s an international body of scientists and medical experts was organized to study the possible problems. Other bodies were formed in this country and most other countries for similar reasons. At the present time the major national and international groups are as follows:

IAEA   International Atomic Energy Agency
ICRP   International Commission on Radiological Protection

UNSCEAR	United Nations Scientific Committee on the Effects of Atomic Radiation
NCRP	National Council on Radiation Protection and Measurements
BEIR	The Committee on Biological Effects of Ionizing Radiation, of the National Academy of Science
EPA	The Environmental Protection Agency

Every major country of the world now has its own national agency to supplement the work of the international bodies.

WHAT IS RADIATION? Many people are confused about radiation. Do we mean the kind of radiation that comes from light and heat sources? No. The radiation of heat from a radiator or of light from a bulb is called *nonionizing* radiation. This means that the rays cannot penetrate and dislodge electrons from atoms. Thus, the examples in *Event 20–G. What Is Radiation?* fit into two groups. Examples of ionizing rays are numbers 1, 6, 7, and 8. The other items produce nonionizing rays.

In summary, radiation that can penetrate an atom to knock off electrons (ionize it) is what we are concerned with when we talk about atomic or *nuclear radiation*. The concern is with ionizing radiation, not nonionizing radiation.

Even with ionizing radiation, there are big differences among various types of rays. The three major types are:

Alpha particles—Very weak. They can be stopped by a sheet of paper or by few centimeters of air. They are no danger unless lodged directly in the lungs or injected into the bloodstream.
Beta rays—Also weak. They can be stopped by a few centimeters of wood or a few meters or air.
Gamma rays—Powerful. These are x-ray type rays. They can penetrate muscle and bone. Very powerful forms of these rays are even used to x-ray heavy metal casings to look for flaws.

WHERE DOES IONIZING RADIATION COME FROM? Ionizing radiation comes from just about everywhere. It comes from the ground we walk on, the air we breathe, the food we eat, the homes we live in, and even (don't say this too loudly) from the person sitting next to you! The sources of ionizing radiation are shown in Table 20–10. Compare it with the student list in *Event 20–H. Ionizing Radiation.*

Table 20–10. **Sources of Ionizing Radiation**

Source	Percentage
Natural background	75.54
Medical diagnosis	24.04
All others except nuclear industry	0.41
Nuclear industry	0.01
Total	100.00

Radiation exposure is measured with a variety of units. Some units indicate the penetrating power of the source; others do not. Some units indicate the biological effects on a body; others do not. The most instructive unit is the millirem (mrem). It measures the biological effect of radiation on the body.

What doses are received by people living in the United States? The exposures differ greatly, but the average is about 360 millirems per person per year. (Until recently the figure most often cited was 200 millirems, but that did not include the exposure to radon in most homes.) Compare the exposure values listed in Table 20–11 with the responses by pupils in *Event 20–I. Average Radiation Doses.* The exposures are those received in 1 year (except where noted otherwise).

One way to gain an understanding of the various exposures is to use a string to measure out some distances on the playground. If you use a scale of 1 meter per millirem, the total average annual exposure (360 millirems) will be longer than three football fields.

On that same scale the exposure to the general public from nuclear power plants measures only 1 *centi*meter. On that same scale, watching television or wearing a watch with a luminous dial gives an exposure that measures a full meter (or one hundred times more than the power plant).

Perhaps most surprising of all, a coal-fired power plant gives a radiation exposure hundreds of times greater than is obtained from the normal operation

Table 20–11. **Radiation Sources**

Sources	Doses in mrem
	Dose per Year
Average dose in the United States	360
Radon in the home	160
Air	5
Food	25
TV watching	1
Grand Central Station	525
Cosmic rays at sea level	35
Cosmic rays at 2,000 m elevation	75
Heart pacemaker (from Plutonium-238)	5,000
Coal-fired power plant (50 km)	50 to 380*
Nuclear power plant (50 km)	0.01
	Dose per Occurrence
Chest x-ray (dose to the bone-marrow)	30 to 80
Chest x-ray (dose to the skin)	1,500
Fluoroscopic x-ray	20,000 to 60,000
Jet airplane flight (per hour)	1

*Depending on the kind of coal used. Coal contains uranium, thorium, and radium—all of which are vented into the air along with smoke and gases when burned. Western coal gives the higher figure.

SOURCES: The data are drawn from UN Report: Ionizing Radiation: Levels and Effects, 1972; EPA report ORP/SID 72-1 from the Office of Radiation Programs; and EPA Report 520-1-77009 Radiological Quality of Environment in the United States.

of a nuclear power plant. Since coal contains radium, uranium, and thorium, those particles are vented into the air and settle in the vicinity of those plants.

According to measurements published by the Environmental Protection Agency (EPA), a person living within 50 kilometers of a coal-fired plant is likely to receive a dose of 50 to 380 millirems per year, depending on the type of coal that is burned in the plant. (Western coal is more radioactive than eastern coal.)

EXPLOSION AND THEFT. The NAEP survey reveals that many people fear that nuclear power stations can blow up in a nuclear explosion. However, there is no scientific basis for that fear. The fuel rods are enriched to about 3 or 4 percent purity. They would have to be enriched to at least 90 percent to sustain an explosive reaction. Thus, the fuel rods *cannot* explode any more than a desk or chair can explode.

There is also some fear that terrorists could steal plutonium from nuclear power plants and make bombs. This fear is also unfounded. First of all, there are no commercial power plants that use plutonium as fuel, so there is no plutonium available to steal.

Some plutonium is gradually formed as a waste product in fuel cells, but that is so difficult to extract for weapons that no country in the world has done it. The fuel rods would have to be processed in a highly sophisticated plant. If thieves possessed such a plant, it would be easier and safer for them to refine the material directly from ore.

Finally, if terrorists wanted to have nuclear weapons, they could probably get them more easily by stealing some of the thousands that already exist instead of trying to build some from spent fuel rods.

WASTE DISPOSAL. The survey shows that there is great fear about the disposal of radioactive waste. Yet, even here, there is much unfounded concern. There are five important considerations that are often overlooked:

1. A nuclear plant does not add any net radioactivity to the earth. Less comes out of the plant than goes into it. Radioactive ore is dug from the ground, is concentrated into fuel, and is burned to make electricity. When spent, there is less radioactive ore than there was in the beginning, and it ends up deeper underground than from where the original ore came.
2. There is very little waste to dispose of. Processed waste from a large power plant totals only 1 to 2 cubic meters of high-level waste per year. A coal-fired plant of the same size produces waste that covers 5 square kilometers to a depth of 2 meters . . . plus adding thousands of tons of waste to the air.
3. Even if nuclear power were ended, the problems, if any, would be unaffected. More than 99 percent of the high-level waste comes from producing weapons for military uses. The total accumulated volume of all high-level wastes in the United States through 1983 was 200,000 cubic meters. Of that total, only 300 cubic meters came from power plants.

4. The radioactivity of spent fuel rods is very intense immediately after being removed from a reactor. The intensity, however, declines quickly—by a factor of 2000 in 10 years. After 30 years no external danger remains from radiation.

5. After 30 years wastes pose a danger only if ingested (by getting into drinking water, for example). Using drinking water standards as a guide, high-level atomic wastes decay below the toxic levels of several natural ores and wastes (such as mercury, pitchblende, chromium, lead, coal wastes, and silver ores) in about 500 years.

DANGER OF A POSSIBLE MELTDOWN. The possibility of a nuclear meltdown is another potential hazard. It was not listed in *Event 20–F. Nuclear Power Survey* and is included now only with reservations.

It was not included in Event 20–F because the National Assessment did not include it. To remain objective, it should be added only with caution.

However, the national survey was prepared prior to the accident at Three-Mile Island (3MI) and the publicity that resulted could now justify its inclusion.

What are those dangers? Let us look briefly at what happens inside a nuclear reactor. Nuclear fuel is inserted into the reactor along with control rods. The fuel produces heat, which, in turn, is used to generate electricity. Control rods are used to keep the reactor from overheating.

Overheating is also controlled another way. The fuel rods are constantly immersed in water. This brings us to the potential danger. What would happen if the core lost its water? First of all, the fuel would stop burning at once because water is necessary to continue the nuclear reaction. Without water the reactor shuts down.

Nevertheless, there would still be latent heat from the natural atomic decay inside partially spent fuel rods. (This does not occur in new fuel rods.) It is this latent heat that could cause a potential meltdown in the reactor core.

How great is that possibility? A look at the Three-Mile Island accident may be instructive. Prior to the accident it was assumed that a meltdown could occur if the fuel rods would lose water for as little as a few seconds or minutes. However, the accident showed that such was not the case. The fuel rods in that accident were exposed to air for up to 8 hours. The temperatures were far lower than expected, and although the core was severely damaged, a meltdown did not occur.

Two special commissions (the Kemeny Commission appointed by the president, and the Rogovan Commission appointed by Congress) investigated the accident. They reported that (1) there was never any danger to the public, (2) there was never any danger of a meltdown, and (3) even if there had been a meltdown, the danger to the public would have been the same—none at all. They reported that the greatest danger to the public was "mental stress" caused by alarmist news reporting.

CAN CHERNOBYL HAPPEN HERE? Ask that question and most students will "admit" that it probably can. However, scientists know that it cannot. Why not? Because of the laws of physics. Or, stated another way, water cannot burn!

The Chernobyl reactor used graphite as a moderator. (A moderator is needed for a nuclear reaction to occur.) It lost its coolant and got so hot that the graphite ignited. Graphite ignites at over 6000 degrees Celsius. Thus, it burned with the intensity of a gigantic arc welder. It vaporized the huge inventory of radioactive fuel and spewed it high into the atmosphere.

American power plants do not use graphite as a moderator. They use water. Thus, if water (the coolant) is lost, so also is water (the moderator) lost. It shuts itself down.

A final note: Students will sometimes ask if the Russians did not know that they could use water instead of graphite. Of course, they knew. Graphite was used because it is especially suited to make nuclear material for weapons. They were using the Chernobyl plant not only to generate electricity, but also to make bomb material.

Discrepant Events and Pupil Investigations

CONSERVATION (EVENTS 20–J THROUGH 20–M)

Event 20–J. Energy Conservation: Home Heating. Have students rank the four items in the following list according to how much energy could be saved. Assume that you are living in a 1200 square foot home (equal to a five-room home or a two-bedroom home). Assume, also, that it had no insulation in the walls or ceiling, no storm windows, and poor weather-stripping.

_____ Add storm windows.
_____ Add 2 inches of fiberglass insulation to ceiling.
_____ Close drapes at night.
_____ Renew weather-stripping.

Pupil Investigations (may include the following processes):
In this event the processes are inherent in responding to the survey. The processes may include comparing, analyzing, interpreting, concluding, and predicting.

Event 20–K. Energy Conservation: Driving. Have students rank the four items in the following list according to how much energy could be saved. Assume that you own a "gas guzzler" that gets 10 miles per gallon (mpg), which is driven 15,000 miles per year.

_____ Drive only 10,000 miles annually instead of 15,000 miles.
_____ Get a compact car (30 mpg) and drive only 10,000 miles annually.
_____ Get a compact car (30 mpg) and drive the same mileage.
_____ Get a standard car (20 mpg) and drive the same mileage.

Pupil Investigations (may include the following processes):
In this event the processes are inherent in responding to the survey. The processes may include comparing, analyzing, interpreting, concluding, and predicting.

Event 20–L. Energy Conservation: Home Appliances. Have students rank the six items in the following list according to how much energy can be saved during a full year:

_____ Each member of a family of four takes a shower daily instead of a bath.

_____ Fix two dripping hot water faucets.

_____ Prohibit the use of outdoor Christmas lights. (Assume the use of 72 bulbs of 7 watts each, turned on for 3 hours each night for 3 weeks.)

_____ Replace 400 watts of incandescent lighting, used 1 hour per day, with fluorescent bulbs of equal light-giving value.

_____ Substitute a window fan for a room air conditioner about 20 percent of the time.

_____ Shave with a blade razor instead of an electric shaver.

Pupil Investigations (may include the following processes):
In this event the processes are inherent in responding to the survey. The processes may include comparing, analyzing, interpreting, concluding, and predicting.

Event 20–M. Energy Use in the Home. Have students rank the 10 following items according to how much energy they use during a year.

_____ blanket (electric)

_____ blender

_____ clock (wall)

_____ clothes dryer

_____ hair dryer (hand held)

_____ range

_____ refrigerator-freezer (14 to 21 cubic feet, side-by-side)

_____ television, color

_____ toaster

_____ washer, clothes

Pupil Investigations (may include the following processes):
In this event the processes are inherent in responding to the survey. The processes may include comparing, analyzing, interpreting, concluding, and predicting.

Events 20–J Through 20–M Explained in Context (Conservation)

Pupils have heard about the importance of conserving energy. Moreover, many do not know how to do so for two main reasons: (1) They don't know where energy is used in significant amounts and (2) they don't know where it can be saved. The preceding events are short, simple exercises that can be used to teach pupils where energy is used and how that energy can be conserved.

Where does the typical American family use its energy? About 80 percent is divided evenly between two major uses: (1) heating and cooling the home and (2) transportation (the family car). So, to be able to save energy, we need to focus attention on where the energy is used. That is done in the first two events in this section.

Most of the remainder of the energy is used to heat water and operate home appliances. Although not nearly so important as heating and transportation, home appliances are the most practical for instructing children. Pupils are not likely to make any decisions about heating and transportation. However, children use appliances all the time. They can form better judgments about how to use them and how energy can be saved. This makes the last two events especially useful in the classroom.

CONSERVING ENERGY IN HOME HEATING. The easiest way to save energy in heating a home is to add insulation to the ceiling. Heat escapes very quickly through the ceiling of an uninsulated home, so adding only 2 inches of insulation saves a great amount of energy (and money). Compare the savings in energy by each of the four practices in *Event 20–J. Energy Conservation: Home Heating.* The results are shown in Table 20–12.

Table 20–12. **Energy Saved in Home Heating**

Rank	Item	Fuel Oil Saved (gal)
2	Add storm windows	290
1	Add 5 cm of fiberglass insulation to ceiling	1044
4	Close drapes at night	58
3	Renew weather-stripping	203

The second best way to save energy in this event is to add storm windows. Glass is a poor insulator; and if there is only a single pane of glass between the inside of a home and the cold outside air, the heat will escape quickly. In fact, heat escapes 10 times as fast through a single window pane than through a typical wall. Storm windows cut in half the heat that is lost through windows.

In third place is the renewal of weather-stripping. Weather-stripping is the lining (usually of soft plastic) around the edges of doors and windows that keeps air from leaking in or out of a home. Unless a lining is used, heat is quickly lost in cold weather, and you can feel the cold draft of air as it enters a home.

Even closing the drapes helps to conserve energy. The drapes act as another layer blocking the movement of air between the outside and inside of a home. In the daytime, however, the drapes should be opened if the sun is shining because sunlight helps heat the house.

You can let some of the students compare the cost of the energy saved with the cost of making the improvements. In many cases the cost of the improvements is gained back within a few years. Thus, conserving energy not only saves fuel, it also saves money.

OBSERVING ENERGY IN DRIVING. Another area of energy use is driving. Two obvious factors influence the amount of energy used: (1) the amount of driving and (2) the efficiency of the car. Both factors are critical to saving energy and are used in *Event 20–K. Energy Conservation: Driving*. The results are shown in Table 20–13.

Table 20–13. **Energy Saved in Driving**

Rank	Item	Gas Saved (gal)
4	Drive only 12,000 mi instead of 15,000 mi	300
2	Get a compact car (30 mpg) and drive the same mileage	1000
1	Get a compact car (30 mpg) and drive only 12,000 mi	1100
3	Get a standard car (20 mpg) and drive the same mileage	750

The figures are obtained by dividing the number of miles driven annually by the miles per gallon. The actual amount of gasoline used for each car at each of the two distances is shown in Table 20–14.

What are the major factors that influence how many miles per gallon you can get from a car? The most important factor is weight. The heavier the car, the more gasoline it needs to operate. A general rule of thumb is that 1 mile per gallon is used for each additional 180 kilograms (400 pounds of weight). Thus, to get the best mileage, a car must be light in weight.

Table 20–14. **Gallons of Gasoline Used per Year**

Distance Driven (mi)	10	20 (mpg)	30
12,000	1200	600	400
15,000	1500	750	500

Perhaps the next most important factor is speed. At a low speed there is very little resistance from air, and a car will get its best mileage at about 40 miles per hour. At high speeds, however, wind resistance becomes important. Beyond 55 miles per hour wind resistance increases so much that most cars suffer substantial losses in gas mileage.

Other factors are important also. Radial tires have lower rolling friction than other types of tires. As a result, there is a small improvement in mileage. Driving habits are important. A "jackrabbit start" will waste gasoline; a smooth start will save it. Underinflating tires will waste gasoline; proper tire pressure saves it. Keeping the engine well tuned saves gasoline while poor maintenance wastes it.

CONSERVING ENERGY IN THE HOME. Energy can be saved by carefully watching how much energy is used by appliances in the home. *Event 20–L. Energy Conservation: Home Appliances* is a good exercise to draw attention to some energy conservation practices. The figures for the items in that event are given in Table 20–15.

Table 20–15. **Energy Savings in Home Appliances**

Rank	Item	Kilowatt-Hours Saved
1	Each member of a family of four takes a shower daily instead of a bath	720
2	Fix a dripping hot water faucet (one drop per second)	625
5	Prohibit the use of outdoor Christmas lights	32
4	Replace 400 W of incandescent lighting, used 1 h per day with fluorescent bulbs	117
3	Substitute a window fan for a room air conditioner about 20% of the time	250
6	Shave with a blade razor instead of an electric shaver	− 44

After the energy needed to heat a home the next biggest energy use in the home is for heating water. That is why the two examples about water use rank first and second in the preceding table. Surprisingly, an average shower uses about 5 gallons less water than an average bath. The added water for an entire year adds up to a savings of 720 kilowatts.

A dripping hot water faucet wastes a surprising amount of energy. The reason for the large loss is the fact that the water drips day and night, every day of the year. The constant drip, drip, drip, uses 625 kilowatts of energy per year (to heat the lost water).

As can be seen in the table, prohibiting Christmas lights (as was done in the early 1970s) will not save much energy. The bulbs are small and use is limited to a few weeks in a year. Changing room lights to fluorescent bulbs is better. They give much more light per watt of energy used than do incandescent bulbs. That is why the change will provide the same amount of light with much less energy.

The item in which the window fan is substituted for a room air conditioner may be misunderstood by students. They sometimes feel that if you want to be uncomfortable, you do not need to use the air conditioner at all. They miss the point of the exercise. There are times when a window fan is just as efficient as an air conditioner in keeping a house cool.

This is especially true after sunset when the outside air often cools off while the inside of a house is like an oven. At a time like this a window fan is very effective in cooling the house. So, it is possible to remain comfortable and still save energy.

The use of a blade razor will not save any energy at all. In fact, it will lose energy. Much more energy is needed to heat the water used for blade shaving than is used with an electric shaver.

Event 20–M. Energy Use in the Home is another good exercise to let students know the energy used by the appliances. The results of that event are shown in Table 20–16.

Table 20–16. **Energy Used by Appliances**

Rank	Appliance	Watts	Kilowatt-Hours*
4	Blanket (electric)	175	504
9	Blender	720	2
10	Clock (wall)	2	17
3	Clothers dryer	5,000	1,044
6	Hair dryer (hand-held)	1,000	120
2	Range	12,200	1,500
1	Refrigerator-freezer (21 cu ft)	180	2,160
8	Toaster	1,100	27
5	Television (color)	200	432
7	Washer, clothes	500	90

*The rankings for the event are based on the amount of energy used during a full year. Energy is measured by units called *kilowatt-hours* (kwh). A kilowatt-hour is 1000 watts used for 1 hour.

You will note that some of the appliances are of high wattage but have low kilowatt-hour figures. This is because they are not used very many hours during the year. A toaster, for example, uses six times more watts but only about 1 percent as much total energy then does the refrigerator-freezer. The biggest users are those appliances that are on most of the time.

Glossary

Absolute zero. The coldest possible temperature; point at which all molecular motion stops; 0 degrees Kelvin, minus 273 degrees Celsius, and minus 459.6 degrees Fahrenheit.

Additive rule (of colors). The color obtained when two or more colored lights are combined; when all colors are combined, they produce white.

Adhesion. An attraction between unlike molecules.

Aerobic. With oxygen; a type of activity in which the body's oxygen needs are met by breathing; it builds endurance.

Air pressure. The pressure of the weight of the atmosphere.

Alpha particles. Weak radiation that can be blocked by a sheet of paper or a few centimeters of air.

Alternating current (AC). A current that goes back and forth; produced by coils and magnets; the type produced by power companies.

Ampere. The rate of current flow; one ampere lights one 100-watt bulb.

Amphibian. A cold-blooded animal that lives on land and water, lays eggs, and has unarmored skin.

Amplitude. The size of waves.

Anaerobic. Without oxygen; vigorous activity that can only be maintained for a short time; it builds strength.

Angle of incidence. The angle of incoming light rays.

Angle of reflection. The angle of outgoing (reflected) light rays.

Appistat (or "set point"). The body's mechanism for maintaining its percentage of body fat; goes down with regular exercise.

Atom. The smallest part of an element, made of electrons and protons.

Beta rays. A stream of electrons with weak penetrating powers.

Block mountain. Mountain formed when one layer of the earth is pushed up and slides over another layer of the earth.

Boiling point. The temperature at which a liquid changes to a gas.

Buoyancy. The lifting force of water; allows some things to float.

Calorie (heat). Amount of heat needed to raise the temperature of 1 gram of water by 1 degree Celsius.

Carbohydrate. An ideal energy food with a value of 4 calories per gram; cannot be used to build tissue.

Celsius scale. A temperature scale with a boiling point of water of 100 degrees and a freezing point of water of 0 degrees.

Charged object. An object with either a surplus or shortage of electrons.

Chemical change. The change of a substance into a new substance; i.e., fire, rust.

Circuit. A path for an electrical current.

Circuit, closed. An electric circuit with the switch turned on.

Circuit, open. An electric circuit with the switch turned off.

Circuit, parallel. An arrangement of two or more batteries or bulbs in which two or more paths exist for current flow.

Circuit, series. An arrangement of two or more batteries or bulbs in which only a single path exists for current flow.

Circuit, short. A sudden drop in electrical resistance; an abnormal condition of excess current.

Circuit breaker. A safety device that cuts off the current when it is too large for the wires in that circuit.

Climate. The long-term condition of the atmosphere.

Cohesion. The attraction between like molecules; it keeps a solid from falling apart.

Cold-blooded. Animals whose body temperatures vary with their surroundings.

Cold front. A large mass of cold air pushing into a mass of warmer air.

Color. The visible effect produced by certain frequencies of light.

Compass. A device with a small pivoting magnet that points to the earth's north pole.

Complementary colors. Two colors that when combined produce white.

Compound. A substance consisting of two or more kinds of atoms; i.e., water (H_2O) or carbon dioxide (CO_2).

Concave lens. A lens that spreads light rays apart; it is thinner in the middle than at the edges.

Conductor (electrical, heat, sound). A substance that is a good carrier of electricity, heat, sound, respectively.

Constructive interference. When two or more waves combine to increase the size of the resulting wave.

Contraction. The shrinking of matter when it cools.

Convection current. The transfer of heat by movement of a liquid or a gas; physical movement of a fluid due to uneven heating and cooling.

Convex lens. A lens that brings light rays to a point; it is thicker in the middle than at the edges.

Current. *See* Alternating current; Direct current.

Cuttings. A means of plant propagation in which a leaf or leaf stalk is cut from a plant and placed into soil where the leaf takes root.

Decibel. A unit of sound loudness.

Destructive interference. When two waves combine to decrease or eliminate the size of the resulting wave.

Dicotyledon. A seed divided into two major parts.

Direct current (DC). A current going in one direction only; obtained from all sources except electromotive.

Discrepant event. An event or activity with a surprising or unexpected outcome.

Drag. The resistance of air on an airplane in flight.

Dry cell. A chemical cell that does not spill when tipped over.

Eclipse, lunar. (Eclipse of the moon) The blocking of the sun's light to the moon by the earth; when the earth goes between the moon and the sun.

Eclipse, solar. (Eclipse of the sun) The blocking of the sun's light to the earth by the moon; when the moon goes between the sun and the earth.

Electrical source of heat. The heat that is generated when an electric current goes through a resistance.

Electromagnet. A magnet made of soft iron and many turns of wire; it can be turned on or off when an electric current is turned on or off.

Electromagnetic spectrum. A range of frequencies that includes radio waves on one end, the visible spectrum in the middle, and cosmic rays at the other end.

Electromotive source of electricity. The current produced with coils and magnets; it produces an alternating current.

Electron. Negatively charged particle in an atom.

Electroscope. A device that can detect a static electrical charge.

Electrothermal source of electricity. The current produced by heating one end of two dissimilar metals and cooling the other end.

Element. A substance made of only one kind of atom; cannot be changed by ordinary chemical means into anything else.

Energy. Resources in oil, natural gas, coal, hydroelectricity and the atom; used to produce food, clothing, and shelter and to protect the environment.

Erosion. The wearing away of the surface of the earth.

Evaporation. Change of a liquid to a gas.

Expansion. The enlargement of matter as it warms up.

Fahrenheit scale. A temperature scale with a boiling point of 212 degrees and freezing point of 32 degrees.

Farsighted. Defect of the eye that results in blurred near-vision.

Fats. Food with an energy value of 9 calories per gram; used for energy, but cannot be used to build tissue.

Fire triangle. The three elements needed to sustain a fire: fuel, kindling temperature, and oxygen.

Fission, nuclear. The splitting of the nucleus of an atom that releases an enormous amount of energy; used in commercial power plants.

Fitness. Being of sound mind and body; being able to engage in vigorous physical activity for a long time.

Food groups. Four categories into which foods are divided: milk, meat, bread-cereal, and vegetable-fruit.

Forced vibrations. Sounds that are made louder when a surface is forced to vibrate at the frequency of the incoming energy.

Freezing point. The temperature at which a substance changes from a liquid to a solid.

Frequency. The number of waves per unit of time.

Fungi. Plant life that needs no sunlight to grow, such as molds, yeasts, mushrooms, and lichens.

Fuse. A safety device that cuts off the current when it becomes too large for the wires in the circuit.

Fusion, heat of. The absorption (or release) of heat when a substance thaws (or freezes).

Fusion, nuclear. Two atoms of hydrogen join (or fuse) to make helium, releasing an enormous amount of energy; the energy of the sun and stars; the energy of the hydrogen bomb.

Galvanometer. A device that detects tiny electric currents.

Gamma rays. Highly penetrating radiation, such as x-rays.

Gas. A substance with no definite shape or volume. It can be held only in an enclosed container.

Geographic poles. The points at the North and South poles around which the earth rotates.

Gravity. The attraction of the earth for an object; the attraction of the sun and moon for objects.

Grounding. Neutralizing an object with a static charge.

Harmony. The pleasing effect of two or more musical notes sounded together.

Heat. The energy a substance has because of the motion of its molecules; measured in calories, Btus, or joules.

Heat of fusion. *See* Fusion, heat of.

Heat of evaporation. *See* Vaporization, heat of.

Humidity. The amount of moisture in the air.

Hydrometer. A device that measures the density of liquids.

Igneous rocks. Rock formed from molten matter.

Induction, charging by. Inducing an opposite charge in an object by grounding it while holding a charged object nearby.

Inertia. *See* Law of motion, first.

Insulator (electrical, heat). Any material that is a poor carrier of electricity, heat.

Isostatic adjustment. The settling or rising of the earth's surface due to massive gains or losses in weight.

Kelvin scale. A temperature scale with the zero point at absolute zero, the freezing point at 273 degrees, and the boiling point at 373 degrees.

Ketones. Toxic by-products formed when fats are broken down for energy.

Kindling temperature. The temperature at which a substance will burst into flame.

Land breeze. A breeze (usually at night) going from land to a body of water.

Law of motion, first (Inertia). An object at rest tends to stay at rest, and an object in motion tends to stay in motion.

Law of motion, third. For each action there is an equal and opposite reaction.

Lens. *See* Concave lens; Convex lens.

Leyden jar. The original device invented to store static electricity.

Lift. The upward force of air exerted on an airplane.

Light. A form of energy in the visible part of the spectrum.

Lightning. A powerful static discharge among storm clouds or between storm clouds and objects on earth.

Lightning rod. A device that protects structures from damage by lightning.

Lines of force. Lines of attraction or repulsion between poles of magnets.

Liquid. A substance with definite volume but no definite shape; it takes the shape of its container.

Lodestone. A natural magnetic rock used in ancient times as a directional aid on ships.

Longitudinal wave. *See* Wave, longitudinal.

Magnet. Iron, nickel, cobalt, and certain alloys with domains in alignment.

Magnet, permanent. A magnet that cannot be turned on or off; it retains its magnetism over time.

Magnet, temporary. *See* Electromagnet.

Magnetic domains. Grouping of atoms into small regions in magnetic substances.

Magnetic field. The region near a magnet through which it extends its force.

Magnetic poles. The concentration of forces at the ends of magnets; the points on the north and south regions of the earth at which the earth's magnetic fields concentrate.

Mammals. A class of warm-blooded animals that possess hair and nurse their young with milk glands.

Mantle. The layer of the earth located between the crust and the core.

Matter. Anything that has mass and takes up space.

Mechanical source of heat. Heat produced by physical action such as bending, friction, pressure, and striking.

Melody. The tune of a musical composition; the effect of single notes in sequence.

Melting point. The temperature at which a solid changes to a liquid.

Metamorphosis. The great change in the life cycle of insects.

Metamorphic rock. Rock that has been changed through the action of heat and pressure.

Mineral. Inorganic matter containing specific elements or combination of elements.

Mixture. Two or more substances that are blended without uniting chemically.

Moh's scale (of hardness). A scale used to measure the hardness of rock.

Molecule. The smallest part of a compound that has the properties of the compound.

Monsoon. A special type of sea breeze that covers a large area of the earth's surface.

Neap tide. *See* Tide, neap.

Nearsighted. Defect of the eye that results in blurred distant vision.

Negative charge. An object with a surplus of electrons.

Nonconductor. Any substance that is a poor carrier of electricity, such as plastic, rubber, glass, and paper.

Nuclear energy. The energy released by splitting an atom (fission) or fusing two atoms into one (fusion).

Ohm. A unit of electrical resistance; resistance affected by length, thickness, temperature, and composition of the material.

Opaque. A substance through which light cannot pass.

Orbit. The path of a satellite around a heavenly body.

Parallel circuit. *See* Circuit, parallel.

Percussion instrument. An instrument played by being struck; includes drums, bells, and piano.

Permeability of soil. The ability of soil to allow water to pass through it.

Persistence of vision. The retention of an image by the eye for a brief instance after the stimulus is gone.

Phases of the moon. The change in the appearance of the sunlit part of the moon during its 28-day orbit of the earth; spells out D-O-C.

Photoelectric effect. Electricity produced when light strikes certain substances.

Photometer. A device that can measure light brightness.

Photon. A bundle of light energy.

Physical change. A change in appearance only, such as tearing paper, breaking glass, or melting butter.

Pitch. The frequency of sound waves; the highness or lowness of sound.

Pith ball. A substance from inside a corn stalk, that is very sensitive to static charges.

Primary colors (of lights). Red, blue, and green; additive; when mixed, make white.

Primary colors (of paints). Red, blue, and yellow; subtractive; when mixed, make black.

Process skills. Skills of investigation such as observing, inferring, recording data, classifying, experimenting, generalizing, measuring, forming theories, comparing, and predicting.

Proteins. A class of foods with an energy value of 4 calories per gram; used for building tissue and for energy.

Radiation (heat or light). The transfer of energy by waves through space.

Radiation (nuclear). Ionizing rays that penetrate matter and knock off electrons from atoms.

Reflection, even. Light bouncing off a smooth surface; image is visible on surface.

Reflection, uneven. Light bouncing off a nonsmooth surface; no image visible.

Refraction. The bending of light as it passes from one medium into another at an angle.

Relative humidity. The amount of moisture in the air compared to the amount it is able to hold.

Reptiles. A class of cold-blooded animals with a backbone and an armored or scaly skin.

Resonance. Sounds that are made louder when an object absorbs energy at its own natural frequency.

Respiration. Breathing; inhaling and exhaling air.

Rheostat. A control device that can raise or lower the current in a circuit.

Rhythm. The timing pattern of music.

Runners. A means of plant reproduction in which growth spreads out from a plant stem and take root.

Sea breeze. The breeze formed on a hot day, going from a body of water toward land.

Sedimentary rocks. Rocks formed by the action of water in which matter is laid down in layers.

Series circuit. *See* Circuit, series.

Set point. *See* Appistat.

Solid. A substance with definite volume and definite shape.

Sonic. At the speed of sound.

Sonic boom. The sound heard on the ground of the pressure wave formed by an airplane traveling at supersonic speed.

Sound. A form of energy caused by vibrating matter.

Species. Any group of related plants or animals that can generally reproduce only with other members of that group.

Spectrum, color. All the colors that make up visible light.

Spectrum, electromagnetic. *See* Electromagnetic spectrum.

Staging. A technique of spaceflight where one or more smaller vehicles hitch a ride, piggy-back style, on a larger space vehicle.

Stalactites. Rocks hanging from the ceiling of a cave; formed by dripping mineral-laden water.

Stalagmites. Rocks built up from the floor of a cave; formed by dripping mineral-laden water.

Static electricity. The buildup of positive or negative charges on an object.

Stringed instrument. An instrument on which a string is set in motion by plucking or bowing, includes violin, banjo, and guitar.

Sublimation. The change of a substance from a solid to a gas without going through the liquid state.

Sub-max test. A test of physical fitness that does not require a maximum effort.

Subtractive rule (of colors). The color obtained when two or more paints are combined; when all colors are combined, they produce black.

Supersonic. Faster than the speed of sound.

Switch. An electrical device that opens or closes a circuit.

Temperature. The average motion of molecules; how hot or cold something is, measured in degrees.

Three-way switch. An arrangement of three wires (three ways) in which a light (or an appliance) can be controlled from two places, such as a light switch at each end of a hallway.

Thrust. A force that pushes an airplane or space vehicle ahead.

Tide, neap. The effect on the tide when the sun and moon are at right angles to each other; low tide.

Tide, spring. The effect on the tide when the sun and moon are in line; high tide.

Trajectory. The path of a thrown (or propelled) object, affected only by inertia and gravity.

Translucent. A substance that permits light to pass through, but through which objects cannot be seen clearly such as frosted or stained glass.

Transparent. A substance through which objects can be seen clearly.

Tsunami (tidal wave). A great water wave caused by a major underwater disturbance.

Uncharged object. An object that has no surplus or shortage of electrons.

Vacuum. A space with nothing in it; absence of matter.

Vaporization, heat of. The absorption (or release) of heat when a substance boils (or condenses).

Volt. A unit of potential difference; or a unit of electrical pressure.

Warm-blooded. Animals whose body temperature remains stable.

Warm front. A mass of warm air driven into a mass of colder air by a large weather system.

Water cycle. The path of water in the atmosphere, from evaporation to clouds to rain.

Wave, longitudinal. A push-pull motion of matter that carries energy.

Wave, primary. Earthquake wave which travels through solids, liquids, and gases.

Wave, transverse. A side-to-side or snakelike motion of matter that carries energy.

Weather. A short-term condition of the atmosphere.

Weathering. The gradual physical and chemical wearing away of rocks.

Wet cell. A chemical cell that produces direct current from dissimilar material and a conducting liquid.

Wind instrument. An instrument in which an air column is used to make the sound; includes reeds, flutes, and horns.

Yeast. A fungus plant used in bread-making and in the production of alcohol.

Index

Events are in italics.

Absolute zero, 30–32
AC (see Alternating current)
Action-reaction principle, 165
Active life-style, 258–259
Adaptations of Nature: Beaks, 239–241
Adaptations of Nature: Eyes, 239, 241
Adaptations of Nature: Feet, 239, 240
Additive colors, 119
Adhesion, 24–25, 28
Aerobic capacity, 265
Aerobic exercise, 261–262
Agriculture, work force in, 282
Aileron, 157, 158
Air:
  capacity for moisture, 141, 145–148
  compressed, 135, 136, 148
  contraction of, 133–136
  expansion of, 135–136, 148
  negative properties of, 125–127
  positive properties of, 127–128
  as real substance, 124–128
Air, The Inviting, 152–153, 155
Air Move In or Out? Does, 41–42
Air pressure, 130–133, 135, 148, 154–155
Aircraft, Approaching, 158, 160–161
Airplane controls, 156–158
Airplane Flying Contest, 156–158
Alpha particles, 293
Alternating current, 74
Ampere, 70
Amphibian, 232, 238
Anaerobic exercise, 261–262
Angiosperms, 219
Angle of incidence, 109
Angle of reflection, 109
Angstrom, 104
Animals:
  adaptations of, 239–244
  with backbones, 239–241
  classification system, 233–234
Ant Farms, 242–244
Antigravity Fountain, 129, 131–133
Antigravity Pail, 168, 170
Appearing Coin! The, 111, 113
Appearing Salt, The, 204, 206
Appistat, 255
Appliances in home, 281–302
Aristarchus, 178–179
Arteries, 267–268
Ascending Cones, The, 166, 169

Astronaut, 174–175
Atom, 9–11, 14
  model of, 9–11
Attraction or Repulsion?, 53–56

Backbones, animals with, 231–239
Baffling Bottles, The, 97, 98
Balancing Ruler, The, 167, 169
Balloon and Its Invisible Shelf, The, 51–53
Balloon Blowup, 133, 136
Balloon Rockets, 163, 164
Baseball Throw, 171, 172
Bay of Fundy (see Fundy, Bay of)
Beaks, 239–241
Bean Power, 217–218, 220
Begonia Beginnings, 222–223
Below zero, 31
Beta rays, 293
Big Splash, The, 82, 83
Bimetallic strip, 44, 46
Birds, 232, 233, 235–237
Block mountains, 191
Blood pressure, 270
Blood sugar, (tables) 257–258
Blow out a candle (activity), 128
Blow through a straw (activity), 128
Blow up a balloon (activity), 127–128
Boil Water in a Paper Cup, 47, 48
Boiling point, 19, 21, 31, 175
Bread-cereal food group, 251, 253, 256
British thermal unit, 30–31, 33
"Broken" pencil, The (activity) 115
Brownian movement, 17
BTU (see British thermal unit)
Build a Power Plant, 283–286
Building Stalactites and Stalagmites, 196, 198
Bulletin board of solar system, (table) 179, 180
Buoyancy, 212

Calorie Counting, 252, 258–259
Calories (food), 252, 261
  expended per activity, (tables) 208, 259
Calories (heat), 31, 33
Can Crusher Number 1, 128, 130–131
Can Crusher Number 2, 128, 130–131
Candle Snuffer, 38, 40
Canning, 229
Capacitor, 50
Capillary action, 25
Carbohydrates, 251, 254–256

Cardiovascular system, 265
Carnation Water Pumps, 224–226
Carrot Plantings, 223–224
Catapult, 165
Caves, 197
Cell (electrical):
    dry, 73–74
    wet, 73
Cell (living), growth of, 245–246
Cells, See, 245–246
Celsius scale, 30, (table) 32
Changes of phase, 17–21
Changing Lights, 106, 107
Changing Spots, 106, 107
Charged objects, 51–53, 56, 67
Charges:
    induction of, 58–59
    like, 53–57
    static, 52–53
    unlike, 57–58
Check Dams, 200–203
Chemical change, (table) 23
Chemical Cleaning of Water, 201, 203
Chemical preservative, 229
    source of heat, (table) 36
Chernobyl, 297–298
Chicken brooder, 237
Chordata, 231–239
Chrysalis (see Cocoon)
Cigarette Money, 277, 279–280
Circling Sawdust, The, 41–42
Circuit, 74–78
    breaker, 77
    closed, 76
    open, 76
    parallel, 75
    series, 75
    short, 74–77
Circulatory system, 266–270
Classifying Animals, 231, 234
Classifying Climates, 137–138
Classifying Foods (Number 1), 251, 253–254
Classifying Foods (Number 2), 251, 254–256
Classifying Insects and Other Animals, 242, 243
Classifying Rocks, 192–194
Cleaning Muddy Water, 201, 203
Climate, 137–151
Cloud, 20
Cloudy Water, 270, 272
Coal, 287, 288
Cocoon, 243
Cohesion, 15, 26–29
Coin in the Cup, 168, 170
Coke-bottle (aircraft) shape, 161
Cold-blooded animals, 232, 235, 237, 238
Cold Currents, 208, 210
Cold front, 141–142
Color:
    additive, 119
    complementary, 119–120
    primary (lights), 119
    primary (paints), 120
    subtractive, 120
Color from White, 116–118
Color? Which Is the "Warmer", 42–43

Colors, Curious, 118, 120
Colors, Fading, 214–215
Compass, 64–66
Compasses and Magnetic Forces, 64–68
Complementary colors, 119–120
Compound, 11, 22–23
Compressed air, 135, 136, 148
Concave lens, 111–115
Concept of Distance, 176, 180–182
Concept of Number, 176–178
Concept of Size, 176, 178–180
Condensation, 146, 148, 149
Condenser, 50
Conduction of heat, (table) 37–40
Conduction Tester, 69, 71
Conductor:
    electrical, 71
    sound, 88–89
Conservation, energy, 297–302
Conservation, Energy: Driving, 297, 299–300
Conservation, Energy: Home Appliances, 298,
    301–302
Conservation, Energy: Home Heating, 297–299
Constructive interference, 103–104
Content, 1–2
Convection, 17, (table) 39, 40–42, 138–143,
    148–149
    box, 138
Convection Contradiction, The, 143, 148
Convection Tester, 41–42
Convex lens, 111–115
Cooling Breezes?, 33, 35
Core of earth, 188, 189
Cork Stay in the MIddle, Make the, 24, 25
Coulomb, 70
Crust of earth, 188–189
Crystal Formation, 192, 195
Current, Cold, 208, 210
Current (electrical):
    alternating, 74
    description of, 69–71
    difference from static electricity, 70
    direct, 74
Current from a Coil?, 72, 74
Current from Coins, 71, 73
Current Generator, 207, 210
Current (ocean), 207, 210, (map) 211
Currents, Curious, 138, 139
Curving parallels! (illusion), 123
Cuttings, 223

Dairy foods, 251, 253, 256
"Dancing" Dimes, 43–44, 46
"Dancing" Salt, The, 85–86, 89
DC (see Direct Current)
Decibel, 94
Deep Drafts, 208, 212
Democritus, 9
Destructive interference, 103–104
Dew point, 146
Dew Point, Discovering the, 143, 146
Diastolic blood pressure, 270
Dicotyledon, 219
Diets, 252, 254, 255, 259, 261
    composition of lost pounds, (table) 261

Diets, Supermarket, 252, 260–261
Direct and Slant Rays, 150, 151
Direct current, 74
Disappearing Coin, The, 111, 113
Discrepant event:
   definition of, 1, 3–7
   usage of, 4–7
Displacement mountain, 191
Dissolving Stones, 196, 198
Distances from sun, (table) 181
Diving Dropper, 133, 136
Does 2 + 2 = 3 1/2?, 11–12, 14
Drag, 154, 156
Drinking Race, 129, 131
Dry-bulb thermometer, (table) 145–146
Dry cell, 73–74
Drying foods, 229

Earth:
   description, 205–206
   distance around, 184–185
   profile, 205
   roundness of, 178, 182, 184
   seasons, 149–151
   size of, 178–181
   structure, 188–189
   surface features, 129–192
Earth-Moon Distance, 182–183, 185
Earthquake, 189
Echo Range Finder, 91, 92
Echo Speed Computer, 90–92
Eclipse of moon, 178, 184–186
Eclipse of sun, 185–186
Egg-in-the-Bottle Mystery, The, 133, 135
Eggs, hatching, 236–237
Einstein, Albert, 104
Electrical source of heat, (table) 36
Electrical terms, 70
Electricity:
   sources of, (table) 72–74
   uses of, 78–80
Electrochemical source of electricity, 73–74
Electromagnetic spectrum, 104
Electromagnets, (table) 79–80
Electromotive source of electricity, 72–74
Electron, 50, 70
Electroscope, 55, 57
   construction of, 59
Electrothermal source of energy, 72–73
Element, 11
Elephant, 241
Elevators on airplanes, 157–158
Embryo, chick, 236
Energy:
   conservation of, 297–302
   definition of, 281–283
   as food, clothing, shelter, 281–282
   generation of electricity and, (table) 287–288
   home heating and, 281, 283, 297, 299
   opinions of scientists about, (table) 290–291
   sources of, 283, 286–287
   survey responses about, (tables) 284–285, 290
   as transportation, 281, 283, 297, 300
   uses, (table) 286–288
      in appliances, (tables) 298, 301–302

   in U.S., (table) 286–288
Energy Conservation: Driving, 297, 299–300
Energy Conservation: Home Appliances, 298, 301–302
Energy Conservation: Home Heating, 297–299
Energy for Electrical Power, 286–288
Energy, Total Use, 286–287
Energy Use in the Home, 298, 301–302
Energy Used? Where Is, 286, 288
Eratosthenes, 184–185
Erosion, 191, 196–200, 202
Erosion on Bare and Grassy Slopes, 200, 202
Evaporation, 142, 144–146
Evaporation Race, 142–145
Exercise, 261–262, 265, 266, 268–270, 272
Expansion, 43–46
   index of, 45
Expansion of Gases, 45, 46
Expansion Meter, 44, 46
Eyes of predator and pursued animals, 239–241

Fahrenheit scale, 30–32
Farsightedness, 114–115
Fast-Falling Paper, 167, 169–170
Fast Friction, 171, 173–174
Fats, 248–251, 254–256
   in foods, (tables) 250, 255, 256
   testing for, 248–250
Feel Magnetic Forces, 64, 65
Feet, 239, 240
Fill the Balloon with an Empty Bottle, 124, 127
Fill the Stocking, 54–55, 57
Fingertip on the Globe, 182, 184
Fire, 47–49
Fire triangle, 48
Fire? What Put Out the, 17–18, 20
Fish, 232–233, 238–239
   as food, 256
Fish in the Bowl, 121
Fitness:
   definition of, 263
   measurement of, 263–265
Flaps on airplane, 157–158
Flat Earth, The, 182, 184
Flight:
   forces of, 152–155
   supersonic, 158–161
Float Metal on Water, 26, 28
Floating Eggs, 208, 212
Floating finger! The, (illusion), 122
"Floating" Ping-Pong Ball, The, 152, 155
Floating Rings, 64, 65
Flower, Parts of a, 224–225, 227
Flowers, 219, 227
Folded Mountains, 189–191
Food:
   groups, 251, 253, 256
   preservation, 229
   tastes, 248–251
   tests, 248–250
Foods, Classifying (Number 1), 251, 253–254
Foods, Classifying (Number 2), 251, 254–256
Foods, Favorite: Helpful or Harmful?, 251, 253
Forced vibrations, 83, 94–95, 97

Four Seasons, The, 149, 151
Franklin, Benjamin, 50–51, 59, 210
Freeze-Fresh Water, 204–205, 207
Freezing, Force of, 197, 199
Freezing point, 31
Frequency, 83, 95–97, 99
Friction, 171, 173–174
Frogs, 238
Fruit Fly Metamorphosis, 242, 243
Fruit-Jar Cultures, 227–229
Fundy, Bay of, 213
Fungi, 229–230
Funnel Magic, 153, 155
Fuses, 75, 77
Fusion, heat of, 33–35

Galvani, Luigi, 68–69
Galvanometer, 71
Gamma rays, 293
Gases, 19–20, 27
Gasoline, usage per year, (table) 300
Geological Maps of Your Area, 189, 191
Germination, 217, 219–221
Get a Lift, 24, 25
Get-the-Kid-to-Smile Box, 108, 109
Ghostly Candle, 107, 109
Giraffe, 241
Glacier, 191–192
Goddard, Robert, 162
Grafting plants, 223
Grass Growing, 222–223
Gravity, 131, 154, 166–173
  center of, 166, 167, 169
Grease-spot photometer, 106, 107
Gripping Chair, The, 166, 169
Ground, electrical, 56
Growth in Light and Dark, 218, 220–221
Growth rates of human, 246–248
Gulf Stream, 210
Gymnosperms, 219

Hands Up and Down, 267, 269–270
Hardness scale, (table) 193–194
Harmony, 99
Hatching eggs, 236–237
Hazards, potential nuclear, 289–291, 295–297
Hearing, range of frequencies, 97
Heart:
  circulatory system and, 266–270
  rates, (table) 266–269
Heat:
  of fusion, 19, 33–35
  measurement of, 30–31
  sources of, (table) 35–37
  travel of, (table) 39
  of vaporization, 19, 33–35
Heat or Temperature?, 30, 32
Height Table, 246–248
Heights, weights and, (table) 247
Highs in weather, 140
Hole in the Hand! (illusion), 122–123
Hot Rod, The, 15, 17
Hot Water Chimney, 208, 210
Hottest Part of a Flame, The, 47, 49
How to use this book, 7–8

Humidity, 145–148
Hurricane Camille, 213
Hurricane Huff!, 93, 96
Hwang Ho (Yellow) River, 198–199
Hydrometer, 209, 212
Hydroponics, 221
Hypertension, 270

Ice Disappear, Make, 17, 19
Ice Preservation Race, 37, 39–40
Ice Water Boil? Can, 38, 40
Iceberg, 207
Igneous rocks, 195
Illuminated object, 105
Incubator, 236–237
Index of expansion, 45
Induce a Charge, 58–59
Induction, charging by, 58–59
Inertia, 166, 169–173
Ink Spread? How Does the, 16, 17
Insect cages, 244
Insect collections, 244
Insects, 242–244
Insects and Other Animals, Classifying, 242, 243
Instant Eye Test, 112–114
Insulator:
  electrical, 7
  heat, 40
Interference, constructive or destructive,
  103–104
Invisible Light, The, 101, 105
Ionizing radiation, sources of, (table) 293
Isostatic Adjustment, 190–192

Jet aircraft, 163, 164
Jetting to the Moon, 163, 164
Join the Water, 26, 28
Joule, 31, 33
Jumping Juice, 44, 46

Kaleidoscope, 110
Keep the Paper Dry Underwater, 125, 127
Kelvin scale, (table) 32
Kemeny Commission, 296
Key, Francis Scott, 162
Killing jar for insects, 244
Kindling Temperatures, 47–49
Kite effect, 154

Land breeze, 140–141
Larynx, 84
Laws of motion:
  first, 170
  third, 165
Layering Action of Water on Soils, 192, 195
Leaping Leaves, 55, 57
Leaves, 226–227
Lens:
  concave, 111–115
  convex, 111–115
  resolving power of, 102
Lesson, steps of, 4–7
Levitation, 62–64
Leyden jar, 50, 51
Lift on airplane, 152, 154

Lifting Forces, 152, 154–155
Light:
  brightness, 106–107
  color, 116–120
  description of, 101–106
  invisible, 105
  reflection of, 107–110
  refraction of, 110–116
  speed of, 105, 113
  theories of, 102–104
  visible, 104, 105
Light the Bulb, 74–76
Lightning rod, 51
Lights, Mixed-Up, 117, 118
Light-Seekers, 224, 227
Like charges, repulsion between, 53–57
Lines of Force, 62, 63
Lingering Images, 117, 120
Lion Roar, Make the, 93, 95
Liquid to Gas to Liquid, 17, 20
Liquids, 19, 20, 27, 29
Listening Tube, 86, 89
Lodestone, 60, 66
Longitudinal wave, 87
Looking at Lenses, 111–114
Loudness of sounds, (table) 94
Lows, in weather, 140
Luminous object, 105
Lung Capacity, Measuring: Inverted Jar, 270–272
Lung Capacity, Measuring: Lung-Volume Bag, 271–273
Lung volumes, (table) 270–273

Magic Tablecloth, 167–168, 170
Magnetic attraction, 61–62
Magnetic domains, 60–61
Magnetic field, 60, 63, 79
Magnetic Forces, Feel, 64, 65
Magnetic lines of force, 62–64
Magnetic Mixup, 65–66
Magnetic poles, 66
Magnetic repulsion, 64–66
Magnetism, 60–67
  causes of, 60–61
Magnetism. What Materials are Attracted?, 61–62
Magnets:
  permanent, 67
  temporary, 67
Magnets, Stop and Go, 79, 80
Mammals, 231–235, 240
Man-in-the-Desert Problem, 164, 166
Mantle of earth, 188–189
Maps of Your Area, Geological, 189, 191
Matter, 9–29
  changes in, (table) 22–23
  phases of, (table) 17–21
Maximum and Exercise Heart Rates, 266–268
Meat group, 251, 253, 256
Mechanical source of heat, 36, 37
Melody, 99
Melt Ice Below its Freezing Point, 33, 35
Meltdown, 296
Melting point, 19

Metamorphic rock, 195
Metamorphosis, 242, 243
Microorganisms, 228–229
Microscopic plants, 227–230
Mildew, 230
Mile Run-Walk, The 1-, 263–265
Milk group, 251, 253, 256
Millirem, 294
Mineral, 193
Mississippi River, 198
Mixed-Up Bottles, The, 40–42
Mixing Pigments, 117–118, 120
Mixture, 22
Moh's scale of hardness, (table) 193–194
Moisture Makers, 224, 226
Mold Farming, 228, 230
Molecules, 9, 11, 17, 22
  motion of, 15–17
  spaces between, 11–15
Molecules, Rearrange Some, 22
Monocotyledon, 219
Monsoon, 141
Moon:
  eclipse of, 178, 184–186
  phases of, 178, 183, 186–187
  size of, 171, 180, 181
Moon, Phases of the, 183, 186
Motions of oceans, 207–214
Mountains:
  block, 191
  displacement, 191
  folded, 189, 191
Multiplying Lines, The, 101–103
Music, 99–100
Musical instruments, (table) 99–100
Musical tumblers, 100
Mysterious Marbles, The, 69, 70

National programs in science, 1, 2, 8
Natural gas, use in U.S., 287, 288
Natural vibrations, 95–96
Neap tide, 213
Nearsightedness, 114–115
Negative charge, 52
Neutralization of static charges, 53, 56, 58
Newspaper Electroscope, 55, 57
Newspaper Stronger than a Board? Is a, 128–129, 131
Newton, Isaac, 102, 104
Nonconductor, electrical, 71
Nontext approach, 3
No-till farming, 202
Nuclear change, (table) 23
Nuclear energy, 288–294
  potential hazards of, 289–290
  as source of heat, 36
  use in U.S., 287, 288
Nuclear Power Survey, 288–291

Ocean:
  currents, 207, 208, 210
  resources, (table) 206, 207
  salinity, 210–212
  sizes and depths, (table) 206
  underwater pressures, (table) 215–216

Ocean (*Cont.*)
  why turn to, 204–207
Ohm, 70
Oil, 287, 288
One-Mile Run-Walk, The, 263–265
One Nose or Two?, 274, 275
Onion, structure of cells from, 246
Opaque materials, 106
Open circuit, 76
Opinion Survey, 283–286
Opinions:
  changes in, 283–286
  of scientists, 290–291
  surveys, 284–285, 289–291
Optical illusions, 120–123
Orbits, 171, 173
Orbits, High and Low, 171, 173
Overfat, 252, 255, 259–260
Overweight, 252, 255, 259–260
Overweight or Overfat?, 252, 259–260
Oxygen in the Air, 133, 135–136

Paper "Dance", Make the, 54, 56–57
Parallel circuit, 77–78
Parallax, 122
Particle theory of light, 102–104
Parts of a Flower, 224–225, 227
Pebble Pinnacles, 196–197, 199
Penny in the Pool, 209, 212
Pepper and Salt, 52, 53
Permanent magnet, 67
Permeability, 195, 200, 202
Permeability of Soils, 200, 202
Persistence of vision, 116, 117, 121–122
Phases of the Moon, 178, 183, 186–187
Photoelectric effect, 73, 104
Photometer, 107
Photon, 104
Phylum, 233
Physical change, (table) 23
Piezoelectricity, 73
Ping-Pong Bounce, 82–84
Pinpointing the Bolt, 110–111, 113
Pitch, 96–99
  definition of, 97
  of object, 98–99
  of string, 97–98
Pith ball, 53, 56
Planets, (table) 180
  distances from sun, 181
  sizes, 178–181
Plant, parts of, 223–227
Playground Solar System, 176–177, 181
Poles:
  like, 62–65
  magnetic, of earth, 65, 66
  unlike, 62–65
Pollen, 227
Pollen Jitter, 15–17
Pop the Fuse, 75, 77
Positive charge, 52
Posture Strains, 273, 275
Potato Power!, 72–74
Pour light (activity), 115
Pour Salt into a "Full" Tumbler, 13–15

Pour Water at an Angle, 26, 28
Pour Water into an "Empty" Bottle, 125, 127
Pouring Air, 124–125, 127
Power-Packed Performer, 78, 79
Primary colors of lights, 119
Primary colors of paints, 120
Process skills, 1–2, 4
Protective coloration, 241
Proteins, 251, (table) 254
Pulse and Exercise, 266, 268

Radiation Doses, Average, 291, 294–295
Radiation (heat), 42–43
Radiation, Ionizing, 291, 293–295
Radiation (nuclear), 291–293
  food preservation, 229
  ionizing, 291, 293–295
  scientific groups, 292–293
  sources, (tables) 293–294
Radiation? What is, 291, 293
Rain, 141, 145–148
Reentry Capsules, 171–172, 174
Reflection:
  even, 107–110
  uneven, 108–109
Refraction, 110–116
Refrigeration, 229
Relative humidity, (table) 145–148
Reptiles, 232, 233, 237
Resolving power of lenses, 102
Resonance, 95–96
Respiration, 270–273
Reverse the Arrows, 112, 114
Rheostat, 80
Rhythm, 99
Rock Erosion, 196, 198–199
Rock Sponges, 192, 195
Rocks, 192–195
  characteristics of, 193
  classification of, 192
  scale of hardness, 193–194
  types of, 193, 195
Rocks, Classifying, 192–194
Rocket-Launching Problem, 163–165
Rockets, 162, 166
Roemer, Olaus, 105
Roentgen, William, 292
Rogovan Commission, 296
Roll (aircraft maneuver), 157, 158
Roots, 225
Roots, Roaming, 223, 225
Rubber-Band Catapult, 163, 165
Rubber-Band Paradox, 96–98
Rubber-Band Riders, 82–84
Rudder, 157–158
Runners from plant, 223
Rutherford, Ernest, 10

Sagging Solid, The, 44, 46
Saline Currents, 208–209, 212
Salting, 229
Satellite, 162, 171, 173
Science, national programs in, 1, 2
Scientists, opinions of, 290–291
Sea breezes, 140–141

Seasons, 149–151
Seawater Gardening, 204, 207
Sedentary life-style, 258–259
Sedimentary rocks, 195
Seed Depth, 217, 219–220
Seedless reproduction of plants, 222–223
Seeds, 217–221
   germination of, 217, 219–221
   travel of, 219, 221
Seeds, Soaking, 217, 219
Seeds Travel? How do, 219, 221
Seeds, Upside-Down, 218, 220
Seeds, Water for, 218, 220
See Through, Shine Through, 101–102, 106
Separate the Materials, 22–23
Series and Parallel Circuits, 75, 77–78
Set point, 255
Shake Heat into a Bottle, 35–37
Short circuit, 74
Shrinking Balloon, The, 14, 15
Silver soot (activity), 115
Singing Wine Glasses, 93, 95–96
Sink the Pepper, 27, 29
Siphon, 131–133
Sit-up Test, The, (table) 246–265
Skin-fold calipers, 260
Smell Box, The, 15, 16
Smoke, Why Adults, 276–278
Smoke, Why Children, 276, 278–279
Smoking cigarettes, cost of, 277
Smoking food, 229
(Smoking), Why Adults Quit, 277, 279
Soaking Seeds, 217, 219
Soft-Drink Gases, 174–175
Soils, 200–203
   conservation of, 202–203
   size and types, (table) 202
Soils, Water-Holding Capacity of, 200, 202
Solar Power Plant, 224, 226
Solar system, 179–181
Solids, 19, 27, 29
Solids to Liquids, 18–19, 21
Sonic Boom, 158, 160–161
Sonic boom, 159–161
Sound:
   caused by vibrations, 83–84
   conductor, 88–89
   definition of, 82–84
   pitch, 96–99
   resonance, 95–96
   speed of, 90–92, 158, 159
   travel of, 84–90
   volume, (table) 92–96
   waves, 87
Sound, Speed of, 158, 159–160
Sources of heat, (table) 36
Sours the Milk? What, 227–229
Space travel:
   astronauts and, 174–175
   history of, 162–163
   power for flight, 163–166
   reentry capsule, 171, 173–174
   staging, 165–166
   travel times, (table) 182
Species, 234, 242

Spectrum:
   color, 118–119
   electromagnetic, 104
Speed Detector, 90, 91
Speed of light, 105
Speed of sound, 90–92, 158, 159
Spiders, 243
Spoon Chimes, 84–85, 88–89
Spring tide, 213
Squeeze-Box Candle Snuffer, 124, 127
Staging (in space flight), 165–166
Stalactites, 196, 198
Stalagmites, 196, 198
Star-Spangled Banner, 162
Starches, Testing for, 248–250
Stars, number of, 177–178
Static charges, 52–53
Stem, 225–226
Step Test, 263, 265
Stoma, 226
Stop and Go Magnets, 79, 80
Stop and Go Signals for Electricity (Switches),
   74–76
Stop the Leak, 130, 133
Strained Strings, 96, 98
Straw Atomizer, 153, 155
Straw Hydrometer, 209, 212
Streamlining for Speed, 155–156
Stringed instruments, 100
Strong Pull, Weak Pull, 168, 170
Sublimation, 19
Sub-max test, 265
Subtractive rule for colors, 120
Sugar, 248–250, 252, 256–258
Sugar: Good or Bad?, 252, 256–258
Sun:
   center of solar system, 178–179
   size, 178–181
Supermarket Diets, 252, 260–261
Supersonic flight, 158–161
Surface tension, 28–29
Surveys on energy, 284–285, 289–292
Suspended Drops, 26, 28
Switches, 74–75, 80
Systolic, 270

Tabletop Messages, 84, 88
Tall Man, Short Man, 120–121
Taste, sense of, 248–251
Taste, Testing for, 248–250
Tastes, Mixed-Up, 249, 251
Teetering Toothpick, 266, 268
Teeth: Sound Detectors, 84, 88
Telegraph, model of, 81
Temperature, 30–33
   measurement of, 30–31
   scales, (table) 32
Temperatures, Two, 143, 146
Testing for Fats, 248–250
Testing for Starches, 248–250
Testing for Sugars, 248–250
Testing for Taste, 248–250
Textbook:
   role of, 2–3
   use of this, 7–8

Three-Mile Island, 296
Thrust, 154, 156
Tidal wave, 214
Tides, 209, 210, 213
Tin-Can Telephone, 85, 89
Tinsel Tree, The, 54, 57
Tiny Tides, 209–210, 213
Tobacco, effects on body, 272, 276–280
Tone of string, 97–98
Top hat (illusion), 123
Tornado Box, 138–139, 142
Touch, sense of, 273–275
Touch Test, 273–275
Traffic light, model of, 81
Trajectory, 171–173
Translucent material, 106
Transparent material, 106
Transverse wave, 87
Travel times in space, (table) 182
Tsunami (see Tidal Wave)
Tuning Fork Amplifier, 92, 95
Turtles, 237–238
Two-Toned Fluid, 117, 120
Two-Toned Paper, The, 37, 40

Undersea living, 214–216
Underwater Distances, 214, 216
Underwater pressures, (table) 215–216
Underwater Sounds, 86–87, 89–90
Unlike Charges Attract, 57–58
Upside-Down Seeds, 218, 220
Upsweep of wings, 158

Vacuum, 131, 132, 135, 136
Vaporization, heat of, 33–35
Vegetable-fruit group, 251, 253–254, 256
Veins, 267, 269–270
Vibrating Air, 93, 95
Vibrating Voices, 83, 84
Vibrations, 83, 94–95, 97
    forced, 94–95
    natural, 95–96
    per second, 83, 95–97, 99
Volt, 70
Volta, Alessandro, 68–69, 73
Volume, (table) 94–96

Warm-blooded animals, 232, 235
Warm front, 141–142

Waste disposal, 295–296
Wastebasket Megaphone, 92–93, 95
Watch that Wink, 107–109
Water Bend, Make the, 52–53
Water Climb? Why Does, 23, 24
Water Cycle, 143–144, 148–149
Water cycle, 142–149
Water displacement method, 260
Water for Seeds, 218, 220
Water from Fire?, 47, 48
Water Go? Where Does the, 12–13
Water-Holding Capacity of Soils, 200, 202
Water In? What Keeps the, 27, 29
Water power, 287, 288
Water? What Pulls Out the, 23, 25
Wave theory, 102–104
Wavelength, 104
Waves:
    constructive interference and, 103–104
    destructive interference and, 103–104
    earthquake, 189
    longitudinal, 87, 189
    motion of water and, 213
    transverse, 87, 189
Weather, 137–151
Weather calendar, 137–138
Weathering, 196–199
Weight Table, 246–248
Weightless Water, 129–130, 133
Wet-bulb thermometers, (table) 145–146
Wet cell, 73
What Am I (Number 1)?, 231, 234–235
What Am I (Number 2)?, 231–232, 235
What Am I (Number 3)?, 232, 235
What Am I (Number 4)?, 232, 237–238
What Am I (Number 5)?, 232, 238
What Am I (Number 6)?, 232–233, 238–239
White from Color, 116, 118, 121
Wind instruments, 100
Wire Heater, 36, 37
Work force in agriculture, 282

X-ray, 292
X-ray Box, The, 108, 109

Yeast Plants, 228, 230

Zero, below, 31
Zero point, 31